REASON AND THE CHRISTIAN RELIGION

Richard Swinburne

REASON
AND THE
CHRISTIAN RELIGION

Essays in honour of
RICHARD SWINBURNE

Edited by

ALAN G. PADGETT

CLARENDON PRESS · OXFORD

*This book has been printed digitally and produced in a standard specification
in order to ensure its continuing availability*

OXFORD
UNIVERSITY PRESS

Great Clarendon Street, Oxford OX2 6DP

Oxford University Press is a department of the University of Oxford.
It furthers the University's objective of excellence in research, scholarship,
and education by publishing worldwide in

Oxford New York

Auckland Bangkok Buenos Aires Cape Town Chennai
Dar es Salaam Delhi Hong Kong Istanbul Karachi Kolkata
Kuala Lumpur Madrid Melbourne Mexico City Mumbai Nairobi
São Paulo Shanghai Singapore Taipei Tokyo Toronto
with an associated company in Berlin

Oxford is a registered trade mark of Oxford University Press
in the UK and in certain other countries

Published in the United States
by Oxford University Press Inc., New York

ISBN 0- 19- 824042- 2

Preface

The essays in this volume have been written in honour of Richard Swinburne on his sixtieth birthday. The editor, contributors, and publisher combine to wish him good health and long life.

The volume is laid out according to the standard *loci* of Christian systematic theology. The theological topics dealt with are faith and reason, revelation, Trinity and Incarnation, atonement, and theological anthropology (or, as it used to be called, the doctrine of Man). While honouring Professor Swinburne, each chapter also demonstrates the importance of the recent renaissance in philosophy of religion for the modern understanding of the Christian faith. Each contribution illustrates the indispensability of philosophy for theology and the interesting philosophical issues that arise in the practice of theological reflection.

Richard Swinburne, Nolloth Professor of the Philosophy of the Christian Religion at the University of Oxford, is an active and vital philosopher who continues to make a very significant contribution to his chosen field of study. His work includes an impressive array of essays and books in several areas of philosophy, such as philosophy of science, epistemology, probability, philosophy of language, and philosophy of religion.

The strength of Swinburne's contribution lies in the rigour of his philosophical method, the clarity of his thought, and the precision of his argument, all of which spring from his grounding in analytic philosophy. This is particularly true when Swinburne focuses his attention on the area of philosophy of religion. His famous trilogy of books, *The Coherence of Theism* (1977), *The Existence of God* (1979), and *Faith and Reason* (1981), standing alone, has made a deep impact upon the philosophy of religion. Professor W. D. Hudson, in a reflection on Swinburne's work, wrote: 'The trilogy . . . is, beyond all doubt, one of the most, if not the most, impressive single achievement in the philosophy of religion during the past decade'.[1] Professor Robert M. Adams likewise feels that

---

[1] From a review of *Faith and Reason*, *Religious Studies*, xix (1983), 93–6.

it comprises one of the finest and most substantial philosophical examinations (and defenses) of theism in our generation. . . . Swinburne has developed that tradition [of apologetics] with great originality and has given it far more sophistication and adequate form than it has had before (especially in his treatment of the design argument in *The Existence of God,* in which I think he rivals Hume).[2]

Such high praise from colleagues on both sides of the Atlantic shows the esteem in which Swinburne's thought is held by philosophers of many stripes.

The significance of this work is reflected in its impact upon current philosophical studies. Indeed, one need only consider the state of philosophy of religion when Richard Swinburne was himself studying at Oxford to understand the importance of his work in shaping philosophical discussion. During his years as a student at Oxford, logical positivism was the dominant philosophical school in the Western world. Philosophy of religion received scant attention, and the little it did receive tended to come in the form of negative attacks upon the viability of such a discipline. The re-emergence of philosophy of religion as the subject of serious philosophical consideration is the result of careful and thorough scholarship, of which Swinburne's work is a primary example. His work on the coherence of the attributes of God in theistic beliefs is the starting-point for the work of other philosophers who continue to publish in this expanding field of philosophy.

Swinburne's sustained intellectual productivity has allowed him to remain at the forefront of the renaissance of philosophy of religion. Not content to rest upon laurels garnered in the 1970s, he has embarked upon a tetralogy of books. The projected four-volume set focuses on philosophical issues arising from specifically Christian beliefs. The first two volumes on *Responsibility and Atonement* (1989) and *Revelation* (1992) have already appeared, with *The Christian God* expected soon. The interest in these issues and the power of Swinburne's argument in this area are evident from the numerous responses which philosophers and theologians have made to the first half of this project. Some of these responses are contained in this volume. Upon completion of this new project, which covers the topics of providence, evil, the Trinity, and the Incarnation, it may very well be that Richard

[2] From a review of *Failth and Reason, Nous,* xix (1985), 626–33.

Swinburne will have accomplished for the twentieth century what Thomas Aquinas did for the thirteenth: a reconciliation of orthodox Christian faith with the rigorous demands of philosophy and science.

The editor is grateful to Blackfriars, Oxford, for permission to print the Aquinas Lecture by Professor Williams in the present forum. Readers will also be interested to know that John Hick's contribution is part of a larger project, *The Metaphor of God Incarnate*. Finally, the editor would like to thank his wife, Sally Padgett, for her encouragement, support, and help with the index and proofs; and Nigel Biggar, Chaplain of Oriel, for his most welcome assistance.

A. G. P.

Azusa, California
All Saints' Day, 1993

Contents

List of Contributors

WILLIAM P. ALSTON is Professor of Philosophy, Emeritus, Syracuse University. A founding editor of *Faith and Philosophy*, Alston has published works in epistemology, philosophy of language, and philosophy of religion. Among his recent books are *Perceiving God* (1993) and *The Reliability of Sense Perception* (1994).

DAVID BROWN is the Van Mildert Professor of Divinity, University of Durham, and a Canon of Durham Cathedral. For fourteen years Chaplain and Fellow of Oriel College, Oxford, Brown has written numerous articles in theology and philosophy of religion. His books include *The Divine Trinity* (1985) and *Continental Philosophy and Modern Theology* (1987).

RICHARD M. GALE is Professor of Philosophy at the University of Pittsburgh. The author of books and articles in epistemology, metaphysics, and the philosophy of religion, he has recently published *On the Nature and Existence of God* (1991).

ROM HARRÉ is a Fellow of Linacre College and Lecturer in Philosophy at the University of Oxford and Professor of Psychology at Georgetown University. Author and editor of over forty books in psychology, general philosophy, and the philosophy of science, he has recently finished his trilogy, *Physical Being* (1991), *Personal Being* (1983), and *Social Being* (1993).

BRIAN HEBBLETHWAITE is Fellow and Dean of Chapel at Queens' College and University Lecturer in Divinity, University of Cambridge. He is the author of articles and books in theology, including *The Incarnation* (1987) and *The Ocean of Truth* (1988).

JOHN HICK is a Fellow of the Institute for Advanced Research in the Humanities, University of Birmingham (England) and Danforth Professor of the Philosophy of Religion, Emeritus, Claremont Graduate School (California). He is the author of some thirty books, two of the most noted being *Evil and the God of Love* (1966), and his Gifford Lectures, *An Interpretation of Religion* (1989).

NORMAN KRETZMANN is Susan Linn Sage Professor of Philosophy, Cornell University. The author of works in medieval philosophy and philosophy of religion, he is the principal editor of *The Cambridge History of Later Medieval Philosophy* (1982) and co-editor (with Eleonore Stump) of *The Cambridge Companion to Aquinas* (1993) and *The Cambridge Translations of Medieval Philosophical Texts* (1988).

J. R. LUCAS is a Fellow of Merton College and Reader in Philosophy at the University of Oxford and a Fellow of the British Academy. His articles and books in philosophy and theology include *Spacetime and Electromagnetism* (with P. E. Hodgson, 1990) and *Responsibility* (1993).

DAVID MCNAUGHTON is Lecturer in Philosophy at the University of Keele. He has published articles in ethics and philosophy of religion, and is the author of *Moral Vision* (1988).

ALAN G. PADGETT is Professor of Theology and Philosophy of Science at Azusa Pacific University. A former doctoral student of Swinburne, he has published articles in biblical studies, philosophy, and theology, and is the author of *God, Eternity and the Nature of Time* (1992) and contributing editor of *The Mission of the Church in Methodist Perspective* (1992).

PHILIP L. QUINN is John A. O'Brien Professor of Philosophy at the University of Notre Dame. He is the author of *Divine Commands and Moral Requirements* (1978), and is currently the editor of *Faith and Philosophy*. He has also written articles in the philosophy of religion, philosophy of science, and metaphysics.

ELEONORE STUMP is Robert J. Henle Professor of Philosophy at St Louis University. She has published articles and books in medieval philosophy and philosophy of religion, including *Dialectic and its Place in the Development of Medieval Logic* (1989), and is co-editor (with Norman Kretzmann) of *The Cambridge Companion to Aquinas* (1993) and *The Cambridge Translations of Medieval Philosophical Texts* (1988).

PETER VAN INWAGEN is Professor of Philosophy, Syracuse University. He is the author of *An Essay on Free Will* (1983) and *Material Being* (1990), as well as other books and several articles.

WILLIAM J. WAINWRIGHT is Professor of Philosophy at the University of Wisconsin, Milwaukee. He has authored and edited books and articles in the philosophy of religion and the history of philosophy, two of which are his major annotated bibliography, *Philosophy of Religion* (1978), and a book entitled *Mysticism* (1981).

C. J. F. WILLIAMS is Professor of Philosophy at the University of Bristol. Among his books and articles in philosophy is his trilogy, *What is Truth?* (1976), *What is Existence?* (1981), and *What is Identity?* (1989).

I

Intellectual Autobiography

RICHARD SWINBURNE

There have been three major influences on my thinking. In order both of increasing time and of decreasing importance, they are the Christian religion, Western philosophy, and theoretical science.

As far back as my memory stretches, I recall having thought in Christian terms. Since neither of my parents was a religious believer, any human contribution to this process must be attributed to my earliest schooling at a time I can no longer recall. By the time I had passed through a British public school (spending most of my time learning Latin and Greek), done my military service (becoming a Russian interpreter), and come up as an undergraduate to Oxford University in 1954, being a Christian was, I claimed to myself, the most important thing in my life.

The world-view of the time, however, then as now, among sophisticated intellectuals was basically anti-Christian. The ethics of sophisticated intellectuals was very different from the ethics of traditional Christians. A materialism, very different from the traditional Christian world-view, was supposed to be what science favoured; and the 'scandal of particularity', God becoming incarnate in Christ in human history, was indeed regarded as a scandal— that is, absurd—by contemporary intellectuals. There was a great belief in progress, and progress seemed to mean leaving Christianity behind. My instincts favoured traditional Christianity. But I was appalled by the fact that the Church didn't seem to take seriously the claims and arguments of the current world-view. Preachers preached pious sermons which simply failed to connect with modern science, ethics, and philosophy; they expounded biblical texts, and preached attitudes. And in answer to such questions as why should one believe the Bible, does it not presuppose an out-of-date science, are not moral truths mere matters of opinion, and why should one suppose that there is a God at all, the answer was given that religion was a matter of 'faith'. But the preachers had nothing to say about why one should take a leap of faith, and why one should take it in this direction rather than that (that is, in favour of this religion rather than that rival world-view). The church's lazy indifference to modern knowledge appalled me; and I saw that, even if in the UK as many as 20 per cent of the population still went to church in 1954, things wouldn't go on like that unless Christianity were seen to fit in better with the intellectual world-view.

In due course I came to realize that behind this lazy indifference, as I saw it, lay a theological attitude. There were theological 'justifications' for why reason had no place to play in establishing the foundations of the Christian theological system. The most influential modern systematic theologians were German, of whom the best known was Karl Barth. They derived their philosophy from the Continental tradition in philosophy of the past 200 years. This included such very diverse figures as Hegel, Nietzsche, Heidegger, and Sartre. But, it seemed to me and has seemed to most Anglo-American philosophers, what characterizes them all is a certain sloppiness of argument, a tendency to draw big, vague general pictures of the Universe, without spelling them out very precisely or justifying them very thoroughly, a kind of philosophy nearer to literature than to science. And the philosopher who above all influenced the theologians was Søren Kierkegaard, who thought that the choice between world-views is a highly non-rational matter.

Now I did not wish to deny that the practice of religion is chosen; it does indeed involve giving your life generously for a supremely worthy purpose. But it needs to be shown that the purpose is in fact worthy, that the Christian way of living on earth is a good way; and this involves showing that the Christian theological system which explains why it is a good way has some reasonable chance of being true. There is no point in confessing your sins to God or worshipping him if he almost certainly doesn't exist. And if the modern world throws up some plausible arguments which suggest that he almost certainly doesn't exist, they need to be treated seriously and shown to be unsound. To ignore them is insulting to God, who has given us our reason and allowed us to use it to such good effect in theoretical and practical science. But, alas, the systematic theology fashionable in the 1950s had no resources for dealing with such matters.

Then, as now, I loved argument, and had a great interest in all big theoretical questions. This led to my reading philosophy, politics, and economics (with the weight on philosophy) for my BA degree, and so to the second major influence on my thinking. The broad stream of careful, rational argument about big metaphysical issues which has characterized most European philosophy since the Greeks had reached an odd stage in 1950s Oxford. In the Anglo-American world at large the scepticism of Hume had given rise to logical positivism, the view that the only real things were sense impressions and (possibly) material objects of a size visible to the naked eye, and that our knowledge was limited to knowledge of how things had been and would be in respect of sense impressions and material objects. And not merely our knowledge. Talk about anything else was meaningless. This view was codified in the verification principle: the only propositions which are meaningful are those which can (in some sense) be verified by observation. And hence, said the verificationists, all claims about the nature of space and time, about which moral views are true, and of course about God are not false but meaningless. In Oxford this logical positivist background had led many philosophers to hold that the only job left for philosophy was to teach people what words mean in ordinary usage, and so to help them avoid using words to state meaningless philosophical theses. If you understood what 'cause' meant—that is, how it was applied in ordinary situations—you wouldn't be tempted to say such a meaningless thing as that God caused the world! The high priest of Oxford so-called ordinary language philosophy was J. L. Austin. I attended many of his lectures and classes, and count myself fortunate to have done so. I learnt something about the subtleties of ordinary language and the need for discussion to begin with words used in their ordinary senses, even if thereafter one introduced new technical terms by means of the former. Metaphysical language must take off from and be explained in terms of ordinary language. Ordinary-language philosophy, however, had no sympathy for anything which went beyond ordinary language. But it taught one clarity of statement and thoroughness of argument. I valued Oxford philosophy greatly for its cultivation of those virtues. But there seemed to me no good reason for believing the dogmas which lay behind the practice. In particular, there seemed no good reason for believing the verification principle; but even if one did assume it, so long as you interpreted 'verified' not as 'conclusively verified' but as 'confirmed or supported by evidence or argument', then why shouldn't great metaphysical theories, including Christian theism, be verifiable and hence meaningful?

So I disliked the Oxford philosophy of the 1950s for its dogmas, but I liked it for its tools of clarity and rigour; and it seemed to me that someone could use its tools to make Christian theology again intellectually respectable. And I came to believe it to be my Christian vocation to try to make a contribution to this process. I was going to become an Anglican priest, but I became a professional philosopher instead. I went on to do graduate work in philosophy—I took the two-year Oxford B.Phil. in philosophy (the normal course at Oxford at that time for intending professional philosophers), and then a one-year diploma in theology.

The centre-piece of the modern world-view was not, however, it seemed to me, Oxford or any other brand of professional philosophy, but modern theoretical science—the physics of relativity theory and quantum theory, the biology of evolution, the genetics of DNA—which many people supposed to count against the traditional Christian world-view. And here I felt very ignorant. I had studied little science at school. I needed to study these great developments thoroughly. I was fortunate in being awarded two research fellowships (at Oxford, then at Leeds); and I devoted the three years (1960–3) which remained of these fellowships after I had taken the B.Phil. in philosophy and the diploma in theology, to learning much modern science and much history of science—how we had got to where we are. And I studied 'philosophy of science', then a very ill-cultivated branch of philosophy in England, which is a study of the meaning and justification of scientific theories, and especially of the criteria which scientists use to judge one theory as well supported and another as ruled out by the data, and of whether those criteria are ultimate or whether they can themselves be justified by some more general principle of rationality or logic.

This third influence on my thinking showed me one thing very quickly and very obviously. The great theories and predictions of modern science concerned matters far beyond observation; they concerned atoms and electrons and later quarks, far too small to be observed in any literal sense; and galaxies and quasars and the 'big bang', far too distant in space and time to be observed in any literal sense. If we insist that to be meaningful a theory has to be 'verifiable' in the sense of conclusively verifiable by observation, modern science is rendered meaningless. Yet, since it quite obviously isn't meaningless—as everyone in any way touched by the modern world-view would admit—theories could be meaningful without, in that sense, being verifiable. I saw, and in due course Anglo-American philosophy itself came to see, that verificationist dogma is fatally flawed. What makes scientific theories *meaningful* is not their verifiability, but the fact that they describe their entities (atoms) and their properties (velocity, spin) with words used somewhat similarly to words used for describing ordinary mundane things. Thus atoms are somewhat like billiard-balls, only very much smaller; they are also somewhat like waves, only not waves in media like water—words have to be used somewhat analogically in order to describe what atoms are like. Any attempt to describe them won't be totally adequate, but it can give us quite a good idea of what atoms are like. And scientific theories (or hypotheses) are *justified* in so far as (1) they lead us to expect the phenomena we observe around us; (2) those phenomena are such as we would otherwise not expect to find; and (3) the theories are simple theories.

The criterion of simplicity is crucial. If the only evidence in favour of a scientific theory was its success so far in leading us to expect what we observe (which was otherwise not to be expected), then we would never have any justification for any prediction about the future. Let me illustrate this by a simple example. Suppose that you are a scientist studying the relation of two variables (x and y) and that you have made a finite number of observations so far (particular values of y for particular values of x). You find, say, the following:

$$x \quad 1\,2\,3\,4\,5\,6$$

$$y \quad 1\,2\,3\,4\,5\,6$$

You seek a general formula connecting x and y which will allow you to predict a future value of y for a new value of x. There are an infinite number of possible formulae, all equally successful in leading you to expect what you have observed so far (which you would otherwise have no reason to expect) but diverging in their future predictions. For example, all formulae of the form $y = x + z(x-1)(x-2)(x-3)(x-4)(x-5)(x-6)$, where z is some constant, are like this. But of course you think that one of them, $y = x$, is better justified than the others; and this is because it is simpler.

The simpler theory is that most likely to be true. The simplicity of a theory is not just a matter of mathematically simple formulae connecting given variables (as in my example), but of few laws, each connecting few variables; the theory postulating few entities, few kinds of entity, few properties, and few kinds of property.

Scientists use this same pattern of argument to argue to the existence of unobservable entities as causes of the phenomena which they observe. For example, at the beginning of the nineteenth century, scientists observed many varied phenomena of chemical interaction, such as that substances combine in fixed ratios by weight to form new substances (for example, hydrogen and oxygen always form water in a ratio by weight of 1:8). They then claimed that these phenomena would be expected if there existed a hundred or so different kinds of atom, particles far too small to be seen, which combined and recombined in certain simple ways. In their turn physicists postulated electrons, protons, neutrons, and other particles in order to account for the behaviour of the atoms, as well as for larger-scale observable phenomena; and more recently they have postulated quarks in order to explain the behaviour of electrons, protons, neutrons, and most other particles. What we postulate must lead us to expect (at any rate with some probability) what we observe, when other theories do not; but the criterion of simplicity remains crucial for choice among the infinite number of theories which do so predict.

We have available to us for explaining phenomena two different kinds of explanation which we use in ordinary life. One is scientific explanation, whereby we explain a phenomenon E in terms of some prior state of affairs F (the cause) and some regularity L in the behaviour of objects involved in F and E. We explain why a stone took 2 sec to fall from a tower to the ground (E) by its having been liberated from rest at the top of the tower 64ft from the ground (F) and the regularity derivable from Galileo's law of fall that all free bodies fall towards the surface of the Earth with an acceleration of 32 ft/sec^2 (L). E follows from F and L. And science can also explain the operation of a regularity or law in some narrow area, in terms of the operation of a wider law in the particular conditions of that narrow area. Thus it can explain why Galileo's law of fall holds for small objects near the surface of the Earth. Galileo's law follows from Newton's laws, given that the Earth is a body of a certain mass far from other massive bodies and that the objects on its surface are close to it and small in mass by comparison.

The other way which we use all the time and see as a proper way of explaining phenomena is what I call personal explanation. We often explain some phenomenon E as brought about by a person P in order to achieve some purpose or goal G. The present motion of my hand is explained as brought about by me for the purpose of picking up a glass. The motion of my legs earlier towards a particular room is explained by my purpose of going there to give a lecture. In these cases I bring about a state of my body which then itself causes by processes susceptible of scientific explanation some state of affairs outside my body. But it is I (P) who bring about the bodily state (E) conducive to producing that further state (G) rather than some other. And the kind of explanation involved here is different from the scientific kind. Scientific explanation involves laws of nature and previous states of affairs. Personal explanation involves persons and purposes. In both cases, however, an explanation is better justified in so far as it invokes few entities (for example, one person rather than many), few kinds of entities, with few, easily describable properties, behaving in mathematically simple kinds of ways (for example, a person having certain capacities and purposes which do not change erratically) which give rise to many phenomena. Detectives and historians use these criteria to judge the worth of personal explanations of their data all the time. In seeking the best explanation of phenomena, we may seek explanations of either kind, and if we cannot find a scientific one which satisfies the criteria, we should look for a personal one.

Once I had seen what makes scientific and other explanatory theories meaningful and justified, I saw that any metaphysical theory, such as the Christian theological system, is a higher-level explanatory theory. Scientific theories each seek to explain a certain limited class of data: Kepler's laws sought to explain the motions of the planets; natural selection seeks to explain the fossil record and various present features of animals and plants. But some scientific theories are higher-level than others, and seek to explain the operation of the lower-level theories and the existence in the first place of the objects with which they deal. Newton's laws explained why Kepler's laws operated; and chemistry has sought to explain why there existed primitive animals and plants in the first place. A metaphysical theory is a highest-level-of-all theory. It seeks to explain why there is a universe at all, why it has the most general laws of nature that it does, and especially such laws as lead to the evolution of animals and humans, as well as any particular phenomena which lower-level laws are unable to explain. Such a theory is meaningful if it can be stated in ordinary words, stretched a bit in meaning perhaps. And it is justified if it is a simple theory and leads you to expect the observable phenomena, when you would not otherwise expect them. Once I had seen this, my programme was in place: to use the criteria of modern natural science, analysed with the careful rigour of modern philosophy, to show the meaningfulness and justification of Christian theology.

It was at this time that I discovered that someone else had the programme to use the best science and philosophy of his day to rigorously establish Christian theology. I read Part I of the *Summa Theologiae* of St Thomas Aquinas. He too started from where the secular world was in his day—the thirteenth century—and used the best secular philosophy available, that of Aristotle, instead of the initially more Christian-looking philosophy of Plato; and he sought to show that reflection on the observable world, as described by Aristotelian science, led inescapably to its creator, God. The *Summa* doesn't start from faith or religious experience or the Bible; it starts from the observable world. After an introductory question, its first main question is *utrum Deus sit*, 'Whether there is a God'; and it provides five 'ways', five arguments from the most evident general phenomena of experience—that things change, that things cause other things, and so on—to show that there is a God. I do not think that those five ways work too well in detail; and it is interesting to note that where the argument goes wrong, it is often not because Aquinas has relied unjustifiably on Christian theology, but because he has relied too much on Aristotelian science. But while I realized that the details were not always satisfactory, it seemed to me that the approach of the *Summa* was 100 per cent right. I came to see that the irrationalist spirit of modern theology was a modern phenomenon, a head-in-the-sand defensive mechanism. It is in general, I believe, the spirit of St Thomas rather than the spirit of Kierkegaard which has been the more prevalent over two millennia of Christian theology. But each generation must justify the Christian system by using the best secular knowledge of its own day; which is why the true disciple of St Thomas cannot rely on the *Summa*—he has to carry out Thomas's programme, using the knowledge of his own day.

Before I could put my programme into practice, I needed to develop thoroughly this understanding of science to which I was coming, and I needed to establish my credentials in this area in order that those who respect such work might listen to what I had to say when I began to write about religion. So after obtaining my first teaching post at the University of Hull in 1963, I devoted most of the next ten years to writing on the philosophy of science. Respect for the pronouncements of science is such a major component of the modern intellectual outlook that investigating the nature, limits, and justification of such pronouncements is a vitally worthwhile task on its own, quite apart from any consequences it might have for religion; it is also a fascinating task. I wrote two substantial books in this area: *Space and Time* (1968) and *An Introduction to Confirmation Theory* (1973). The former worked up from an analysis of our talk about distance and temporal interval to such big questions as whether there is only one space and time, why space has three dimensions and time only one, and why causes precede their effects. It had a lot to say about the interpretation of relativity theory, and was in that way a case-study of the meaning and justification of a famous scientific theory. The book on confirmation theory was crucial for my later thinking. Confirmation theory is the axiomatization of what makes what probable, or confirms it (that is, increases its probability). I sought to show that the criteria by which scientists and others judge the worth of theories, which I described in words a few pages back, can be captured by the mathematical calculus of probability, and especially by a famous theorem of that calculus—Bayes's theorem.

Apart from a short book, *The Concept of Miracle*, and a few articles, I had published nothing on the philosophy of religion before 1972. I was then ready to change gear. In that year I became Professor of Philosophy at the University of Keele, and began to write a trilogy on the philosophy of theism, the claim that there is a God. The first book of that trilogy, *The Coherence of Theism*, was concerned with what it means to say that there is a God; the second book, *The Existence of God*, was concerned with whether there is a God, and it argued that it is significantly more probable than not that there is; and the third book, *Faith and Reason*, was concerned with the relevance of arguments about the existence of God to the practice of religion.

The basic idea of the central book, *The Existence of God*, was that (with the one exception of the ontological argument) the various traditional arguments for theism—from the existence of the world (the cosmological argument), from its conformity to scientific laws (a version of the teleological argument), and so on—are best construed not as deductive arguments but as inductive arguments to the existence of God. A valid deductive argument is one in which the premisses (the starting-points) infallibly guarantee the truth of the conclusion; a correct inductive argument is one in which the premisses confirm the conclusion (that is, make it more probable than it would otherwise be). Science argues from various limited observable phenomena to their unobservable physical causes, and in so doing it argues inductively. My claim was that theism is the best justified of metaphysical theories. The existence of God is a very simple hypothesis which leads us to expect various very general and more specific phenomena which otherwise we would not expect, and for that reason is rendered probable by the phenomena. Or rather, as with any big scientific theory, each group of phenomena add to the probability of the theory; together they make it significantly more probable than not.

The cosmological argument argues from the existence of a complex physical universe to God who keeps it in being. The premiss is the existence of our universe for so long as it has existed (whether a finite time or, if it has no beginning, an infinite time). The universe is a complex thing. There are lots and lots of separate chunks of it. The chunks each have a different finite and not very natural volume, shape, mass, and so on—consider the vast diversity of galaxies, stars, and planets, and pebbles on the sea-shore. Matter is inert, and has no powers which it can choose to exert; it does what it has to do. There is a limited amount of it in any region, and it has a limited amount of energy and velocity. There is a complexity, particularity, and finitude about the universe which looks for explanation in terms of something simpler. The existence of the universe is something evidently inexplicable by science. For, as we saw, a scientific explanation as such explains the occurrence of one state of affairs in terms of a previous state of affairs and some law of nature which makes states like the former bring about states like the latter. It may explain the planets being in their present positions by a previous state of the system (the Sun and planets being where they were last year) and the operation of Kepler's laws, which specify that states like the latter are followed a year later by states like the former. And so it may explain the existence of the universe this year in terms of the existence of the universe last year and the laws of cosmology. But either there was a first state of the universe, or there has always been a universe. In the former case, science cannot explain why there was the first state; and in the latter case it still cannot explain why there was ever any matter (or, more correctly, matter-energy) for the laws of nature to get a grip on, as it were. By its very nature, science cannot explain why there are any states of affairs at all.

But a God can provide an explanation. The hypothesis of theism is that the universe exists because there is a God who keeps it in being and that the laws of nature operate because there is a God who brings it about that they do. He brings it about that the laws of nature operate by sustaining in every object in the universe its liability to behave in accord with those laws (including the law of the conservation of matter, that at each moment what was there before continues to exist). The universe exists because at each moment of finite or infinite time, God keeps in being objects with this liability. The hypothesis is a hypothesis that a person brings about these things for some purpose. He acts directly on the universe, as we act directly on our brains, guiding them to move our limbs (but the universe is not his body—for he could at any moment destroy it, and act on another universe, or do without a universe). As we have seen, personal explanation and scientific explanation are the two ways we have of explaining the occurrence of phenomena. Since there cannot be a scientific explanation of the existence of the universe, either there is a personal explanation or there is no explanation at all. The hypothesis that there is a God is the hypothesis of the existence of the simplest kind of person which there could be. A person is a being with *power* to bring about effects, *knowledge* of how to do so, and *freedom* to make choices of which effects to bring about. God is by definition an omnipotent (that is, infinitely powerful), omniscient (that is, all-knowing), and perfectly free person; he is a person of infinite power, knowledge, and freedom; a person to whose power, knowledge, and freedom there are no limits except those of logic. The hypothesis that there exists a being with infinite degrees of the qualities essential to a being of that kind is the postulation of a very simple being. The hypothesis that there is one such God is a much simpler hypothesis than the hypothesis that there is a god who has such and such limited power, or the hypothesis that there are several gods with limited powers. It is simpler in just the same way that the hypothesis that some particle has zero mass or infinite velocity is simpler than the hypothesis that it has 0.32147 of some unit of mass or a velocity of 221,000 km/sec. A finite limitation cries out for an explanation of why there is just that particular limit, in a way that limitlessness does not. God provides the simplest stopping-point for explanation.

That there should exist anything at all, let alone a universe as complex and as orderly as ours, is exceedingly strange. But if there is a God, it is not vastly unlikely that he should create such a universe. A universe such as ours is a thing of beauty and a theatre in which humans and other creatures can grow and work out their destiny, a point which I shall develop further below. So the argument from the universe to God is an argument from a complex phenomenon to a simple entity which leads us to expect (though does not guarantee) the existence of the former far more than it would be expected otherwise. Therefore, I suggest, it provides some evidence for its conclusion.

The teleological argument, or argument from design, has various forms. One form is the argument from temporal order. This has as its premisses the operation of the most general laws of nature: that is, the orderliness of nature in conforming to very general laws. What exactly these laws are, science may not yet have discovered—perhaps they are the field equations of Einstein's General Theory of Relativity, or perhaps there are some yet more fundamental laws. Now, as we have seen, science can explain the operation of some narrow regularity or law in terms of a wider or more general law. But what science by its very nature cannot explain is why there are the most general laws of nature that there are; for, *ex hypothesi*, no wider law can explain their operation.

Yet the conformity of objects throughout endless time and space to simple laws cries out for explanation. For let us consider what this amounts to. Laws are not things, independent of material objects. To say that all objects conform to laws is simply to say that they all behave in exactly the same way. To say, for example, that the planets obey Kepler's laws is just to say that each planet at each moment of time has the property of moving in the ways that Kepler's laws state. There is, therefore, this vast coincidence in the behavioural properties of objects at all times and in all places. If all the coins of some region have the same markings, or all the papers in a room are written in the same handwriting, we seek an explanation in terms of a common source of these coincidences. We should seek a similar explanation for that vast coincidence which we describe as the conformity of objects to laws of nature—for example, the fact that all electrons are produced, attract and repel other particles, and combine with them in exactly the same way at each point of endless time and space.

Again, there is available the simple explanation of the temporal orderliness of the universe: that God makes protons and electrons move in an orderly way, just as we might make our bodies move in the regular patterns of a dance. He has, *ex hypothesi*, the power to do this. But why should he choose to do so? The orderliness of the universe makes it a beautiful universe, but, even more important, it makes it a universe which men can learn to control and change. For only if there are simple laws of nature can humans predict what will follow from what—and unless they can do that, they can never change anything. Only if they know that by sowing certain seeds and weeding and watering them they will get corn, can they develop an agriculture. And humans can only acquire that knowledge if there are easily graspable regularities of behaviour in nature. It is good that there be human beings, embodied mini-creators who share in God's activity of forming and developing the universe through their free choice. But if there are to be such, there must be laws of nature. There is, therefore, some reasonable expectation that God will bring them about; but otherwise, that the Universe should exhibit such very striking order is hardly to be expected.

A similar pattern of argument from various other phenomena, such as the existence of conscious beings, the providential ordering of things in certain respects, the occurrence of certain apparently miraculous events in history, and the religious experiences of many millions, is, I claimed in *The Existence of God*, available to establish theism (when all the arguments are taken together) as overall significantly more probable than not.

My trilogy was finished in 1981. It concerned mainly bare theism—the meaning, justification, and relevance of the claim that there is a God. But Christianity claims a lot more than that. Along with many other religions, Christianity involves a view of human beings which distinguishes them sharply from ordinary material objects. And here I knew that there was entrenched very deeply in the modern world-view a materialist doctrine—that a human being was nothing but a very complicated material object, a highly sophisticated robot. That doctrine seemed to me, on grounds quite independent of theology, to be totally mistaken.

When a conscious human being continues to exist for a period of time, however short, there are two things going on. His body has continued to exist, with its physical characteristics of shape and mass realized in the arrangements and rearrangements of its chemical molecules. Also the human has had thoughts and feelings; and the description of a person as having thoughts and feelings neither entails nor is entailed by his having a body. A true and full description of the world will therefore list two things as continuing: a part of the human, let us call it the soul, having thoughts and feelings; and his body, having shape and mass. That there are two substances, two entities, involved—body and soul—is the doctrine of substance dualism, clearly stated by Descartes, among other philosophers. The essential part of the human person is the soul; for it is being the same subject of thought, not having the same body, which makes the same person. Soul and body interact, of course, and—while embodied—the soul depends on the body for its ability to function. But that makes no difference to the fact that there are two things involved. Modern materialism tries to pretend otherwise, saying that *really* the soul is the body; and *really* thoughts are movements of molecules. But this is newspeak, defining away some evident feature of experience by definition. I find the arguments for substance dualism overwhelmingly strong, and the reluctance of some philosophers and scientists to recognize here what stares them in the face something deeply worrying, to be explained only by a process of irrational culture conditioning.

I devoted the next five years to articulating the case for substance dualism, and my defence of that doctrine and of connected doctrines about the nature of human beings (for example, their possession of free will) was published in final form in *The Evolution of the Soul* in 1986. Christian theology vitally needs the doctrine of substance dualism—for if there is to be life after death, the essential part of the person must be something other than the body, which can be reduced to ashes or even chunks of energy.

My treatment of this issue was a prolegomenon to treatment of specifically Christian doctrines; and having finished it, I began work on a tetralogy on the philosophical issues involved in Christian doctrines. I write the 'philosophical' issues, because Christianity is a historical religion, and some of its doctrines require historical evidence to support them. A philosopher is not competent to treat of that; but he can show where we need historical evidence and how much relevance it has to an overall case, for which other grounds can also be provided; and that I have sought to do. My treatment of specifically Christian matters coincided with my move back to Oxford to a chair entitled 'The Nolloth Professorship of the Philosophy of the Christian Religion'.

The first volume of this planned tetralogy, entitled *Responsibility and Atonement* was published in 1989. When we do good or harm to each other, various of a set of moral notions have application: we are guilty or meritorious; we need to repent and apologize and make reparation; others need to forgive us, or, as the case may be, express gratitude or reward us; or they may punish us. Part I of *Responsibility and Atonement* was devoted to analysing these notions and seeing when they apply to the dealings of humans with each other. Part II then directed the results of part I to analysing the meaning and justification of those Christian doctrines which utilize these notions to describe the relations between God and human beings: for example, doctrines of sin and original sin, the Atonement, eternal punishment and eternal reward.

The second volume, *Revelation*, was published in 1991. Christianity has traditionally claimed to announce truths revealed by God. *Revelation* investigates what would be evidence that creeds and the Bible are revealed. There are prior philosophical questions about how meaning can be conveyed by analogy and metaphor within the false scientific and historical presuppositions of an ancient culture; and I treat of these in part I of that work before applying my results to the Christian claim. I conclude that if the Christian revelation, properly interpreted, is to be credible, its contents must have a certain prior probability and there must be some reasonable historical evidence to show that the miracle of the Resurrection took place, to give them divine authentication. I argue that some New

Testament scholars have had quite unreasonably high standards for assessing the worth of historical evidence about the occurrence of particular events; and my own belief is that when reasonable standards are applied, there is sufficient historical evidence to support the view that the Resurrection took place in roughly the way described in the Gospels.

The third volume, *The Christian God*, should be published at the end of 1994. It moves quickly through some of the issues discussed in *The Coherence of Theism* about what it means to say that there is a God, before applying the resulting account of the divine nature to the Christian doctrines of the Trinity and the Incarnation. I argue that there is significant prior probability that each of these doctrines (and especially the doctrine of the Trinity) is true, before we turn to the witness of revelation (that is, the teaching of the Church) in confirmation of them. Part I of this book is concerned with crucial metaphysical notions like substance, property, cause, time, and necessity; I develop theses about these matters before utilizing them in discussion of the divine nature.

Although I devoted some two and a half chapters of *The Existence of God* to the problem of evil, I have since then felt the need for a much fuller discussion of this topic, in the light of specifically Christian doctrines (such as life after death and the suffering of Christ). This I intend to provide in the final volume of my tetralogy, probably to be entitled *Providence*. Christianity badly needs a well-articulated theodicy, explaining why God allows pain and suffering to occur. I believe that the clue to theodicy is the realization that thrills of pleasure are not the only good states of affairs, nor are twinges of pain the only bad ones. There are many and far better good states than thrills of pleasure, and many and far worse bad states than twinges of pain. One of the best things that can happen to a person is to be of use to others; another is to have a free will able to influence the way things go in the world. Once one sees this, one comes to understand that pain and suffering of limited intensity and duration make possible for oneself and others the greater goods of free choice and service. But to show this in watertight detail is, I believe, a lengthy and difficult philosophical enterprise, which I shall try to achieve in *Providence*.

In all my works on the philosophy of religion, the approach has been to start from where secular humanity stands in some area of thought, develop a coherent philosophy of that area, and then consider whether that philosophy leads to a Christian understanding of things in some respect. I like to think that I have approached each topic without taking any theological position at the start, and prepared to follow where the argument leads. There is no other way to proceed in the philosophy of religion if its results are to be made rationally acceptable to those who are initially non-religious and also to those who, while religious, are more convinced of the secular starting-points than of their religious beliefs. Hence the philosopher of religion needs to be more than an amateur in other areas of philosophy; and I have written, at least at article length, on most other such areas. All philosophy concerns exciting and important issues; and, hard work though it is, I have enjoyed discussing the issues with colleagues and students, learning from their work, and, I hope, advancing things a bit further in all the areas of philosophy in which I have worked.

It has been an enormous privilege to be allowed to spend my working life doing philosophy, and especially being allowed to try to contribute in a small way towards making Christian theology intellectually respectable again. I am immensely grateful for this privilege—grateful to God, grateful to my atheistic philosophy friends for their tolerance and open-mindedness towards an odd colleague, and grateful to the public who, unknowingly and indirectly, have paid my salary for philosophizing all these years. Nor, or course, have I been alone in trying to do this. A considerable number of philosophers in the Anglo-American empiricist tradition, mainly in the United States, have been working in their various ways to relocate Christianity in its proper place at the centre of a rational, scientifically sensitive world-view. I am greatly indebted to their work and their personal friendship, and also to the work and personal friendship of the graduate students whom I have supervised in recent years.

I am very conscious that my intellectual development has been largely a matter of systematizing and justifying what I believed in a very vague way forty years ago. Although my views on lesser matters have changed, my world-view has not changed. I remain convinced that there is a significant balance of evidence in favour of Christian theism. I am well aware that I do not like changing habits or attitudes, and that there is another explanation of my intellectual development which has some initial plausibility—that I am simply too 'pig-headed' to change my mind under the pressure of experience and the force of the arguments of my philosophical opponents to which I have been exposed during my philosophical career. All that I can plead in defence is that holding a true view about very big metaphysical issues matters to me enormously, and that I have continually sought out objections to my position and tried to explore their force. I do honestly believe that if I had judged that experience or argument led to a position contrary to that of my youth, I would not have concealed that fact from myself. I have no wish to worship a God who does not exist, and in consequence I have sometimes found myself *beginning* to pray 'O God, if you do not exist, help me to see that fact'!

When my book on *Providence* is finished, I do not see myself as having anything further to say at book length on the philosophy of religion. I shall have said what I have to say. But I hope to continue to publicize and defend what I have already said, in various ways; as well perhaps as writing books on certain philosophical theses— for example, about simplicity and necessity—underlying some of my writing on the philosophy of religion but which fall centrally within other branches of philosophy. I am an impatient person, and have never enjoyed the present moment as much as I ought to have done. I have always looked forward. I continue to look forward to completing academic projects; and, please God, I look forward also to what God will do with me when this life is over. But fear and trembling are the only proper attitudes with which a creature may appear before his creator. And I pray that God may give me the time and the grace to prepare for That Day.

PART I

Faith and Reason

2

Swinburne on Faith and Belief

WILLIAM P. ALSTON

I

In *Faith and Reason*[1] Swinburne sets out an ambitious and impressive account of religious faith and the epistemology thereof, one that is based on a general account of belief and of rational belief in particular. In this chapter I will take issue with his general theory of belief, arguing that it is untenable. I will also make a few remarks on his discussion of the rationality of belief, but, though I do have some rather serious reservations about this account, I will refrain from going into them in detail. Since I will have given what I take to be conclusive reasons for rejecting Swinburne's account of the nature of belief, I feel called upon to consider what modifications, if any, this demands in his admirably balanced, acute account of religious faith. Fortunately, so far as I can see, little change is called for. Aside from some minor rewriting, the treatment of faith survives unscathed the demise of the general theory of belief on which it is putatively based.

II

In the second paragraph of chapter 1 Swinburne enunciates his most basic thesis concerning the nature of belief, one in terms of which a great deal of the book is set.

So, then, what is it to believe that so-and-so, that today is Monday or that there is a God? I suggest that the primary concept of belief picked out by public criteria is the concept of believing so-and-so more probable (or more likely) than such-and-such. (pp. 3–4)[2]

---

[1] Oxford: Clarendon Press, 1981. References to this book are included in the body of the text.
[2] See also pp. 8, 11, 18, 21, 25, 119, and many other such passages.

As this formula implies, and as Swinburne goes on immediately to make explicit, belief is always relative to alternatives.

> You believe of one proposition as against another proposition, or propositions, that the former is more probable than any of the latter; and what your belief in the former amounts to depends on what are the latter. (p. 4)

Thus, if my belief before the last US presidential election that Bush would win was the belief that his winning was more likely than that either of the other serious contenders would win, it was a different belief from believing that Bush's victory was more likely than his failing to win (here the alternative is just the negation of the specified proposition) or that his victory was more likely than Clinton's. Swinburne opines that normally the alternative with which a proposition is contrasted is its negation (p. 4). But he fully acknowledges that other contrasts are sometimes in the picture, and, as we will see, he makes an important application of this point when he considers religious belief.

What concept of probability is employed in this account? It is the concept of 'epistemic probability'.

> The epistemic probability of a proposition is a measure of the extent to which evidence renders it likely to be true. Epistemic probability is relative to evidence. Whether a proposition is epistemically probable or not depends on the evidence-class relative to which the probability is assessed. . . . In statements about an individual's beliefs it is presumably the evidence available to the man himself rather than the evidence available to any community which is involved. So my claim that S believes that *p* if and only if S believes that *p* is more probable than any alternative amounts to the claim that S believes that *p* if and only if S believes that the total evidence available to him makes *p* more probable than any alternative. (pp. 18–19)

According to Swinburne a subject's evidence consists of the set of propositions that are 'basic' for that subject (p. 20). And what is it for a proposition to be basic for a subject?

> I shall call those propositions which seem to a man to be true and which he is inclined to believe, but not solely on the ground that they are made probable by other propositions which he believes, his basic propositions. Among a man's basic propositions are those propositions which report his perceptions ('I see a clock') or what he perceives ('the clock reads 5.10'), his memories ('I remember going to London yesterday') or what he remembers ('it rained in London yesterday'). (p. 20)

A basic proposition will acquire the status of a belief (and we may then call it a basic belief) unless other of a man's basic beliefs render it improbable. Most of a man's basic propositions acquire the status of beliefs, but some do not. (p. 21)[3]

Note that Swinburne's criterion for basicality is only that the person not be inclined to believe the proposition *solely on the grounds that it is made probable by other propositions the person believes*. This leaves open the possibility that the proposition might be believed, in part, because of its support from other beliefs. Thus Swinburne's classification of (many) perceptual beliefs as basic is compatible with the view that those beliefs are partly based on other, 'background' beliefs, so long as there is a non-doxastic basis—for example, experience—in the picture as well.

Although the examples of basic propositions Swinburne gave in the above passage were taken from (one version of) the 'canon', he makes it explicit that he

puts no restriction on the kind of propositions which can function as basic propositions. A man's basic propositions may include not merely ordinary reports of things perceived and remembered, but his 'hunches' and 'intuitions' which he thinks are justified by the experiences to which he has been subjected but cannot justify in terms of propositions. (p. 22)

Indeed, he goes so far as to say that 'Where a man's belief has no evidence expressible in words, we just say that the proposition believed is one of the man's basic propositions which acquired the status of a belief because he had such confidence in it that it was not overruled by any other evidence' (p. 23).[4]

Why should Swinburne restrict a person's evidence to the set of basic propositions for that person? Can't I believe that a given proposition is rendered more likely than its negation by evidence that consists, in whole or in part, of propositions that themselves are believed solely on the basis of further evidence? Perhaps I

---

[3] Swinburne is undoubtedly attributing much too much rationality to his fellow human beings in supposing that a proposition I am inclined to believe not wholly on the basis of evidence will not actually be believed by me if it is rendered improbable by the set of my basic beliefs. Clearly, people are not always so perspicacious as to withhold belief when that condition is satisfied. This point could be taken care of by replacing 'unless other of a man's basic beliefs render it improbable' with 'unless the person sees that other of his basic beliefs render it improbable'.

[4] Note that in this last sentence Swinburne is implicitly recognizing the point made in n. 3. If I have enough confidence in the truth of a proposition, I will believe it even if the rest of my beliefs make it improbable.

thought it more likely than not that Clinton would lose the election because of the results of certain polls, where my belief that those polls have those results is itself accepted solely on the basis of evidence—for example, reports in the newspapers. Swinburne would not wish to deny this obvious fact. His restriction of evidence to basic propositions reflects a foundationalist assumption that the support for all non-basic beliefs can ultimately be traced back to basic beliefs.

Normally . . . men do not consider directly whether their evidence makes some proposition probable (or rules out some would-be basic belief), but only whether their other beliefs do this, but this is on the assumption (which can be questioned) that those other beliefs are rendered probable by evidence. Once a proposition . . . is admitted into the belief-corpus, it plays its part in promoting further beliefs, without the extent of its own evidential support very often being brought explicitly into question. (pp. 21–2)

Note that what Swinburne is committing himself to here is what we might call 'psychological foundationalism', the view that all non-basic beliefs are based, directly or indirectly, on basic beliefs,[5] rather than epistemic foundationalism, the view that in order to be *justified* a non-basic belief must be based, directly or indirectly, on basic beliefs. Psychological foundationalism would seem to be a more difficult thesis to defend. It implies the denial of one kind of (foundationally) unjustified belief, one that is not basic and is not based, even indirectly, on basic beliefs. It does seem plausible to suppose that people do have such beliefs. Consider various superstitious and prejudiced beliefs. To be sure, psychological foundationalism does not go so far as to imply that there are no foundationally unjustified beliefs. A non-basic belief could be based, directly or indirectly, on basic beliefs, without its being so related to the latter that they provide adequate support for it.

I have been representing Swinburne as applying the concept of epistemic probability only to non-basic beliefs, and that does seem to be the general tenor of his discussion. As we saw, he held that a basic proposition will be believed unless one's other basic beliefs render it improbable. Thus it would seem that basic belief does not fall under the view with which we started and which is presented as a general account of belief: namely, that to believe that *p* is to believe that *p* is more probable than———. For that was explained in

---

[5] See Robert Audi, 'Psychological Foundationalism', *The Monist*, lxii (1978), 592–610.

terms of *p*'s being rendered more probable than——by one's evidence; and basic beliefs were not described in this way. Even if, as we have seen Swinburne allow, a basic belief could be partly based on one's evidence, he never suggests that to have a basic belief that *p* is to believe that *p* is rendered more probable than some alternative by one's evidence. On the contrary, to have a basic belief that *p* is for one's intuitive inclination to believe that *p* not to be checked by one's seeing that *p* is rendered improbable by one's other basic beliefs. Probability comes in here only in a negative, not in a positive, role.[6] I do not find Swinburne explicitly recognizing that his general account of belief does not apply to basic beliefs on his account of the latter. He could, of course, treat basic beliefs as a limiting case of the general account, a case in which the belief is held to be rendered probable by one's evidence because it is part of that evidence. But I don't find Swinburne doing this either.

In any event, Swinburne is obviously most interested in non-basic beliefs, both as to their nature and as to their epistemic evaluation. This is, no doubt, because he is assuming that all religious beliefs, or at least the more prominent ones, are non-basic (Plantinga notwithstanding[7]).

Swinburne also has a fair amount to say about the relation of belief and action. Though he holds that a person's beliefs have consequences as to how that person will seek to bring about his or her purposes, consequences of a very complicated sort, he denies that that is all there is to belief (p. 12). There is also 'an inner attitude toward a proposition' (p. 16). I find this discussion exemplary, and I will proffer no criticisms of it.

III

Returning to Swinburne's view of non-basic beliefs with which I began, I now want to explain why it seems to me untenable. The

---

[6] But consider the following: 'When a man is asked why he is initially inclined to believe some basic proposition, with the degree of confidence in question, the only answer which he can give is that his experiences have been such that it seems to him to be probable to that degree' (p. 20). This naturally suggests that basic beliefs (are taken to) acquire epistemic probability on experience in a way analogous to that in which non-basic beliefs acquire probability on evidence. But Swinburne does not develop the suggestion.

[7] See Alvin Plantinga, 'Reason and Belief in God', in A. Plantinga and N. Wolterstorff (eds.), *Faith and Rationality* (Notre Dame, Ind.: University of Notre Dame Press, 1983), 16–93.

most obvious objection is that it is too sophisticated to stand as a general account of even non-basic belief. Confronted with such a view, my first critical reaction is that at the most basic and rudimentary level cognitive subjects have beliefs about things they encounter in their environment, without having any beliefs at all about the extent to which various propositions are rendered more or less probable by evidence. In thinking about this, let us recognize that Swinburne makes it explicit that the beliefs about probability he takes to constitute non-basic beliefs are not supposed to involve specific numerical probability assignments (p. 19). Comparative probability judgements would be sufficient. But even these are much too sophisticated for many believers. I will leave aside lower animals, to many of whom I am prepared to ascribe beliefs. Let us take it that Swinburne's target is restricted to believers of at least a human level of intellectual capacity. But even this territory is not peopled solely by those who have the resources to form beliefs about epistemic probability. Leaving primitive cultures to one side, let us just consider very small children and persons with diminished mental capacity. I take it to be clear that children, virtually from birth, form beliefs about their surroundings, and it is equally clear that they do not begin to make even rudimentary probability judgements until they have reached a stage of mental development considerably beyond that. And even restricting ourselves to those with the conceptual resources for making comparative probability judgements, how often do they do so? Every time they form a (non-basic) belief, according to Swinburne. But that seems wildly implausible to me. Every day I form innumerable, usually short-lived non-basic beliefs. I glance out of my window and note that the new building opposite is not finished yet. That is a non-basic belief, based on the (possibly basic) belief that no windows have yet been installed on the side facing me. Did I form the belief that the proposition that the building is not yet finished is rendered more probable than some alternative— such as its negation—by my set of basic propositions? If so, I regularly carry out such doxastic operations in a way ideally calculated to escape my notice. I am not opposed on principle to positing unconscious cognitive operations, where there is good and sufficient reason to do so. But I can think of no reason here more respectable than the desire to save a theory from refutation.

To be sure, Swinburne backs off from the most extreme possible version of his thesis. He assures us that he does not claim that 'men make very explicit calculations' when forming beliefs regarding comparative probabilities (p. 21). 'Nor do I imply that a man who on some evidence believes a proposition, can say why his evidence makes the proposition probable, can state explicitly the inductive standards (i.e., standards for one proposition making another probable) which he uses' (p. 22). But none of this touches the dual implausibility of supposing that all believers have the conceptual resources for making probability judgements and of supposing that those who do are making use of them whenever they come to believe anything (non-basically).

It is worth noting in this connection that when Swinburne argues for his account, he totally ignores the possibility that someone believes that p and yet lacks any belief about the probability of p.

What can be said in favour of this claim? To start with, if I do not believe that p is probable, I cannot believe that p is true. If I believe that it is more probable that non-p than that p, I cannot believe that p. (p. 4)

Here Swinburne is obviously taking 'I believe that it is more probable that not-p than p' to be equivalent to 'I do not believe that p is probable', thus ignoring the other way in which the latter may be true: namely, by not having any belief about the probability of p at all.

A somewhat less obvious, but more obviously fatal, objection to Swinburne's view is that it involves an infinite regress. Swinburne notices that he has a problem here.

It may be objected to my account that it leads to an infinite regress. For on that account normally to believe that p is to believe that p is more probable than not-p, i.e., to believe that p is probable. If S believes that p, then S believes that p is probable. So, by substitution, it follows that S believes that it is probable than p is probable. And so on. (p. 6)

Swinburne holds that this regress is not harmful on the grounds that it would be vicious only if it occurred in a definition, and the view in question was not intended to be a definition of 'believe that p' (p. 6). But I can't see that the regress constitutes a difficulty only if it arises from a definition. The difficulty is that, on Swinburne's own showing, the view implies that one cannot believe anything without having an infinitely complex belief, something that is presumably beyond human powers. This implication holds for the very reason he gives: namely, that any belief that p is construed to be the belief that it is probable that p (roughly speaking). That is, whatever propositional object we specify for a belief, the belief is not that *that* proposition is true, but rather the more complex belief that that proposition enjoys a certain comparative probability status. And the view will apply in just the same way to this enriched specification of the propositional object. The belief isn't the belief that *that* proposition is true either; rather its propositional object is of a still greater complexity. And so on *ad infinitum.* We never succeed in saying what the propositional object of the belief is. No matter how complex we make it, it is always something still more complex. No proposition of merely finite complexity will do the trick. (And perhaps no proposition of infinite complexity either!) It is an understatement to say that the view makes it impossible to *say* what the propositional object of any belief is. Worse, it implies the impossibility of any finite propositional object, any object that is within human ken. In short, it has the disastrous implication that no finite creature believes anything.

To avoid this disaster, Swinburne would have to cut off the regress at a certain point by saying that his view no longer applies beyond that point. From that point on, believing that p no longer consists in believing that p is more probable than some alternative, but just consists in believing that p, full stop. But what possible rationale could be given for the choice of such a point, beyond the starting-point? If sooner or later we are forced to say that to believe that p is just to believe that p, why shouldn't we say that at the outset? Why were we launched on this wild-goose chase in the first place?[8] If one were to choose some point beyond the start at which believing that p is just believing that p, the most reasonable (least unreasonable) choice would be the second level—the first specification of a probability assignment as the propositional object of the belief. This does seem to be Swinburne's basic conviction. The only things we can believe are comparative probabilities. Whenever some belief content other than a comparison of probabilities is specified, that object turns out on analysis to be a comparison of probabilities after all. But where the propositional content is already specified as a comparison of probabilities, there is no need to add to the content to give it that shape; it already wears that

---

[8] As we have seen, Swinburne's attempts to motivate the initial move are far from convincing.

character on its face. When the view is put in that stark a form, its absurdity becomes apparent. Surely it is obvious that probability comparisons are, at best, among the (many different sorts of) things we can believe; and it would seem that they occupy a rather minor place in the variety, at that.

Here is something about which we have to be careful. On the view in question, to believe that *p* is to believe that X is more probable than Y, Z,... What sorts of items are these probability-bearers? If you say 'beliefs', you are in trouble. If to believe that *p* is to believe that the *belief* that *p* is more probable than——, we will never be able to say what belief it is we are believing to be more probable than——. The trouble is that the phrase 'the belief that *p*' occurs as part of an explanation of what the belief that *p* is. This means that when we substitute the *explanans* for 'the belief that *p*', we get 'the belief that *p*' as part of that again. The belief that *p* is a proper part of itself! Usually Swinburne's exposition of his view simply uses the dummy letter *p* without any further specification. 'Normally to believe that *p* is to believe that *p* is more probable than not-*p*' (p. 4). If we interpret *p* as standing for a proposition, as Swinburne sometimes explicitly indicates, we are not in this particular difficulty. The (so-called) belief that *p* could be the belief that the proposition that *p* is more probable than——, without forcing us to chase our tail in the above fashion. But sometimes Swinburne talks as if the belief that *p* is the belief that the *belief* that *p* is more probable than, for example, the belief that not-*p*. 'The normal alternative with which a belief is contrasted is its negation.' Emphasize 'its', and you get the false step that the belief that *p* is the belief that the belief that *p* is more probable that the belief that not-*p*. But it would be more charitable, as well as more accurate, to put this down to the common and (usually) harmless ambiguity of 'belief' between a psychological state and the propositional object of said state.

IV

Before examining the effects of the abandonment of Swinburne's account of the nature of belief on his treatment of religious faith, I will glance briefly at his account of rational belief. He first gives a preliminary indication of how he is using the term 'rational belief' by saying: 'Roughly a man's belief is a rational belief if he is justified in holding it—for epistemological reasons.' He then explains 'epistemological reason' as follows: 'the only reasons which concern us here are reasons which concern the likelihood of it [the belief] being true—these I will call epistemological reasons' (p. 45). He then distinguishes five kinds of rationality, as follows:

1 'A subject S who believes that p will have what I shall call a rational$_1$ belief if and only if his belief that p is probable, given his inductive standards and given his evidence' (p. 45).

2 'A subject who believes that p has what I shall call a rational$_2$ belief if and only if p is in fact rendered probable by his evidence, and his evidence consists of basic propositions which he is in fact justified in holding with the degree of confidence with which he does hold them' (p. 46).

3 'A subject S who believes that p has, I shall say, a rational$_3$ belief if and only if S's evidence results from past investigation which was in S's view adequate, his inductive standards have been subjected to criticism by S which was in S's view adequate, and S has checked in his view adequately that p is made probable by his evidence' (p. 49).

4 'A subject S who believes that p has a rational$_4$ belief if and only if S's evidence results from past investigation which was by S's own standards adequate, and his inductive standards have been subjected to criticism by S which is by S's own standards adequate, and S has checked adequately by his own standards that p is made probable by his evidence' (p. 53).

5 'S's belief that p is a rational$_5$ belief if and only if S's evidence results from past investigation which was adequate and inductive standards which have been submitted to adequate criticism, and S has investigated adequately whether his evidence makes his belief probable' (p. 54).

The dominant direction in this list is toward greater objectivity and greater critical-reflective validation. R_2 differs from R_1 in that the latter requires probability relative to S's evidence and inductive standards, while the former requires that the evidence be made up of justified beliefs and that the standards be the correct ones. R_3, R_4, and R_5 differ from the first two in that the subject has engaged in critical examination of the evidence and/or the standards, with positive results. R_3 requires only that it be S's opinion that the checking was adequate, R_4 that the checking be adequate by S's standards for such investigation, and R_5 that the checking has, in fact, been adequate. Thus we get increased objectivity when we move from R_3 to R_5.

There are several troubling features of this account. First, and most glaring, is that it would seem to be restricted to non-basic beliefs, since it all has to do with the probability of the belief on evidence, something that Swinburne considers only in relation to non-basic beliefs. Some of the definitions themselves indicate that Swinburne is prepared to speak of basic beliefs as 'justified' or not. Then why not 'rational'? Remember that he led off the discussion by explaining 'rational' as 'justified for epistemological reasons', those reasons that concern the likelihood of the belief's being true (p. 45). But, on his account, what renders a basic belief justified—that it is held not wholly on the basis of evidence and that it is not rendered improbable by other basic beliefs—certainly has to do with the likelihood of the belief's being true. So why restrict the account of rationality to non-basic beliefs?

Second, the account is wholly in terms of how the belief is related to what evidence the subject has. Nothing is said about what the belief is *based on*, the reasons for which it is held. So long as I have (justified) evidence on which my belief that p is probable, then I am rational₂ in believing it, whether my belief is based on that evidence, held because of it, or not. That leaves us open to counter-examples like the following. I have considerable evidence that a colleague is trying to get me dismissed from my position, and I believe that he is. But I believe this not because of the evidence, which I have never put together properly, but because of strong paranoid tendencies that, for evidentially irrelevant reasons, have fastened on him. By Swinburne's criteria I am—or could well be—rational₂ in this belief, despite its disreputable provenance. Because of that provenance the belief is clearly lacking in some important dimension of rationality, one not provided for in any of Swinburne's definitions.

Third, why do R_3, R_4, and R_5 speak of S's evidence as having resulted from *investigation*? Remember that, as Swinburne sets things up, one's evidence consists of the set of one's basic beliefs, and it seems clear from Swinburne's explanation of 'basic belief' and from the examples he gives that basic beliefs would not usually be acquired by anything properly called 'investigation'. One's perceptual and memory beliefs, as well as one's beliefs in self-evident propositions, typically just come to one willy-nilly, not as a result of an attempt to answer some question. Of course, one can perceive and remember things in the course of an investigation, but ordinarily, whether one is justified in holding the perceptual or memory belief has nothing to do with the adequacy or other evaluative status of the investigation. If I am investigating a mysterious death, the epistemic status of the conclusion I come to concerning how the person died (a non-basic belief) will be sensitive to good- or bad-making features of the investigation. But the various perceptual beliefs I form in the course of the investigation will be justified, or not, independently of the merits of the investigative procedures. Perhaps when Swinburne was constructing these definitions he had slipped back into a more ordinary use of the word 'evidence', in which anything one believes—basic or non-basic—can function as evidence. That would at least make the adequacy of investigation relevant to the epistemic status of some of the territory.

If I were concerned here with Swinburne's treatment of rationality for its own sake, I would go further into these issues. But the above will suffice as a basis for the discussion of faith, to which I now turn.

V

Swinburne's account of faith is nicely balanced. He begins with the point that 'The faith which the Christian religion commends is basically faith in a person or persons, God (or Christ) characterized as possessing certain properties and having done certain actions; and secondarily perhaps in some of the deeds which he has done, and the good things which he has provided and promised' (p. 104). The question then is 'what this "belief in" or "faith in" amounts to' (ibid.). He proceeds by expounding three views of faith: Thomist, Lutheran, and what he calls 'pragmatist'. He claims that all the views take faith to involve both propositional belief and trust, though the relative emphasis and the role assigned to these components differ across the views (p. 118). He also points out that on all these views 'the sort of faith which is meritorious involves . . . a good character, normally shown in good actions' (ibid.). With all that on the table I can proceed to point out that my concern here is with the propositional belief component of faith, and more specifically with how Swinburne's treatment of it is or is not dependent on his account of belief, which we have seen ample reason to reject.

The main use Swinburne makes of his conception of belief in his account of faith concerns the point that 'the strength of belief that a proposition is true is ... a matter of the alternatives with which the proposition is contrasted'. Both in chapter 1, on the nature of belief, and again in chapter 4, on the nature of faith, he derives this claim from his most basic thesis concerning belief: 'To believe a proposition is to believe it more probable than any alternative. So what the belief amounts to depends on what are the alternatives' (p. 119). As we saw earlier, he holds that to believe that *p* is more probable than not-*p* is to make a stronger claim than to believe only that *p* is more probable than some of its contraries. And since any (non-basic) belief is a belief that some proposition is more probable than some alternative or other, we must always determine what the alternatives are before we can determine just what belief we have on our hands.

The application to religious belief, more specifically Christian belief, runs as follows:

It follows from this that there are really two different things which believing a creed such as the Nicene Creed might amount to. It may be a matter of believing each item of the Creed to be more probable than its negation.... Alternatively, believing a creed such as the Nicene Creed might be a matter of believing each item of the Creed to be more probable than each of a number of specific heretical or non-Christian alternatives. A man in affirming his belief in 'the resurrection of the body' may be claiming that it is more probable that men rise embodied than that (as some other religions claimed) they rise disembodied, and so on. (p. 119)

Swinburne calls the former kind of belief in a creed 'strong belief' and the latter kind 'weak belief'. As these terms imply, it takes more to make it rational to believe that the creed, or some portion thereof, is more probable than its negation than it does to make it rational to believe that the creed, or some portion thereof, is more probable than one or more specific competitors. Hence the way in which this ambiguity is resolved has important—indeed crucial—consequences for what it takes for religious belief to be rational and for whether such belief merits this appellation in a particular case.

Swinburne goes on to suggest that,

in earlier centuries, men tended to assume that Christianity was being contrasted with various other religions and philosophical systems; and that in expressing belief in Christianity you were expressing a belief that it as a whole was more probable than each of those other systems. . . . Religious belief then does seem to have been relative to fairly specific alternatives. In later centuries there seems to be a change. The post-Renaissance centuries saw the emergence and steady growth, among intellectuals to start with and then more widely, of a vast pool of 'agnostics'. . . many of these agnostics must have felt that one religion was more probable than others, and yet they still felt themselves unqualified for entry to it. . . . Clearly men supposed that there were stronger conditions for belief than those which, I have claimed, existed in early centuries. (p. 123)

Swinburne then proceeds in chapter 5 to argue that the kind of belief needed for the pursuit of the aims of religion and the kind of belief a Church ought to demand of its adherents is the weaker sort. He does not deny that it would be good, if possible, to rationally believe that each of the items of, for example, the Christian creed is more probable than its negation. But this, he seems to think, is very difficult to attain. And, fortunately, he avers, the aims of religion can be amply attained with only the weaker sort of belief that each article of the creed in question is more probable than certain live alternatives.

Swinburne's distinction between believing that p is more probable than its negation and believing that p is more probable than a restricted number of contraries is an important one, and his use of it in connection with religious belief is a major contribution to the study of the epistemology of religious belief. At first sight it looks as if we will have to do without these riches if we jettison Swinburne's account of the nature of belief. For the treatment of religious belief in question derives from the view that to believe that p is to believe that p is more probable than certain alternatives, with its implication that since those alternatives can be set in different ways, what is called a belief that p can amount to something different, depending on how those alternatives are chosen. Nevertheless, I believe that one can accept the earlier criticisms of the general theory of belief and still reap the benefits of Swinburne's distinction between different degrees of strength with which one can believe articles of faith (as well as other items).

How can this be? It's very simple. One doesn't have to hold that all (non-basic) belief is belief in comparative probabilities in order to hold that some is. There was nothing in my criticism of Swinburne's general account of belief to suggest that no one ever believes that some proposition is more probable on his or her evidence than some other propositions(s). And it is quite obvious that people do have such beliefs. My criticism was directed solely at the claim that *all* (non-basic) beliefs are of this sort. Once we recognize that beliefs may or may not be of this form, we are free to follow Swinburne in distinguishing degrees of strength of belief in terms of which propositions it is whose probability is being compared with the kernel proposition, where the beliefs are such as to make this appropriate. In this connection we should note that it is not only beliefs of the form '*p* is more probable than *q* on evidence *E*' that will vary in content, force, or import with different substitutions for *q*. There are other ways in which comparisons of other propositions with *p* can come into (what would naturally be called) a belief that *p*. Thus one can believe that *p* is a better explanation of certain data than other attempted explanations. One can believe that *p* has a greater initial plausibility than certain alternatives. One can believe that *p* coheres better with a certain body of background knowledge than various alternatives. And so on. However, in this discussion we will stick with Swinburne's comparative probability judgements.

To return to the main thread of the discussion, having abandoned Swinburne's general account of the nature of belief, the applicability of his 'what are the alternatives?' treatment depends on whether what we are dealing with can be correctly construed as beliefs in comparative probabilities. To what extent is this the case with religious belief? I don't believe there is any simple answer to this question. Religious belief presents a much more variegated scene than Swinburne would have us believe, though he does, of course, recognize certain distinctions. In particular, it seems clear to me that in religion, as elsewhere, people often just straightforwardly and unselfconsciously believe something—for example, that Jesus did the things attributed to him in the Gospels and that what the Church proclaims about his nature and his mission is true. They have read and heard these things; they find people around them, including those for whom they have the most respect, appar-

ently accepting all this without question. And so they unhesitatingly follow suit. They just find themselves believing these things,
much as they just find themselves with beliefs about the identity
and nature of their parents, siblings, and associates. Swinburne
might try to accommodate such cases by terming them 'basic beliefs'. But it need not be so. The people in question, or some of
them, might believe that Jesus miraculously multiplied the loaves
and fishes because it says so in the Bible. Here the belief is accepted
on the grounds of another belief (that it says so in the Bible). And
yet it might be accepted in the unreflective, unselfconscious way
that involves no comparison with alternatives, whether in terms of
probability on one's evidence or otherwise.

But even if I am right about this, we must also recognize
other, more sophisticated forms of religious belief that better fit
Swinburne's model. When doubts arise, when people become
aware of incompatible alternatives to their system of religious belief, when people begin to wonder why they should suppose that all
this is true, it is natural to take a more critical, more reflective
stance toward the beliefs of one's religion. This can lead to one's
doxastic relation to the creed becoming something like a belief that
articles of the creed are or are not more probable on one's evidence
than certain alternatives, whether it is the denial of the article in
question or something more specific. We find the same phenomenon in many other areas. Up to a certain point, and past every
point for some people, one tends to accept the views of the world,
nature, history, society, and morality that are dominant in the
circles in which one lives, assuming that one's social and cultural
environment is homogeneous enough to display a single dominant
view on each topic. But when one gets exposed to other, conflicting
views, or when one acquires the habit of raising critical questions
about such matters, one undergoes a sea change. Instead of taking
all this unhesitatingly as a given, one considers what reasons there
are for accepting a given view, whether it is more likely, on the
available evidence, to be true than its competitors.

Thus I would say that Swinburne's account is suited to a certain
type or a certain stage of religious belief, one at which the more
basic unselfconscious internalization of the faith has given way—
under the stress of doubt, competing alternatives, and critical
reflection—to an attitude of more detached investigation, in
which the articles of faith are viewed as proposals or possibilities

for belief, each of which has to be evaluated on its epistemic merits. It is relative to this stage of religious belief that his account in terms of the comparative probability of alternatives is powerfully illuminating.

3

Swinburne's Argument from Religious Experience

RICHARD M. GALE

I have long admired Richard Swinburne's work, not only for the way it has raised the level of discussion in the philosophy of religion by the introduction of technical sophistication and rigour, but even more for its courageous honesty in espousing and defending to the hilt his deepest beliefs and convictions, regardless of whether they are currently in vogue. He is a true professor whose concern is not to look good but to seek the truth, and for this he deserves our deepest respect as a philosopher.

Of all his many important contributions to philosophy, the one for which he is most likely to achieve lasting fame is his empirical argument for the existence of God in *The Existence of God*, a book that will become a classic in my opinion.[1] As a result of this work, a return visit from Hume's Philo is needed, but he had better come loaded for bear, because the weapons that he used so effectively to stop poor Cleanthes in his tracks will be of no avail.

While Swinburne's overall aim is to establish that the probability that God exists is greater than one-half, he does not want the probability to be too high, for he fears that this would necessitate belief in God on the part of whoever accepts the argument, thereby negating the accepter's freedom to choose not to believe. 'If God's existence, justice, and intentions became items of evident common knowledge, then man's freedom would in effect be vastly curtailed' (p. 245). An ontological argument would do even greater violence to the traditional Christian view of God as wanting men to come to know, love, and obey him of their own free will. If someone were to come up with a really convincing version of the ontological argument, Swinburne might not be crushed if we followed the example

---

[1] Oxford: Clarendon Press, 1979. References to this book are included in the body of the text.

of the Pythagoreans, who set adrift *sans* supplies the person who demonstrated the existence of irrational numbers. Swinburne, therefore, must tread a very narrow line indeed, possibly a vanishing one.

I believe that Swinburne has created a needless difficulty for himself. First, he has mislocated the point at which creaturely free will enters into the relationship between man and God. It does not concern the freedom with which we believe that God exists, for it is dubious that in general we can believe at will, be it for conceptual or only causal reasons. Our free endeavouring, rather, concerns the efforts we make to adopt and adhere to a religious way of life, part of which is doing that which will help to self-induce a belief that God exists. One could accept the ontological argument, as Russell once did, and yet have no inclination to follow a religious way of life.

Second, there is much more free play between belief and assessment of probabilities than Swinburne allows. He has claimed that 'S believes that *p* if and only if he believes that *p* is more probable than any alternative', in which the alternative normally is not-*p*.[2] It certainly is possible for someone to believe a proposition while believing that it is improbable, even highly improbable. I need not go back to Kierkegaard or Tertullian for an example, since I can appeal to my own case as a young boy when I believed with all my heart that the Giants would win the pennant, even though I believed that their chances were extremely remote; I wouldn't have bet my piggy bank on it. Furthermore, one can believe that one horse in a race with a thousand horses in it has a better chance of winning than any other horse but not believe that it will win, since its chances of doing so are slight. And this holds even when the context is such that the alternatives to this proposition are propositions asserting that some other horse in the race will win. If we are to bet on one of these horses, naturally we will bet on the one that has the best chance of winning, however, slight this, assuming that the pay-offs are the same; but this just shows that believing cannot be analysed in terms of readiness to bet. Swinburne's analysis is hardly an analysis of our ordinary concept of belief, but at best of our concept of *rational* belief. Thus, Swinburne's worry about giving too good an argument for the existence of God is unfounded.

---

[2] *Faith and Reason* (Oxford: Clarendon Press, 1981), 5–6.

His real worry should be that he hasn't given a good enough argument.

There is a beautiful architectonic to his overall argument, replete with a surprising ending. Up until chapter 13, in which he presents the argument from religious experience, he appears to be making a cumulative case for the existence of God being probable, based on an agglomeration of the premisses of many probabilistic arguments that severally appeal to a wide range of evidence: namely, that there is a world at all, that it displays widespread law-like uniformity and simplicity in its governing laws and theories, that there exist organisms and—in particular—conscious ones, that men have great opportunities for freely co-operating in gaining knowledge and shaping the universe, and that history displays certain meaningful patterns, including the apparent existence of miracles. This counters the divide-and-conquer strategy of the theologian who considers each of these arguments in isolation, and shows that alone it doesn't amount to very much.

For each of the above arguments a Bayesian-based case is made out that the evidence appealed to in its premisses makes it more likely than otherwise that God exists, which he calls a good 'C-inductive argument'. Using P for probability, h to stand for the proposition that the God of traditional theism exists, e for the empirical evidence contained in the premiss of the argument, and k for background knowledge, the claim is that, for each of these arguments, the empirical evidence, e, that it appeals to is such that $P(h/e \text{ and } k) > P(h/k)$. He also argues that the kinds and amounts of evil we find in the world do not form the basis for a good C-inductive argument for not-h, since they do not lower the probability of h.

After he has completed this task at the end of chapter 12, the reader wonders what will result when the empirical premisses of all these arguments are agglomerated. Let us call the resulting argument the 'cumulative probabilistic argument'; the question is whether it renders h more likely to be true than not (called a good P-inductive argument). Using e' to stand for the conjunction of all these premisses, the question is whether $P(h/e' \text{ and } k) > 1/2$. The reader is getting ready to respond by saying, 'Who knows?' Since each of the arguments is a C-inductive argument, it is only comparative; and because each fails to assign any numerical value to the probability of h, there is no procedure for determining what happens when we add them together.[3] There can be several good C-inductive arguments for a proposition *p* which together do not bestow a probability of greater than 1/2 upon *p*. But the reader realizes that it would be premature to engage in this bottom-line assessment, since there is another argument to come, the one in chapter 13, from religious experience. But the expectation is that the addition to the list of yet another C-inductive argument for *h* will not dispel our uncertainty about what to say. Mush added to mush gives mush.

It is here that the argument takes an unexpected turn. Instead of making out the usual Bayesian case that the evidence consisting of numerous religious experiences renders *h* more probable than it would otherwise be, which would be yet another good C-inductive argument, it appeals to an a priori presumptive inference rule, the 'Principle of Credulity' (hereafter PC), which renders it prima facie probable that the apparent object of religious experience, God, exists, and which can be defeated only if our background knowledge makes it is very improbable that God exists. And it is here that the foregoing highly intuitive cumulative case is appealed to for the purpose of defeating this lone possible defeater, thereby rendering it probable without qualification that God exists. Thus, Swinburne's overall P-inductive argument for the existence of God is as follows:

(1) For any person S and any object *x*, if S, on the basis of an apparent experience of *x*, takes it that *x* exists, then prima facie it is probable that S's experience is veridical and thereby *x* exists. (PC)

(2) If any person S, on the basis of an apparent experience of God, takes it that God exists, then prima facie it is probable that God exists. (From (1) by universal instantiation)

(3) Numerous persons, on the basis of apparent experiences of God, take it that God exists. (Premiss)

(4) Prima facie it is probable that their experiences are veridical and thereby God exists. (From (2) and (3) by *modus ponens*)

---

[3] The very use of Bayes's theorem is suspect. According to this theorem:

$$P(h/e.k) = P(e/h.k)/P(e/k) \times P(h/k)$$

Since a numerical value can be assigned neither to *h*'s prior probability—$P(h/k)$—nor to *h*'s explanatory power—$P(e/h.k)/P(e/k)$—it is unclear what it means to multiply them together.

(5) That it is prima facie probable that their experiences are veridical, and thereby the claim that God exists can be defeated only if it is significantly more probable than not that God does not exist. (Premiss)

(6) The cumulative argument shows that it is not significantly more probable than not that God does not exist. (Premiss)

(7) It is probable without qualification that their experiences are veridical, and thereby God exists. (From (3), (4), and (5))

It is the purpose of this chapter to critically evaluate this argument. It will turn out that the fatal step in the argument is the deduction of (2) from (1), the reason being that the PC applies only to perceptual-type experiences, and religious experiences, on conceptual grounds, fail to qualify as perceptual. Instead of faulting (2) with an improper universal instantiation of the PC, it could just as well be charged that the PC is not properly restricted in (1) to perceptual-type experiences. These objections come to the same thing.

For the purpose of evaluating this argument, we will restrict ourselves to non-sensory experiences that the subject takes to be 'directly' of God in the sense that, relative to our human epistemic circumstances—the manner in which we humans experience the world and process information—they involve a minimum amount of interpretation and inference, unlike the experience of some empirical state of affairs as God-caused, for example, a sunset as an expression of God's love or an evil as a test set for us by God. The latter are the religious experience analogue of the highly 'interpretative' and theoretically laden perception of a track in a Wilson cloud chamber as a movement of an electron, while 'directly' perceiving God is a 'recognitional' perceiving-as similar to perceiving something as a chair.[4]

Before I press my objection to Swinburne's argument, it must be further fleshed out, beginning with the PC in premiss 1. Swinburne

---

[4] I think that Swinburne errs in making both recognitional and inferential perceivings of God subject to the PC. In regard to seeing a sunset as an expression of God's love he writes: 'That God is at work is no inference for these men but what seems . . . to be happening' (p. 253). People in our human epistemic circumstance who say that they perceive a sunset as an expression of God's love, unlike those who say that they simply feel God's presence or God's comforting them, are making inferences to the existence of God as witnessed by the fact that they are willing to give inductive backing to their assertion, such as is supplied by Swinburne's cumulative P-inductive argument.

describes this principle as follows: 'I suggest that it is a principle of rationality that (in the absence of special considerations) if it seems (epistemically) to a subject that x is present, then probably x is present,' in which an epistemic seeming is one that serves as a basis for the subject to believe that the apparent object of the seeming exists and is as it seems to be (p. 254). Does this PC apply to any epistemic seeming, so that if it non-perceptually seems to a person that some proposition is true, then probably it is, unless there is reason to think otherwise? Such an unrestricted form of the PC is quite dubious. However, it seems clear that Swinburne means to restrict it to perceptual seemings, for immediately upon giving the above formulation of the PC he adds this paraphrase of it: 'what one seems to perceive is probably so. How things seem to be is good grounds for a belief about how things are.' And when he later recaps his argument from religious experience he writes: 'My conclusion about the considerable evidential force of religious experience depends on my Principle of Credulity that apparent perceptions ought to be taken at their face value in the absence of positive reason for challenge' (p. 275; see also pp. 272 and 276).

Another indication that he intends to restrict the PC to perceptual seemings is that he applies it to religious experiences, which in turn are defined as perceptual. Initially he defines a 'religious experience' as one 'which seems (epistemically) to the subject to be an experience of God ... or some other supernatural thing' (p. 246).[5] But he then goes on to say that the person who veridically experiences God will 'in the very general sense . . . perceive God', and talks 'of such awareness of God as a perception without implying that the awareness is necessarily mediated by any of the ordinary senses' (p. 247). Herein Swinburne allows for the possibility of non-sensory perceptions. They alone will concern us, since religious experiences that have a sensory content are highly inferential.

Notice that Swinburne's PC is a retail principle that applies piecemeal to individual perceptual-type experiences. This contrasts with William Alston's wholesale approach, according to which any well-established social practice for forming objective beliefs on the basis of certain types of perceptual inputs, subject to certain

---

[5] This definition is too broad if we take every non-spatio-temporal entity to be supernatural; e.g., we would not want to call Plato's intuitive experience of triangularity a religious experience.

overriders, which he calls a 'doxastic practice', is to be taken to be reliable unless its outputs are either internally inconsistent or inconsistent with those of better-established doxastic practices. Since a reliable doxastic practice has belief outputs that are generally true, it would follow that any one of its perceptually based beliefs is probably true, which is exactly what results from the piecemeal application to it of Swinburne's PC. Alston claims superiority for his approach on the grounds that 'Swinburne's principle applies to experience–belief pairs individually, in isolation, while in my approach a principle of justification that applies to individual beliefs is grounded in a defense of the rationality of socially established doxastic practices. This provides support for my position that is unavailable to Swinburne.'[6] Swinburne's retail form of justification is open to supplementation by Alston's wholesale approach, unless Swinburne doesn't trust people who tell him that they can get it for him wholesale.

Furthermore, both claim an a priori status for their respective innocent-until-proved-guilty justificatory principle, and see it as our only alternative to complete scepticism. According to Swinburne, any attempt to inductively justify the PC on the grounds that most past perceptually based beliefs are true would have to assume a version of the PC which applies to beliefs based on apparent memories, since only through memory could we have access to this inductive evidence. But, obviously, the latter version of the PC does not admit of any non-circular inductive justification, and thus must be accepted if complete scepticism is to be avoided. 'And if it is justifiable to use it when other justifications fail in memory cases, what good argument can be given against using it in other kinds of case when other justifications fail?' (p. 256). Alston's justification is similar in that it is based on the impossibility of giving a non-circular justification for any doxastic practice, again presenting us with the alternative of accepting the PC, now in its wholesale form, or embracing scepticism.

The prima-facie probability that the PC bestows upon perceptually based beliefs is subject to various sorts of possible defeating conditions—conditions that lower the probability that the experience is veridical and that its apparent object therefore exists. A defeating condition is really a flunked test. It is essential that there be possible defeaters, for otherwise it would be meaningless to

---

[6] William P. *Perceiving God: The Epistemology of Religious Experience* (Ithaca, NY: Cornell University Press, 1991), 195.

speak of prima-facie justification. Swinburne lists four generic defeating conditions: (i) the subject or conditions under which the
apparent perception were made are of a sort that have proved to be
unreliable; (ii) there is inductive evidence that it is not possible for
the subject to have perceived what he or she claimed to perceive;
(iii) background evidence shows that very probably the apparent
object was not present; and (iv) there is evidence that the apparent
object probably was not part of the cause of the perception.

Having clarified premiss 1's PC, it can now be asked how
Swinburne justifies its application to religious experiences in premiss 2. Immediately upon stating the PC, he instantiates it with
religious experiences: 'From this it would follow that, in the absence of special considerations, all religious experiences ought to
be taken by their subjects as genuine, and hence as substantial
grounds for belief in the existence of their apparent object—God'
(p. 254). His justification for so instantiating the PC is given at the
end of the chapter.

Initial scepticism about perceptual claims—regarding them as guilty until
proved innocent—will give you no knowledge at all. Initial credulity is
the only attitude a rational man can take—there is no half-way house.
However, claims which can subsequently be shown unreasonable can be
weeded out. But the onus remains on the challenger. Unless we take
perceptual claims seriously, whatever they are about, we shall find ourselves in an epistemological Queer Street. Religious perceptual claims
deserve to be taken as seriously as perceptual claims of any other kind.
(p. 276)

Here we see the basis for a rearguard action argument from
analogy with sense experience for the applicability of the PC to
religious experiences. Having shown that we readily apply the PC
to beliefs based upon apparent memories and sense experiences so
as to avoid scepticism, he states: 'And if it is all right to use it for
other experiences, they need a good argument to show that it is not
all right to use it for religious experiences' (p. 254). Herein
Swinburne is placing the onus on those who refuse to extend the PC
from sense- and memory-based beliefs to beliefs based on religious
experiences: show some relevant disanalogy that would justify such
restrictiveness, or shut up. And he is committing himself to neutral-
izing any proffered disanalogy, which task occupies the remainder
of the chapter. Herein the analogy between religious and sense
experiences is not given up front but in the course of shooting down

alleged disanalogies. It is my intention to accept his challenge, but first I must complete my fleshing out of his argument.

There is little to question in (3)—Numerous persons, on the basis of apparent experiences of God, take it that God exists—since the experiences of these persons are being described in a way that does not entail the existence of their apparent object, called an 'internal description' by Swinburne. He claims that 'all arguments from religious experience must be phrased as arguments from experiences given internal descriptions' so as not to beg the question (p. 245). To accept the reports of others to have had certain internally described experiences, we need not appeal to Swinburne's Principle of Testimony—'Other things being equal, we think that what others tell us that they perceived, probably happened' (p. 271)—which employs an 'external', or existentially committed, description of their experiences. A weaker, internalized version of it—namely, that other things being equal, we think that what others tell us that they apparently perceived probably was apparently perceived by them—will suffice as justification for the acceptance. It need only be added that the other things are in fact equal, since there is no good evidence that all those who reported having apparent perceptions of God are untrustworthy. Wouldn't you be willing to buy a used car from Saint Teresa?

Pace Swinburne, his strong Principle of Testimony is not needed to justify either the acceptance of (3) or the transferability of the evidential value that these religious experiences have for their subjects to others. To show that if S's apparent perception of x gives S a prima-facie justification for believing that it is probable that x exists, then it bestows a prima-facie justification for anyone to believe likewise, appeal need be made only to my weakened version of the Principle of Testimony and the principle of the universalizability of being-evidence-for, which Swinburne spells out as holding that 'if e is evidence for h, this is a relation which holds quite independently of who knows about e' (p. 260). The subject of the experience is more certain of its occurrence than is the hearer who must take the subject's word for it by appeal to my weakened Principle of Testimony, and thus there is, as Swinburne points out, some small decrease in the probability of the proposition relative to the hearer over what it has relative to the subject—'if S reports that it seems (epistemically) to S that x is present, then that is reason for others also to believe that x is present, although not as good reason as it is for S if in fact he is having the experience which he reports' (p. 274).

Since there is no mystery as to how (4)—prima facie it is probable that their experiences are veridical and thereby God exists—follows from (2) and (3) by *modus ponens*, we can skip to (5)—that it is prima-facie probable that their experiences are veridical, and thereby the claim that God exists can be defeated only if it is significantly more probable than not that God does not exist. Swinburne's argument for (5) consists in attempting to show for each of the above four generic defeaters that the only way in which they could apply to religious experiences, given the actual facts about such experiences, is if it could be shown that it is significantly more probable than not that God does not exist.

The test set for religious experiences by defeater (i) requires that 'Most religious experiences are had by men who normally make reliable claims, and have not recently taken drugs' (p. 265). And this test is in fact passed by most religious experiences. It is unclear how their reliability in 'normal' cases, such as making claims based on ordinary sense experience, has any relevance to their competence or ability to have veridical non-sensory perceptions of God. The cases are too unlike, because we can specify what constitutes a normal perceiver and standard conditions for sense experience but not for religious experience, a point that Swinburne himself emphasizes (see pp. 262 and 269). God is a supernatural being who freely decides upon whom to bestow grace by making himself an object of their experience. What Swinburne really does is to argue that religious experiences cannot run afoul of (i) because the test it poses is conceptually inapplicable to them. A lot more will be said about this when an attempt is made to show cognitively relevant disanalogies between sense and religious experiences that destroy his rearguard analogical argument.

Defeater (ii) requires that normally claims based on religious experience are true. But the only way in which it could be shown that religious experiences fail to satisfy this requirement is 'If there was a good proof of the non-existence of God. . . . But the point here is that the onus of proof is on the atheist; if he cannot make his case the claim of religious experience stands.' The prima-facie probability it bestows on the claim to have perceived God is yet to be defeated.

Swinburne considers another way in which the veridicality of religious experiences might be impugned—by appeal to the conflicting claims that are made on the basis of religious experiences within different religious traditions. Swinburne's strategy is to argue that the extent of the conflict has been exaggerated, and that for the most part these claims can be shown to be compatible, since God could choose to present himself under different guises to persons who are in different cultural circumstances. He even gets down to why it is reasonable that a Portuguese peasant would 'see' Mary as attired in the manner in which she is pictured on the walls of Portuguese churches rather than as she was in the old days in Palestine.

That seems to me to count not at all against the peasant's claim. For if Mary has survived death, what reason is there to suppose that she has now to dress the way she did in Palestine? If she is to manifest herself in bodily form the obvious way for her to dress is the way in which she would be recognized by those to whom she appears. (p. 268)

This raises the intriguing question of where she does her shopping. I could have sworn that I saw her the other day in the clothing section of a K-Mart in Pittsburgh, and thus I suspect that there will shortly be reports of visions of Mary in this area. It will be seen that Swinburne fails to neutralize the challenge posed by religious diversity because he considers only apparent inconsistencies between the claims based on religious experiences within diverse religious traditions and not the seeming clash between their different tests for the veridicality of such experiences. Again, he fails to detect a damaging disanalogy that would justify not extending the PC from sense to religious experience.

The requirement set by defeater (iii) would be flunked by religious experiences only if it could be shown

that very probably God was not present to be perceived, and so the subject could not have perceived him. But if there is a God, he is everywhere. He is only not present if he does not exist. So to use this challenge, you have to prove that very, very probably there is no God, and, as stated above, the onus is on the atheist to do so. (p. 269)

The prima-facie probability that apparent perceptions of God are veridical is not defeated by the fact that most other perceivers fail to have similar experiences, the reason being the above stated one that we do not know that all persons with certain equipment and concepts could be expected to have experience of God, if he was there . . . the fact that there are no obvious disconfirming observations (no observations of the absence of God) which could be made, has the consequence that the original perceptual claim is, on its own, somewhat less evidence of the existence of God. (p. 269)

But it does not lessen the claim so much that it becomes less than one-half, and thus its initial claim to being prima facie probably true is not defeated. Again Swinburne is really showing that some potential defeating test is conceptually not applicable to religious experiences, thereby raising doubt about their cognitivity.

He holds that if theism is true, religious experiences cannot run afoul of (iv), which requires in this case that they be caused by God. God is the ultimate cause of everything, and moreover is omnipresent, not in the sense of being physically present everywhere, which would make him a cosmic fat man, but in being able to bring about effects at any place, including a perception of himself by those upon whom he bestows this grace. 'If there is a God, any experience which seems to be of God, will be genuine—will be of God' (p. 270). Thus, religious experiences pass the test imposed by (iv) with flying colours, assuming theism.

This is much too quick. Many religious experiences are caused in ignoble or devious ways, as for example by the ingestion of LSD or unconscious sexual desires.[7] What are we to say about such experiences? Some would see them as forming the evidential base for a good C-inductive argument for the non-existence of God. For, if God exists, he is their ultimate cause. But, given the causal theory of perception, it would follow that they are veridical perceptions of him; however, it would be inconsistent with his goodness to bring about veridical experiences of himself in such ignoble and devious ways. A more reasonable way of dealing with them is to say that, although it is true that if God exists he must be at least a necessary

---

[7] In regard to the latter, consider Nouet's description of a religious experience, quoted in Anton Poulain, *The Graces of Interior Prayer*, trans. L. Y. Smith (London: Kegan Paul, Trench, Trubner, 1950), 111: 'God, who was formerly in the soul of the just *as a hidden treasure*, by way of sanctifying grace, now presents Himself to her as *a Treasure that is found*. He flows into her faculties. He *gives Himself to her*. He *fills* her with the fullness of His Being. The soul, in return, ravished by His charms and by the spectacle of His beauty, *holds Him*, *embraces Him*, *clasps Him* closely, and all on fire with love, she flows, she plunges, she buries and loses herself deliciously in God with sentiments of inconceivable joy.' Why, this is nothing but smut, and we should take steps to have Poulain's book banned from our schools.

cause of them, it does not follow that they are veridical perceptions of God, the reason being that they are not caused by God *in the right way*. God, moreover, could have some morally exonerating excuse for permitting there to be unveridical apparent perceptions of himself, such as that they were caused by the subjects *freely* ingesting LSD or not doing everything in their power to rid them- selves of sexual lust. This allows for the possibility that a religious experience may flunk the being-caused-in-the-right-way-by-God requirement, even if God exists.[8]

Swinburne fails to see this possibility because his mistaken causal theory of perception—'S perceives *x* (believing that he is so doing) if and only if an experience of its seeming (epistemically) to S that *x* is present was caused by *x*'s being present' (p. 247)—fails to include a caused-in-the-right-way requirement. The presence of a chair can cause my apparent perception of it without my perceiving it if, for example, it caused someone who was probing my brain with electrodes so as to deceive me to see it and as a result produce in me the experience of seeming to see a chair. The causal chain that goes from the presence of the chair to my subsequent seeming to perceive it is too kinky or devious. While Swinburne is mistaken in his claim that religious experiences, on the assumption of theism, cannot fail (iv)'s causal requirement, *properly understood*, no serious damage is done to his overall argument; for it is reasonable to say that there are many religious experiences that do not in fact flunk this requirement. There is no evidence that the great mystics were high on something or had minds filled with smut or the like. Of course, if God does not exist, then any apparent per- ception of him flunks the caused-in-the-right-way requirement. Therefore, if the prima-facie probability that this experience bestows on the existence of God is to be defeated, the onus again is on the atheist to show that it is significantly improbable that God exists.

Before considering whether premiss 6's claim that the cumulative argument is strong enough to defeat this defeater, it must be asked with what right Swinburne makes the strong demand of the defeater that it is *significantly more probable* than not that God

---

[8] I failed to see this possibility in my book *On the Nature and Existence of God* (Cambridge: Cambridge University Press, 1991), 315, when I said that 'it is imposs- ible for God to cause an of-God experience in the wrong way'. I am thankful that there are no malpractice suits in philosophy, or I would have been reduced to the state of pauper a long time ago.

does not exist. Why wouldn't it suffice if it is only probable that God does not exist? There are some, like Gary Guting, who would demand even less of the defeater, since they reject Swinburne's strong version of the PC in favour of a weaker one according to which an apparent experience of x merely constitutes 'significant but not sufficient evidence' that x is present, hereby departing from Swinburne, who takes it to be alone sufficient to justify an assertion that x is present, since it bestows a probability of greater than one-half on x's being present.[9] Although I agree with Guting's objection, for the sake of argument I will accept Swinburne's PC, and thus will confine myself to the objection that it is not required of the defeater that it is *significantly* improbable that God exists but only that it is improbable that he does.

To see how Swinburne justifies his strong demand, we must begin with his generic account of defeater iii that the apparent object x of S's experience wasn't present or existent. 'It has to make it very improbable that x was present if it is to outweigh the force of S's experience sufficiently for it to remain more probable than not that x was not present' (p. 261).[10] Because religious experiences have an apparent object that is qualitatively remote from the subject's past experiences and do not admit of the possibility of disconfirming experiences, Swinburne lowers his demand on the defeater so that it need show only that it is significantly more probable than not, rather than very probable, that God does not exist. 'But for these qualifications, I would have concluded that a religious experience apparently of God ought to be taken as veridical unless it can be shown on other grounds that very, very probably God does not exist' (p. 270).

There certainly is nothing intuitively obvious about this. Consider the generic case in which Swinburne requires the defeater to show that it is 'very improbable that x was present'. It would seem to be sufficient for the defeater to show that relative to certain background evidence e_1 the probability that x was not present be equal to or greater than that of the probability that x was present relative to the apparent experience of x. And since the probability of x's being present relative to an apparent perception of it need

---

[9] Gary Guting, *Religious Belief and Religious Skepticism* (Notre Dame, Ind.: University of Notre Dame Press, 1982), 149.

[10] I have corrected a typo in the text: an 'S' incorrectly appears in place of my final 'x'.

be only more than one-half according to the PC, however slight that might be, the improbability that x was present relative to e_1 need be only less than one-half, and thus not very improbable. Similar considerations apply, only more so, to the case of religious experiences.[11]

If this objection is sound, Swinburne's premiss 5 will have to be weakened to something like

(5′) That it is prima facie probable that their experiences are veridical and thereby God exists can be defeated only if the probability that God does not exist relative to evidence e_1 is equal to or greater than the probability that God exists relative to the apparent experiences of him.

This will require a corresponding change of 6 to

(6′) The cumulative argument shows that it is not the case that the probability that God does not exist relative to evidence e_1 is equal to or greater than the probability that God exists relative to the apparent experiences of him.

The demands that are made upon the cumulative argument, therefore, will depend upon whether it must counter (5) or (5′). My objection to (5) is far from conclusive, and thus both cases must be considered. Any neutralizer of (5)'s defeater also functions in the same way for (5′), but not vice versa. Thus, (5) makes the weaker demand, and is more easily neutralized. There are two main grounds for doubting that the cumulative probabilistic argument is up to even the less demanding task.

First, its account of the a priori prior probability of h relative to the tautological background knowledge k rests on a radical abuse of the concept of simplicity. It is claimed that although the $P(h/k)$ is very low, since for any contingent being, of which God is one, it is extremely unlikely that it exists, God is far more likely to exist than is any other contingent being. This is because the only relevant consideration in such a case of prior probability is simplicity, and

---

[11] Swinburne claims that the probability that the apparent experience of x is veridical is increased if either the experience is forceful (p. 265) or others have similar experiences (p. 263). Forcefulness would seem to have nothing to do with the case, especially since many unveridical experiences are very forceful, and the vast majority of our waking veridical experiences are quite unforceful, *pace* Hume. Furthermore, it is highly suspect to allow for confirmatory experiences of the presence of x when the possibility of disconfirmatory experience is ruled out.

God is far and away the simplest of all beings, the reason being that since God has all his perfections to an infinite extent it can't be asked, as it can be for possession of any finite degree thereof, why it has that degree rather than some larger or smaller degree. 'A finite limitation cries out for an explanation of why there is just that particular limit, in a way that limitlessness does not. There is a neatness about zero and infinity which particular finite numbers lack' (p. 283).

Herein Swinburne is confounding the simplicity of a being or its manner of possessing a property with its not requiring an explanation. Certainly, from a mathematical point of view, infinity is more complex than finitude, since it is defined in terms of an operation upon finite or natural numbers. And from a conceptual point of view, God's infinite possession of perfections is far more complex and troubling than is the finite possession thereof. It was not for no reason that Swinburne felt a need to write a book entitled *The Coherence of Theism*. God's omni-properties are far more problematic and paradox-prone than are their finite counterparts. Conceptually speaking, God is the most complex and difficult to grasp of all possible beings.

Second, Swinburne fails to do justice to the challenge posed by natural evils to his cumulative probabilistic argument. He argues with extreme implausibility that the amount and distribution of natural evil does not even lower the probability of God's existence over what it would otherwise be. Swinburne constructs a theodicy for these evils based on their being necessary for our having the requisite knowledge to make morally significant choices, a knowledge of which can be gained only by inductive reasoning from past experiences of actual instances of natural evils.

if men are to have the opportunity to bring about serious evils for themselves or others by actions or negligence, or to prevent their occurrence, and if all knowledge of the future is obtained by normal induction, that is by induction from patterns of similar events in the past—then there must be serious natural evils occurring to man or animals. (p. 211)

In response to the objection that God could simply tell us what are the consequences for good or evil if we make certain choices, he responds that by doing so he would make his existence and intentions so manifest that it would usurp our freedon, since we 'would have little temptation to do wrong—it would be the mark of both prudence and reason to do what was virtuous. Yet a man only has a genuine choice of destiny if he has reason for pursuing either good or evil courses of action' (p. 212).

There are two fatal flaws in this theodicy. First, it fails to realize that it is only a *contingent* fact, if it is a fact at all, that all human knowledge of empirical matters of fact is gained via inductive reasoning from past experience. Certainly, God's omnipotence would enable him to instil in us innate knowledge of the good and evil consequences of different acts, and, moreover, to do so in a way that did not reveal his existence or intentions; it would then be up to us to freely decide what to do on the basis of this knowledge. That Swinburne fails to see this alternative is further evidence of his failure to properly locate the point at which creaturely free will is operative.[12] The other flaw is that it fails to deal with specific instances of natural evil that do not seem to be necessary for our gaining the requisite knowledge for functioning as moral agents. In effect, his theodicy is little more than a defence which offers a *possible* exonerating excuse for God's permitting a certain *kind* of evil without any attempt to show that this excusing condition actually applies to *all known instances* of this kind of evil.

For these reasons Swinburne has completely failed to show that the many actual cases of apparently gratuitous natural evils do not significantly lower the probability of God's existence. According to the intuitions of many, a good P-inductive, no less than a good C-inductive, argument can be based on such evils. If the cumulative argument, when purged of its abuse of simplicity in determining the prior probability of *h*, is sufficiently strong, the conjunction of its premisses with a premiss reporting all known instances of apparently gratuitous evil could still result in a good C-inductive argument or, less plausibly, a good P-inductive argument.[13] If we are to be fully honest, I think we must admit that we do not have clear-cut intuitions about what to say about this enlarged and purified cumulative argument, and, as a result, have no basis for saying whether it suffices to neutralize either the strong defeating condition of (5)

---

[12] Another place at which this failure becomes evident is in his attempt to deduce God's omnibenevolence from his omniscience and perfect freedom, on the assumption that there are objective moral truths (p. 101). What this Socratic all-virtue-is-knowledge approach overlooks is that someone could know what is the morally right thing to do and still perversely choose the immoral alternative.

[13] For an excellent discussion of this issue which supplies the technical details missing in my account, see Robert M. Adams, 'Plantinga on the Problem of Evil', in I. Tomberlin and P. van Inwagen (eds.), *Plantinga* (Dordrecht: Reidel, 1985), 225–55.

or even the weaker one of (5'). Thus, we are no better off than we were at the end of chapter 12. We are still mired in the mush.

This completes my critical exposition of Swinburne's overall argument. While many objections have been lodged against it, none is really decisive. An attempt will now be made to give such an objection based on its being illegitimate to extend the PC to religious experiences, as is done in premiss 2. In the course of making it, relevant disanalogies between sense and religious experience will be unearthed that will more than answer the challenge issued by Swinburne's rearguard argument from analogy to either produce such disanalogies or permit the extension of the PC from sense to religious experience.

It has already been seen that Swinburne himself seems to confine the PC to perceptual experiences. But what is a perceptual experience? It will not do to say that it is an involuntary experience in which some object is presented to the subject, for certain paradigmatic subjective experiences, experiences that take cognate or internal accusatives and do not admit of the veridical–unveridical distinction, such as sensations of pain and after-images, along with dreams and certain kinds of feelings, share these features. Nor will it do to define it as 'an awareness of something apart from oneself', as Swinburne does (p. 247). I could be thinking of Jones, and thereby be aware of him without perceiving him. Fortunately, it is not necessary for present purposes to give a definition of 'perceive'. It will suffice to say that the conditions specified by the PC are at least necessary conditions for being such an experience.[14]

According to the PC, an apparent experience of x renders it prima facie probable that x is present, subject to challenge by certain defeaters. Both a metaphysical and an epistemological requirement for being a perceptual experience can be extracted from this. The metaphysical condition requires that the apparent object of the experience admits of the possibility of 'objective' existence, meaning that it can exist unexperienced and is capable of being the common accusative of different perceptions. The epistemological condition requires that the experience admit of the veridical–unveridical distinction by appeal to background defeaters or tests.

---

[14] For a fuller discussion of this, see my article. 'Why Alston's Mystical Doxastic Practice is Subjective', in the *Philosophy and Phenomenological Research* symposium book on William Alston's *Perceiving God* (forthcoming).

It is crucial that my account of these conditions be generic, so as to apply to all species of perception, including non-sensory perceptions of God. Were it to be confined to the case of *sense* perception I could rightly be charged with illegitimately taking features of one species of perception as normative for all other species. But because sense perception is both a clear-cut and a paradigmatic case of perception, for each of these conditions I will first give an account of how it is satisfied by sense perception. Abstraction then will be made from sensory qualities or anything that entails having sensory qualities, thereby rendering the account generic. It will be seen that religious experiences satisfy neither of these necessary conditions and thus fail to qualify as perceptual, and, as a consequence are not subject to the PC.

The metaphysical requirement. The object of a veridical sense perception can exist unperceived and be the common object of perceptions by different perceivers at the same time and the same perceiver at different times.[15] This is because the object, along with the perceivers, are housed in the dimensions of space and time within which they are hooked up to this object by different causal chains. The tests for the veridicality of a sense perception—having the right sort of causal hook-up (which involves, among other things, a normal perceiver in standard circumstances), agreement among perceivers, and predictive success—presuppose this worldview of a common space-time receptacle in which the objective accusatives of veridical sense perceptions are the common causes of the, for the most part, nomic-type coherence among the contents of the sense perceptions of the differently positioned perceivers. That there are such tests is not a contingent fact about sense perception but a conceptual fall-out from the concept of a sense perception as having an objective accusative.

These accusatives are ultimately individuated by their position in the space-time receptacle, it being a conceptual truth that numerically distinct individuals of the same kind cannot coincide spatio-temporally. In order to perform this individuating function for empirical entities, these dimensions must not themselves be empirically determined. As Plato said about his Receptacle, 'that which is

---

[15] For a fuller account of this, see ch. 8 of my book *On the Nature and Existence of God.*

to receive in itself all kinds must be free from all characters.'[16] This receptacle creates the possibility of there being counter-examples to the principle of the identity of indiscernibles when restricted to fully general properties. Any such property admits of the possibility of multiple instantiations at different regions in this receptacle. As a consequence, we are able to distinguish between perceptions that are of numerically one and the same particular and those of particulars that are only qualitatively similar. In the latter case there are non-coincident particulars that are hooked up with different perceptions via different causal chains.

With this all too brief sketch of the conceptual requirements for sense perception having an objective accusative, the generic requirements for *any* perceptual experience, including non-sensory religious experiences, having an objective accusative can be derived by abstracting from the features of these requirements that involve or entail having sensory qualities. It cannot be demanded that the objective accusative of religious experiences occupy the spatial dimensions, since being spatial entails having sensory qualities. This requirement, when made properly generic, is that the accusative of a veridical perception of *any* species occupy some non-empirical dimension(s), though not necessarily those of space and time, by which it is individuated and within which it is causally hooked up with different perceivers, thereby explaining how it is possible both for it to be the common accusative of different perceptions and for the distinction to be drawn between perceptions of one and the same object and those of only qualitatively similar objects.

It is obvious, and readily acknowledged in different things that Swinburne says, that none of these metaphysical requirements, even when divested of all sensory elements as has just been done, are satisfied by religious experiences. To begin with, God is a spiritual being whose individuation is not dimensionally based, not even on time, which he occupies, according to Swinburne. God's individuation is based instead on his uniquely satisfying certain properties, such as being the sole creator of the world and the

---

[16] Plato, *Timaeus*, 50E–51; quoted from F. M. Cornford, *Plato's Cosmology* (New York: Liberal Arts Press, 1952). This issue is dealt with more fully in my book *Negation and Non-Being*, American Philosophical Quarterly Monograph no. 10, 1976.

determiner of what happens in it, possibly subject to certain limitations due to creaturely free will.

This raises the problem of how we can experientially identify God. To know that one is experiencing God, and not just any old very powerful, loving, non-human person, of which there could be several, it is necessary to know that what one is experiencing completely and solely determines every feature of the world. But this requires knowing the negative fact that there does not exist any being other than this who determines any of these features. The same considerations hold for God's omni-properties; to know that the apparent object of your experience is omnipotent, you must know the negative fact about it that there is no possible state of affairs that it cannot bring about. Swinburne rightly restricts the PC to positive-seeming experiences: 'The principle is so phrased that how things seem positively to be is evidence of how they are, but how things seem *not* to be is not such evidence' (p. 414; his emphasis). But he fails to see that this restriction to positive-seeming experiences precludes his applying the PC to religious experiences, since they are in part negative. Furthermore, because religious experiences are not dimensionally hooked up to God, there is no way of indexically identifying God. Since we are unable to identify God experientially either indexically or as the unique satisfier of some description, we cannot identify God experientially at all. And this has the consequence that we are unable to determine whether different religious experiences are of one and the same or only qualitatively similar accusatives.

The epistemological requirement. The PC applies to experiences that not only take an objective accusative but also are cognitive in that they count as evidence, even rendering it prima facie probable, that the apparent object of the experience exists and is as it appears to be. But to play this sort of cognitive role, they must be subject to defeaters, tests, or checks, failure of which lowers this prima-facie probability. Roughly speaking, the tests for the veridicality of sense perceptions are being caused in the right way, agreement among observers, and predictability. Since it is reasonably clear how they apply to sense perceptions and how they enable us to distinguish between veridical and unveridical sense perceptions, we can go directly to the question of whether they also apply to religious experiences, bearing in mind that we must drop any feature of these tests that involves sensory qualities.

Being caused in the right way requires a normal observer in a standard situation causally hooked up in 'the right way' to the apparent object of the perceptual-type experience. It has already been seen that none of these considerations apply to an experience of God, in virtue of God's being a non-dimensional (save for time) supernatural being who freely bestows his grace on persons when he causes them to have an experience of him. Thus, the causal test does not apply to religious experiences. And if Swinburne should reply that a religious experience cannot be caused in the wrong way by God, the proper counter is that a test that cannot be failed is no test at all.

Swinburne obviously thinks that religious experiences are subject to the agreement test, for he counts agreement among different observers as confirmatory of the veridicality of their religious experiences (p. 263). But whereas the failure of a sense perception to satisfy the agreement test is taken to be disconfirmatory of its veridicality, Swinburne does not take the failure of a religious experience to pass this test to be disconfirmatory. The reason that failure of agreement is not disconfirmatory for religious experiences but is so for sense perceptions is that only in the latter case do we know what counts as a normal observer and as standard conditions.

If we do not know what experience would count against some perceptual claim (because we do not know which observers could have been expected to have had an experience apparently of *s* if *s* had been there), that somewhat lessens the evidential force of an apparent perception—but only somewhat. This is because in that case we cannot have confirming evidence of failure to find evidence which counts against the claim. (p. 275)

The basis of Swinburne's 'somewhat lessens the evidential force of' is obscure. But this slight concession on his part hides the seriousness of the challenge posed to his analogical argument by evidential asymmetry. The in principle impossibility of disconfirming the veridicality of a religious experience by appeal to the testimony of other observers, rather than just lessening the probability of its veridicality, calls into question the very applicability of the agreement test, for it is a strange test indeed that can be passed but not failed. Swinburne seems to have forgotten that he is supposed to be justifying his extension of the PC to religious experience in premiss 2 on the ground that there are no cognitively relevant disanalogies between sense and religious experience. The same considerations hold for his failure to neutralize the disanalogy between them based on the caused-in-the-right-way test being applicable only to sense experiences.

Another example of Swinburne's failure to face up to a damaging cognitively relevant disanalogy between sense and religious experience is seen in his attempt to neutralize the challenge posed by religious diversity by showing that, for the most part, the statements made on the basis of religious experiences within different religions are compatible, this sometimes, requiring a visit to K-Mart as we saw (pp. 265 ff.). But this overlooks the more serious challenge posed by religious diversity: namely, that whereas all persons who engage in the doxastic practice of making physical object claims on the basis of sense experience agree on what are the relevant tests for veridicality, this blatantly is not the case for all participants in the doxastic practices of basing claims about God on religious experiences: the tests for veridicality employed within the different religious traditions are mutually incompatible, as, for example, in what they count as growing in sanctity and the revealed truths that are recognized as normative.

It is to William Alston's credit that, in *Perceiving God*, he recognized that this is the real challenge posed by religious diversity. Unfortunately, his attempt to counter it by arguing that since the rival religious traditions do not share a common method for warranting or overriding claims based on religious experiences, the epistemic discreditation is far less than it would be if they shared the same method but differed in their output beliefs, fails. Certainly persons holding rival beliefs would be more seriously divided if they could not agree on a method for resolving their disagreement than if they did; for in the latter case they can at least argue with each other, unlike the former, in which they can resort only to non-epistemic means to resolve their differences. Furthermore, someone impugns my epistemic soundness far more if they question the very method by which I arrive at and warrant my beliefs than if they only question some of my beliefs.

There still remains the prediction test. There are two issues here: being able to predict who will have the type of perceptual experience in question and being able to predict future events that will confirm the veridicality of a given experience of that type. Both can be done for sense, but not for religious, experience. Because a religious experience is *freely* brought about by God, there is no way to predict who will have such an experience and under what conditions. It is for this reason that Swinburne calls religious experiences 'private' (p. 269). The best that he can offer in response is: 'if there is a God, there is a greater probability that men will have such experiences' (p. 275); and it is more likely that the person of faith, rather than the atheist, will have them, for 'there are no grounds for supposing that if there is a God, the atheist would have experience of him' (p. 310).

Both of these extremely vague probabilistic predictions can be challenged. A religious experience is often so psychologically overpowering that the subject is forced to believe that God exists, which goes counter to Swinburne's requirement that such belief be free. Such an experience would not exert as coercive a force upon an atheist, since it would be counterbalanced by his initial disbelief. The atheist, furthermore, being far more in need of God's grace than the person who is already launched along the path of faith, would seem to be more likely to have a religious experience if God exists than would the believer, *pace* Swinburne. I am not, of course, altogether sincere in these probabilistic pronouncements, but merely wish to show how little basis there is for making any probabilistic predictions at all in this area.

As for being able to predict future events that would be confirmatory, Swinburne appeals to the traditional test based upon the subject's growth in sanctity (p. 273). Given God's omnibenevolence, we would expect that a veridical experience of him would result in the subject becoming more God-like. Not only does this encounter the problem posed by religious diversity, due to there being incompatible criteria for growth in sanctity within different religions, it also strikes out on Bayesian grounds. The prior probability that S has a veridical religious experience (p) relative to background knowledge k is very low, and p's explanatory or predictive power in conjunction with k of the fact that S becomes more sanctified (e) is no greater than that of k alone in respect of e— $P(e/p.k) = P(e/k)$. The reason for this is that k includes known facts about the psychological causes of human behaviour that explain why someone who believes that she veridically experiences God is likely to become more holy. Thus, on Bayesian grounds, $P(p/e.k)$ is very low.

In conclusion, religious experiences not only do not have any defeaters analogous to those for sense experience, they have no defeaters at all. For this reason alone, they fail the epistemological requirement for being perceptual-type experiences. And when this failure is combined with their failure to pass the metaphysical requirement, there is more than ample justification for refusing to extend the PC to them. We have thereby met Swinburne's challenge to produce a relevant disanalogy between sense and religious experience that would justify applying the PC to the former but not to the latter.

4

Mystical Perception: St Teresa, William Alston, and the Broadminded Atheist

NORMAN KRETZMANN

According to Richard Swinburne's well-known Principle of Credulity, 'How things seem to be is good grounds for a belief about how things are. From this it would follow that, in the absence of special considerations, all religious experiences ought to be taken by their subjects as genuine, and hence as substantial grounds for belief in the existence of their apparent object.'[1] Naturally, Swinburne subjects his principle to several refinements in the course of carefully considering objections against it, but its fundamental simplicity is a very important aspect of its appeal. A more recent, fundamentally more complex attempt to establish a result very much like Swinburne's application of his principle to religious experience is what I want to consider here.

1. A Paradigm Case of Mystical Perception

In her autobiography St Teresa gives this report of her first 'intellectual' vision of God:

One day when I was at prayer... I saw Christ at my side—or, to put it better, I was conscious of Him, for I saw nothing with the eyes of the body or the eyes of the soul [the imagination]. He seemed quite close to me and I saw that it was He. As I thought, He was speaking to me. Being completely ignorant that such visions were possible, I was very much afraid at first, and could do nothing but weep, though as soon as He spoke His first word of assurance to me, I regained my usual calm, and became cheerful and free from fear. All the time Jesus Christ seemed to be at my side, but as this was not an imaginary vision [i.e., a vision seen by 'the eyes

[1] Richard Swinburne, *The Existence of God* (Oxford: Clarendon Press, 1979), 254.

of the soul'] I could not see in what form. But I most clearly felt that He was all the time on my right, and was a witness of everything that I was doing.[2]

In his book *Perceiving God*,[3] William Alston understandably includes this experience of St Teresa's among what he calls 'paradigm cases of experiential awareness of God' (p. 12). Alston distinguishes between 'focal' and 'background' awareness of God. St Teresa's experience is of the focal sort, 'in which the awareness of God occupies one's attention to the exclusion of all else' (p. 32). Background awareness is described as 'a sense of the presence of God that is of much lower intensity and persists for long periods of time as a constant background for the flux of everyday experience' (ibid.). As Alston's book develops, background experience becomes more important than focal experience for his purposes. This shift of emphasis seems to me to have a significant effect on his position, but on this occasion I'm going to ignore it, because I'm concerned only with Alston's central thesis and main argument, which are essentially developed in the earlier chapters of *Perceiving God*. Leaving the later development out of account for now is further warranted by the fact that Alston himself sees 'no reason to think that these long-lasting background awarenesses of God are a radically different sort of phenomenon from the overwhelming momentary awareness that blots out all else' (p. 33). So I will take St Teresa's focal experience as my single paradigm of all experi-

---

[2] St Teresa of Avila, *The Life of St Teresa of Avila by Herself*, trans. J. M. Cohen (London: Penguin Books, 1957), 187–9; quoted (at greater length) in William P. Alston, *Perceiving God: The Epistemology of Religious Experience* (Ithaca, NY: Cornell University Press, 1991), 13. Here is another translation of the same passage, by Kieran Kavanaugh, OCD, and Otilio Rodriguez, OCD, from *The Collected Works of St Teresa of Avila*, i (Washington, DC: ICS Publications, 1976), 174: 'Being in prayer on the feastday of the glorious St Peter, I saw or, to put it better, I felt Christ beside me; I saw nothing with my bodily eyes or with my soul, but it seemed to me that Christ was at my side—I saw that it was He, in my opinion, who was speaking to me. Since I was completely unaware that there could be a vision like this one, it greatly frightened me in the beginning; I did nothing but weep. However, by speaking one word alone to assure me, the Lord left me feeling as I usually did: quiet, favored, and without any fear. It seemed to me that Jesus Christ was always present at my side; but since this was not an imaginative vision, I didn't see any form. Yet I felt very clearly that He was always present at my right side and that He was the witness of everything I did.' A note by the translators explains that 'St Teresa will distinguish at least three kinds of visions: intellectual (like the present one . . .); imaginative (perceived with what she calls "the eyes of the soul," that is, the imagination or phantasy . . .); and corporeal (seen with the bodily eyes and which, she says, . . . she never experienced)' (p. 298).

[3] See n. 2 above. Page references are included in text from here on.

ence (awareness, perception) of God, which Alston more often calls 'mystical perception', carefully distinguishing it from sense perception.[4]

For Alston's purposes in *Perceiving God*, the primary significance of mystical perception is not spiritual but epistemological.[5]

a person can become justified in holding certain kinds of beliefs about God by virtue of perceiving God as being or doing so-and-so. The kinds of beliefs that can be so justified I shall call 'M-beliefs' ('M' for *manifestation*). M-beliefs are beliefs to the effect that God is doing something currently vis-à-vis the subject—comforting, strengthening, guiding, communicating a message, sustaining the subject in being—or to the effect that God has some (allegedly) perceivable property—goodness, power, lovingness. (p. 1)

St Teresa's experience, then, clearly deserves its status as a paradigm for Alston's purposes. She reports that she perceived God ('I saw Christ at my side'), that the perception of him was not sense perception ('I saw nothing with the eyes of the body'), and that on the basis of her mystical perception she formed such M-beliefs as that God was reassuring her ('as soon as He spoke His first word of assurance to me, I regained my usual calm, and became cheerful and free from fear').

Alston's claims in *Perceiving God* are bold, his arguments intricate and challenging. Readers who give the book the careful attention it demands and deserves will, I think, find much to admire in it, as I have done. Of course, attending carefully to a philosophy book inevitably raises questions too.[6] On this occasion, taking St Teresa's

---

[4] The term 'mystical perception' is introduced first on p. 5, more fully on p. 11. The distinction between mystical perception and sense perception permeates the book, beginning in ch. 1, sec. iii, entitled 'Experiential Presentations of God—Sensory and Non-Sensory' (pp. 14–20).

[5] He is, of course, keenly aware of its ordinarily far more important spiritual significance; see e.g. p. 2.

[6] Thanks to Professor Alston and to Mr John Ackerman of Cornell University Press, I was able to use the typescript of *Perceiving God* as the basis for a graduate seminar at Cornell in the spring of 1991. I am grateful to all the members of the seminar—Hugh Gauch, Bill Kraybill, Steve Maitzen, Tim O'Connor, Bob Pasnau, David Robb, David Slutsky, and Michael Wakoff—and especially to Bill Alston, who sent written replies to all the weekly hand-outs, discussion questions, and critical notes. Naturally, the seminar turned up many more questions than those I am considering in this chapter, but those at issue here are fundamental to Alston's project in *Perceiving God*. I look forward to seeing other questions developed further by members of the seminar, as in Pasnau's 'Justified Until Proven Guilty: Alston's New Epistemology', *Philosophical Studies*, lxxii (1993), 1–33, and Maitzen's review of the book, *The Philosophical Review*, cii (1993), 430–2.

experience as my paradigm of mystical perception, I want to consider some questions about the book's 'central thesis': 'that experiential awareness of God, or as I shall be saying, the *perception* of God, makes an important contribution to the grounds of religious belief' (p. 1). What, exactly, is the important contribution that mystical perception is supposed to make to the grounds of religious belief, and does Alston succeed in showing that it does or can make that contribution? I'm led to raise these tendentious questions by my conviction that what Alston calls the perception of God can make an important contribution to the grounds of religious belief only subjectively. Objective grounds of religious belief are still to be sought mainly or solely in the old, familiar, still vital enterprises of natural and philosophical theology.[7]

2. A Plausible Appraisal of the Paradigm

Because Alston is focusing on epistemological issues, as he prominently declares in subtitling his book 'The Epistemology of Religious Experience', he intends to address philosophers generally, not just those who are initially ready to take as veridical at least some perceptions of the sort that St Teresa reports. He says so expressly on page 1: 'the book is designed for a general audience that includes those who do not antecedently accept those presuppositions'—namely, 'that God exists' and 'that people are sometimes genuinely aware of God and do genuinely perceive God'. Accordingly, he begins by disarmingly 'specifying the experiences in question as those that are *taken by the subject* to be an awareness of God (or would be so taken if the question arose). One can agree that there are experiences that satisfy this description even if one does not believe that God exists or that people ever genuinely perceive Him' (p. 1).

In the setting provided by Alston's stipulation regarding the relevant experiences and by his expressed intention to address a wide academic audience, imagine presenting St Teresa's report to a knowledgeable, philosophical, broadminded atheist—one who acknowledges that some people sometimes have experiences of the

[7] For some development of this observation, see e.g. Eleonore Stump and Norman Kretzmann, 'Theologically Unfashionable Philosophy', *Faith and Philosophy*, vii (1990), 329–39.

sort St Teresa describes, even though he does not believe that God exists or, consequently, that anybody ever genuinely perceives God. And suppose that this atheist knows enough about St Teresa to accept her report as altogether honest. Now imagine asking him, outside any particular philosophical context, whether the experience St Teresa describes justified her in believing that God reassured her. It is at least very likely that he would say yes. An experience with the content and force St Teresa describes, had by a person with her expressed beliefs and with the beliefs a sixteenth-century Spanish Carmelite nun may be expected to have held antecedently, would strike nearly everyone as *justifying* the belief she expresses, even someone who takes the belief justified in that way to be provably *false*. This same atheist reading chapter 1 of *Perceiving God* might get the impression that Alston himself would endorse this plausible appraisal, especially when he finds Alston saying that 'a belief that X is present can be justified by an experience even if that experience is not a veridical experience of X. I might be justified by my visual experience in supposing that there is a lake in the distance, even though it is only a mirage' (p. 12).

But, whatever Alston's attitude towards it turns out to be, I want to begin with the broadminded atheist's plausible appraisal of the Teresan paradigm, as a putative perception of God that justifies the perceiver's M-belief that God reassured her. It is an appraisal that can easily be extended, for my atheist would readily agree that St Teresa's more fundamental belief that God exists was also justified by her putative experience of God's speaking to her and witnessing everything she was doing, just as he would agree that her experientially justified belief that God reassured her presupposes that God exists. He could borrow Alston's own words in order to express this extension of his appraisal: 'if beliefs "about God", entailing or presupposing that God exists, are justified by being based on putative experiential awareness of God, then so is the belief that God exists' (p. 9). Indeed, some of Alston's formulations of 'the main aim of the book' would strike the broadminded atheist as altogether uncontroversial—for example, 'to show that putative perception of God can provide justification for certain beliefs about God and thereby contribute to a basis for religious belief' (p. 68)— although the atheist's appraisal of the Teresan paradigm would leave him wondering why a whole book was needed to show what seems to be a plain truth.

3. Trouble for the Plausible Appraisal

But the broadminded atheist and everyone else who finds his appraisal plausible should be brought up short by a passage I've already quoted in part, a passage that appears on the first page of the first chapter of Alston's book:

> I will not argue that God exists. Such argument for this as will be found in the book is indirect; if beliefs 'about God', entailing or presupposing that God exists, are justified by being based on putative experiential awareness of God, then so is the belief that God exists. (p. 9)

So, although Alston will not argue directly that God exists, his book does contain an indirect argument for that conclusion, an argument he summarizes here in this conditional proposition:

> (C) If (a) beliefs about God, entailing or presupposing that God exists, are justified by being based on putative experiential awareness of God, then (b) the belief that God exists is justified on that basis.

But the broadminded atheist who, as we've just seen, has no difficulty accepting (C) will be astonished to find it presented as a sketch of even an indirect argument that God exists. And his astonishment will grow when he finds that the book's main argument, the argument for its central thesis, is an argument for (Ca), the conditional proposition's antecedent, which the atheist readily granted on the basis of no argument at all: 'most of [the book] (chaps. 2–7) is one long argument for the thesis that certain kinds of belief about God can be justified by being based on putative perception of God' (p. 10).

Perhaps these discrepancies between the broadminded atheist's attitude and Alston's pronouncements and promises are already enough to show that when Alston says that he means to show that mystical perception 'makes an *important* contribution to the grounds of religious belief' (p. 1, emphasis added), he is alluding to a contribution quite different from the psychologically natural response to a putative experience of God that is acknowledged in the atheist's plausible appraisal. The conditional proposition, C, can represent the argument Alston says it represents only in case at least some mystical perception is veridical. And so the book's main argument, supporting its central thesis, must include support for the *veridicality* of perceptions of God and, in that way, for the *existence* of God. Alston promises the inclusion of such support when he says, for instance, that 'the case for the *reality* of perception of God will emerge from the book as a whole' (p. 10, emphasis added). And he sketches the nature of the support to be supplied when he summarizes the main argument in these words:

I am conducting the discussion from a standpoint outside any practice of forming beliefs on the basis of those alleged perceptions [of God]. And so far as I can see, the only way of arguing, from that standpoint, that people do genuinely perceive God is to argue for the epistemological position that beliefs formed on the basis of such (putative) perceptions are (prima facie) justified. If that is the case, we have a good reason for regarding many of the putative perceptions as genuine; for if the subject were not often really perceiving X why should the experience involved provide justification for beliefs about X? (p. 10)[8]

This summary of the main argument can be presented even more clearly in the following form:

(1) Putative experiences of God provide justification for beliefs about God.

(2) Putative experiences of X provide justification for beliefs about X only if many of those experiences are veridical.

∴ (3) Many putative experiences of God are veridical.

The broadminded atheist, in acknowledging that the belief St Teresa formed on the basis of her putative perception of God was justified, was in effect accepting premiss 1. Indeed, he manifested his broadmindedness in accepting premiss 1 despite his

---

[8] I find it hard to distinguish this from an argument for God's existence, despite what Alston says in the passage quoted just above from the first page of ch. 1 and in this passage from his introduction: 'I want to make it explicit at the outset that my project here is to be distinguished from anything properly called an "argument from religious experience" for the existence of God. [Footnote omitted.] The thesis defended here is not that the existence of God provides the best explanation for facts about religious experience or that it is possible to *argue* in any way from the latter to the former. It is rather that people sometimes do perceive God and thereby acquire justified beliefs about God' (p. 3). But, as we have already seen, on Alston's own interpretation of this thesis defended in *Perceiving God*, it implies that God exists. Moreover, he himself describes his defence of the thesis as an indirect argument for the proposition that God exists (p. 10, quoted above). There's more than one way to argue from religious experience for the existence of God, and I see no reason why only arguments to the best explanation should be *properly* called arguments from religious experience.

conviction that God does not exist, and that, consequently, no putative perception of God can be veridical and no M-belief about God can be true. So, of course, he will reject premiss 2 out of hand. St Teresa went on to have hundreds more putative experiences of God, and the atheist might well have appraised each of them just as he appraised the first one; but he would certainly not have taken himself to be thereby in the slightest degree committed to accepting *any*, much less *many*, of those experiences of hers as veridical. And he would have a ready answer for Alston's rhetorical question: 'if the subject were *not often really* perceiving X, why should the experience involved provide *justification* for beliefs about X?' He would say that his broadminded acknowledgement that one of St Teresa's experiences provides justification for one or more of her beliefs about God amounts to no more than acknowledging that she violated none of her epistemic obligations relevant to forming that belief on the basis of that putative experience of God; and acknowledging that the subject was within her epistemic rights in forming that belief on this basis is utterly independent of assessing the veridicality of her perception or the truth of her belief.

4. Alston's Concept of Epistemic Justification

Everyone who knows Alston's work, even if he or she has not yet read *Perceiving God*, will feel confident that he must have anticipated and blocked the moves I've been making on behalf of the broadminded atheist. And, of course, he does so—but not (or at least not clearly) until chapter 2, sixty-seven pages into the book.[9] He begins chapter 2, entitled 'Epistemic Justification', by restating the summary argument (pp. 68–9), this time including a fuller version of what I've designated premiss 2, which he associates here with a clarification of the much earlier, easily misinterpreted example of the lake mirage:

I may be perceptually justified in believing that there is a lake in front of me even if I am a victim of a mirage and no lake is being perceived. But this

---

[9] The only earlier hint I have noticed is easily overlooked. It is in the introduction's 'Preview of Chapters', where he says that 'since we are working with a reliability constraint on justification (a mode of forming beliefs is justificatory only if it is reliable), we are faced with the question of whether this mode of forming M-beliefs [on the basis of religious experience] is sufficiently reliable' (p. 6).

is just an isolated incident that occurs against the background of innumerable cases in which perceptual justification involves authentic perception
of the object. (p. 68)

His willingness to acknowledge that such a false belief may be
justified depends entirely on that background of innumerable
veridical perceptions of lakes and other ordinary objects of sense
perception, as he shows in this restatement of premiss 2:

It strains credulity to suppose that an entire sphere of putatively perceptual experience could be a source of justification for perceptual beliefs,
while there is no, or virtually no, genuine perception of the objects involved. (p. 68)

Of course, such a supposition puts not the slightest strain on credulity as long as the broadminded atheist's concept of justification is
operative. But immediately after this summary of the main argument Alston introduces his own concept of epistemic justification,
which lies behind premiss 2 and blocks the atheist's plausible appraisal of the Teresan paradigm:

To be sure, this all depends on the sense of justification in which it is shown
(or rendered reasonable to suppose) that putative perception of God can
provide justification for beliefs about God. In particular, it depends on
whether the concept of justification involved exhibits 'truth conducivity',
that is, on whether my being justified in believing that *p* entails that it is at
least likely that it is true that *p*. (p. 69)

Alston readily concedes that anyone who, like my broadminded
atheist, employs a concept of justification that does *not* exhibit
truth-conducivity will naturally be compelled to *deny* that the 'justificatory relation has any tendency to show that the experience in
question is genuine perception of those objects'—that is, to deny
premiss 2 of the summary argument. But this concession gives
Alston no trouble at all because, as he observes, 'if, on the other
hand, our conception of justification does exhibit truth conducivity,
as mine will, the argument does go through' (p. 69).

So at this point our assessment of the book's main argument
appears to turn on a choice between two concepts of epistemic
justification.[10] One of them, the one at the heart of the atheist's
plausible appraisal of the Teresan paradigm, is the view that 'being

[10] For an excellent, full, critical survey, see William P. Alston, 'Concepts of
Epistemic Justification', in Alston (ed.), *Epistemic Justification, Essays in the Theory
of Knowledge* (Ithaca, NY: Cornell University Press, 1989), 81–114.

justified in believing that *p* consists in some sort of "deontological" status, for example, being free of blame for believing that *p* or having satisfied one's intellectual obligations in doing so' (pp. 72–3). A deontological concept of justification renders Alston's main argument utterly unacceptable, as he himself points out. For of course, as we have seen, acknowledging that the subject of an experience has fulfilled her intellectual obligations in believing that *p* on the basis of her experience provides absolutely no support for concluding that such experiences are *ever*, never mind often, veridical experiences.

On the other hand, Alston's own concept of justification is the quite different view that 'to be justified in believing that *p* is to be in a *strong position* for realizing the epistemic aim of getting the truth'; that 'to be in an epistemically strong position in believing that *p* is to have an adequate ground or basis for believing that *p*' (p. 73), a ground on which one's belief that *p* is actually based (p. 74); and that 'If the ground is to be adequate to the task [assigned it in this concept], it must be the case that the belief is very probably true, given that it was formed on that basis' (ibid.).

The most important and perhaps most obvious consequence of this concept in the context of my investigation so far is that in accordance with this concept of epistemic justification 'the argument does go through', as Alston points out. For if justification is construed as truth-conducive in this way, then of course the belief that God exists *is* rendered highly probable if *any* particular belief about God based on a putative perception of God is justified.

Almost as obviously, Alston's own concept of epistemic justification is strictly 'nondeontological'. Since it maintains that 'justification requires that the ground be adequate in the *objective* sense that the ground be such as to render it objectively likely that the belief be true', it is 'an *externalist* conception, since there is no reason to suppose that these objective probability relations are ascertainable just on reflection. They have to do with the lawful structure of the world, and I can't expect to discern that just by looking within my breast' (p. 75, emphasis added). By the same token, deciding whether a person is truth-conducively justified in believing something or other has nothing to do with considering what is to be expected of someone in his or her epistemic situation, with its attendant advantages and disadvantages—the sort of consideration on which the atheist's plausible appraisal of the Teresan paradigm was based. No atheist, no matter how broadminded, would even consider saying that St Teresa's experientially based belief that God had reassured her was justified in Alston's sense of 'justified'. If Alston is not to lose his intended wide audience at this early stage of the development of his central thesis, he will have to set about filling the tall order of rendering his concept of truth-conducive justification appropriate to the Teresan paradigm.

Given the drastic discrepancy between the two concepts of justification we've encountered, it might seem crucially important for Alston at this juncture to provide conclusive reasons for rejecting the deontological concept and adopting his externalist, strong-position concept of epistemic justification. But, having already under-taken that job elsewhere,[11] Alston has earned the right to do no more here than allude briefly to his two most important considerations against the deontological concept: 'I reject all versions of a deontological concept on the grounds that they either make unrealistic assumptions of the voluntary control of belief or they radically fail to provide what we expect of a concept of justification' (p. 73). More significantly for my present purposes, he also takes a second approach to the discrepancy between his concept of justification and the deontological concept, one that provides a special excuse for saying no more about the deontological concept in this book. 'I feel', he says, 'that the requirements for justification are more stringent on my conception than on that of its most prominent competitors,' and he is unquestionably entitled to that feeling. 'Hence,' he continues, 'if I can successfully defend the position that (some) M-beliefs are justified on my conception, I will have shown that they can pass one of the most difficult tests in the field' (p. 76). That's putting it mildly. If he can successfully defend the position that *any* given M-belief—a belief about God based on a putative perception of God—is justified on his conception of justification, he will have shown that that M-belief 'is very probably *true*, given that it was formed on that basis' (p. 74, emphasis added), and that, consequently, putative perceptions of God 'are, at least frequently, *genuine* perceptions of God' (p. 69, emphasis added), and that, consequently, God exists.

So the assessment of Alston's main argument in *Perceiving God* turns on the question of whether he can successfully defend his

[11] See 'The Deontological Conception of Epistemic Justification', in Alston (ed.), *Epistemic Justification*, 115–52.

position that some M-beliefs, based on putative perceptions of God, are justified on his stringent, truth-conducive concept of epistemic justification.

5. Alston's Case-Study of the Reliability of Sense Perception

Like other ingenious defensive tacticians, Alston begins by preparing the ground in front of his position. The broadminded but by now disconcerted atheist, intent on assessing Alston's strong claims for the justifiedness of some M-beliefs such as St Teresa's and for the associated reliability of some mystical perceptions of the sort she had, must first consider 'The Reliability of Sense Perception: A Case Study', Alston's chapter 3. And since my purposes require me to follow the development of Alston's main argument, which is intimately associated with his study of sense perception, I must consider that study in some of the limited space allotted to this chapter. I won't be able to draw expressly and justify all its consequences for mystical perception in general and the Teresan paradigm in particular. Still, I believe that, in the end, at least some of those consequences will be clear.

The fact that sense perception is to be considered first is not the only respect in which a reader's expectations may have to be temporarily postponed, for it very soon becomes clear that the reliability at issue in the case-study will not attach to particular sense perceptions or even to types of sense perceptions, but only to what Alston calls a belief-forming, or 'doxastic', practice, for which particular sense perceptions are the input. The reliability directly at issue, then, is only the reliability of

The practice of forming perceptual beliefs about the physical environment on the basis of sensory experience (together, sometimes, with suitable background beliefs) [, which] we may term 'sense-perceptual practice' ('SP' for short). (p. 103)

Although Alston often writes simply about 'sense perception' in this case-study, his examination of its reliability is clearly concerned primarily with the reliability of the doxastic practice SP.[12] And the

---

[12] See p. 106: 'talk of the reliability of a source [such as sense perception or mystical perception] is to be understood as shorthand for the reliability of a certain doxastic practice that takes that source as input, a certain way of going from that source to beliefs related to it in a certain way.'

examination of the reliability of mystical perception to which this case-study leads is likewise concerned primarily with the reliability of the doxastic practice MP, 'mystical perceptual practice' (p. 103):

At the end of Chapter 2 I said that the basic problem of the book could be formulated as follows. 'Is the standard or customary practice of forming M-beliefs a source of prima facie justification for those beliefs?' And since the concept of justification we are using is both truth-conducive and source-relevant, this involves the question 'Is that practice a reliable one, one that generally will or would yield true beliefs?' [Footnote omitted.] Rather than tackle that straight off, I will approach it indirectly. In this chapter and the next I will concentrate on the parallel question concerning our standard practice of forming sense-perceptual beliefs. (p. 102)[13]

Alston provides two reasons for trying SP before putting MP in the dock. 'First, sense perception is a much more familiar, intelligible, and well-studied topic. We all constantly form perceptual beliefs on the basis of sense experience, and, in practice, we all take this to be highly reliable. Whatever results we attain here may throw light on the more obscure and controversial area of theistic perception' (p. 102). This first reason cites only features of SP that seem likely to sharpen one's assessment of the reliability of the less well understood MP, and so, on the basis of this first reason alone, the tactic seems altogether untendentious.

But the second reason puts the first in a different light:

Second, philosophers typically contrast the epistemic status of M-beliefs unfavorably with the status of sense-perceptual beliefs. It is widely believed that we are in a much better position to judge that sense perception is a source of justification than we are in the case of theistic perception. Many even believe that we can *show* that sense perception is reliable, but not that mystical perception is. [Footnote omitted.] These convictions are used as a basis for downgrading the epistemic status of the latter and for denying that beliefs formed on the basis of theistic perception are justified. (pp. 102–3)

Since this second reason focuses on the use that philosophers make of allegedly reliable SP as a stick with which to beat MP, the tactic of beginning with SP now looks tendentious. Even the apparent credentials of SP itself, which formed the basis of the first reason,

---

[13] It is the primary attachment of reliability to the doxastic practice that warrants Alston's saying, as we've seen him saying (on pp. 69 and 72–3 above), that even on his concept of truth-conducive justification the mirage victim's belief that there is a lake in the distance may be justified, because the innocent victim is engaging in SP, a putatively reliable doxastic practice.

now seem called into question. And it is this second reason that sets the tone for Alston's case-study of SP:

> In this chapter I shall argue that none of the attempts to show that sense perception is a reliable source of belief, or at least none that are not otherwise discredited, escape what I call 'epistemic circularity'. This suggests that, contrary to the usual supposition, the epistemic credentials of sense-perceptual beliefs are not so different from those of M-beliefs. (p. 103)

Epistemic circularity, then, appears to be a principal charge brought against MP by its detractors. Even someone not yet sure what Alston means by 'epistemic circularity' may begin to suspect that the nature of his central thesis and the structure of his main argument have suddenly taken on a different appearance. Evidently we are not to be shown, or at least not yet, that some M-beliefs are truth-conducively justified by being based on putative experiential awareness of God. Instead, it now looks as if Alston, adopting an entirely defensive stance, is going to fend off attempts to show that the doxastic practice MP is not reliable, or even just not as reliable as SP is, by simply developing a *tu quoque* argument against any philosopher who cites epistemic circularity in rejecting MP.

I think the charge of epistemic circularity figures rarely, if at all, in philosophers' attacks on reliability claims for MP. Alston certainly does develop such an argument, at length. If that is all he does by way of defending mystical perception, he surely will not have substantiated his earlier claims regarding the reliability of putative experiential awareness of God.

What does Alston mean by 'epistemic circularity' in connection with SP?[14] In assessing a particular attempt to show that SP is reliable, he makes remarks that turn out to be in his view generally applicable to attempts of that sort:

> Any such argument is infected by a kind of circularity. . . . we are, so to say, assuming the reliability of sense perception in using it, or some source(s) dependent on it, to generate our premises. If one were to challenge our premises and continue the challenge long enough, we would eventually be driven to appeal to the reliability of sense perception in defending our

---

[14] He provides a detailed general account in his article 'Epistemic Circularity', in Alston (ed.), *Epistemic Justification*, 319–49. It is virtually indispensable for an understanding of *Perceiving God*, esp. ch. 3.

right to those premises. . . . Since this kind of circularity involves a commitment to the conclusion as a presupposition of our supposing ourselves to
be *justified* in holding the premises, we can properly term it 'epistemic
circularity'. . . . In this chapter we will assume that epistemically circular
support fails to give us what we are looking for [establishing the reliability
of a doxastic practice], and we will take epistemic circularity to be disquali-
fying. (p. 108)

For this reason his case-study of SP leads him to conclude in chapter 3 that it is *not* 'possible to give adequate reasons for supposing
that practice to be reliable' (p. 102). Although MP is not directly at
issue in chapter 3, Alston takes up this case-study of SP just because he is 'concerned to contest the common supposition that we
have sufficient reason to trust SP, but not MP. By showing that any
otherwise impressive argument for the reliability of SP suffers from
epistemic circularity, I have rebutted this attack' (p. 143). And
where does this defensive tactic leave MP? Well, like SP, 'MP
cannot be shown noncircularly to be reliable' (p. 145). And so at
this stage of the development of Alston's argument he has replaced
the common supposition that we have sufficient reason to trust SP
but not MP with the reasoned conclusion that we have no sufficient
reason to trust *either* SP *or* MP.

Alston's assessment of SP constitutes a formidable critique,
though I'm not entirely convinced by it.[15] For my primary purpose
in this investigation I'm perfectly willing to let the negative result of

---

[15] I am one of those who believe that 'we are in a much better position to judge
that sense perception is a source of justification than we are in the case of theistic
perception' (p. 102). I want to point out one form of support for SP against which I
think Alston's charge of epistemic circularity doesn't stick. He devotes an entire
section of chapter 3 to the consideration of a formidable pragmatic argument in
support of the reliability of SP. A superficially similar argument considered earlier
was dismissed 'as infected with epistemic circularity. *This* argument is specifically
designed to avoid that disability. The earlier argument appealed to our success
in making accurate predictions of external, physical states of affairs. Hence it required reliance on SP to determine that those predictions are often correct. But
this argument appeals to our success in predicting *the course of our sense
experience*. . . . Hence no reliance on the perception of external states of affairs is
presupposed by the argument. [Footnote omitted.] . . . The argument is quite
straightforward: we can effectively anticipate our experience by taking it as
revelatory of the external world in accordance with SP; therefore, SP is quite
probably reliable. What could be more direct or convincing?' (pp. 136–7, first
emphasis added). It turns out that this attractive, definitive-seeming synopsis of the
argument is expressed too strongly from Alston's point of view. What strikes him as
unwarranted is the use of the first-person plural. 'If we are to avoid epistemic
circularity *I* cannot appeal to the success of *other* people in predicting *their* sense

his case-study of SP stand. But, of course, his argument does not end with that result. He goes on, as he must, to argue that we are, after all, justified in believing MP to be reliable.

6. The Reliability of Doxastic Practices

The only reliability now at issue is the reliability of the doxastic practices SP and MP, but neither SP nor MP can be shown to be reliable in a way that does not involve epistemic circularity; and so it appears to be impossible to show that either SP or MP is reliable. We seem to be farther than ever from being shown that any M-belief is ever truth-conducively justified, that any mystical perception is veridical.

If, as Alston argues, 'with respect to even those sources of belief of which we are normally the most confident we have no sufficient noncircular reason for taking them to be reliable', then in the aftermath of his appraisal of the reliability of SP (and, by implication, MP) his project is indeed in what looks to be 'a desperate situation' (p. 146). For, as we have seen, his main argument appears to require him to show that some M-beliefs are justified in the sense that the believer is 'in a strong position for realizing the epistemic

experience. For apart from reliance on SP I have no reason to think that there are other people, much less that they make use of SP and enjoy predictive success thereby. Hence the explanandum is restricted to *my* predictive success when using SP. . . . So far as the argument goes, I might be the only person who enjoys such success from using SP . . . [and] if all the other billions of human beings who have existed have failed to reap such benefits from the use of SP, we could hardly conclude that SP is reliable. . . . Of course, I am not suggesting that this is actually the case. The point is that if I am to avoid epistemic circularity I can't assume either that it is or that it isn't' (pp. 137–8, some emphasis added).

In introducing this argument Alston says that its 'whole point' is that 'by taking individual sense experiences as revelatory of external physical realities and connecting up our sense experiences through a detour into the physical world, we can do an incomparably better job of predicting those experiences than we could by looking for purely phenomenal patterns' (p. 137). And even in objecting to the argument, he concedes that it can show that SP is reliable *for the person employing the argument.* It seems clear to me, then, that I can legitimately put these observations together to yield an epistemically non-circular assurance that the other people I seem to experience in SP do exist and behave pretty much as I perceive them to do. And since I often perceive them succeeding in predicting their experiences when they appear to be using SP, and since SP is reliable for me, I think that this argument's use of the first-person plural is *not* unwarranted. Consequently, I'm not convinced that Alston has shown that all attempts to support SP's reliability are characterized by epistemic circularity.

aim of getting at the truth'—that is, the believer forms such beliefs on a basis that is 'adequate'—where a basis is adequate only if 'the belief is very probably true, given that it was formed on that basis' (pp. 73–4).[16] Showing that any M-belief is truth-conducively justified in that way strikes the broadminded atheist as impossible, of course. And the task must impress even the defender of mystical perception's epistemic importance as at least extremely difficult *before* Alston sets his project in the context of doxastic practices. But it is as a consequence of that move that the difficult looks desperate, even from a defender's point of view.

We have already seen that Alston's doxastic-practice approach ties the justification of a belief to the reliability of the doxastic practice of which that belief is an output. He makes this connection plainer in developing that approach in chapter 4:

What is, factually, a more or less fixed habit of going from inputs of type I to a belief output of correlated type B, is also, evaluatively, a principle of justification for beliefs so formed. The principle says that when a belief of type B is formed on the basis of an input of type I, that belief is thereby (prima facie) justified. (p. 158)

Each practice . . . carries its own distinctive modes of justification [for its belief outputs], its own distinctive principles that lay down sufficient conditions for justification, not only prima facie justification but also, through its overrider system, unqualified justification as well. (p. 162)

If we adopt a truth-conducive concept of justification and situate the justification of a belief within a doxastic practice in this way, then, as Alston acknowledges, 'we want practices to be subject to epistemic evaluation in terms of *reliability*' (p. 166, emphasis added), a necessary condition for truth-conducive justification of belief. And his project looks desperate because in his own view 'we have no sufficient noncircular reason for taking them [doxastic practices] to be reliable' (p. 146).

The first ray of hope Alston offers comes in a subtle observation that epistemic circularity does not, after all, 'prevent us from being justified in believing sense perception to be reliable by virtue of basing that belief on the premises of a simple track-record argument' (p. 147):

a belief is justified if and only if it is based on an adequate ground. That is, it is necessary only that the ground *be* adequate, not that the subject know

---

[16] See also p. 74 above.

or justifiably believe this, much less that the subject know or justifiably believe that all requirements for justification are satisfied. [Footnote omitted.] But then I can be justified in accepting the outputs of a certain doxastic practice without being justified in believing that the practice is reliable. . . . SP must *be* reliable if I am to be justified in holding perceptual beliefs, but I don't have to be justified in supposing this to be the case. But then *if SP is reliable*, I can use various (justified) perceptual beliefs to show that SP is reliable, for I need not already be justified in holding the conclusion in order to be justified in holding the premises [of a track-record argument in support of SP]. . . . [And so] Epistemic circularity does not in and of itself disqualify the argument. (pp. 147–8)

Of his accomplishment in this passage Alston says, 'I have removed an allegedly crippling disability, but I have not given the [track-record] argument a clean bill of health' (p. 148). Most readers would certainly agree; for 'the argument will not do its job unless we *are* justified in accepting the premises; and that is the case only if sense perception is in fact reliable. And this is to offer a stone instead of bread. We can say the same of any belief-forming practice whatever, no matter how disreputable. . . . So the situation is fairly desperate after all' (ibid.).

Before proposing his way out of the desperate situation, Alston resolutely refuses to take one way that might seem open to him: he 'might weaken the concept of justification, disembowel it of its implications of likelihood of truth. In that case our inability to satisfactorily establish the reliability of SP would not prevent us from showing SP to be a source of justification' (ibid.). The deontological concept of justification employed by the broadminded atheist in his plausible appraisal of the Teresan paradigm is just such a weakened concept, and would have just such results. But, as Alston clearly sees, that way out would scuttle rather than salvage his project:

apart from attachment to my theory of epistemic justification, I do not choose to take this way out. The main reason is that, apart from the question of how to think about *justification*, the question of the reliability of whatever doxastic practice we are concerned with is itself a matter of the highest importance, since our chief concern, after all, in belief formation, and in cognition generally, is to get the truth. (Ibid.)

I am calling attention to this passage not because it is in itself at all surprising or damaging to Alston's case; on the contrary, it says just what he must say in these circumstances, and it is entirely consistent with what he has been saying. My reason for citing it in this way is that I'm convinced that Alston's way out *does* 'weaken the concept of justification, disembowel it of its implications of likelihood of truth'. Moreover, and more surprisingly, the weakened concept he adopts is, I think, unmistakably a *deontological* concept of epistemic justification.

I'll now try to back up these convictions of mine. For if the justification of beliefs formed within a doxastic practice ultimately depends on the justification of believing that that practice is reliable, and if that latter justification is not truth-conducive but deontological, Alston's project will look no more viable on his doxastic-practice approach than it did in the light of the broadminded atheist's plausible appraisal of the Teresan paradigm.[17]

7. Alston's Account of Accepting a Doxastic Practice as Reliable

The way Alston finally accommodates epistemic circularity provides early indications of a deontological approach to justification:

Given that we will inevitably run into epistemic circularity at some point(s) in any attempt to provide direct arguments for the reliability of one or another doxastic practice, . . . what alternative is there to employing the practices we find ourselves using, to which we find ourselves firmly committed, and which we could abandon or replace only with extreme difficulty if at all? The classical skeptical alternative of withholding belief altogether is not a serious possibility. In the press of life we are continually forming beliefs . . . , whether we will or no. . . . we are just not in a position to get beyond, or behind, our familiar practices and criticize them from . . . [a] deeper or more objective position. Our human cognitive situation does not permit it. [Footnote omitted.] Again, we cannot take a step in intellectual endeavors without engaging in some doxastic practice(s) or other, and what reasonable alternative is there to practicing the ones with which we are intimately familiar? These considerations seem to me to indicate that it is eminently *reasonable* for us to form beliefs in the way we standardly do. (pp. 149–50)

---

[17] Someone might wonder what doxastic practice would or could provide the justification for the belief that this or that practice is reliable, especially given the way Alston goes on to justify the belief in the reliability of practices.

Much of what Alston says in this passage is plainly true, and for present purposes I will simply accept his whole assessment of our cognitive situation and the practical conclusions he draws from it. But in the framework of his project in *Perceiving God* the point of this passage is, or ought to be, to provide justification for the belief that this or that doxastic practice is reliable. Does it do so? Obviously not, if justification involves truth-conducivity. There is absolutely nothing in these familiar observations about our cognitive situation that has any tendency to suggest that the practices we can't avoid engaging in are really reliable.[18] On the other hand, there are abundant grounds for excusing us from insisting that any adopted practice puts us in a strong position from which to get truth, abundant grounds for condoning our more relaxed epistemic stance toward doxastic practices as one to which we have no alternative, one that we could abandon or replace only with extreme difficulty if at all, one that it is 'eminently *reasonable*' for us to have. It strikes me that these characteristics are all unmistakably indicative of a deontological justification of our belief that this or that doxastic practice is reliable.

A deontological concept of justification seems clearly to be in force also when Alston describes in more detail what it is for a belief to be justified in accordance with his doxastic-practice approach; and in this context the deontological consideration attaches directly to the justification of a particular belief within a practice, not simply to the acceptance of the relevant practice as reliable.

A belief is unqualifiedly justified (by the standards of the practice in question) provided it is prima facie justified (formed on the right kind of basis in accordance with the built-in principles of the practice), and there are no sufficient overriders. . . . It is not necessary for unqualified justification that the subject has *determined* that there are no sufficient overriders, only that there *are* none. That requirement is not perfectly precise. We can't restrict there being an overrider to its already being

[18] In any case, it seems plainly false that the unavoidability of a doxastic practice has, or should have, any bearing on our attitude toward its reliability. Since we form beliefs in dreams and sometimes briefly retain dream-beliefs when we wake up, dreaming may well qualify as a doxastic practice even if the dreams are not supplemented, as in certain primitive societies and Freudian psychoanalysis, by interpretative rules for the formation of waking-life beliefs on the basis of the dream experience. If ordinary dreaming, without systematic interpretation, is a doxastic practice, it certainly is one that we can't normally avoid engaging in. Yet, all sane people almost always consider at least uninterpreted dreaming to be an unreliable belief-forming practice.

present in the subject's existing system of belief. We must also allow that an overrider exists provided it is something that the subject could ascertain fairly easily. How easily? That's where the vagueness enters. Nevertheless, this criterion is, I believe, sufficiently precise to be usable. (p. 159)

Again, I have no interest in disputing any claim Alston makes in this account of the justification of a belief on the doxastic-practice approach. I do, however, want to call attention to the fact that in this account the '*unqualified* justification' of a particular belief depends ultimately on the plainly deontological consideration of whether or not the particular believer may be excused for not ascertaining that there is an overrider that would prevent that belief's being part of the output of that practice. Just think of a particular committed ancient Greek practitioner of the then well-established doxastic practice of discovering the will of the gods by examining sacrificed animals' entrails; and suppose that the shape of this particular sheep's liver is the practitioner's basis for forming the belief that Zeus favours the Spartans. Since the practitioner would not have easy access to overriders of that belief, his particular perceptual belief about the will of Zeus would be unqualifiedly justified. If unqualified justification can—indeed, must—be culturally and historically relativized in this way, the designation seems dangerously misleading.

I don't need to collect more passages to bolster my conviction that Alston is finally dependent on a deontological concept of justification if his prominent use of the notion of 'practical rationality' in this connection gets the interpretation I think it requires.[19] Returning to his conclusion that it is *rational* for us to engage in established doxastic practices, Alston says:

It is a kind of practical rationality that is in question here. In reflecting on our situation—what considerations are available to us, what we can and can't know, can and can't prove, what alternatives are open to us—we come to realize that we are proceeding rationally in forming and evaluating beliefs in ways that are established in our society and that are firmly embedded in our psyches. . . . *I call this rationality 'practical' to differentiate it from the rationality we would show to attach to a belief if solid grounds for its truth were adduced, or to attach to a doxastic practice if sufficient reasons were given for regarding it as reliable.*[20] I have forsworn the attempt to carry

[19] Ch. 4, sec. v (pp. 168–70) is entirely devoted to 'Practical Rationality'.
[20] Alston is certainly not to be suspected of vagueness or uncertainty about the sharp difference between showing that a doxastic practice is reliable and showing

out anything like that for our familiar doxastic practices. I only claim that
we cannot be faulted on grounds of rationality for forming and evaluating
beliefs in the ways we normally do (absent any sufficient overriding consid-
erations), since there are no alternatives that commend themselves to ra-
tional reflection as superior. (p. 168, emphasis added)

Alston is presenting here his account of the ultimate epistemic
justification for engaging in established doxastic practices, the
foundational justification on which the justification of any particular belief depends. In it he forthrightly announces that it provides
not the reliability of our belief-forming practices (which a reader
might well have been led to expect) but only the practical rationality of their practitioners. As such, it is a thoroughly deontological
account. What else could it be? His use of the deontological designation 'practical rationality' and the things he says by way of explaining it make its deontological nature perfectly clear. For
instance:

A question of practical rationality arises only when we are dealing with
what we *do*. If we were speaking of the truth (validity, acceptability . . .) of
principles or the adequacy of grounds, then there could be no question of
what it is rational to do, since we would not be discussing doings'. (p. 174,
Alston's dots)

The claim to practical rationality . . . [is] that where doxastic practices are
firmly rooted in our lives, it would be *folly* to cease practicing them without
very strong reasons for doing so; and we have no such reasons. This could
be the case even if the practice were in fact unreliable. (p. 178, emphasis
added)

We have shown, at most, that engaging in SP enjoys a *practical* rationality;
it is a reasonable thing to do, given our aims and our situation. . . . We have
not shown that it is rational in an *epistemic* sense that SP is reliable, where
the latter involves showing that it is at least probably true that SP is
reliable. (p. 180, second and third emphases added)

It seems right to say, then, that the kind of acceptance of a doxastic
practice as reliable that is dictated by considerations of practical
rationality amounts simply to *acting as if* that practice is reliable.

that we are practically reasonable to engage in it. The difference is the subject of ch.
4, sec. ix, 'Practical Rationality and Reliability', and it crops up repeatedly in other
places in the chapter—e.g., 'I am taking significant self-support to function as a way
of strengthening the prima facie claim of a doxastic practice to a kind of practical
rationality, *rather than* as something that confers probability on a claim to reliability'
(p. 174, emphasis added).

Since it is Alston himself who offers these observations, he presumably considers his central thesis and main argument to be unaffected by the bad news he seems to be conveying in offering them. I will conclude by trying to show how they really do damage his thesis and argument.

8. Alston's Main Argument and Justification by Practical Rationality

Alston has reduced the justification of the belief in a particular doxastic practice's reliability to the reasonableness of engaging in that practice, and he has explained that practical rationality on the basis of the practice's being 'established in our society' or 'firmly embedded in our psyches' or simply unavoidable. In a passage I've already quoted he gives as the sole explanation for our blamelessness in 'forming and evaluating beliefs' in SP the fact that '*there are no alternatives that commend themselves to rational reflection as superior*'. I need to stay with Alston's preliminary consideration of SP, but I can't forgo asking here how anyone could suppose that such an explanation could be seriously proposed for our blamelessness in forming and evaluating beliefs on the basis of *MP*.

In any case, once the nature of practical rationality as the ultimate justification emerges, it has an effect on later summaries of the main argument—for example, in this apparently casual revision of premiss 2: 'It is a reasonable supposition that a practice would not have persisted over large segments of the population unless it was putting people into effective touch with some aspect(s) of reality and proving itself as such by its fruits' (p. 170).[21] 'Putting people into effective touch with some aspect(s) of reality' may not be significantly weaker than there being 'genuine perception of the objects involved'. But the place occupied in this version of premise 2 by a practice having 'persisted over large segments of the population' contained in earlier versions by the much braver description of 'an entire sphere of putatively perceptual experience' being 'a source of justification for perceptual beliefs'. Worse yet, although this weakened claim does seem to deserve the modest designation of 'a reasonable supposition', it reckons without the unreasonable-

[21] See e.g. p. 68, quoted on p. 21 above.

ness of 'large segments of the population', among whom such doxastic practices as seances and newspaper horoscopes have long persisted. Reasonable though it is, this weakened supposition now standing in for premiss 2 is simply false: seances have not been putting people into effective touch with any aspect of reality. And so whatever force the main argument may seem to have promised for its robust conclusion of veridicality has not been delivered.

In the concluding section of chapter 4 Alston himself sounds at first like his own severest critic:

despite the initial tough talk [in chapter 2] about justification entailing reliability, it would seem that . . . we have finally settled for an epistemic status for SP (and derivatively for the epistemic status of perceptual beliefs) that falls far short of likelihood of truth. So why didn't we begin with a weaker notion of justification, instead of initially holding out hopes that were eventually to be dashed? Why didn't we begin with a more 'internalist' notion of justification that does not entail the likelihood of truth? (p. 181)

Of course Alston does not leave these questions hanging in the air, but before going on to his response, I want to call attention to the fact that the questions imply concessions of points I have been stressing in this section of the chapter. Here is his response:

So far as this charge is applied to perceptual beliefs, it is vitiated by a level confusion.[22] The lower epistemic status we have settled for attaches to the *higher-level* claim that SP is reliable, not . . . [to] the particular perceptual beliefs that issue from that practice. As for the latter, what we are claiming is still the full-blooded (prima facie) justification of Chapter 2 that involves likelihood of truth. . . . At the higher level we have settled for showing that it is (practically) *rational* to take SP to confer justification in the full-blooded sense. But it would be a level confusion to suppose that this implies that perceptual beliefs themselves are not justified in the stronger sense. (pp. 182-3)

He's right, of course, about its *not* implying that perceptual beliefs *aren't* justified in the stronger sense. But his settling for the lower epistemic status at the higher level also leaves us without *any* justification for believing that perceptual beliefs *are* non-deontologically, truth-conducively justified. Finding ourselves committed by our inescapable cognitive circumstances to *acting as if*

---

[22] For a detailed account of this useful notion, see his article 'Level Confusions in Epistemology', in Alston (ed.), *Epistemic Justification*, 153-71.

some doxastic practices are reliable, we are left utterly without justification for believing that their products are strongly justified. All we can say is that it would be practically *un*reasonable for us to act as if its products are *not* strongly justified. There's a natural tendency for the reasonable attitude toward the doxastic practice to be extended downward to its output beliefs, but the practically reasonable refusal to reject those beliefs is a far cry from truth-conducive justification for accepting them. The practically reasonable, but epistemically scrupulous, practitioner of the practice can recognize that in theory the epistemic status of the products themselves is left open.

Alston sums up his defence by trying to drive home the lesson: 'Once more, according to our account of justification, the justification of perceptual beliefs requires that it is *true* that SP is reliable, not that we are truth-conducively justified in believing this' (p. 182). But surely this situation is irreversibly changed for us reflective practitioners just by Alston's having let the cat out of the bag. Now that we've found out that we can't be truth-conducively justified in believing that SP really is reliable, what warrants our claim that that requirement of the justification of perceptual beliefs is satisfied—that is, that it *is* true that SP is reliable? Could our warrant for that claim simply be the fact that it would be practically unreasonable for us to act as if SP were not reliable? Surely not. The practical rationality imposed on us by our epistemic limitations is not to be confused with the fact required for the justification of perceptual beliefs.

In another place and in another connection Alston says very aptly what I think must be said here as well:

I can justify, and *be* justified in, taking the source [of belief] to be reliable and to be a source of justification. But as soon as I direct a critical scrutiny on this happy state of affairs, it disappears before my eyes; it eludes my reflective grasp. . . . I can justify, or be justified in, accepting either particular perceptual propositions or a general principle of perceptual justification or reliability, only by practically accepting that principle of reliability. But in the enterprise of seeking to answer critical questions whenever they arise, one is driven to convert that practical acceptance into theoretical justification. . . . All is well so long as we rely on justification that obtains in fact and do not insist on demonstrating it. But as soon as we look back with a critical eye, we meet the fate of Orpheus.[23]

[23] Alston, 'Epistemic Circularity', 343.

And anyone bent on bringing truth-conducive justification safely into the workaday world will meet the fate of Orpheus if he or she reads Alston's chapter 4, where the author *makes* the reader look back with a critical eye.

I've finished my examination of Alston's main argument, but I shouldn't end without at least mentioning some of the differences between MP and SP that raise further problems when Alston turns to consider directly the reliability of MP and the justification of M-beliefs within MP. Many relevant differences are likely to have occurred to the reader as various features of SP came up in this investigation. For instance, where SP presents a universal, constant abundance of perceptual inputs, MP's inputs seem relatively rare, scattered, intermittent, and few; where SP's outputs exhibit consistency across cultural divisions, MP's don't . Of course Alston recognizes these and other such differences, and tries to accommodate them in the latter half of his book. But perhaps the most salient difference from the standpoint of practical rationality as we have seen that concept employed in this investigation is the fact that while we cannot rationally reject or suspend judgement on most sense-perceptual experience, even devout theists often conscientiously reject or suspend judgement on putative mystical perceptions. And since it is the absence of 'alternatives that commend themselves to reflection as superior' that Alston offers as the linchpin of the practical rationality of acting as if SP is reliable, it looks as if he cannot argue along the same line for the practical rationality of acting as if *MP* is reliable.

I conclude that on the basis of this investigation it seems at least unlikely that Alston could succeed in showing that mystical perception makes an important contribution to the objective grounds of religious belief.[24]

[24] I am grateful for comments on an earlier draft of this chapter from Claudia Eisen, Carl Ginet, Steve Maitzen, Sean Murphy, Tim O'Connor, Bob Pasnau, George Rudebusch, Sydney Shoemaker, David Slutsky, and Eleonore Stump. And for discussing the earlier draft with me and generously providing written comments I owe special thanks to Bill Alston, whose friendly advice in this as in other matters I may not have followed as closely as I should.

5

The Nature of Reason: Locke, Swinburne, and Edwards

WILLIAM J. WAINWRIGHT

I

In *An Essay Concerning Human Understanding*, John Locke defines reason as 'the discovery of the certainty or probability of such propositions or truths, which the mind arrives at by deduction made from such ideas, which it has got by the use of its natural faculties; viz. by sensation or reflection' (iv. 18. 2).[1] Rational belief is proportionate to the strength of the evidence at one's disposal. 'The mind, if it *will proceed rationally*, ought to examine all the grounds of probability, and see how they make more or less for or against any proposition, before it assents to or dissents from it; and upon a due balancing of the whole, reject or receive it, with more or less firm assent, proportionably to the preponderancy of the greater grounds of probability on one side or the other' (iv. 15. 5). What is true of beliefs in general is true of religious beliefs in particular. They are rational only if (1) they are properly basic (immediately grounded in the mind's intuitive awareness of its own ideas), or (2) inferred from those ideas by sound deductive or inductive standards, or (3) are the content of a revelation whose credentials are certified by beliefs meeting the first or second condition. While modern intellectuals may doubt whether religious beliefs meet these standards, Locke did not. God's existence can be demonstrated, and the evidence at our disposal makes it probable that the Bible is God's revelation.

Richard Swinburne would agree with the substance of Locke's remarks. His books *The Existence of God* and *Faith and Reason* persuasively argue that the evidence at our disposal makes God's

---

[1] John Locke, *An Essay Concerning Human Understanding* (2 vols., New York: Dover Publications, Inc., 1959).

existence probable and the Christian revelation credible.[2] Swinburne's work as a whole is informed by a conception of reason which is similar to Locke's in spirit if not always in letter. 'To believe that *p* is to believe that *p* is more probable than any alternative.... The kind of probability at stake here is ... epistemic probability,' and 'epistemic probability is relative to evidence' (*FR* 18). Belief is (fully) *rational* when it is *properly* based on the best evidence at one's disposal. 'S's belief that *p* is rational if and only if S's evidence results from past investigation which was adequate,' his 'inductive [that is, inferential] standards ... have been submitted to adequate criticism, and S has investigated adequately whether [given his inductive standards] his evidence makes his belief probable' (*FR* 54).[3]

Evidential (probability) relations are objective. While probabilities can't always be given an 'exact numerical value' (*FR* 19, 65), there are objectively true propositions of the form $P(h/e_1.k) > P(h/e_2.k)$ or $P(h/e.k) > 1/2$, where *h* is our hypothesis, *e* our evidence, and *k* our background knowledge.[4] There are also objectively true answers to questions like 'Are S's basic beliefs justified?', 'Are his inductive standards justified?', 'Does his evidence result from an adequate investigation?', and 'Have his inductive standards been subjected to adequate criticism?' (see *FR* 45–54). Although Locke doesn't explicitly discuss the matter, he would undoubtedly agree.

Swinburne recognizes, of course, that apparently rational people differ over such things as the prior probability of hypotheses. For example, he thinks that although a hypothesis's prior probability is determined by its simplicity, scope, and fit with our background knowledge, scope is relatively unimportant. (An increase in scope decreases probability, but 'if a theory loses scope it loses simplicity too, because any restriction of scope is often arbitrary and compli-

---

[2] *The Existence of God* (Oxford: Clarendon Press, 1979); *Faith and Reason* (Oxford: Clarendon Press, 1981); hereafter *EG* and *FR* respectively.

[3] Locke and Swinburne may differ in one respect. Swinburne thinks not only that the mind *should* proportion its belief to the evidence at its disposal, but that it *must* do so in the sense that it can't believe *p* unless it rightly or wrongly thinks that (given its inductive standards) the evidence at its disposal makes *p* probable. Whether Locke also thought this is uncertain, but I believe he did not.

[4] See e.g. *EG* 67, where Swinburne argues that if the probability of *h* depended 'on whether we had thought of *h* before we saw *e*', probability would be 'a highly subjective matter instead of an objective relationship between evidence and hypothesis'.

cating'.) Simplicity and fit are what are important in practice. Yet fit *isn't* an important determinant of a *large-scale* theory's prior probability, for as a theory's application widens, 'there are less and less other fields with whose theories it has to fit' (*EG* 52–3). Since the scope of the theistic hypothesis includes *all* contingent facts, fit with background knowledge (of contingent facts) is irrelevant. Swinburne concludes that because of its simplicity, its prior probability is comparatively high. J. L. Mackie, on the other hand, restricts the theistic hypothesis's scope to the origin of the universe, and argues that fit is the most important criterion in determining its prior probability. He concludes that, because it conflicts with other things we know, its prior probability is low.[5]

Swinburne also notes that people's beliefs in reports of experience, deliverances of reason, and other basic propositions differ 'in the degrees of confidence with which they hold' them. Peter and John may have similar experiences, be inclined to report them in the same way (as sightings of a UFO, for instance), be aware of the same defeaters, and acknowledge that they *are* defeaters. Yet Peter may be more confident in his report than John is. Nor are differences of this sort confined to belief in basic propositions. For example, some find the statement 'Every event has a cause' obvious, while others do not (*FR* 35–7).

People's inferential standards also differ. Sometimes one or more of the conflicting standards are obviously irrational (for example, a rule which would license inferring that a fair coin will probably turn up heads on the next toss because it has turned up tails the last five times). But sometimes they are not. Two people may differ, for example, 'as to how far they may extrapolate from evidence obtained in a narrow spatio-temporal region' without either being clearly irrational.

Finally, people's assessments of the *overall* probability of theories and hypotheses differ. As Swinburne points out, 'when it gets anywhere near the border between the probable and the improbable', qualified enquirers typically disagree as to whether a theory is more probable than not. There is a dearth 'of examples of theories which, it is intuitively obvious, are more probable than not, without being overwhelmingly probable; or less probable than not

---

[5] J. L. Mackie, *The Miracle of Theism* (Oxford: Clarendon Press, 1982), 5. For a good discussion of this dispute see Robert Prevost, *Probability and Theistic Explanation* (Oxford: Clarendon Press, 1990), ch. 2.

without being overwhelming improbable'. 'Is Quantum Theory more probable than not? Or is the General Theory of Relativity? The answer is in no way clear' (*EG* 280).

Swinburne admits that these disagreements are very much the product of our 'upbringing', but insists that if progress is to be made in rational enquiry, 'we must make the judgements which seem to us to be intuitively right'. The relativity of our understanding 'does not mean that our understanding is in error' (*EG* 56).[6]

I believe that this is correct. But I also think that differences over prior probability, the overall probability of a hypothesis, and so on, are differences in judgement, and that differences in judgement are typically affected by what William James called our 'willing' or 'passional' nature—our temperament, needs, concerns, fears, hopes, passions, and 'divinations'. Simplicity, for example, is partly a matter of intelligibility or naturalness.[7] But the conviction that a hypothesis is intelligible or natural is partly a product of familiarity, and is affected by our attachments and attitudes. A hypothesis that seems intelligible or natural to a traditional Christian theist like Swinburne may not seem intelligible or natural to a J. L. Mackie.

Our assessments of the overall probability of a hypothesis like theism are also affected by our passional nature; for when it comes to 'the question, what is to come of the evidence, being what it is', each of us must finally decide 'according to (what is called) the state of his heart'.[8] In the last analysis, I can only view the evidence 'in the medium of *my* primary mental experiences, under the aspects which they spontaneously present to *me*, and with the aid of *my* best illative sense'.[9] Our assessments of the evidence depend on our view of prior probabilities, of the evidence's overall weight, and so on. But because these 'have no definite ascertained value and are reducible to no scientific standard, what are such to each individual,

---

[6] In the passage quoted, Swinburne is specifically speaking of our assessments of prior probabilities and differences in our 'scientific and mathematical upbringing'. I believe that he would nevertheless accept my generalization of his remarks.

[7] See *EG* 94, where 'all material bodies attract each other with forces proportional to mn^1/r^2' is said to have a 'naturalness' which 'All bodies attract each other with forces proportional to $mn^1/r^{2.000142}$' lacks. Or see *EG* 103, where Swinburne says that the theistic hypothesis is intelligible because we are familiar with the type of causality it postulates from our experience of bringing things about by making choices.

[8] John Henry Newman, 'Love the Safeguard of Faith against Superstition', in *University Sermons* (Westminster, Md.: Christian Classics, 1966), 227.

[9] Newman, *Grammar of Assent* (Garden City, NY: Image Books, 1955), 318.

depends on his moral temperament' and personal history, as well as investigation and argument.[10]

Swinburne would not deny that our willing nature affects our judgement,[11] but would, I think, insist that its influence is epistemically harmful. Good arguments employ premises which are 'known to be true' by those who dispute over the conclusion (*EG* 7). A good argument is also presumably one which the disputants can see makes its conclusions certain or probable.[12] But if it is, they must abstract from their passional differences. For example, in the controversy in which he is engaged in *The Existence of God*, Swinburne must abstract from the influence of his specifically Christian dispositions, since many of those whom the book addresses lack them. His opponents, on the other hand, must try to prevent their hostility to religion or secular sentiments from affecting their assessments of his arguments.

This attitude towards the effect of 'passion' on reason is hardly unusual. But is it correct? The remainder of the chapter will offer a partial defence of the claim that the influence of the heart can be epistemically benign.

II

The position I will defend was once a Christian commonplace: that reason is capable of knowing God—but only when one's cognitive faculties are rightly disposed. It should be distinguished from two others which have dominated modern thought. The first[13] claims that God can be known by 'objective reason'—that is, by an understanding that systematically excludes 'passional factors' from the process of reasoning. The other insists that God can be known only 'subjectively', or by the heart. Both views identify reason with

---

[10] Newman, 'Faith and Reason Contrasted as Habits of Mind', in *University Sermons*, 191. Whether Newman meant that there aren't any objective probabilities is unclear. In any case, what *I* mean is that even if there *are* objective probabilities, we have no algorithm for determining what they are. Our assignments of probabilities ultimately rest on judgement and intuition (although judgement and intuition can be more or less reasonable or instructed), and these are infected by temperament, values, etc. I have argued for this thesis at more length in 'World Views, Criteria, and Epistemic Circularity', in James Kellenberger (ed.), *Interreligious Models and Criteria* (London: Macmillan, 1993), 87–105.

[11] Although he might accuse me of exaggerating its influence.

[12] Or raises its probability.   [13] Which I take to be Swinburne's.

ratiocination. They also assume that reasoning is objective only
when unaffected by wants, interests, and desires. The tradition I
will discuss steers between these two extremes. It places a high
value on proofs, arguments, and inferences, yet also believes that a
properly disposed heart is needed to see their *force*. The most
articulate spokesman for this position is Jonathan Edwards.

Edwards was strongly influenced by Continental rationalists
like Malebranche, by some of the Cambridge Platonists (Henry
More, for example), and by the empiricists (especially Locke). He
was also excited by Newton and the new science. Although these
traditions were diverse, they had an important common feature—
an almost uncritical confidence in reason's power and scope.
Edwards's practice reflects this confidence. Philosophical arguments are deployed to demolish critics, justify the principal Christian doctrines, and erect a speculative metaphysics (a subjective,
idealism like Berkeley's). But Edwards was also a Calvinist who
shared the Reformed tradition's distrust of humanity's natural capacities and its scepticism about natural theology.

These diverse strands are reflected in the apparent ambiguity of
Edwards's remarks on reason. Thus, he can say, on the one hand,
that 'arguing for the being of a God according to the natural powers
from everything we are conversant with is short, easy, and what we
naturally fall into' (Misc. 268, T 78), and yet, on the other hand,
insist that, in thinking about God, reason is baffled by 'mystery',
'paradox', and 'seeming inconsistence'. (Examples are an omni-
presence without extension, an immutability (which Edwards
thinks implies duration) without succession, and the idea of a 'perfect knowledge of all . . . things of external sense, without any
sensation or any reception of ideas from without' (Misc. 1340, T
231).)[14]

Again, Edwards claims that we can know that a just God governs
the world by the 'light of nature'; conscience, which sees 'the re-

[14] Edwards's principal discussions of reason are located in the 'Miscellanies' (a
number of which can be found in *The Philosophy of Jonathan Edwards from his
Private Notebooks*, ed. Harvey G. Townsend (Eugene, Oreg.: University of Oregon
monographs, 1955), hereafter Misc., T; 'A Divine and Supernatural Light' and
'Miscellaneous Observations', in *The Works of President Edwards* (1968 repr. of
Leeds edn. reissued with a 2-vol. supplement in Edinburgh, 1847), viii), hereafter
DSL and Misc. Obs., respectively; 'The Mind', 'Subjects to be Handled in the
Treatise on the Mind', and 'Of the Prejudices of Imagination', in *Scientific and
Philosophical Writings*, ed. Wallace E. Anderson (New Haven, Conn.: Yale Univer-
sity Press, 1980), hereafter 'Mind', 'Subjects' and 'Prejudices', respectively, and

lation and agreement there is between that which is wrong or unjust and punishment,' and finds unpunished wrongs 'shocking', naturally leads us to conclude that God is 'a just being' (Misc. 353, T 110–11). But he also says that while 'the invisible things of God are indeed to be understood by the things that are made', uninstructed reason invariably errs (Misc. 986, T 212). It is 'almost impossible for unassisted reason' to demonstrate 'that the world, and all things contained therein, are effects, and had a beginning'. If a person were 'left to himself', he 'would be apt to reason' that since causes and effects must be 'similar and conformable, matter must have a material cause' and 'evil and irregularity . . . must be attributed to an evil and unwise cause'. Indeed, without assistance, 'the best reasoner in the world . . . might be led into the grossest errors and contradictions' (Misc. Obs. 185–6). If 'God never speaks to or converses at all with mankind', we would most likely think that 'there is no being that made and governs the world' or that, if there is, it is not 'properly an intelligent, volitive being' (Misc. 1298, T 218).

Finally, although reason *can* prove God's existence, determine the nature of many of his attributes, discern our obligations to him, and establish the credibility of Scripture, grace is needed to help 'the natural principles against those things that tend to stupify it and to hinder its free exercise' (Misc. 626, T 111). It is also needed to 'sanctify the reasoning faculty and assist it to see the clear evidence there is of the truth of religion in rational arguments' (Misc. 628, T 251).

In many respects, Edwards is simply restating Puritan commonplaces. While 'some of the things "plainly proved" by scripture could also be detected by the "light of natural reason"', Puritans emphasized reason's powerlessness.[15] For example,

Original Sin (New Haven, Conn.: Yale University Press, 1970), hereafter *OS*. Other relevant material can be found in *Religious Affections* (New Haven, Conn.: Yale University Press, 1959), hereafter *RA*; *The Nature of True Virtue*, in *Ethical Writings*, ed. Paul Ramsey (New Haven, Conn.: Yale University Press, 1989), hereafter *TV*; and *History of the Work of Redemption* (New Haven, Conn.: Yale University Press, 1989). The 'Miscellaneous Observations' must be used with caution. It was originally published in 1793, and consists of material from the 'Miscellanies'. The editor (John Erskine) 'took great liberties with the text, disregarded all chronological order, patched together widely separated excerpts, and added whatever connections or conjunctions seemed appropriate to him' (Townsend, p. xi, n. 14).

[15] John Morgan, *Godly Learning; Puritan Attitudes towards Reason, Learning and Education* (Cambridge: Cambridge University Press, 1986), 51.

Robert Bolton thought that if 'a man looke upon Gods ways onely with the eye of reason they are foolishnesses to him'. Richard Greenham said, 'there is no greater ods in the world than between our owne reason and God's wisdome.' According to the great Puritan divine William Perkins, one 'must reject his owne naturall reason, and stoppe up the eyes of his naturall minde, like a blinde man, and suffer himself wholly to be guided by God's spirit in the things of God'. And the Puritan mystic Francis Rous commended those who 'have . . . quenched their owne naturall lamps, that they might get them kindled above by the Father of Lights'.[16] As John Morgan points out, Puritan strictures on reason reflect the Reformed (and ultimately Augustinian and Pauline) insistence upon human corruption. Reason isn't exempt from the consequences of the Fall. While natural reason may discover some truths about God (along with many errors), it is incapable of discerning his saving actions on our behalf. Puritan strictures also reflect their emphasis upon an 'experimental knowledge' of God's favour towards us. According to Arthur Dent, 'the knowledge of the reprobate is like the knowledge which a mathematical geographer hath of the earth and all the places in it, which is but a generall notion and a speculative comprehension of them. But the knowledge of the elect is like the knowledge of a traveller which can speake of experience and feeling, and hath beene there and seene and known the particulars.'[17]

Edwards shares these attitudes. What distinguishes him from other Puritan divines isn't his learning or his use of philosophical resources,[18] but his philosophical acumen and the fact that the intellectual currents which most influenced him (Continental rationalism and British empiricism) are those that have both shaped modern philosophy and underlie the dominant view of rationality.

III

Edwards uses 'reason' in two closely related senses. Sometimes the term refers to 'ratiocination, or a power of inferring by arguments'

---

[16] The quotations are found in ibid. 51–3.   [17] Quoted in ibid. 59.

[18] In spite of their strictures on reason, Puritans insisted on a learned clergy, and Puritan divines commonly drew on the ancient philosophers, the schoolmen, Ramus, etc.

(DSL 18). At others it refers to 'the power . . . an intelligent being has to judge of the truth of propositions . . . immediately by only looking on the propositions' as well as to ratiocination (Misc. 1340, T 219).[19] The difference between these characterizations isn't important; in both cases, 'reason's work is to perceive truth and not excellency' (DSL 18). Excellency and what pertains to it are perceived by the heart. While Edwards concedes that there is a more extended sense in which 'reason' refers to 'the faculty of mental perception in general' (DSL 18), he clearly prefers the stricter usage. His official view is that of other modern philosophers who deny that reason has an affective dimension (a love of the good, for example, or a delight in excellence).[20]

Grace affects reason as well as the heart. 'Common grace' helps the faculties 'to do that more fully which they do by nature,' strengthening 'the natural principles [for example, conscience] against those things that tend to stupify it and to hinder its free exercise'. 'Special grace', on the other hand, 'causes those things to be in the soul that are above nature; and causes them to be in the soul habitually' (Misc. 626, T 111). Special grace sanctifies by infusing benevolence or true virtue—namely, the love of being in general. Infused benevolence is the basis of a new epistemic principle; a sense of the heart which tastes, relishes, and perceives the beauty of holiness (that is, benevolence). By its means, the sanctified acquire a new simple idea (the idea of 'true beauty') which the unredeemed lack. Because this idea is needed to properly understand divine matters, the 'saints' are in a superior epistemic position.[21] One can't rightly understand God's moral attributes, for example, if one doesn't perceive their beauty. Nor can one adequately grasp truths which logically or epistemically depend on

[19] *Freedom of the Will* (hereafter *FW*) asserts that propositions are self-evident when they express necessary truths or things present to (immediately perceived by) the mind. Examples are mathematical propositions, analytic truths, metaphysical principles, true moral statements, and reports of present ideas and sensations (see *FW* 153, 181 ff., and 259).

[20] Although Edwards's identification with this tradition isn't entirely straightforward. His sense of the heart, e.g., is a *cognitive* faculty, whereas (e.g.) Hutcheson's is not. Furthermore, while Edwards normally assigns the sense of the heart to the will (i.e., to our affective nature) he sometimes assigns it to the understanding. See e.g. *RA* 206.

[21] The saints aren't wholly passive with respect to the reception of this new simple idea, for they can increase its clarity and intensity. They can do so, however, only 'by the practice of virtue and holiness—for we cannot have the idea without the adapted disposition of mind' (Misc. 123, T 246).

God's holiness and its splendour such as the infinite heinousness of sin or the appropriateness of God's aiming at his own glory. The saints also behold old data with new eyes. They perceive the stamp of divine splendour on the world's order and design and upon the events recorded in sacred history. They thereby acquire a more accurate sense of this evidence's force and impressiveness.

Since I have discussed the new sense of the heart elsewhere,[22] I will focus on another epistemic effect of special grace. The new principle that God infuses

sanctifies the reasoning faculty and assists it to see the clear evidence there is of the truth of religion in rational arguments, and that in two ways, viz., as it removes prejudices and so lays the mind more open to the force of arguments, and also secondly, as it positively enlightens and assists it to see the force of rational arguments . . . by adding greater light, clearness and strength to the judgment. (Misc. 628, T 251)[23]

There is nothing intrinsically supernatural about many of these benefits. The *cause* of the mind's reasoning soundly is supernatural, but the effect (sound reasoning) often is not;[24] the spirit simply helps us use our natural epistemic faculties rightly.

What sorts of 'prejudices' interfere with reason's 'free exercise'? 'Opinions arising from imagination' are one example. They

take us as soon as we are born, are beat into us by every act of sensation, and so grow up with us from our very births; and by that means grow into us so fast that it is almost impossible to root them out, being as it were so incorporated with our very minds that whatsoever is objected to them, contrary thereunto, is as if it were dissonant to the very constitution of them. Hence, men come to make what they can actually perceive by their senses, or immediate and outside reflection into their own souls, the standard of possibility and impossibility. ('Prejudices', 196)

Biases arising from temperament, education, custom, and fashion furnish other examples ('Mind', 68, and 'Subjects', 384 and 387).

Sin's essence is a failure to obey the love commandment. Those who don't love being in general love 'private systems'. Their loves are partial, extending to only some beings. They are also inordi-

---

[22] William J. Wainwright, 'Jonathan Edwards and the Sense of the Heart', *Faith and Philosophy*, vii (1990), 43–62.

[23] In so far as special grace simply strengthens natural principles, its effects are the same as those of common grace.

[24] The exceptions will become clear as we proceed.

nate; lives are centred on the self or more extensive private systems rather than on God (who is 'in effect' being in general) and the creatures who are absolutely dependent on him and reflect his glory.[25]

Sin has noetic consequences. Edwards refers, for example, to 'the great subjection of the soul in its fallen state to the external senses' (Misc. 782, T 122). (This subjection is presumably a consequence of the soul's inordinate love of temporal goods.[26]) Again, self-love blinds us to everything that doesn't bear on immediate self-interest (*OS* 145–57). In addition, 'the mind of man is naturally full of enmity against the doctrines of the gospel' which cause 'arguments that prove their truth . . . to lose their force upon the mind' (*RA* 307). (God crosses our self-love and love of temporal things, and this arouses hostility.)

Our corrupt inclinations even affect our sense of what is and isn't reasonable. 'Common inclination or the common dictates of inclination, are often called common sense.' A person who says that the doctrine of eternal damnation offends common sense is using the expression in this way. But the inclinations behind this judgement have been shaped by an insensibility to 'the great evil of sin'. They are therefore corrupt (Misc. Obs. 253).

William James has suggested that our judgements of credibility reflect what we have a use for, what vitally concerns us. 'In . . . the sense in which we contrast reality with simple *un*reality, and in which one thing is said to have *more* reality than another, and to be more believed, reality means simply relation to our emotional and active life. This is the only sense which the word ever has in the mouths of practical men. In this sense whatever excites and stimulates our interests is real.'[27] 'The natural propensity of man is to believe that whatever has great value for life is thereby certified as true.'[28] Our judgements of truth and reality, in other words, are (partly) functions of our emotional engagement. Edwards would

---

[25] For a fuller treatment of these points see my 'Original Sin', in Thomas V. Morris (ed.), *Philosophy and the Christian Faith* (Notre Dame, Ind.: University of Notre Dame Press, 1988), 31–60.

[26] Cf. Plato in the *Phaedo* and elsewhere. There is an important Platonic strand in Puritanism.

[27] William James, *The Principles of Psychology*, (Cambridge, Mass.: Harvard University Press, 1981), ii. 924 (James's emphases).

[28] William James, *The Varieties of Religious Experience* (New York: Modern Library, c.1902), 500n.

agree. If our interests are badly misdirected, our judgements of what is and isn't credible will be correspondingly distorted.

Grace frees the mind from these 'prejudices'. An unprejudiced reason, however, isn't dispassionate. For it is affected by *epistemically benign* feelings and inclinations. A love of wider systems alone checks self-interest. Nor is it sufficient to replace hostility towards religion with indifference or neutrality; the heart must be receptive to it. An unprejudiced reason is also affected by natural motions of the heart—gratitude for one's being, for example, or a sense that it would be unfitting for the injustice that evades human tribunals to escape punishment.[29] And since our love of temporal goods is inordinate because it isn't subordinate to a love of eternity, the latter is needed to correct it.[30]

Another point is relevant as well. Natural reason reveals many truths about God and our relation to him. Yet even at the level of nature these truths aren't properly understood if the heart lacks a due sense of the natural good and evil in them[31] (a proper sense of the natural unfittingness of disobeying the world's sovereign, for example, and a horror of the natural evils consequent upon offences against him, or a proper sense of the natural benefits he has bestowed upon us and of the obligations these gifts create).

I conclude, then, that *common* grace not only inhibits the action of passional factors corrupting reason; it (at least temporarily) causes better affections to influence it. *Sanctifying* grace replaces the effects of corrupt affections by the influences of true benevolence. A reason that is exercising itself 'freely' and without 'prejudice', therefore, is affected by passional factors.

But grace does more than remove the impediments ('prejudices') hindering reason's free exercise by restructuring our affections. It adds 'greater light, clearness and strength to the judgement'. Edwards refers us to Miscellany 408 for 'one way' in which it does so.[32] Here he argues that ideas of spiritual things

[29] See Misc. 353 (T 110 ff.) for an instance in which a natural sentiment legitimately affects the reasoning process. Our sense of justice (rightly) leads us to suppose that the world is governed by it.
[30] This needn't involve an infusion of supernatural principles. A love of God for his holiness is saving and truly supernatural. A love of God based on disinterested admiration of his greatness and gratitude for his temporal benefits is not.
[31] Natural goods and evils are those which can be appreciated without the help of infused supernatural principles (i.e. without a love of being in general and the sense of divine beauty which is rooted in it).
[32] There is no indication of what other 'ways' Edwards had in mind—if any.

'appear more lively and with greater strength and impression' after conversion, and that, consequently, 'their circumstances and various relations and connections between themselves and with other ideas appear more' (T 249 ff.).

How does the Spirit accomplish this? By focusing the mind's attention on 'actual ideas'. Thought has a tendency to substitute signs for ideas—that is, to use signs without having the 'actual' (lively, clear, distinct) ideas they signify. The signs may be words or (confused) ideas of 'some sensible part, . . . effect, . . . or concomitant, or a few sensible circumstances' of what we are thinking about (Misc. 782, T 116).[33] Our ability to make this substitution is advantageous because some actual ideas aren't easy to elicit, and because thought would be too slow without it; it serves us well for 'many of the common purposes of thinking'. Nevertheless, it is a *dis*advantage when 'we are at a loss concerning a connection or consequence, or have a new inference to draw, or would see the force of some new argument'; for the 'use of signs . . . causes making to run into a multitude of errors' (Misc. 782, T 1178). The tendency to make this substitution is strongest when the ideas which terms signify are ideas of 'kinds and sorts', or things 'of a spiritual nature, or things that consist in the ideas, acts, and exercises of minds' (Misc. 782, T 115). This tendency infects *all* (not merely religious) thinking, and can be remedied by attending to ideas instead of the signs that express them.[34]

Actual ideas and attention are closely connected. An idea won't become actual unless one 'dwells' upon it; 'attentive reflection' is necessary. Indeed, 'attention of the mind' itself consists 'very much' in 'exciting the actual idea and making it as lively and clear as we can' (T 118). But attention is difficult. Even in temporal affairs, taking an 'ideal view' (having actual ideas) often depends 'not merely on the force of our thoughts but the circumstances we are in, or some special accidental situation and concurrence of things in the course of our thoughts and meditations, or some particular incident in providence that excites a sense of things' (T 121 ff.). As for *eternal* matters, our attention is distracted by 'the great subjec-

---

[33] Why must the parts, effects, and so on be sensible? Presumably because sensible ideas are easier to excite and because sensible things are the kind 'we are mainly concerned with' in ordinary life (T 117).

[34] Cf. Locke's chapters on the imperfection and abuse of words *(Essay Concerning Human Understanding*, III, ix–xi). In xi. 8–9 Locke tells us to avoid terms which don't stand for clear and distinct, or determinate, ideas.

tion of the soul . . . to the external senses', and by 'the direction of the inclinations . . . [away] from . . . things as they are' (T 122). Grace remedies this defect, for one of its effects is to 'engage the attention of the mind, with more fixedness and intenseness to that kind of objects; which causes it to have a clearer view of them' (DSL 9 ff.). Grace 'makes even the speculative notions more lively' by assisting and engaging 'the attention of the mind' (RA 307). Yet why should such extraordinary measures be necessary?

Actual ideas of kinds or sorts are clear and distinct ideas 'of those things that are principally essential' in the idea, those things wherein it 'most essentially consists' (T 113, 114). Edwards is undoubtedly thinking of Locke's theory of ideas. Our ideas of God, human nature, and perplexity (Edwards's examples) are complex. The idea of God, for instance, is constructed from the ideas of 'supremacy, of supreme power, of supreme government, of supreme knowledge, of will, etc.' (T 113). Actual ideas of complex ideas like these involve actual ideas of the ('principally essential'?) simple ideas which compose them.

Actual ideas of things pertaining to good or evil present another difficulty. One can't have them without being suitably affected, pleased or displeased as the case may be. Actual ideas of these things involve the heart.

Finally, actual ideas of 'the ideas, acts, and exercises of minds' are 'repetitions of those very things'. One can't have them without experiencing what they are ideas of (Misc. 238, T 247).[35] (Actual ideas of the will or inclination, or the affections, and of things pertaining to them, will thus also involve the heart. An idea of love, for example, is a repetition of it, and love's seat is the heart.)

Our failure to attend to actual ideas has two causes. Sometimes we substitute words and images for ideas we have. Sometimes we lack relevant simple ideas. Both can adversely affect religious reasoning. Those parts of the idea of God which everyone has (ideas of his power, knowledge, and justice, for instance) aren't attended to, or, when they are, don't affect us with a proper sense of the natural good or evil associated with them. Other parts are

---

[35] Although Edwards overstates his case, there is a measure of truth in it. The idea of an idea isn't another instance of it, but does include it. The ideas of fear and love aren't fear or love, but an experience of these emotions may be needed to acquire them or to have the same ideas of fear and love that others do. Perhaps, too, ideas of this sort only become lively and vivid when we recall the relevant experiences—i.e. when how they 'feel' comes back to us.

simply missing. Without the simple idea of true beauty, people can't understand God's holiness and the facts that depend upon it, such as the infinite heinousness of sin or the infinite importance of holiness. Nor can the 'carnal' understand genuine benevolence and other properties and qualifications which the elect share with God. Because the idea of true benevolence is a repetition of it, the truly benevolent alone have an actual idea of it. Those who aren't truly benevolent discern only its circumstances, effects, and so on, 'explaining' it to themselves and others in 'general terms' which don't adequately delimit it (Misc. 123, T 245 ff.).[36]

It should by now be clear how sin affects reasoning. Our immersion in temporal concerns distracts us so that we don't attend to our ideas. Our subjection to the senses aggravates the tendency to substitute words and other sensible signs for ideas, and our disordered lives make it difficult for us to appreciate even the natural goods and evils associated with religion. (For example, our blunted conscience blinds us to the natural fittingness of obeying God's commands, and our inordinate attachment to the present life leads us to neglect more important natural goods that extend beyond it.) A lack of true benevolence (which is sin's essence) makes it impossible to understand God's holiness (which consists in it) or to appreciate its beauty.

We are now also in a position to understand why rational arguments for religious truths aren't always convincing. Miscellanies 201 (T 246 ff.) and 408 (T 249 ff.) imply that a conviction of reality is created (1) by an idea's clarity and liveliness, (2) by its internal coherence and its coherence with our other ideas, and (3) by its agreement with 'the nature and constitution of our minds themselves'. Why, then, do religious ideas so often fail to carry conviction? Partly because the clarity and intensity of spiritual ideas is a function of 'the practice of virtue and holiness' (Misc. 123, T 246) and our own practice falls woefully short, and partly because the

---

[36] 'Apprehension', or 'an ideal view or contemplation of the thing thought of' (i.e. having an actual idea of it), is closely connected with a sense of the heart, but isn't identical with it. The former is contrasted with 'mere cogitation', 'which is a kind of mental reading wherein we don't look on the things themselves but only on those signs of them that are before our eyes'. The latter is contrasted with 'mere speculation or the understanding of the head', which includes 'all that understanding that is without any proper ideal apprehension or view' and all understanding that doesn't 'consist in or imply some motion of the will'—i.e. that doesn't involve the heart (Misc. 782, T 118–19). A sense of the heart isn't needed to 'apprehend' (take 'an ideal view' of) mathematical objects.

'tempers' or 'frames' of the ungodly aren't suited to them. (Compare William James's claim that what seems true and real to us is what we have use for.) It is possible that those without spiritual frames can't even discern their coherence. Sang Hyun Lee argues that because beauty, in Edwards's view, consists in harmony or proportion, a perception of beauty is a perception of harmony.[37] If proportion and pleasing order are included in coherence, unaided reason may have difficulty grasping it; for it may miss the 'sweet harmony' among the ideas of religion and between those ideas and other ideas. (Compare those who reject religion because it doesn't seem to 'fit' or 'hang together' with science, although they concede that there isn't any formal inconsistency.)

Special, or sanctifying, grace remedies these defects by enabling us to attend more easily to the actual ideas that the words of religion stand for and by disposing the heart to be suitably affected by the natural and supernatural good and evil associated with them. Common grace has similar effects, but (because it doesn't replace the love of private systems with true benevolence) doesn't furnish the mind with actual ideas of true virtue and true beauty, affecting it only with a sense of the relevant *natural* goods and evils.

The sense of divine beauty alone is intrinsically supernatural. A reason which has been freed from the bonds of imagination, prejudice, and narrow self-interest, attends to ideas of God's being, power, knowledge, justice, munificence, and other 'natural' attributes, and is suitably affected by the natural good and evil associated with them isn't, functioning above its nature.[38] A reason which has been strengthened in these ways is capable, however, of seeing the force of rational arguments for the truths of 'natural religion'—that is, truths about God which neither logically nor epistemically depend on the ideas of holiness and true beauty. A suitably disposed natural reason is thus capable of establishing

[37] Sang Hyun Lee, *The Philosophical Theology of Jonathan Edwards* (Princeton, NJ: Princeton University Press, 1988). For a slightly different account, see my 'Jonathan Edwards and the Sense of the Heart'.

[38] Although, if I understand Edwards correctly, our bondage to the senses and self-interest can be fully eliminated only by God's infusing in us true virtue—i.e. by his infusing a new supernatural principle. Without a supernatural principle to govern them, our natural principles fall into disorder. 'Man's nature, being left to itself, forsaken of the spirit of God . . . of itself became exceeding corrupt' (*OS* 279). 'The absence of positive good principles [holiness or true virtue] . . . leaving the common natural principles of self-love, natural appetite, etc. (which were in man in innocence) . . . will certainly be followed with corruption' (*OS* 381).

God's existence and general nature. Truths which depend on the ideas of holiness and true beauty can also be established by rational arguments, but the force of these can be appreciated only by people with spiritual frames.

IV

Edwards was the philosophical heir to rationalists and empiricists whose confidence in reason was relatively unqualified. He was the theological heir to a Reformed tradition which distrusted humanity's natural capacities. Did he succeed in coherently weaving these apparently inconsistent strands together? The answer, I believe, is a qualified 'Yes'.

The key is a distinction between good rational arguments and the conditions necessary for their acceptance. I may have a good argument against smoking, for example, but my desire to smoke may prevent me from appreciating its force. What is needed isn't a better argument, but a reorientation of my desires.

Edwards's position is roughly this. While reason is capable of generating good rational arguments for God's existence, his providential government of human affairs, predestination, and many other theological and metaphysical doctrines, self-deception, prejudice, self-interest, and other passional factors make it difficult for us to see their force. These faults can't be corrected by applying Descartes's rules for correct thinking, Locke's 'measures . . . to regulate our assent and moderate our persuasion',[39] or other methods of this sort. What is needed is a set of epistemic excellences which are themselves expressions of morally desirable character traits and rightly ordered affections. The defects distorting human reasoning are deeply rooted in human nature, and can only be eliminated by the appropriate virtues.

Two features of Edwards's position are especially significant. First, the epistemic virtues aren't merely negative; they involve more than the exclusion of the passions and selfish partialities which subvert reason. Nor are the epistemic virtues confined to non-controversial excellences like the love of truth. They include properly ordered natural affections such as gratitude and a love of

---

[39] Locke, *Essay*, introd., 3.

being in general which God infuses into the hearts of his elect. These affections not only cast out others which adversely affect reasoning; they affect it themselves. Under their influence, we reason differently and more accurately.

The other significant feature is this. Two views should be distinguished. One is that there are circumstances in which it is legitimate for people's passions and affections to make up deficiencies in the evidence. Although the (objective) evidence isn't sufficient to warrant belief, one is entitled to let one's passional nature tip the balance. The other is that a person's passional nature is sometimes needed to evaluate the evidence properly (to accurately assess its force). The first view is often attributed to James. Edwards holds the second.

Edwards's position differs significantly from the more familiar positions of James, Kierkegaard, and others who appeal to passional factors. Edwards is an evidentialist. A proper, and therefore rational, religious belief must be self-evident or based on adequate evidence.[40] But, unlike most evidentialists, Edwards believes that passional factors are needed to appreciate the evidence's *force*. Only those with properly disposed hearts can read the evidence rightly.

Edwards's view thus also differs from Locke's and Swinburne's. Fully rational judgements are determined not only by one's evidence and inductive standards; they are also determined by feelings and attitudes that express theological virtues.

But perhaps this difference is illusory. For aren't the promptings of true benevolence *themselves* pieces of evidence?[41] Or (alternatively) isn't 'True benevolence should affect our assessment of the evidence' *itself* an inductive standard? I suggest that the answer is 'No'.

---

[40] One must remember, however, that the most compelling evidence is the divine beauty or splendour which the elect see in the Gospel, in Christ, in the saints, and so on. (The belief that these are truly beautiful is properly basic.)

[41] If our passional nature is a reliable guide to reality, aren't its promptings being regarded as 'reliable *evidence*, a type of credible testimony'? If so, the basis of one's belief is 'evidential' (Louis Pojman, *Religious Belief and the Will* (London: Routledge & Kegan Paul, 1986), 177, my emphasis). That Swinburne might be sympathetic to this move is suggested by his broad construal of evidence. A person's evidence includes '"hunches and intuitions" which he thinks are justified by the experiences to which he has been subjected but cannot justify in terms of propositions' (*FR* 22). Mightn't he regard true benevolence's assessment of the force of the evidence as a hunch or intuition of this sort?

The promptings of true benevolence in this context just *are* the assessments of the force of a body of evidence, e, made by a truly benevolent heart.[42] Suppose that one treats this assessment as a new piece of evidence, e_1. If one does, one must now assess *its* force (or the force of one's other evidence plus e_1). But this new assessment also reflects the state of one's heart. It too, therefore, must be treated as a new piece of evidence, e_2, whose force (or the combined force of $e + e_1 + e_2$) must in turn be assessed. Hence, if one's assessment of the force of a body of evidence is itself part of one's evidence, then either the force of some of one's evidence isn't assessed or one's evidence includes an infinite number of items.

Treating true benevolence's assessment of the force of the evidence as a piece of evidence, or regarding 'To properly assess evidence, cultivate a benevolent heart' as an inductive standard, is a mistake. It is as misguided as treating an intellectually honest, critical, and fair-minded person's assessment of a body of evidence as part of his or her evidence or including 'In assessing the evidence, be intellectually honest, critical, and fair-minded' among his or her inductive standards. Rules prescribing intellectual virtues should be distinguished from rules of evidence, and one's evidence should be distinguished from one's take on it.

It doesn't follow that true benevolence's take on the evidence is a 'non-rational ground of belief' in Swinburne's sense. A non-rational ground for belief that p is a reason for 'believing it to be true other than that it [is] likely to be true'. It might be (intrinsically) good, for instance, to hold a certain belief although the evidence seems to count against it. (For example, respect for persons might entail a duty to think well of them in spite of appearances.) Or it might be prudentially worthwhile to hold a belief. But even if you have a non-rational ground for believing p, you can't believe p unless you believe that your evidence makes p probable. To get yourself to believe p, you must therefore get yourself to believe that your evidence supports p. Yet, 'to get yourself to believe that your evidence makes p probable' when it (now) seems to you that it doesn't involves 'getting yourself to change your inductive standards by adopting standards which you now believe to be incorrect, or . . . getting yourself to forget about some of the unfavourable evidence, or . . . getting yourself to acquire new

---

[42] The assessments made by a truly benevolent heart must be distinguished from its perception of true beauty. The latter *is* a new piece of evidence.

favourable evidence through looking only where favourable evidence is to be found and then forgetting the selective character of your investigation'. It thus involves deliberately inducing beliefs which are irrational by your present standards (*FR* 88–92).[43]

True benevolence's assessment of the evidence isn't a non-rational ground for belief in this sense. It doesn't lead the saints to construct new inductive standards, to forget about some of the evidence, or to engage in selective investigation. Nor does it provide them with a *reason* for doing so. True benevolence isn't a non-rational ground for belief in Swinburne's sense, because it isn't a *ground* for belief at all, although its presence *does* partially explain why the saints hold the beliefs they do. In the same way, a good scientist's impartiality, intellectual honesty, and desire for truth help explain why she holds the beliefs she does and not the views of some less scrupulous or more credulous colleague. But they aren't *grounds* for her belief.

The position Edwards represents must be distinguished, then, from other more familiar views. Is it true or plausible? I am not sure. But I am convinced that the two strongest objections to it are inconclusive. I will discuss the more serious of the two in the following section.

V

That passional factors *should* affect reasoning strikes most philosophers as epistemically, or even morally, objectionable. Louis Pojman's recent *Religious Belief and the Will* is a forceful expression of this view.[44] Because his objections are representative, I shall focus on several of the most important. I will show that they rest on a common assumption that our passional nature isn't a reliable guide to objective truth. Since Edwards (and also, I think, Pascal, Kierkegaard, and James) denies this, these objections beg the question.

---

[43] Though they won't *seem* irrational once you have acquired them, and though (after you have acquired them) they will be rationally held in the sense that they follow from the evidence you will then have by the inductive standards you will then hold.

[44] All page references in this section are to Pojman's book unless otherwise noted. I shall use a certain freedom in interpreting his arguments, since my primary target isn't Pojman but the view he represents.

Let me begin with two preliminary comments. First, people like Edwards aren't recommending that we cultivate certain beliefs by viewing the evidence selectively. Edwards isn't advising us to *ignore* evidence, but to view *all* the evidence (assess its force) in a certain way. Second, the sort of partiality exhibited by those with holy dispositions doesn't exclude other intellectual virtues closely associated with impartiality. A truly benevolent person, too, can 'seek out evidence and pay attention to criticism and counter claims . . . support his judgment with recognizable good reasons', 'be open to the possibility that he might be wrong', 'revise and reject his belief in the light of new information' (pp. 198, 203), and yet *still* 'let his wants or self-interest [or other passional factors] enter into the judgment he makes' (p. 199) by allowing them to affect his evaluations of the evidence's overall force.

The truly benevolent *are* partial in the sense that they allow their judgements to be influenced by their new wants and interests. Whether this sort of selectivity or partiality is undesirable is another matter. Consider four arguments which purport to show that it is.

First, Pojman borrows one argument from Richard Gale.[45] 'To be an autonomous person is to have a high degree of warranted beliefs at one's disposal upon which to base one's actions. There is a tendency to lower one's freedom of choice as one lowers the repertoire of [evidentially] well-justified beliefs regarding a plan of action.' Allowing one's beliefs to be determined by passional factors is also 'a sort of lying [to oneself] or cheating [oneself] in that it enjoins believing against what has the best guarantee of being the truth'. (Swinburne shares this view.) 'Cognitive-voliting',[46] then, 'decreases one's own freedom and personhood.' 'Since . . . it is wrong to lessen one's autonomy or personhood, it is wrong to lessen the degree of [evidential] justification of one's beliefs on important matters' (pp. 188–9).

Several things are wrong with this argument. Cognitive voliting doesn't involve lying to oneself if one doesn't deceive oneself about the real force of the evidence. James, for example, takes the same

---

[45] Richard Gale, 'William James and the Ethics of Belief', *American Philosophical Quarterly*, xvii (1980), 1–14.

[46] Pojman uses this term 'to signify "directly obtaining a belief by willing to have it"' (p. viii). I will use it more broadly to signify '(knowingly) allowing one's beliefs to be influenced by passional factors'.

view of the evidence's force as his critics. He allows passional factors to determine beliefs which he, too, thinks aren't evidentially justified. It is difficult to see how this involves self-deception unless 'Seeing that the evidence for p is insufficient' entails 'not believing that p is true'—an entailment James would deny.[47]

Even if the entailment holds, it is difficult to see why someone must be deceiving herself when she consciously allows passional factors to affect her assessment of an argument's real strength. We could, of course, *identify* the evidence's real force with the force it seems to have when we abstract from the influence of subjective qualities like hope, faith, true benevolence, and other holy dispositions. But to do so begs the question.

Nor is it clear that 'Being an autonomous person involves having a high degree of warranted beliefs at one's disposal' is more plausible than 'Being an autonomous person involves having a high degree of true beliefs at one's disposal'. Consider two people A and B. A has a high degree of warranted but false beliefs. B has a high degree of true but insufficiently warranted beliefs. Is it obvious that A is more autonomous? Only if autonomy is (partly) *defined* in terms of rational belief formation. Is acting on the basis of one's passional nature heteronomous? Is the behaviour of a person who acts in this way constrained by something external to the self? It *is* if (as Kant thought) reason is one's real self. But Edwards, James, and Kierkegaard believe that it isn't. In *their* view, our heart or passional nature is the deepest thing about us. Nor is it obvious that B's freedom of choice is less. (B is, after all, in a better position to satisfy his desires.) The underlying assumption, of course, is that beliefs which are determined by 'impartial' assessments of relevant evidence are more likely to be true. That this holds of *all* subject-matters, however, is precisely what is at issue. James and Edwards, for example, think it doesn't when the propositions at stake are

---

[47] James talks this way in *The Will to Believe and other Essays in Popular Philosophy* (New York: Dover Publications Inc., 1956), 1–31, and elsewhere, but on other occasions expresses a view more like Edwards's. Our passional nature affects our assessment of the *force* of the evidence. The explanation for this apparent inconsistency, I believe, is James's identification of the 'objective' force of the evidence with the force attributed to it by disinterested (or even hostile?) enquirers rather than with what he regards as its *real* force. If I am right, then (contrary to standard interpretations of James) 'volitional believing' does express what seems to one to be the evidence's real force. See my 'James, Rationality, and Religious Belief', *Religious Studies*, xxvii (1991), 223–38.

'generic' hypotheses about the metaphysical shape of reality (James) or statements about God and our relation to him (Edwards).

Second, another argument derives from William Clifford. 'General truthfulness is a desideratum without which society cannot function' (p. 189). Unwarranted beliefs which don't directly injure ourselves or others may do so indirectly. 'Beliefs do not exist in isolation from each another, so that to overthrow one belief may have reverberations throughout our entire noetic structure, affecting many of our beliefs. . . . Cognitive-voliting, as Bernard Williams has pointed out', may be the sort of project that ' "tends in the end to involve total destruction of the world of reality, to lead to paranoia" '. It injures society as well, because it impairs the habit of truth seeking, which, 'if it is to be effective at all . . . must be deeply engrained within us' (p. 190).[48]

There are also problems with this argument. In the first place, it isn't obvious that people's beliefs are that tightly connected. It is significant, I think, that Pascal, Kierkegaard, and James were probably *less* credulous with respect to most matters than others. (All three had deeply sceptical temperaments.) Nor was Edwards more credulous than his educated contemporaries. It is also difficult to see how a Jamesian will to believe (as usually interpreted) could impair one's evidence-evaluating faculties when one of its *presuppositions* is a clear view of what James *and* his critics agree is the evidence's real strength (that it doesn't clearly point to a belief or to its denial).[49] As for Edwards, we may concede that wilfully believing that the evidence has a force it lacks can impair our evidence-evaluating faculties. Identifying the evidence's real strength with the force it has in the eyes of the 'impartial', however, begs the question.

Pojman's second argument, of course, rests on the same assumption as his first—that beliefs determined by passional factors are less likely to be true. Why should we believe this?

Third, 'The very concept of having a belief entails the belief that if the belief is true, there must be some connection between it and

---

[48] The internal quote is from Bernard Williams, 'Deciding to Believe', in *Problems of the Self* (Cambridge: Cambridge University Press, 1972), 151.

[49] James's official position is that 'cognitive voliting' is in order only when an issue is 'intellectually undecidable'—i.e. when the 'so-called objective evidence' is (by commonly agreed standards) inconclusive.

states of affairs in the world' (p. 172). In other words, 'belief that *p* seems to imply the thought of a causal chain stretching back from the belief to a primary relationship with the world and so faithfully representing the world' (p. 175). Allowing one's beliefs to be determined by passional factors severs this connection. 'It is a confusion to believe that any given belief is true simply on the basis of being willed. As soon as the believer discovers the basis of his belief—as being caused by the will alone—he must drop the belief' (p. 172). Beliefs arising from passional factors are like beliefs based on imagination. When we discover their origins, we discard them as worthless.

Several things need sorting out. It is certainly true that except for a few cases in which the future depends on our current attitudes, 'wishing doesn't make it so' (p. 171). Neither does wanting, needing, willing, nor feeling. Beliefs are made true by the states of affairs they represent and not by the wishes, wants, feelings, and volitions of the people who have them.[50] But neither Edwards nor James, for example, would deny this. Nor would they deny the existence of some sort of causal link between true beliefs and the world they faithfully represent. What, then, is their position? Although a need for meaning, a desire for significant action, or holy dispositions do not *make* the beliefs they (partly) determine true, they are *correlated* with states of affairs that do. For these needs, desires, and feelings are causally connected (in the right way) with the way the world is. James, for example, thinks that our 'willing nature' has evolved as it has because following its dictates has enabled us to more successfully adjust to reality. Behaviour based on our passional nature wouldn't be so successful if it egregiously misrepresented things as they are.[51] Similarly, Edwards's *The Nature of True Virtue* attempts to show that the 'mechanism' underlying the new sense of heart—namely, true benevolence—'agrees' with reality. Reality's core is an infinite benevolence—the world's only true substance and its only true cause. The benevolence of the saints is grounded in this, and mirrors it. Edwards concludes that benevolence isn't 'arbitrary' but agrees 'with the necessary nature of things' (*TV* 620).[52] Assuming that cognitive voliting invariably

---

[50] To place this in perspective, however, we should remember that cognitions and perceptions don't make beliefs true either.

[51] See my 'William James, Rationality and Religious Belief'.

[52] The force of these arguments becomes clearer when one notes that Edwards is

severs the connection between beliefs and the states of affairs they represent begs the question against views like these.

Fourth, the best argument against cognitive voliting is inductive. Extensive experience has shown that need, desire, and other passional factors can adversely affect judgement. It has also shown that methodical efforts to reduce their influence can serve the cause of truth. Science is the most impressive example.

This argument, however, is also inconclusive: Edwards would agree with James. 'Almost always' in science, 'and even in human affairs in general', we should 'save ourselves from any chance of believing falsehood, by not making up our minds at all till objective evidence has come.'[53] They would agree, in other words, that passional considerations are out of order in most cases *like those in the sample.*[54] Both would deny that we can legitimately extrapolate from these cases to others with different subject-matters (the metaphysical and moral structure of reality, for example, or things of the spirit). As we have just seen, they have arguments purporting to show that, with respect to these subject-matters, some passional factors *are* reliable guides to truth. To simply assume that the generalization concerning the adverse effects of passional factors can be extended to areas like these begs the question. It may not, for example, apply to ethics. Aristotle argued that moral reasoning goes astray when it isn't informed by a correct understanding of the good life. The latter, however, depends on properly cultivated dispositions as well as sound reasoning. If one's emotional temper is defective or has been perverted by corrupt education, one can't appreciate the good. As a result, one misconstrues the nature of the good life, and one's practical deliberations miscarry. Now according to classical theism, God *is* the good. One would therefore expect a properly cultivated heart to be a necessary condition for grasping truths about him.[55]

---

an occasionalist, a subjective idealist like Berkeley, and a mental phenomenalist. For a more detailed discussion, see my 'Jonathan Edwards and the Sense of the Heart'.

[53] James, *Will to Believe*, 20.

[54] The qualification ('most') is designed to accommodate cases in which there may be special reasons for overriding our prima-facie duty to exclude 'subjective' factors in science and everyday life—cases, e.g., in which we have moral obligations to trust others.

[55] If God isn't the good but is 'only' a perfect instance of it (or its supreme exemplar), this argument is less compelling. The fact remains that dispassion and disinterest are sometimes epistemically harmful.

If theism is true, and if it is also true that subjective qualifications would be needed to know God if God existed,[56] then there is reason to think that cognitive voliting is sometimes reliable. In refusing to allow our passional nature to affect our judgement on religious matters, we may, therefore, be prejudging the case against people like Edwards. Indeed, we may be unwittingly assuming that theism is *highly* improbable or that it is unlikely that subjective qualifications would be needed to know God if theism were true. For suppose that John is reluctant to trust his passional nature but that the evidence suggests to him that theism has a significant chance of being correct—0.3, for example, or even 0.5. Suppose he also has good, although not conclusive, reasons for thinking that if theism is true, refusing to trust his passional nature is likely to permanently debar him from acquiring a vitally important truth. Suppose finally (as seems plausible[57]) that it is more important for us to believe theism if theism is true than to believe it false if it is false. Is it unreasonable for John to trust his passional nature in these circumstances? It is difficult to believe that it is.[58]

The arguments examined in this section seem, then, to beg the question by implicitly assuming that theism is false or that subjective qualifications aren't needed to know God. Still, theists like Edwards and James may be no better off. For attempts to show that our passional nature is sometimes reliable may also beg the question; arguments like theirs aren't likely to persuade those who suppress the promptings of their hearts or refuse to be guided by them. A fully adequate defence of positions like Edwards's must therefore show that they aren't vitiated by circularity. I have attempted to do this in another place.[59]

---

[56] On the latter, see C. Stephen Evans, 'Kierkegaard and Plantinga on Belief in God: Subjectivity as the Ground of Properly Basic Religious Beliefs', *Faith and Philosophy*, v (1988), 25–35. Cf. Edwards, who argues that if a divine glory distinguishes the Gospel from merely human books, sin 'would blind men from discerning' it (*RA* 301). 'It is not rational to suppose, if there be any such excellency in divine things, that wicked men should see it', since the power of their 'filthy lusts' prevents them from 'relishing' it (DSL 16).

[57] And as Swinburne admits (*FR* 81).

[58] There may be even less reason to think that I shouldn't engage in cognitive voliting to *strengthen* my belief in God when the evidence seems to me to make it (even slightly) more probable than not.

[59] See my 'World-Views, Criteria, and Epistemic Circularity'. Its apparent circularity is, of course, the other major difficulty alluded to at the end of sec. IV.

VI

Why should Edwards's account of the proper use of our epistemic faculties still interest us? For two reasons. First, his account is the most carefully articulated version known to me of an epistemic theory deeply embedded in important strands of the Christian tradition. Calvin, for example, thought that rational arguments for the authority of Scripture 'will not obtain full credit in the hearts of men until they are sealed by the inward testimony of the Spirit'.[60] And while Aquinas believed that there is good evidence for the divine origin of Christian teaching, he didn't think that it was sufficient to compel assent without the inward movement of a will grounded in a 'supernatural principle'.[61] Similarly, seventeenth-century Anglican divines argued that 'the gospel can only obtain "a free admission into the assent of the understanding, when it brings a passport from a rightly disposed will" '.[62] The notion that a proper disposition is needed to appreciate the force of rational arguments for the authority of the Gospel can be easily extended to rational arguments for the truths of 'natural religion' when these, too, come under attack. John Spurr has argued that this process was well under way by the end of the seventeenth century.[63]

The other reason for taking Edwards seriously is this. I suggest that theists who think that there are rational arguments for the truths of religion and who, in the light of their beliefs, think through the implications of their disagreements with intelligent, well-informed, honest, and philosophically astute critics will be forced to draw similar conclusions. They believe that these critics' assessment of the overall force of the evidence is in error. This error can't plausibly be attributed to such things as lack of intelligence, unfamiliarity with relevant evidence, obvious prejudice, or an unwillingness to consider counter-claims. Edwards would ascribe it to a failure of the heart. Modern theists may be reluctant to agree. (Partly because of their respect for these critics.) Yet if theism *is*

---

[60] John Calvin, *Institutes of the Christian Religion* (Grand Rapids, Mich.: Eerdmans, 1957), 1.1, 7.4.

[61] St Thomas Aquinas, *The Summa Theologica* (New York: Benziger Bros., 1947), vol. 2, part II-II, q. 6, a. 1.

[62] John Spurr, ' "Rational Religion" in Restoration England', *Journal of the History of Ideas*, xlix (1988), 580. The internal quote is from Robert South.

[63] Ibid.

true, and there *is* good evidence for it, what other explanation could there be of the failure of so many to appreciate its force?[64]

---

[64] I think one reason why so many theists are reluctant to accept this implication is that it smacks of intellectual phariseeism. This is a real danger. Its proper corrective, I believe, is to focus on the ways in which one's *own* sinful proclivities infect and distort one's thinking about God. (On this point see Merold Westphal's excellent 'Taking St Paul Seriously: Sin as an Epistemological Category', in Thomas P. Flint (ed.), *Christian Philosophy*, (Notre Dame, Ind.: University of Notre Dame Press, 1988), 200–26.)

PART II
Revelation

6

Did Revelation Cease?

DAVID BROWN

In the second work of his tetralogy devoted to philosophical issues raised by Christian doctrine, Richard Swinburne has written persuasively on the theme of revelation.[1] The middle section of this book considers what evidence we might use to justify belief in such a revelation, while its two outer sections concentrate on rules governing its interpretation. Thus part I is devoted to general issues of meaning, and in particular draws our attention to the way in which truth conditions are affected not only by how the language is employed (literal, metaphorical, analogical, and so on), but also by its wider context, the genre to which it belongs, the presuppositions of the audience or society, and so forth. This implies, he argues, that poetic licence should not be seen as undermining truth (different standards apply), nor should false cultural assumptions. The latter sounds more controversial, but in support Swinburne invites us to consider the case of a man drinking sherry, of whom we declare 'That man drinking a Martini seems very cheerful'. Russell would have declared the sentence false, Strawson neither true nor false, whereas Swinburne argues plausibly (following Donnellan) that the sentence should be taken as true, provided the context makes it clear to whom we wished to refer.[2] The relevance of this to the Bible, which seeks to convey truth through long-discarded scientific presuppositions, should be obvious.

This is but one example of a number of helpful points which he makes in part I. It is part III, however, which has generated my provocative title. Certainly it is by far the most surprising section of the book. For Swinburne displays at one and the same time both a healthy engagement with modern biblical criticism and a highly unfashionable desire to reinstate traditional allegorical readings.

---

[1] Richard Swinburne, *Revelation: From Metaphor to Analogy* (Oxford: Clarendon Press, 1992).
[2] Ibid. 28–32.

The latter is generated by his assumption that the meaning of the Bible is given by its being, so far as possible, rendered consistent with itself in matters of doctrine and morals: 'Putting the books together into the whole Bible involved giving them a change of context and, in consequence, . . . a change of meaning.'[3] The result is that the moral savagery with which Psalm 137 concludes would seem to brook no other interpretation than the 'metaphorical': it is 'forced on the text' and 'must be adopted'.[4] Again, to give a doctrinal example, all passages which like John 14: 28 seem to imply the subordination of the Son to the Father '*have* to be interpreted with other than their normal meanings (i.e. their meanings in isolation)'.[5] Such emphatic language could easily mislead the reader into supposing that Swinburne was concerned to identify a single, true meaning for each verse. But the acknowledgement of a more literal meaning is made: 'God inspired the human authors to see things which had quite a bit of truth in them; but what they wrote down, taken on its own, had quite a bit of falsity too. However, what they wrote down was ambiguous in the sense that a fuller context could give it a different meaning from what it would have on its own.'[6] None the less, this fuller meaning should in no sense be seen as the creation of the Church: 'revelation came to an end with the death of the last apostle.'[7] The Church merely 'discovers' meaning that is already there, as 'understanding of revelation grows in the community through reflection'.[8] God imbued the text with his intended meanings; 'but, if the intended audience of Scripture is the Church, not only of the first century . . . but of later centuries and millenniums, then . . . truth evident to the latter . . . must also be allowed to force a reinterpretation on the text.'[9]

Though dissenting from some of his specific examples, with Swinburne's general desire to reinstate more traditional patterns of exegesis I have much sympathy. However, his claim that thereby one is simply discovering already implicit intended meanings seems to me to generate more problems than it solves. What I shall argue is that he has confused the closure of the canon with the closure of revelation. Theologians of the past have of course sought to differentiate sharply between revelation and tradition, but I shall argue

---

[3] Ibid. 175; cf. also 180.
[4] Ibid. 184.   [5] Ibid. 138, my emphasis.
[6] Ibid. 197; cf. also 190 and n. 43.   [7] Ibid. 102; cf. 140.
[8] Ibid. 223; for 'discovers', 221.   [9] Ibid. 194.

in what follows that a combination of factual and conceptual considerations forces a weakening of this contrast. The underlying
factual element (which of course some may wish to dispute) is the
understanding of the biblical text now common among biblical
scholars; the conceptual element, the resultant changes required in
our notions of revelation and divine intention. Whereas the second
of my two arguments (the 'providential') focuses on the divine
perspective, on what might constitute a plausible account of divine
intention in the light of such facts, the first (the 'analogical') examines the actual use of the revelatory text in its process of transmission and the notion of revelation thereby implied.

The Analogical Argument

In some ways my argument here will strengthen Swinburne's hand.
For I shall maintain that the same principles of exegesis are to
be found within Scripture itself as came to predominate in later
ecclesiastical understandings, and so one cannot be condemned
without condemning the other. Where I would differ from him,
however, is in the conclusions to be drawn from such parallel,
'analogical' patterns of behaviour. The implausibility of describing
such rereadings within the canon as 'discovery' argues against a
parallel use of the image for post-biblical interpretations. In both
cases the imposition of fresh understandings on the text needs
stronger classification than the mere discovery of already latent
meanings. There is a disclosure, a 'revelation' which is inexplicable
in terms of the text alone.

To establish the initial analogy, all one need do is take the heart
of each of the two Testaments, the Pentateuch in the Old and the
Gospels in the New, and observe the way in which their principles
of reinterpretation can now be seen to observe essentially the same
symbolical rules as are to be found in the subsequent life of the
Church. In saying this, one draws attention to a splendid irony. The
objective behind much biblical criticism until fairly recently has
been essentially historical: either to probe beneath the text in order
to ascertain what really happened (for example, the 'quest for the
historical Jesus') or to disclose the original meaning as intended by
the human authors at each stage of the text's transmission (as in
source, form, and redaction criticism). What has seldom been ob-

served is the way in which this systematic search for the historical
has thoroughly undermined itself. The dominant value assigned to
the historical by the biblical scholar finds no comparable reflection
in the authors of the text. For what we repeatedly discover is the
subordination of historical accuracy to something deemed much
more important, some interpretation of how the story of Moses or
Jesus was supposed to apply in new circumstances, in the life of the
author's contemporaries. To us, of course, such liberties with the
historical facts seem deceptive; but not only does Jewish literature
generally indicate this to be common practice, even the ancient
world's nearest equivalent to professional historians were not immune.[10] So it is hardly surprising that such a motivation would be
still more prominent among those who saw their primary task as
evangelisation, explaining how events of the past could be good
news for today. Against such a backdrop, Swinburne's remarks on
the relation between presupposition and truth condition could
scarcely be more apposite.

Consider, first, the Pentateuch. Though the theory continues to
have its detractors, the majority of scholars still subscribe to the
hypothesis according to which four sources underlie our present
text—J, E, D, and P—with dates of composition ranging from
approximately 1000 BC to 500 BC. That there is a historical core to
the patriarchal and Mosaic traditions I would not in any way wish
to challenge. However, more pertinent to the argument here is the
extent to which all four, though agreeing in giving definitive status
to Moses and in expressing God's concern for Israel in terms of a
covenant relationship, none the less differ radically in their presentation of these ancient times, which they feel is necessary if that
relationship is to continue to be a reality for their own times. Thus
J, writing at the time of the nation's greatest prosperity under
Solomon, finds his (or her, if Harold Bloom is right in *The Book of
J*) most natural response in celebration and gratitude for this inti-
macy; whereas E, writing a hundred or more years later, with Israel

---

[10] For an excellent introductory treatment of the use in Jewish literature of
ancient figures to convey contemporary truths, see D. F. Russell, *The Old Testament
Pseudopigrapha* (London: SCM Press, 1987); for its wider application to all Jewish
literature, see J. Neussner, *Torah through the Ages* (London: SCM Press, 1990).
Historians like Livy and Tacitus may have indulged to a lesser degree, but there can
be no dispute that the presentation of their material has been considerably affected
in the one case by a desire to enhance Augustus's principate and in the other by the
wish to underscore the corrupting effects of absolute power.

now divided into two small separate kingdoms of Israel (in the north) and Judah (in the south), realizes that the main challenge to be faced is the danger of assimilation to the pagan practices of their large pagan neighbours. Accordingly, to counteract that threat, all the anthropomorphisms that had been popular in the time of J are eliminated. So, for example, J's charming image of God walking in the Garden of Eden in the cool of the day[11] could never have been tolerated by E because of its openness to an over-literalistic misunderstanding. Again, D is writing at a time of hope for a religious revival in the southern kingdom, so he attempts to reinforce this by envisaging Moses as insisting that the covenant needs to be renewed afresh in each generation, and he duly provides a ritual for doing this.[12] Finally, P performs his task at a time when both nations have fallen subject to foreign domination, and his antidote is to suggest that the only way of ensuring the continuance of national identity is by careful observance, and indeed intensification, of all the traditions of the past, ritual as much as ethical—hence the strange mixture of both in the book of Leviticus.

The result also includes four different versions of the Ten Commandments, which, though in essence the same, give four different reasons for observing a day of rest. The version with which we are all familiar, in Exodus 20, comes from P, and so, not surprisingly, given what I have already said about his stress on rules, he puts it very much in terms of a sabbath rule ordained by God's having rested on the seventh day of creation; whereas, by contrast, J in Exodus 34 gives no reason, while E in Exodus 21 and D in Deuteronomy 5 refer us to the need to be compassionate to those less fortunate than ourselves, and so the stress is less on what we ourselves do and more on how we treat those for whom we are responsible.

If one looks only to historical fact, it is inconceivable that all four are always right: they are too often saying different things. Rather, as I have already tried to indicate, what they are doing is seeking to apply the same general principles in what are often a very different set of historical circumstances. It is, for instance, extremely unlikely that Moses ever gave detailed instructions for an agricultural community. None the less, D attributes this to him, not in order to deceive, but because he honestly believes that the legislation he

---

[11] Gen. 3: 8.   [12] In Deut. 6: 20–5.

advocates is that which will best further the Mosaic covenant in a world in which the Hebrews are no longer insecure, runaway slaves but settled farmers. Again, the prominence given to the sabbath in P is unlikely to go back to Moses; but, once more, this does not mean that he is doing something dishonest: rather, he is seeking to preserve the identity of the Jews when they are in danger of being swamped by alien cultures,[13] and indeed, in that role it has worked admirably throughout the centuries.

If the Pentateuch provides an obvious instance of Swinburne's claim that truth claims are intelligible only against the backdrop of existing cultural assumptions, so too do the Gospels themselves. Here I shall confine myself to two examples, one trivial, the other more substantial.

Consider, first, Jesus's remark about the necessity of our lamp not being hid under a bushel, so that it can give light to all in the house. The phraseology in Matthew's version ('put it on a stand and it will give light to all in the house')[14] assumes the typical one-roomed Palestinian house, and so must be original; whereas Luke alters what were almost certainly Jesus's actual words to reflect the larger Hellenistic house of the day, with its separate entrance passage from which light would shine on those entering it ('put it on a stand so that those who enter may see it'). Though trivial, the example well illustrates the freedom of the evangelists. Luke was clearly determined that the illustration should immediately come alive, as it were, for his non-Jewish readers, and so does not hesitate to alter the words actually spoken.

Nor are more substantial examples wanting. Suffice it to consider one example in detail: Luke's response to a decline in expectation of the imminence of the world's end. Mark, in common with the early Paul,[15] seems to have thought that the world would soon end, and that this was somehow bound up with the impending destruction of Jerusalem; this is the belief which we find reflected in chapter 13 of his Gospel. But by the time Luke came to write, Jerusalem had in fact been destroyed in the great revolt of AD 70. So he rewrites Jesus's words to make clear that they referred to this

[13] As R. De Vaux observes in *Ancient Israel*, 2nd edn. (London: Darton, Longman and Todd, 1965) 482: 'after the destruction of the Temple, and during the Exile, the other feasts were no longer observed; hence the sabbath acquired a new importance, for it then became the distinctive sign of the Covenant.'
[14] Matt. 5: 15; Luke 11: 33.   [15] Cf. 1 Cor. 7: 29: 'The time is short.'

recent destruction,[16] thereby, of course, divorcing the event from any connection with the end of the world. Indeed, he even rewrites Jesus's words before the High Priest to avoid any exclusive concentration on Jesus's future coming as distinct from his present reign in heaven. Whereas Mark had written, 'You will see the Son of Man sitting at the right hand of Power, and coming with the clouds of heaven,' Luke offers: 'From now on the Son of Man shall be seated at the right hand of the power of God.'[17]

None of this should be taken to imply that Mark or Luke are distorting the truth to suit their own convenience. Rather, it discloses their interest in something much more important than mere historical fact: how to convey the relevance of the Gospel to the immediate situation of their readers. Jesus no doubt had said something about the terrible fate which was in store for Jerusalem. Having had two former terrorists among his disciples, he could not but have been aware of the passions which existed among so many of his fellow nationals and their inevitably destructive consequences. Mark, by linking such comments to predictions of the end of the world, sought to use them to reinforce a major thrust of his Gospel, the demand for decision and conversion; whereas Luke not only writes after the event, but realizes that the Church, if it is to spread successfully throughout the Empire, cannot be too closely identified with a longing for the world's end, with expectations of a world catastrophe, as though it were a force implacably opposed to the might of Rome. So not only does he change some of the emphases of Mark, but the continuation of his Gospel in Acts symbolically ends in the heart of the Empire itself, in Rome.

It would not be difficult to continue with such examples, *ad infinitum*, and indeed to offer still more radical instances of the evangelists' methods. Many biblical scholars, for example, believe that the author of the Fourth Gospel not only restructures the events of Jesus's life to bring out the full significance of who he was, but also that the long discourses, so unlike the material in the Synoptic Gospels, are themselves meditative expansions of words of Jesus invented by the evangelist with a similar end in view.[18]

---

[16] Contrast Luke 21: 20–4 (esp. v. 24) with Mark 13: 14–20.

[17] Mark 14: 62; Luke 22: 69.

[18] See, e.g., C. K. Barrett, *The Gospel according to St John*, 2nd edn. (London: SPCK, 1978), 15–21, 42–6; J. Ashton, *Understanding the Fourth Gospel* (Oxford:

Clearly this is not the place to arbitrate regarding the degree to which such practices are to be found within the biblical canon. That it happened to some degree would be an all but universal view, with the examples given above fairly representative of a general scholarly consensus. One should not of course draw the wrong implication from all this. A God who acts in history remains central to the understanding of both Testaments. It is precisely because God acting in Moses and in Jesus was seen as so decisive that the authors wrestled with what their actions and words might mean for their own day. It is thus an indifference not to history as such, but to historical detail, which is disclosed, and here considerable liberties are certainly taken, with the detail constantly made subordinate to the significance, to what might be called the symbolic as distinct from the literal. So, whether we consider the original revelatory event or the original revelatory text, it is just not the case that their meaning was seen as fixed in stone. Rather, both were treated as a medium towards further disclosures, not themselves simply a function of the meaning of the original.

That said, we may observe that it was exactly the same exercise in which post-biblical exegesis was engaged. The classical four senses of Scripture (literal, allegorical, moral, anagogical) which developed from Origen's original three (literal, moral, spiritual) had the same objective in view: to render possible an understanding of the original events and words that would continue to have meaning for the commentators' own day. Swinburne notes the presence of moral motives, as in Psalm 137, but other factors of course played their part: some positive, some negative. The christological reading of the book of Joshua, for instance, was in part no doubt motivated by the purely fortuitous coincidence of him having the same name as Jesus (the initial impetus perhaps having been given by Hebrews 4: 8), but in part also by a genuine desire to assign some permanent meaning to this record of battles fought in the long-distant past. Again, the christological reading of the Psalms was in part motivated by the conviction that

Clarendon Press, 1991), esp. 162–6, 425–30. Barrett proposes a meditative adaptation and expansion of the synoptic tradition, with John probably aware of both Mark and Luke, whereas Ashton goes further, both admitting and defending the invention of specific incidents. On the other side, for a defence of a more traditional view of the Gospel's historicity (from an atheist), see R. Lane Fox, *The Unauthorised Version* (Harmondsworth: Penguin, 1991), who describes it as of all the Gospels 'historically the most valuable' (p. 205).

anticipations of Christ must lurk everywhere beneath the text (the evangelists' use of Psalm 22 here providing the precedent); and although this often produced absurd results, as in Augustine's deduction from Psalm 109 that Judas Iscariot was married with a family,[19] yet also present was the laudable desire to intensify the believer's identification with Christ through an *imitatio Christi* of the emotions as well as of one's actions. Once more, examples could be multiplied, but sufficient has perhaps been said to indicate the plausibility of postulating a parallel subordination of the literal to the symbolic both within the canon and beyond, though of course with the significant difference that post-biblical writers gave themselves less latitude, in that they no longer felt themselves free to alter prior versions of the text.

The way in which biblical scholarship has transformed our understanding of how Scripture came to be written, however, seems to me not only to demonstrate the essential continuity between pre- and post-canonical treatment of the events of revelation (and hence the legitimacy of the latter, at least in theory), but also to call into question whether the discovery model is the best approach to elucidating what happens in either case. For most of the history of Christianity we have, of course, operated with a very simple model: that God spoke to the authors of the books as we have them, and thereby communicated through them more than they understood, with very little personal contribution from them or their specific historial circumstances. Leo XIII in his encyclical of 1893 *Proventissimus Deus*, in speaking of 'all the books and the whole of each book . . . written at the dictation of the Holy Spirit',[20] was thus merely encapsulating the common assumption of both Protestant and Catholic. But as biblical scholarship produced progressively more complex accounts of the human element, so systematic theologians struggled to produce a more adequate model for the nature of the divine involvement. These have ranged from various modifications to the notion of divine speech to very different understandings, such as mediation through events or normative images; and each has generated its corresponding critique.[21]

[19] Deduced from Ps. 109: 9: 'May his children be fatherless, and his wife a widow', in *Enarrationes in Psalmos*, CCSL 40, 1583, 1590.
[20] H. Denzinger and A. Schönmetzer, *Enchiridion Symbolorum* (Freiburg: Herder, 1965), para. 3292, my translation.
[21] For a modified divine speech model, see W. Abraham, *The Divine Inspiration of Holy Scripture* (Oxford: Clarendon Press, 1981). For revelation as event, see

My aim here, however, is of necessity much more limited: simply to draw attention to the inadequacy of any model whatsoever which continues to be contained within the category of discovery alone.

Thus, it surely places impossible strains upon the imagination to suppose that later strands in the biblical tradition do no more than 'discover' what is already latent in the earlier revelatory texts which they employ or to which they relate. So, for instance, E can hardly just have discovered in J reasons for rejecting the former's anthropomorphism, any more than can D his concern for the details of agricultural life or P his attention to the codification of every aspect of life. The same surely applies to Luke's rejection of Mark's imminentist eschatology and John's fully developed christology, whether or not he was aware of the existence of any of the other Gospels.

In each case, in addition to the existence of the earlier more primitive text or kerygma, we must surely postulate at least three other factors which make the development possible: a new set of circumstances generating new questions, the perception of principles in the original revelation which at least permit this further development, and creative insight that enables the original events or words to be read in a new way. It is, of course, this last factor which would constitute for the believer the work of the divine revealer. If to the application of such an understanding beyond the biblical canon, it is objected that such new insights appear to come without any dramatic confirmation through audition, vision, or miracle, the obvious response is that this is equally true of many developments within the canon itself, and in any case there is no reason why divine causation should be taken as any less decisive simply because of being less dramatic.

But for some, the principal objection to any such account may well not yet have been faced. My argument, it will be said, is beside the point, since revelation resides in the canon as a whole, not in individual books, far less the sources that contributed to their formation. Though a traditional view and one which has received much support recently in the canonical criticism of Brevard

W. Pannenberg (ed.), *Revelation as History* (London: Sheed and Ward, 1969). For revelation as normative images, see A. Farrer, *The Glass of Vision* (London: Dacre Press, 1948). For a good general discussion of the issues, see A. Dulles, *Models of Revelation* (Dublin: Gill and MacMillan, 1983).

Childs,[22] its difficulty is that modern theology frequently uses the Bible in ways which challenge this criterion: for instance, in giving priority to the original teaching of Jesus on marriage over the Matthean exception clause, or in insisting upon the importance of eschatology because of its centrality to Jesus's teaching, even though demoted in later strands of the New Testament. Once more, examples could be multiplied. Yet, even if all were to be rejected as instances of bad exegesis, the discovery model still will not work, as becomes obvious when we consider the New Testament's use of the Old Testament.

Consider Matthew's repeated refrain upon the theme of the fulfilment of prophecies. Biblical scholarship has made us fully alive to the oddness of them when read as predictions in their original context. Swinburne is aware of this, but gives the following response: 'Now which verses of the Old Testament are to be interpreted as prophecies of a Messiah is not a matter of how the original author of the strand of the Old Testament book intended them to be taken. It is a matter of what their meaning is as part of the Scriptures of the old Israel, and that is a matter of how Israel in the centuries immediately before and after Christ understood them.'[23] But the difficulties in fact run deeper than this. For instance, at the beginning of chapter 21 Matthew assumes that Jesus needs both an ass and a colt to fulfil the prophecy of Zechariah 9: 9, thus contradicting Mark 11: 2; whereas in fact the original is a case of parallelism, a common feature of Hebrew poetry whereby the same thing is said twice, but in a slightly different way each time. Again, on one occasion he even inserts a negative that gives the opposite sense to the original![24] In fact, as study of the Targums and the Dead Sea scrolls is increasingly making clear, there was considerable variety within contemporary scriptural interpretation, and, while some examples have antecedents elsewhere, some must also be entirely the creation of the early Church, if not Matthew himself. A clear case in point is the prediction of Judas's thirty pieces of silver at 27: 9, even if Matthew muddles up who said what and attributes to Jeremiah what again comes from Zechariah.[25]

---

[22] B. S. Childs, *Introduction to the Old Testament as Scripture* (London: SCM Press, 1979). Further developments in his position are to be seen in *Old Testament Theology in a Canonical Context* (London: SCM Press, 1985) and still more so in *Biblical Theology of the Old and New Testaments* (London: SCM Press, 1992).

[23] Swinburne, *Revelation*, 113–14.   [24] Cf. Mic. 5: 2 and Matt. 2: 6.

[25] Zech. 11: 12.

So, once again, the notion of discovery makes little sense. Matthew's 'prophecies' are a creative imposition upon the text, whose value lies not at all in their predictive value but in their encouragement of a Christian rereading of the Old Testament as leading in its entirety under God to the decisive revelation which was Jesus Christ.

Once it is conceded that within the canon revelatory texts (whether in part or taking the Old Testament as a whole) are treated in a way which exceeds what might legitimately be described as discovery, it becomes hard to defend treatment of the canon as a whole in this way. Of course, the definitive events of salvation are described therein, so any fresh insights into them would inevitably be secondary and, moreover, would need the authorization of the community of faith as a whole to be seen as revelatory; but this does not mean that it cannot, or has not, happened. In a moment I shall consider two possible cases, one from the patristic world and one contemporary; but first let me emphasize that none of what follows should be taken as denying the existence of more obviously continuous developments. For instance, because some of the Fathers believed that miracles had ceased to happen in their own day,[26] eventually all of Jesus's miracles came to be given a symbolic interpretation. But that had a natural precedent in John's description of them as 'signs', the abundance of wine at Cana clearly being meant to refer to the fullness of new life which Christ could bring. Indeed, some commentators now suggest that even the Synoptics may also have had such dual motives in recording them.[27]

But in other cases discontinuity is much more evident. Consider first the story of Abraham's sacrifice of Isaac in Genesis 22. As early as Origen (who raised the possibility that the angel in question was not from God but an evil demon),[28] Christians were experiencing moral difficulties with the story. Kant was later to argue that even if we thought that God were issuing such a command, we ought to disobey it, because it is impossible that so callous an injunction

---

[26] e.g., the early Augustine and John Chrysostom. An excellent discussion of the patristic attitude to miracles is offered by R. A. Greer in *The Fear of Freedom* (University Park, Pa.: Pennsylvania State University Press, 1989).

[27] e.g., Morna Hooker, *The Gospel according to St Mark* (London: A. and C. Black, 1991), 71–5, where she remarks that 'there is thus a sense in which Mark's miracles function as "signs", very much like the Johannine signs' (p. 73).

[28] Origen, *De Principiis*, 3. 2.

could ever issue from a good God.[29] By contrast, Kierkegaard gloried in the story's apparent irrationality: Abraham is the great knight of faith prepared to go unquestionably wherever God calls.[30] Should one wish to defend the appropriateness of the story, that would seem the obvious direction in which to go, especially as the test element is reinforced by various key features in the narrative. Even so, the moral difficulties surely remain. The only potentially alleviating factor lies in acknowledging that children in the period from which the narrative originally dates were regarded as property, as an extension of oneself, and so the offer of one's son in sacrifice would not have had the same moral significance as it has for us. Yet, in another sense that merely intensifies the problem since, presumably, we would now want to add that Abraham was wrong to treat his child in this way. One can only sympathize therefore with the biblical commentator James Crenshaw when he remarks that 'no acquisition of fresh insight seems sufficiently precious to justify the private hell initiated by these words: Take your son, and offer him as a burnt offering'.[31]

This is no doubt why in the history of the passage's exegesis, in both Jewish and Christian tradition, alternative accounts have been sought. The Targums solve the moral problem of abandoning an innocent child to death by insisting that the decision was as much Isaac's as Abraham's: the initial impression of the narrative that Isaac was a mere infant needs correcting, since Isaac was in fact thirty-seven years old at the time.[32] The argument given to justify this claim is that Sarah's death (recorded in the following chapter) must have been in response to what happened, and Isaac was in fact thirty-seven when she died. Medieval Judaism even went a stage further, as one can see from the great Cabbalistic work the *Zohar*. For along with a complicated argument which removes Abraham altogether from the text, one finds this pertinent question: 'Who has ever seen a compassionate father turn cruel?'[33] Christian exegesis exhibits a parallel development. For, though the New Testa-

---

[29] Kant, *Religion within the Limits of Reason Alone*, 4. 4. Kant is even more emphatic in *The Conflict of the Faculties*.

[30] Kierkegaard, *Fear and Trembling*, ed. H. V. Hong and E. H. Hong (Princeton, NJ: Princeton University Press, 1983), *passim*, but esp. 22.

[31] J. L. Crenshaw (ed.), *Theodicy in the Old Testament* (London: SPCK, 1983), 8.

[32] Targum of Pseudo-Jonathan; quoted, e.g., in P. Grelot (ed.), *What are the Targums?* (Collegeville, Minn.: Liturgical Press, 1992), 27.

[33] *Zohar*, trans. D. C. Matt (London: SPCK, 1983), 74.

ment shows no knowledge of a middle-aged Isaac, it too tries to lessen the impact of Abraham's decision by making the historically implausible suggestion that Abraham knew that God could raise his son from the dead.[34] But of course the pattern adopted for most of Christian history has been rather different. The story became a symbol or type of the Crucifixion, with Isaac and the ram in the thicket either separately or jointly representing the sacrifice of God the Son as the Lamb of God.

Those who have no moral difficulties with the story can of course follow the lines indicated by Kierkegaard. But if, instead, one follows the predominant direction of later exegesis, then to justify doing so, it seems to me, is stretching the bounds of probability, to claim that such a meaning is somehow either implicit in the text or required by biblical revelation as a whole. Not only are there many other passages in the Old Testament which seem unedifying or morally problematic and which have failed to generate comparable 'solutions'; but in this case the solution involves a deliberate rejection of what was clearly the central feature of the original story in generating its testing character, the youth of Isaac. Yet, can one fail to describe as revelatory what in the Jewish tradition of the Akedah became the inspiration for numerous martyrdoms or in the Christian tradition, through sermon and icon, a key image in conveying the compassion of God, and not his unreasonableness?

My second (and modern) example concerns the equality of the sexes. We are so used to hearing Galatians 3: 28 quoted in support that it is salutary to remind ourselves that for almost the whole of Christian history the passage was seen as meaning that Christ brings not absolute equality in everything but simply an equality of access to the most important thing of all—salvation. Nor is there a shortage of arguments which might be used in support. Certainly in respect of another pair mentioned in the verse, Paul, in Romans 11, leaves us in no doubt about the continued privileged position of the Jew: the Gentile wild olive shoot has been grafted on to the cultivated olive tree that is the Jew, and we are not to boast, since it is not we who support the Jewish root but the Jewish root that supports us.[35] Again, even if 1 Timothy 2 and 1 Corinthians 14 are

---

[34] Heb. 11: 17; implausible because almost all biblical scholars are agreed that a positive conception of the afterlife as distinct from a shadowy existence in Sheol is a late development.

[35] Cf. Rom. 11: 17–18.

declared not to be from the hand of Paul, that still leaves I Corinthians 11, where Paul uses the second Genesis creation story (with the man created first) to argue for a prioritizing of male over female. Add to that his omission of women in parallel uses of the contrasting pairs,[36] as also their absence as first witnesses to the resurrection in 1 Corinthians 15, and one begins to perceive a very strong case against, especially given the strength of Jewish attitudes at the time.

None of this is meant to deny the legitimacy of belief in the equality of the sexes; rather, it is to call into question whether this can be portrayed as simply discovering a meaning already inherent in Scripture. For what appeared to be good scriptural and biological grounds, both Jewish and Christian traditions assumed the dependence of the female on the male, and it is really only the discovery of the extent to which such apparent dependence is merely a product of cultural conditioning that has generated a change of view. In other words, the important causative factor in now using Galatians in this way is not discovery of an already inherent meaning but change in our natural knowledge. Initially it may seem odd to describe this too as revelation, but appeals to natural knowledge are of course already part of the canon, most obviously in the Wisdom literature and Romans 1. So in deciding to read the verse in this new way, the Christian community would simply be continuing a practice, as old as the Bible itself, of attempting to integrate all our knowledge, natural and otherwise, into a common framework.

The Providential Argument

Hitherto we have examined the plausibility of the discovery model from the human perspective, from what biblical scholarship suggests the character of the Bible and the history of its development to have been. Now, however, I want to consider the issue from the divine perspective. For to all I have said thus far it may be objected that it ignores the providential, controlling hand of God over the entire process of transmission and eventual interpretation. My response proceeds by two stages: first by observing generally

---

[36] As in Col. 3: 11.

the way in which our understanding of providence has been transformed in other areas; then, more particularly, by applying similar
questions to the Bible in the light of what we now know of its
development.

Consider first the transformation which has occurred in Christian
understandings of medicine, economics, and theodicy. For most of
Christian history almost everyone, Protestant as much as Catholic,
has opposed contraception. Even as late as 1908 the Lambeth
Conference of Anglican Bishops was still unreservedly condemning all forms of birth control. Because modern Roman Catholic
objections tend to be put almost exclusively in terms of natural law,
it is easy to lose sight of the more underlying concern to which that
appeal points, one which was once shared by Protestantism. There
is believed to be a law or pattern in nature operating at its best
which reflects the underlying divine will and which it is our job to
obey, except where we can see opportunities for facilitating this
natural operation where it is prevented by illness or disease.
Children were thus seen as essentially a providential gift, and only
minimally as the result of human choice. But nowadays choice has
become primary in the thinking of many Christian moralists, most
obviously perhaps with the endorsement of *in vitro* fertilization,
where it is hard to speak of the facilitating of natural processes
when the technique itself involves bypassing the source of the
problem.

Similarly, in the modern interventionist state it is hard to recall
just how dominant notions of specific providence once were. Just as
God determined when children would be born, so he was thought
to determine who would be wealthy, who poor. Of course, further
distinctions were then drawn, as, for instance, between the deserv-
ing and the undeserving poor, the latter the object of divine judgement, the former an incentive to charity on the part of the rich and
a means of grace for themselves.[37] But amidst all the qualifications
we should not lose sight of the very tight notion of providence
which was being assumed. Every event providentially serves the
divine will, either directly or in spite of human sin.

Even as late as 1832 it was still possible to persuade the British
Parliament to decree a National Fast Day on the grounds that a

---

[37] For a detailed investigation of the extent to which conceptions of providence
still affected economic thinking, even in the first half of the nineteenth century, see
B. Hilton, *The Age of the Atonement* (Oxford: Clarendon Press, 1988).

cholera epidemic had been sent upon the nation as a visitation for its sins; whereas today, whether we think of illness, poverty, or children, Christians have by and large moved to a very different understanding. The difference may be expressed by saying that we have moved from a directive to a permissive approach. This is emphatically not to say that the notion of specific providence has been abandoned (except among a minority of theologians), but it is to say that a very different conception now prevails, one in which, over and above God's general providential ordering of the world, it is entirely up to the individual concerned whether he or she responds to the offer of divine grace or help in the specific situation. So, for instance, that pain occurs would remain as part of the general divine ordering of the world, but whether this or that specific individual suffers would not be seen as a matter of providence; rather, where specific providence enters is in the grace always available from God to bring good out of the evil in question.[38] What has led to such a transformation of consciousness is too complex a matter to enter into here. Suffice it to observe that one key factor must be the rise of the freewill defence as the most popular 'solution' to the problem of evil.

I turn now to the specific case under consideration. Of course, there can be no objection in theory to the notion of God behaving very differently with respect to revelation as compared to his pattern of action elsewhere. After all, it is not a small matter—the salvation of the world—with which we are concerned. None the less, it does seem to me that reflection forces upon us a similar pattern of transformed understanding to what I have indicated has occurred elsewhere.

Fortunately, whether we conceive of God as within or outside time is not pertinent to this particular issue. For even if we think of God deciding everything from a timeless perspective, it still remains true that some, at least, of his decisions would require specific dating, not of course in the sense that they were made (temporally) at that date, but in the still significant sense that, though decreed outside time, they must still be read as a response

---

[38] Antipathy between philosophers and theologians on the question of theodicy seems to me due in part to confusion (on both sides) between issues of general and special providence. I have tried to highlight these in my essay 'The Problem of Pain', in R. Morgan (ed.), *The Religion of the Incarnation* (Bristol: Bristol Classical Press, 1989).

to what is datable within time. Perhaps the most obvious instance is answer to prayer. Whether we think of extraordinary coincidence or miracle, that natural laws and/or human decisions should have coalesced in this way or that a violation of a natural law should have occurred, is only fully explicable once the datable prayer of petition has been fed into the equation. Clearly, too, there is a sliding scale of need for such datability, with response to prayer at one extreme and the general system of natural laws at the other. In between lies much room for debate. For instance, if we follow Duns Scotus's position on the Incarnation (that this would have happened whether or not humanity had sinned), then clearly the fact of its occurrence has as little dependence on datable events as natural laws. But even with Aquinas's stance (that it was a consequence of Adam's sin), it would be misleading to talk of dependence in the same way as in response to prayer. For the Thomist position surely requires only that human beings in general or some human beings have sinned, not that all have done so, still less a specific datable pair. However, in some Catholic theology the key role of Mary's free response to the angel is stressed; clearly, the more this is done, the more we have, after all, the dependence of the Incarnation on a datable event. Yet against this may be set the contrary tendency present in the doctrine of the Immaculate Conception, which brings the existence of a suitable *Theotokos* or 'God-bearer' once more totally under the control of God: any woman could presumably have been so predestined.

The issues are thus far from simple. As already noted, Swinburne does of course concede one dated element, the point at which historical circumstances require or make possible an alternative reading. So, for instance, our very different scientific presuppositions require a metaphorical reading of Genesis 1, just as prophecy has to be interpreted in the light of subsequent events.[39] But in holding to the model of 'discovery', he then seems to retreat. For on that assumption the datable element can in fact be elided. It becomes datable only in the same way as Einstein's discovery of the theory of relativity. The truth was always there; but it required a specific set of circumstances for it to become known. In short, the element of divine response is in no sense required, as with prayer.

But the question is whether the divine intentions and, with them, revelation can be made at all plausible without similar

---

[39] Swinburne, *Revelation*, 184, 195.

interactionist assumptions. The difficulty is that, if we say that it is all a matter of divine anticipation (that the meanings were put there to be discovered in due course), it is hard not to see much of the result as very ham-fisted—surely an odd result if we are speaking of the source of all wisdom! Of course, sometimes the transition is an entirely natural one, For instance, most biblical scholars now believe that the phrase 'Son of God' was used in the Gospels (as in the Old Testament where it is applied to the king[40]) to indicate not divinity as such, but merely someone in a special relationship with God. None the less, its subsequent use to refer to Christ's divinity is an entirely natural one. Or again, to give a more philosophical example, a similar claim might be made for Aquinas's interpretation of the name of God in Exodus 3. Most biblical scholars seem to be agreed that in its original context it was intended to express divine faithfulness and constancy ('I will be what I will be').[41] But there could scarcely be any greater constancy than that of a God like Aquinas's whose very being is immutable, with his existence identified with his essence. So once again one could argue that there is a natural transition.

But the same cannot be said of many other expressions and passages. Reference has already been made to Matthew's strange use of Old Testament 'prophecy'. If the divine meaning had simply been planted there by God to be discovered subsequently by Matthew, would he not have made a better job of it, even conceding that it was to remain hidden till then? Nor is Matthew's transformation of Micah the only instance of a New Testament writer giving exactly the opposite sense to an Old Testament verse. Much the same happens with Paul's use of Habakkuk 2: 4 to endorse his argument for justification by faith in Romans 1: 17. Whereas Paul quotes the prophet as saying that 'he who is righteous by faith will live', Habakkuk appears to have written that 'the righteous shall live by his faithfulness', a quite different meaning.[42] Nor, if scholars of the calibre of Stendahl and Sanders are right,[43] does the transfor-

[40] As in 2 Sam. 7: 14 and Ps. 2: 7.

[41] So G. von Rad in *Old Testament Theology* (Edinburgh: Oliver and Boyd, 1962), who none the less cautions: 'nothing is farther from what is envisaged in this etymology . . . than a definition of his nature in the sense of a philosophical statement about his being' (i. 180).

[42] So, e.g., J. D. Dunn, *The Living Word* (London: SCM Press, 1987), 118.

[43] K. Stendahl, *Paul among Jews and Gentiles* (London: SCM Press, 1977), esp. 2–4 and 28–9; E. P. Sanders, *Paul and Palestinian Judaism* (London: SCM Press, 1977), 442–7 and 474 ff.

mation end there. For, according to them, the heart of the argument of Romans lies elsewhere, and it is really only Luther who makes justification central to its interpretation.

My objective in rehearsing these points is in no way to challenge the doctrine. Rather, it is to question the plausibility of any idea of God foreordaining that the verse should appear in the text of Habakkuk with a significance unknown to the prophet, yet one subsequently to be discovered by Paul through a misreading, and then in turn to be more deeply understood by Luther through a narrowing of focus unknown to Paul. Not only does it sound excessively manipulative, but it again conjures up the image of a specific providence bordering almost upon the incompetent. Would it not, after all, have been a relatively simple matter to ensure identity of text between Habakkuk and Paul's quotation?

At all events, it is such factors as these that lead me to propose datable intentions in the much stronger sense already indicated. God at each stage of the development of the canon and beyond has been interacting with the recipients of his revelation, and how they read it is a function not just of the divine will or of historical circumstances but of what God can get the individual to see on the basis of his reflection both upon his context and upon the biblical text. In other words, there is an inspired imposition of meaning rather than its discovery, and so the crucial dependence is not upon a meaning already inherent in the text but upon a datable individual(s) being inspired to propose that meaning.

If it be objected that this still leaves us with as ham-fisted a God as ever, my response would be that this is not at all the case. For now, instead of God arbitrarily creating verses which he intends be given some very different sense in the future, it is more a case of God accommodating himself to the historical circumstances of the individuals concerned and advancing their perceptions through whatever means happen to be available, including misunderstandings of the text or implausible systems of exegesis.

My conclusion is thus that the usual sharp contrast made between revelation and tradition is no longer sustainable. Within the Bible itself we have under God a history of interpretation and reinterpretation, and this continues within the subsequent life of the Church. The definitiveness of the text is thus not at all the same thing as the definitiveness of its interpretation. The Bible is already a history of revelatory texts and their reinterpretation under God in changed circumstances within a community of faith, and it is precisely this interaction between a community of faith and God which has continued to yield fresh reinterpretations in the Church's subsequent history. Only the text became fixed; how it is to be interpreted continues to depend upon inspired individuals and the community of faith's response to them. Of course, the revelation of what is definitive of Christianity, as expressed in its two creeds, lies in the past; but this does not mean that there is no more to learn through the Scriptures, whether it be a proper appropriation of justification by faith in the sixteenth century or the equality of the sexes in the twentieth. Ironically, though he is quick to modify his comment back towards his discovery model, almost the last words of Swinburne's book well express the position adopted here: 'the revelation goes on.'[44]

[44] Currently it is the German-speaking world which seems to be showing the greatest interest in later, ecclesiastical interpretations of Scripture. U. Luz, *Das Evangelium nach Matthäus* (Zürich: Benziger, 1985–), is a fine example, one volume of which has been translated into English: *Matthew 1–7: A Commentary* (Edinburgh: T. and T. Clark, 1989). Witness too the joint discussions between Lutheran and Roman Catholic theologians on the relation between Scripture and tradition, only the first volume of which has appeared so far: W. Pannenberg and T. Schneider (eds.), *Verbidliches Zeugnis* (Freiburg: Herder, 1992).

7

The Communication of Divine Revelation

BRIAN HEBBLETHWAITE

To say that a theology is perspectival is to acknowledge that it necessarily embodies a particular cultural approach to the world. To say that something has been 'revealed' does not imply that it escapes this necessity. Many believers assume that it does and some contemporary philosophers of religion support that assumption. But it is simply false to say, in the words of one such philosopher of religion, that 'there are things that can be known to be "true without qualification" on the authority of a prophet who can be known to speak with the authority of God', or, in the words of another, that 'once one believes God has really revealed something, one is bound to believe it on simple authority'. Any revelation, real or otherwise, finds its expression in the context and the thought forms of some specific and contingent cultural tradition. All theology is in that sense perspectival. No manner of divine authorization can override that feature of the human situation.

Thus Maurice Wiles in his *Christian Theology and Interreligious Dialogue*[1]—a rather surprising foray by the Regius Professor Emeritus of Divinity at Oxford into the world of comparative religion. But the point here—that we do not, and cannot, get divine revelation neat—is characteristic of this liberal theologian's work throughout his career. The first of the philosophers of religion mentioned is Richard Swinburne, the second Keith Ward—ironically, Wiles's successor in the Oxford Chair.

Swinburne's view—that some things can be known to be true without qualification if said by a prophet known to speak with God's authority—is in fact quoted by Wiles from *Faith and Reason*, the third book of Swinburne's highly influential philosophy of re-

---

[1] M. Wiles, *Christian Theology and Interreligious Dialogue* (London: SCM Press, 1992), 64 ff.

ligion trilogy.[2] More recently, Swinburne has begun to publish a series of philosophical theology books, the second of which, *Revelation: From Metaphor to Analogy*,[3] might be held to have dealt with the topic in a more nuanced way. But, although Swinburne recognizes God's self-revelation through historical manifestation (especially by incarnation), he still restricts his analysis to revelation by God of propositional truth. And, although he does recognize the indirect and mediated way in which God's Word is given in Holy Scripture, he still thinks in terms of the spoken and written word, authenticated by miracle—notably by Christ's resurrection—as the heart of special revelation.

It is true that Anglo-Saxon philosophers of religion tend to favour the model of communication between persons by speech in their analysis of special revelation. In addition to Swinburne and Ward—at least the Ward of *Divine Action*[4] as cited by Wiles—one might mention Basil Mitchell in his dispute with Wiles himself[5] and W. J. Abraham in *Divine Revelation and the Limits of Historical Criticism*,[6] the latter being of particular interest on account of its careful distinction of its position from fundamentalism and its recognition of the problem set for traditional ideas of revelation by the rise of historical criticism.

For it is this problem—our awareness of the all too human, culturally and historically conditioned nature of the Jewish and Christian scriptures—that has led many modern theologians to reject the traditional view, as is clear from Wiles's brusque dismissal of Swinburne and Ward. And Ward's own volte-face in his very next book, *A Vision to Pursue*,[7] in which, belatedly, he acknowledges mistakes in the Bible, not least regarding Jesus's own expec-

---

[2] R. G. Swinburne, *The Coherence of Theism* (Oxford: Clarendon Press, 1977); *The Existence of God* (Oxford: Clarendon Press, 1979); and *Faith and Reason* (Oxford: Clarendon Press, 1981).

[3] R. G. Swinburne, *Revelation: From Metaphor to Analogy* (Oxford: Clarendon Press, 1992). Swinburne's views on revelation may be gleaned in summary form from an article entitled 'Revelation', written shortly before the book and partly incorporated into it, but published the same year, in K. J. Clark (ed.), *Our Knowledge of God. Essays on Natural and Philosophical Theology* (Dordrecht: Reidel, 1992), 115–29.

[4] Keith Ward, *Divine Action* (London: Collins, 1990).

[5] Basil Mitchell, 'Does Christianity Need a Revelation? A Discussion', *Theology*, lxxxiii (1980), 103 ff.

[6] W. J. Abraham, *Divine Revelation and the Limits of Historical Criticism* (Oxford: Oxford University Press, 1982).

[7] Keith Ward, *A Vision to Pursue, Beyond the Crisis in Christianity* (London: SCM Press, 1991).

tation of an imminent end, and, on that ground, comes right over to Wiles's 'perspectival' relativism, is an indication of the seriousness of the problem.

This last example shows that the controversy is not just one between philosophers and theologians. Philosophers can succumb to the lure of historical relativism too. And equally there remain theologians, not only fundamentalist ones, convinced of the centrality of the Word of God for a theology of special revelation. But I take Wiles's comment on Swinburne and the earlier Ward as indicative of the mutual suspicion or hostility that prevails between many contemporary theologians and many contemporary philosophers of religion.

The dispute tends to polarize, perhaps more unfairly from the theologians' side than from the philosophers'. For, while the theologians tend to read the philosophers as being more extreme than they really are—Wiles clearly thinks of Swinburne and the earlier Ward as historically insensitive crypto-fundamentalists, and this, as Swinburne's book *Revelation* shows, is unfair—the theologians, at least theologians such as Wiles, are pretty extreme in their historical relativism and, in some cases, Wiles included, in their rejection of the need for special revelation in the Christian scheme of things. In his debate with Mitchell, Wiles suggests that Christian theology should treat the Bible not as something new and *sui generis*, but just as part of the human religious data requiring interpretation.[8]

Interestingly, Wolfhart Pannenberg, in his brief discussion of the Mitchell/Wiles debate,[9] sides with the theologian against the philosopher, without, apparently, realizing the extremity of Wiles's view. Pannenberg has his own reasons, over and above those of historical/critical awareness, for opposing the primacy of the verbal communication model—in particular his opposition to the irrationalism and authoritarianism of Barthian 'Word of God' theologies.

---

[8] Another example of the asymmetrical polarization evident between theologians and philosophers of religion is to be found in some recent issues of the journal *Faith and Philosophy*. In the January 1989 issue, Gordon Kaufman tried to spell out why he, as a modern theologian, was not much interested in the topics debated with such analytic sharpness by members of the Society of Christian Philosophers, whose journal *Faith and Philosophy* is. An acute and trenchant reply by Eleonore Stump and Norman Kretzmann appeared in the July 1990 issue. But again it has to be pointed out that Kaufman is, if anything, a more extreme relativist and constructivist than Wiles, while Stump and Kretzmann can hardly be labelled fundamentalist.

[9] W. Pannenberg, *Systematic Theology*, i, trans. G. W. Bromiley (Grand Rapids, Mich.: Eerdmans, 1991), 233 ff.

But in no way does he renounce the place of special revelation in specifically Christian systematic theology. As we shall see, he locates the presence of special revelation in certain key historical events within the context of universal history.

But before we examine the more mainstream theological alternative to the verbal communication model for divine special revelation—namely, the conception of particular divine action in and through certain key events in history—let us consider further the pros and cons of the verbal communication model, which philosophers of religion such as Swinburne defend, and which theologians such as Wiles reject. The idea that God speaks to humankind, making his will and something of his nature known, disclosing, through verbal communication, say, to prophets and Gospel-writers, his plan of salvation and his intentions regarding human destiny, is quite common in the history of religions. It plays a central role, of course, in Islam. Restricting ourselves to the Judaeo-Christian tradition, we may think of what God said to Moses on Mt Sinai, including the giving of the Ten Commandments, of the prophets' confident declaration, 'Thus saith the Lord . . .', and especially of the teachings of Jesus of Nazareth, believed to be the incarnate Son of God. All this is recorded, sometimes allegedly verbatim, in the multifarious books of the Bible. The Bible itself has been thought of as divinely inspired and constituting the Word of God, God's special revelation. And, although a certain, public, fixed quality came to be accorded to the canonical scriptures, special revelation in this public sense being restricted to these particularly inspired books, countless other individuals within the Christian tradition have claimed to experience private revelations, auditions as well as visions, all supposedly coming from God. And while the Church has been suspicious of private revelations, subjecting such claims to rigorous tests, as William Alston has pointed out in his study of religious experience, *Perceiving God*[10] the idea that God can and does speak to men and women is central to the personal theism of the biblical and Judaeo-Christian tradition, whatever else may be believed about the hidden, interior working of the divine Spirit in the human heart and soul. Indeed, it is the model of verbal communication that is held to

[10] W. Alston, *Perceiving God* (Ithaca, NY: Cornell University Press, 1993). Alston examines here not only visions and auditions but also wordless, unmediated forms of awareness of God reported in the literature.

preserve the interpersonal character of divine/human encounter, a central feature of Judaeo-Christian religion allegedly lost in Wiles's rejection of special revelation, as Mitchell made clear in their debate. And if the Christian doctrine of the Incarnation is true, we have in the words of Jesus the very words of God made man—human words no doubt, but the human speech of the incarnate Word, words of undeniable divine authority.

But the difficulties of the verbal communication model are only too clear. Not only do we have the problems of historical criticism stressed by Wiles. Comparative religion and the psychology of religion have brought out both the commonalities between the religions of the ancient Near East (and elsewhere) and the developing religion of Israel and the psychologically intelligible nature of phenomena such as 'auditions'. James Barr has shown the difference it makes to our reception of the Hebrew law when we become aware of the parallels and common background in the ancient Near East,[11] and countless studies of the varieties of religious experience across cultures have made it much more difficult to read a story such as that of Eli and the boy Samuel literally. Moreover, the actual content of the Bible is so varied—trivial and profound, local and universal, morally dubious and morally searching, contradictory and factually wrong in places, as well as religiously innovative and challenging in others. Earlier generations of interpreters were already selective in their reading of Holy Scripture and well versed in typological and other means of accepting the unacceptable. Historical critical method only supplemented these devices, and helped to bring out the very human, fallible nature of these extraordinarily powerful religious documents. And even where the words of Jesus are concerned, there are problems as to whether they have been accurately handed down and recorded, of their often indirect and parabolic nature anyway, open to diverse fruitful and less fruitful interpretations, and of their embeddedness in an all too human first-century cultural form, unprotected from error. By the very principle of true incarnation, the man Jesus thought in contemporary demonological and apocalyptic categories, which may have been vehicles of practical and religious insight, but were not devoid of factual error, as Ward has come to recognize.

[11] See, e.g., J. Barr, *Biblical Faith and Natural Theology* (Oxford: Clarendon Press, 1993), 95–101.

Beneath all these difficulties lies the theologians' sense of a certain basic naïvety in the supposition that it is God's way to dictate, infallibly, to prophets, apostles, or even to the incarnate Son a number of true propositions or eternally valid injunctions. It is not only the nature of the biblical material, its historical and cultural embeddedness and its extreme heterogeneity, out of which profound convictions about God's nature, God's acts, and God's plan have to be extracted, but the alleged modality of God's revelatory acts—dictation, the immediate causation in people's minds of dreams, visions, auditions, or even of profound convictions—that comes to seem so implausible, not only to the rational but to the theological mind.

It is not that the idea of such direct dictation is logically impossible. It is an aspect of Wiles's extremism that he seems to think that God *could* not give us direct, unmediated verbal directives. The fact that 'an articulate voice from the clouds'—to cite David Hume's extravagant example[12]—would have to be in a particular language and the fact that language would have a particular history and cultural context do not of themselves preclude direct divine causality behind its occurrence. Suppose that articulate voice uttered the words, 'Thou shalt do no murder' (or their equivalent in whatever language a potential murderer spoke) immediately prior to any such premeditated deed. The meaning and authority of the prohibition would surely be trans-cultural, independent of any particular 'perspective'. And even if a minimal cultural context is required for the concept of murder to be intelligible, it could be argued that the fostering of such minimal cultural contexts would itself be a providential dispensation whereby the conditions of intelligibility for such direct prohibitions are created. Indeed, setting aside this extravagant example, we may observe that the idea of the providential preparation of a particular cultural context for the gift and reception of special revelation through the Incarnation is part and parcel of mainstream Christian theology. The presence of a particular 'perspective', far from constituting a relativist objection to the idea of special revelation, plays an integral part in the very notion, as actually instantiated in Christianity.

The objection to the idea of direct verbal communication is not logical. It results rather from a combination of reflection on the all

---

[12] D. Hume, *Dialogues Concerning Natural Religion*, pt. III.

too human, fallible nature of the Scriptures and recognition of the inappropriateness, even naïvety, of the direct dictation model. Not only do we not in fact get articulate voices heard from the clouds (once we come to appreciate the genre, we cannot take 'Saul, Saul, why persecutest thou me?' literally, at least in any public sense), we also learn to see the point of indirect communication in and through fallible human media. Spelling out the rationale of that indirect communication is a necessary task for both philosophy of religion and theology, if special revelation without divine dictation is to be defended and explained.

Before this task is attempted, something must be said about the alternatives to the verbal communication model that have come to the fore in twentieth-century theology. This, too, is a controversial matter, but it will be argued here that the main alternative is not the fashionable notion of narrative, as urged in Ronald Thiemann's book, *Revelation and Theology*,[13] but remains that of God's acts in history culminating in the events of Christ's life, death, and resurrection, as urged by Wolfhart Pannenberg, first in the co-operative volume *Revelation as History*[14] and latterly in his *Systematic Theology*.[15] Narrative undoubtedly plays a role in the communication of divine revelation. The story of God's saving acts has to be told and heard, written down and read; but, as Christof Schwöbel has insisted in a useful analysis of the concept of revelation,[16] the ontological implications of what is narrated are not spelled out in Thiemann's book. And it is the merit of Pannenberg's work, by contrast with that of Thiemann, that neither ontology nor experience is allowed to fade from view. It is, incidentally, quite extraordinary that a book on revelation such as Thiemann's, published in 1985, should make no mention of Pannenberg's work.

The insistence that history itself discloses the revelatory activity of God to the attentive rational mind was the thesis of Pannenberg's earlier co-authored book. We cannot discuss here the details of that argument—the significance, once positive history is rejected, of the history of religions within the context of universal history; the significance of the history of Israel, including the eschatological

---

[13] R. Thiemann, *Revelation and Theology. The Gospel as Narrated Promise* (Notre Dame, Ind.: University of Notre Dame Press, 1985).

[14] W. Pannenberg *et al.*, *Revelation as History*, trans. D. Granskow and E. Quinn (New York: Macmillan, 1968).

[15] See n. 9.

[16] C. Schwöbel, *God: Action and Revelation* (Kampen: J. H. Kok, 1992), ch. 4.

horizon to her understanding of world history, within the context of the history of religions; and the significance of the life, teaching, and fate of Jesus and its aftermath, within the context of Jewish faith and eschatology. All this, according to Pannenberg and his colleagues, is suggestive of construal in revelatory terms without any special appeal to authority or inspiration. Pannenberg's recent treatment is more sensitive to the experiential elements involved both in the formation of the particular historical traditions, which stand out as providing the interpretative key to the meaning of universal history, and to the verbal witness, including proclamation and liturgical response which the special acts of God in question evoke if rightly understood; but the fact that the revelatory events require mediation by words if their signifiance is to be grasped and communicated does not mean that the words, rather than the events, are the primary vehicles of revelation. On the contrary, it is what God has done for humanity's salvation in the series of events that culminate in the Incarnation that constitute special revelation in the primary sense. The fact that the events, including the forma- tion of the faith traditions that interpret them, are set within the context of a wider history and show common features and points of contact, as well as idiosyncratic and original developments, has led some, such as James Barr, to question the distinction between general and special revelation and between natural and revealed theology.[17] Certainly the renunciation by Pannenberg of the re- quirement of special inspiration or divinely guaranteed authority for scriptural (and other) witness to the events in question renders all the data open to debate and critical enquiry. Special revelation has no particular privilege in this respect. But we still need the distinction between general and special if we are to do justice to the differences between those aspects of God's nature and will open to experience and inference the world over and at all times and that particular series of acts and events culminating in the Incarnation which, in the nature of the case, constitute a unique series and inevitably raise the so-called scandal of particularity.

How are we to evaluate this preference for the model of special revelation by God's acts in and through a series of historical events over the model of special revelation by verbal communication? Certainly it has the advantage of locating special revelation firmly in the public domain, in a particular life lived within a particular

---

[17] Barr, *Biblical Faith.*

historical context and in the particular effects of that sequence of events. All this is discussible and open to interpretation without appeal to any authority other than the moral and religious force of what emerged from that context. The Scriptures can then be seen as essential documentary sources for our knowledge of the revelatory events, but not as the immediate vehicles of special revelation in and of themselves. This is not to disparage the philosopher's interest in propositional truth. The truth content of special revelvation must of course be stated in propositional form, as it is in creeds and theologies. But no one wishes to identify these as constituting special revelation. Not even Barthians give the *Church Dogmatics* that exalted status. Creeds and theologies, including rudimentary examples in the Scriptures themselves, are eminently discussible human attempts to extract and state the meaning and truth of what is revealed in and through the historical events, the tradition, and the life and fate that constitute special revelation. And it needs to be stressed again that rudimentary creeds and theologies form only a small part of Holy Scripture. Thiemann was quite right to see the core of Scripture in such categories as those of narrated promise. His error was to locate special revelation in the narrative itself rather than in what is narrated—namely, the acts of God in history, culminating in the Incarnation.

To locate special revelation primarily in act, event, and presence, rather than in word, is not to escape the problem of the fallible, all too human media of divine action. The history of the chosen people was a pretty messy affair, and the development of their ethical monotheism to the heights of second Isaiah's servant songs was an arduous struggle. Mention has already been made of the limitations of first-century Jewish categories, which may have enabled the incarnate Son to carry out his mission and achieve God's saving purpose, but which cannot simply be taken over without question after 2,000 years of further history, including the rise of modern science. The same question, of why God should act indirectly through such a history and tradition and in and through that particular first-century Jewish rabbi, arises here as arose in the case of the verbal communication model. We still need a theological rationale of indirect communication.

Moreover, the contrast between revelation as history and revelation as word has been overdrawn, as Pannenberg himself has come to recognize. The series of events to be construed in terms of God's self-revelatory acts includes Israel's reception of the Law, the prophets' powerful declarations of God's will and promise, and, above all, the teaching as well as the example, Passion, death, and resurrection of Jesus. No doubt, more stress will be placed on the literary genres that are exemplified by the law codes and the prophetic oracles. No doubt, the emphasis will lie much more with the development of Israel's self-understanding in the face of her experience of prosperity and adversity from exodus to exile and beyond. Where the words are not themselves seen as the primary locus of special revelation, their context in the event series leading to the Incarnation will seem more central, and less difficulty will be found in their fallibilities, their inadequacies, and their, in part, alien, irrecoverable features. But, in so far as the legal system, the Wisdom writings, and the prophets' visionary experiences and insights contributed to the tradition of faith which was to provide the context for the Incarnation, these more verbal elements belong to the event series, and are part of the history which reveals God in a special way. And if Jesus Christ was indeed God incarnate, his teaching, so far as it can be recovered and interpreted aright, must indeed be deemed revelatory, notwithstanding the limitations of the first-century categories in terms of which it was expressed.

When George Mavrodes distinguishes, therefore, in his book *Revelation in Religious Belief*[18] between the communication model (tied to notions like saying and telling), the manifestation model (more like showing, irrespective of what is said), and the causation model (where God is held simply to bring about awareness of some fresh truth), we are bound to detect some artificiality in keeping these three forms apart, as well as some naïvety in failing to address the problem of the modality of divine action in revelation. If preference is given to manifestation through history and a life, this will include elements of verbal communication; and both aspects—acts in history and speech-acts—will involve some conception of divine causality at work behind, or in and through, the creaturely causality of the human agents whose fallible human story constitutes the vehicle or medium of divine self-disclosure.

This brings us back to the question of the rationale of indirect communication. We require not only a plausible theory of special providence—an account of God's action in and through fallible

---

[18] G. Mavrodes, *Revelation in Religious Belief* (Philadelphia: Temple University Press, 1988).

creaturely action—but also a plausible account of why God acts thus indirectly, and gradually, over a long period of time, in providence and revelation alike. Such a theory and such an account may be developed along the lines suggested by Austin Farrer in a series of short books published in the 1960s.[19] In order to create and enter into relations with a world of genuinely free, independent yet interdependent, finite persons, God has to fashion his creatures gradually from below, in and through a regularly structured, yet open, evolving and innovative world. In Farrer's words, God 'makes the creatures make themselves', thus giving them room to be themselves, to form their own characters and build their interpersonal relationships. The fact that the regular, reliable conditions of learning, growth, freedom, and personality at the same time render finite creatures at risk to accident and loss constitutes a theodicy, an extension of the 'free-will defence' back into an explanation of our vulnerability to natural evil. For these are necessary conditions of the creation of the values of human existence.[20]

By the same token, human knowledge and experience of God cannot be immediately given and imposed. The point of human life—our learning by experience, our growth in understanding, our development of character, our enjoyment of a unique life history and of particular interpersonal relations—would be lost if God overwhelmed us with his glory and imposed his reality and will by direct public manifestation or dictation. The method of indirect communication, whereby men and women are drawn into seeking God and finding him throughout a lifetime's experience, is appropriate to the nature of those being drawn out of nature into spirit and fashioned gradually for eternity. No more in respect of their relations with their Maker than in respect of their formed character and personality can human persons be created complete and perfected as they will be in the end. The hiddenness of God behind and within the structures of creation and the gradualness of the process of indirect communication are not only appropriate but necessary if the story of creation—pictured by Farrer on the analogy of the

---

[19] A. M. Farrer, *Love Almighty and Ills Unlimited* (Garden City, NY: Doubleday, 1961); *Saving Belief* (London: Hodder and Stoughton, 1964); *A Science of God?* (London: Bles, 1966) (US title: *God Is Not Dead* [New York: Morehouse-Barlow, 1966]); and *Faith and Speculation* (London: A. and C. Black, 1967).

[20] I have explored these arguments in my contribution, 'The Problem of Evil', to G. Wainwright (ed.), *Keeping the Faith, Essays to Mark the Centenary of Lux Mundi* (Philadelphia: Fortress Press, 1989).

novelist who does not force or fake his narrative but resolves the plot out of the natural behaviour and interactions of his characters—is to be allowed to take its natural and intended course under God's supervenient providence. This is not a deistic picture of the relation between God and the world. Nature is not left to its own devices; but the divine Spirit operates in providence, revelation, and grace within the parameters of what has been set in motion by the creation of a person-producing cosmos.

Moreover, this process of indirect communication is held in the Christian tradition to have reached an unrepeatable climax in the Incarnation, conditions having reached the point where God himself, in the Person of his Son, was able to manifest his nature and his love in an actual human life and death. This apogee of indirect communication was captured classically by Søren Kierkegaard with his parable of the king and the humble maiden.[21] To woo the maiden and win her love for himself and not for his kingly state, the king had to put on a peasant's clothes and live the life of a peasant in the village.

The key notion employed by Farrer in his articulation of the concept of divine action is that of double agency.[22] God's action takes place in and through creaturely action. The divine Spirit realizes God's intentions and manifests God's nature and saving plan in and through creaturely energies and acts, including what fallible humans do and say, under the inspiration of the divine, and eventually by incarnation. This notion of double agency is often misunderstood, as by Ward in *Divine Action*.[23] That God's universal creative and sustaining hand underlies all creaturely existence and action is taken for granted. Double agency refers to God's action in special providence, revelation, incarnation, and grace as mediated by creatures with all their limitations and fallibilities. In all these cases, a purely natural, purely human story can be told. But the puzzling, inadequate character of the purely naturalistic accounts is suggested, if not demonstrated, by their actual characteristics and by their results, often when viewed in retrospect. Not always so, since a man's experience of grace may be such as to lead him to say,

---

[21] S. Kierkegaard, *Philosophical Fragments*, trans. D. F. Swenson (Princeton, NJ: Princeton University Press, 1942), 19–21.

[22] On this, see essays by O. C. Thomas, Roger Forsman, and Michael McClain, in Brian Hebblethwaite and Edward Henderson (eds.), *Divine Action. Studies Inspired by the Philosophical Theology of Austin Farrer* (Edinburgh: T. T. Clark, 1990).

[23] Ward, *Divine Action*, 51.

there and then, 'it is no longer I who live, but Christ who lives in me' (Gal. 2: 20)—although of course it is his own life and his own act, even though the act goes beyond his known abilities.

The fact that Farrer used the grace/free will relation as a paradigm case of double agency shows that this analysis of special providence is much wider in its scope than is involved in the case of special revelation which is the concern of this chapter. But Farrer had already, in his Bampton Lectures, *The Glass of Vision*,[24] and in a subsequent response to criticism, 'Inspiration: Poetical and Divine',[25] attempted to explore just this problem of the modality of divine action in special revelation. Despite his recognition of the fact that we do not have access to that modality—that, as he later put it, in the nature of the case, 'the hand of God is perfectly hidden'—he was still prepared to speculate, with great imaginative power, about the vehicles of divine revelation in the minds of the prophets and in the thought and teaching of Jesus of Nazareth. Farrer suggested that what enabled them to be bearers of special revelation was the inspired development of certain images that came, for instance, in the parables of Jesus, to open up some novel vision of the nature and the will of the divine. What differentiates divine inspiration from poetic inspiration and indicates its ultimate divine control is not the psychological mechanism involved but the extraordinary religious significance of the product—in the case under consideration, the teaching of Jesus as recorded in the Gospels. Again we note that there is no suggestion of unmediated dictation or direct divine causation behind such inspired teaching. Inspiration is not to be thought of as something direct and unmediated. The images have a history in the development of Israel's faith. They become vehicles of innovative disclosure through imaginative development and novel use. Just such human creativity and imagination in the context of a particular tradition of faith are interpreted as the media of divine revelation. And what suggest this interpretation are the quality and authority of what emerges from this process: namely, the prophetic and dominical teachings themselves. It is not the process of inspiration that is to be construed as revelation. Rather, it is what results from it.

Further illumination on these matters may be gained from recent writings by David Brown. In chapter 2 of his book *The Divine*

---

[24] A. M. Farrer, *The Glass of Vision* (London: Dacre Press, 1948).
[25] In A. M. Farrer, *Interpretation and Belief* (London: SPCK, 1976), 39–53.

Trinity,[26] he develops a view of revelation as a divine dialogue, in which God always respects the freedom and humanity of the recipients and the stage of development they have reached. As Brown puts it in the course of a later summary, 'this will explain why failures of moral insight sometimes occur, even for example in the prophets or psalms. It is because God values something more, that the individual comes to appreciate for himself what the truth is.' Brown makes it clear in his exposition of this dialogue model for divine revelation that the rationale behind the conception of gradual revelation in and through fallible human recipients is akin to the freewill defence in theodicy. So we find in Brown an account of indirect communication developed along similar lines to the one adumbrated here.

In a subsequent paper[27] Brown defends his earlier analysis by means of the analogy with teaching. The good teacher adapts and accommodates his instruction to the pupil's level and capacities, and gradually, through dialogue, raises the level of insight and understanding.[28] Then, in response to objections regarding the lack of analogy with speech in the divine case, Brown takes up Farrer's treatment of inspired images as the vehicle of revelation, and extends it in a very interesting way to the creative transformation of certain natural symbols present in the unconscious. He stresses the point that such transformation is experienced in religious contexts—perhaps, as Farrer suggested, by contrast with poetic inspiration—not purely in subjective terms as the achievement of new insight, but as encounter and interaction with the divine source of transformation and new insight.

Clearly, these tentative explorations by Farrer and Brown will cover only aspects of the divine/human 'double agency' involved in special revelation. The transformation of images and symbols in the minds of the prophets and of Jesus is only one strand in the history of Israel and the events of Christ's life, death, and resurrection. On the other hand, especially in Brown's case, the extension of the range of the purported vehicles of revelation from the biblical images to natural symbols suggests that we are dealing with

[26] D. Brown, *The Divine Trinity* (London: Duckworth, 1985).

[27] D. Brown, 'God and Symbolic Action', in Hebblethwaite and Henderson (eds.), *Divine Action*, 103–22.

[28] A similar analogy was used by W. J. Abraham in an earlier book, *The Divine Inspiration of Holy Scripture* (Oxford: Oxford University Press, 1981).

much more than special revelation. James Barr would doubtless observe that we are once again being drawn into the sphere of natural theology and general revelation. This two-pronged difficulty, that the analysis applies only to aspects of special revelation—its media in individual minds—but that it nevertheless applies to a wider range of divine/human encounter than that of special revelation, should lead us back to the crucial question of what differentiates special revelation in the Christian scheme of things from other elements in divine providence and divine grace, all of which share the characteristics of double agency and indirect communication. After all, God may address and claim a person's heart and mind through the words of a friend or a preacher. But such words and such an event are not what the Christian tradition means by special revelation.

Commentators on Farrer's Bampton Lectures raised the not unreasonable question of what justified his restriction to biblical images. Brown's development of Farrer's approach entails no such restriction. But either way, the defining parameters of special revelation, in contradistinction to providence, inspiration, and grace more generally, have not been successfully indicated, even though both authors have made a valiant attempt to focus attention on the media of indirect communication undoubtedly involved in all revelation. That is why we must return at this point to the notion of locating special revelation in the public events of Israel's history, the historical growth of her distinctive form of religious faith, and the life and teaching of Jesus that were enabled by that historical context, even though they greatly transcended and transformed it. That these events can be construed as salvation history and, as such, locus of special revelation still requires justification. And undoubtedly this public event series, not least its culmination in the story of Jesus Christ, includes a great deal of mediated verbal communication of the sort explored by Farrer and Brown. But it is the product of that dialogue—the public facts to which the Scriptures (and any other relevant evidence) bear witness—that constitutes special revelation. These facts are as rationally scrutinizable as any other facts. What makes them special is the particular story they tell—a story inaccessible elsewhere.

How, then, in conclusion, does Swinburne's account of revelation compare with the account offered here? We have seen reason to question Swinburne's decision to concentrate on propositional truth rather than the incarnate life in which God was especially self-revealed. Propositional truth must indeed be striven for, analysed, and justified. But the words of Jesus, integral though they are to the revelation that came to us through all he was and did, can hardly be thought of as religious—let alone metaphysical—information. The parables certainly illuminate God's nature and God's plan. The moral injunctions reflect and reveal God's love and God's demand. But none of this can easily be classified as propositional truth. As already insisted above, the ethical, religious, and metaphysical propositions which the Church and her theologians extract from the story of Jesus Christ, including his teaching, are indispensable, but they are not themselves revelation.

That said, we can surely read even the sentence from *Faith and Reason* quoted so disparagingly by Wiles with a more sympathetic ear. 'There are things that can be known to be true without qualification on the authority of a prophet who can be known to speak with the authority of God.' If we read the word 'known' in both its occurrences in this sentence more in the sense of 'knowledge by acquaintance' than in that of 'knowledge that', then we may indeed suppose that one who comes to recognize the Christ event as specially revelatory of God's love for the world will 'know' something of that love. However mediated, that knowledge brooks no qualification. And Christ's authority in these matters cannot be questioned by those—his Church—who have come to appreciate who he was and is. That Swinburne's sentence deserves a more sympathetic reading than that given to it by Wiles is clear from his later *Revelation* book, where one finds, perhaps to one's surprise, most of the points adumbrated here about the gradual communication of divine revelation through fallible human media recognized and expounded with clarity and plausibility. But the book's concluding sentence still does not quite ring true: 'the revelation spoken by and the deeds acted by Christ will be interpreted by human witnesses under the guidance of the Spirit of God. The revelation goes on; it is their witness and yet their witness to an original source which forms the revelation.'[29] What leads to the implausible remark 'The revelation goes on' is precisely that preference for propositional truth as itself constituting revelation rather than the deeds done—and the words spoken—by Christ. On the account given here, the

---

[29] Swinburne, *Revelation*, 224.

original source—the Christ event—is what constitutes special revelation, and that does not go on. By contrast with general revelation, providence, inspiration, and grace, special revelation took place once for all in the past—mediated, like those other forms of divine/human encounter or dialogue, by fallible human words and deeds—but constituting an identifiable, public event series, to which the Bible and the Church bear witness in ever developing, though equally fallible, interpretations.

8

Revelation and Biblical Exegesis: Augustine, Aquinas, and Swinburne

ELEONORE STUMP

Introduction

Christianity, like the other major monotheisms, is committed to the claim that God has revealed himself to human beings and that his revelation is written down in a text. This claim gives rise to a host of questions. We might, for instance, wonder about the means by which this revelation is supposed to have been made. Does Christianity intend us to think that God himself talked, face to face, with individual human beings at some period in history? Or is Christianity committed rather to some weaker claim about the way in which human doctrines and narratives have been given divine significance? We might also wonder about the means by which the divine revelation is set down in writing. According to Beryl Smalley, some early Montanists supposed that God dictated every syllable of Scripture.[1] Contemporary Biblical scholars, on the other hand, assume that the biblical texts were formed in human, culture-bound ways. We might also want to examine particular parts of the biblical texts which seem to pose problems for the claim that the text is revealed, because they seem to conflict with something we believe to be true on other grounds—something drawn from science, for example—or because they offend our moral sensibilities or because they seem to conflict with other passages in the texts. These and other questions like them are interesting and worth pursuing, but in this chapter I want to look at a different kind of question raised by the Christian claim about revelation. However much they may differ otherwise, virtually all Christians have supposed that although God's revelation was made at particular points

[1] Beryl Smalley, *The Study of the Bible in the Middle Ages*, 2nd edn. (Notre Dame, Ind.: University of Notre Dame Press, 1970), 22.

in history, it was meant somehow to be available to people at subsequent times. What I want to consider here is the availability of revelation to people other than those to whom the revelation was originally made. How does Christianity suppose this to occur?[2]

There is an answer to this question now commonly accepted both by those who believe the Christian claim that God has revealed himself to human beings and by those who reject it. Christianity is taken to hold that, by one means or another, God originally communicated a true and important message (or messages) to particular people at some time in the past and that divine revelation is available to us in so far as we have access to the original message(s). Of course, views about the nature and extent of our access vary widely. Some conservative Christians, for example, suppose that the current biblical texts are virtually identical with God's original message and that we have access to revelation just in virtue of understanding what the texts mean. On the other hand, historically oriented biblical scholars who don't reject the idea of revelation suppose that, in order to have access to the divine message, we have to locate the core of revelation within the human accretions built up around it; we have, for example, to determine which sayings attributed to Jesus are genuine and which are the product of later editorial efforts. On this view, revelation isn't necessarily presented by the texts as we have them but is more likely to be found in earlier traditions which we excavate from the texts. Extending this thought, Peter van Inwagen has recently argued[3] that not even the original revelation consisted entirely in a true message from God to human beings. Because the divine message is sent to particular people at certain times, the message needs to be adapted to their understanding. It will therefore incorporate all sorts of inaccuracies in order to seem plausible to them; it will, for instance, presuppose a cosmology which seems right to those people, even though their views are not scientifically accurate. Only in those areas directly related to salvation will the original revelation be altogether true. On this view, to get the message which God intends for us now, not only do we need the original revelation, but we also

---

[2] It is, of course, possible to ask a similar question of Judaism or Islam, each of which, I suspect, would give different answers, and neither of which would take just the positions that Christianity does. I pick Christianity as my sample monotheism because it is the religion whose theology and biblical commentaries I know best.

[3] Peter van Inwagen, 'Genesis and Evolution', in Eleonore Stump (ed.), *Reasoned Faith* (Ithaca, NY: Cornell University Press, 1993), 93–127.

need to confine ourselves to that portion of it involving moral or theological teaching.

The common approach underlying these diverse views is well represented in a recent book by Richard Swinburne on revelation.[4] Since this common approach undergirds historically oriented biblical scholarship, which is still the dominant form of current academic research on biblical texts, it will be helpful to pause here and spell out Swinburne's approach in some detail.

Swinburne's Account of Revelation

'The obvious way', Swinburne says, for one person to communicate a message to another 'is to use sentences of normal grammatical forms containing words having their literal senses' (p. 1). There are also other ways, he says, and among these he recognizes metaphors, parables, and models. The first third of his book on revelation is given over to a careful examination of these ways of communicating a message. His concern is to show what we have to know in order to retrieve the message that the message-giver has put into words. First, Swinburne asks how we know what a sentence in a message means or expresses, and his answer is this: 'the statement which a token sentence *s* expresses is that element of claim in what is said which is made by any other token sentence *r* which predicates the same properties of the same individuals, at the same times and places (however the individuals, times and places are picked out); when the properties are the same if and only if the predicates which designate them are synonymous' (p. 11). In order to understand the meaning of a message, however, we need to know many other things in addition. We must understand any metaphors and other figures of speech which the author of the message is employing. The author will also be relying on a host of presuppositions common to his culture or the culture of his audience. We need to be able to separate a statement from the presuppositions behind it, and to do that 'we must ask . . . what were the common beliefs of the culture which they could reasonably presuppose that the speaker shared with them' (p. 31). Furthermore, Swinburne says, 'sentences are normally uttered to convey infor-

---

[4] Richard Swinburne, *Revelation: From Metaphor to Analogy* (Oxford: Clarendon Press, 1992). References to this book are included in the body of the text.

mation in certain particular contexts of enquiry' (p. 37), and we need to know something about the context of enquiry with respect to which sentences are uttered. Messages conveyed in written form have the further complexity that they fall into genres. The message of a written work is dependent on its genre, and genre is in part a function of the 'context of the society in which the work is written' (p. 55).

In order to know what statements the sentences of a particular written work express, we need to be familiar with the social context of that work. In particular, we need to know 'the immediate context of the surrounding sentences (. . . the literary context), the authorship and intended audience (. . . the social context), and the context of the wider culture within which the sentence appears (. . . the cultural context)' (p. 64).

In order to know all the things that Swinburne says we need to know to retrieve a written message, then, we clearly need to know quite a lot of philology, history, and sociology for any text which comes from a culture and language other than our own.

Since a written revelation is tied to a particular culture in these ways, and since a benevolent God would in any case take account of the culture of the people to whom he made the original revelation, it is clear, Swinburne says, that 'the message of a revelation will inevitably become less clear as it is passed from one culture to another' (p. 80). But it helps revelation to be flexible to the needs of different cultures, he says, if God provides for the original revelation to be recorded by different people at different times and in ways which are 'overlapping, stressing different aspects of revelation, and occasionally contradicting each other' (p. 83). In order to have access to revelation, then, each generation will have to determine 'which historical documents contain the original revelation' and to 'ferret out the original teaching'. They will also need to 'make the distinction between the presuppositions of the original documents and their informative content' and 'reinterpret the revelation into the terms of their own culture' (pp. 83–4). In part because of the difficulty of this process, Swinburne argues, a benevolent God would provide for the authority of a Church which would help to interpret revelation to people in subsequent ages.

Here is how Swinburne describes the investigation for learning about the teachings of Jesus, which he takes to be the fullest or most important of God's revelations. 'How are we to know what Jesus Christ did teach?', he asks. 'The primary process for finding that out must be historical investigation of just the same kind as that which would be pursued by historians investigating the teaching of any other teacher. This is the kind of work which New Testament scholars have been doing so very well with rich energy and ingenuity for the past hundred or so years' (p. 103). According to Swinburne, who is here echoing historically oriented biblical scholars, 'the Gospels cannot be taken without caution as straightforward accounts of the teaching or actions of Jesus' (ibid.). We need source criticism to draw our attention to 'the diversity of sources whose information transmitted through various channels reached its final form in the four Gospels. The normal historical tests for accidental error and doctrinal bias must be applied' (pp. 103–4). Then form criticism is required to show us the 'source of distortion' constituted by the use to which Gospel stories were put in teaching or liturgy. We will also need to correct for distortions introduced by the theological use made of Gospel stories; we will need a biblical critic 'to discern the original material underlying its transformed version'. With the help of all the expertise of biblical criticism, Swinburne says, 'the task of discovering some vague outlines of what Jesus said and did, and what happened to him is not . . . an impossible one' (p. 105). Partly because of the slenderness of this evidence, on Swinburne's view, we need to rely on the Church as the divinely appointed interpreter of Jesus' teachings. On Swinburne's view, 'we know a lot more about what Jesus taught than normal historical enquiry reveals. For it would follow [from Swinburne's arguments about the authority of the Church] that he taught what the Church said he taught' (p. 113).

Swinburne's position here is somewhat difficult to understand, I think. He holds simultaneously that the Gospel texts are full of error and distortion, so that it is next to impossible to discern the original message of Jesus in them, and also that the Church is the divinely appointed interpreter of revelation, so that we may safely take our understanding of Jesus' teaching from the Church. But, of course, for most of the history of Christianity the Church (at least in the form of the Roman Catholic Church) taught that the Gospel texts were entirely accurate (even if in need of interpretation on several levels), and it derived its interpretation of Jesus' teaching from the very texts Swinburne finds so deficient. My purpose in this chapter, however, is not to evaluate Swinburne's position. Instead, I want to call attention just to certain features of his account which I think he shares with most historically oriented biblical scholars.

Presuppositions of Swinburne's Account

The first thing to notice about Swinburne's account is that it relies, at least in part, on what we might call a deistic picture of revelation. According to Swinburne, God needs to reveal certain things to human beings, because those things are important for salvation but are otherwise difficult or virtually impossible for people to discover on their own; and the process by means of which God provides this needed revelation, on Swinburne's account, is in one sense (although maybe not in another sense) oddly reminiscent of deistic conceptions of God's creation. The deists supposed that God intervened once to create the world, but after that he let nature take its own course and didn't interfere. Swinburne supposes that at certain points in history God revealed things to particular human beings, but that after those times God let human nature take its course, with the result that the original revelation soon became distorted, confused by cultural misconceptions, and mingled with error to such a degree that the original revelation was hard to discern in it. In the course of Swinburne's book on revelation, it becomes clear that he wants to dissociate himself to some degree from this deistic conception, and it is for this reason that he places a great deal of emphasis on the claim that the Church is the divinely appointed interpreter of revelation, whose views about God's original message may be taken as authoritative. It is not easy to see how that claim is to be reconciled with the deist elements in his account of revelation, but what is most interesting for my purposes here is just the deistic elements themselves.

The deistic picture is the view of revelation taken by most contemporary historically oriented biblical scholars who connect the biblical texts with revelation, and it helps to explain their quest for earlier versions of texts and traditions.[5] On this view, the earlier a document of, or a source for, a particular text, the more likely it is to contain information which is significant or authoritative.[6] The

---

[5] Another explanation for this quest might be a secular attitude towards the texts and a desire to learn about the society in which the text arose or the process by which the text was composed. This explanation, however, doesn't account for the *value* biblical scholars have accorded this quest, which has in the past crowded out virtually all other approaches to the texts, since it is also possible to learn about ancient societies by looking at the final stages of text composition and at the societies which adopted the texts in their final, edited form.

[6] The prima-facie (and perhaps only prima-facie) sense in which this notion is

deistic conception of revelation also underlies the scholarly enterprise of dissolving biblical texts into disparate chunks that can be
sorted by doctrine or ideology, and it provides the motive for
attempting to separate the text into strands associated with different cultural subgroups. On the deistic conception of revelation, we
need to get behind the later or ideologically motivated accretions in
the text and find our way back to the original events or messages in
order to have access to God's revelation.

Furthermore, this deistic conception of revelation accounts for
the emphasis on *historical* biblical scholarship. The historical approach to biblical texts is relatively recent in the long tradition of
biblical studies, and the deistic picture illuminates its concerns. The
scholarship Swinburne discusses—for example, investigations of
the cultures in which the texts arose—is necessary to give us access
to revelation in case God revealed his message at certain points in
time and then left it alone to drift through human history (with or
without the divinely appointed authority of the Church which
Swinburne emphasizes). In order for us now to have access to the
original revelation, we must not only strip away all the accumulated
human noise in the divine signal, but also gain insight into the
attitudes of those to whom the divine message first came. That is
why we need form criticism and source criticism, and that is the
point of requiring expert understanding of all the contexts (literary,
social, and cultural) in which the biblical texts stand. Even the
emphasis on philology and textual criticism characteristic of historically oriented biblical scholarship is explained on the deistic
picture of revelation. As Swinburne holds, unless we have the
correct form of the divine message, in the best manuscripts, and
unless we have expertise in the languages in which the message was
transmitted, the meaning of the message will not be clear to us.

So on the deistic conception, in periods other than that in which
the original revelation occurred, human access to the divine mess-

true is, of course, that documents purporting to record historical events are more
authoritative if they're firsthand and written as soon as possible after the events
were witnessed. I say 'perhaps only prima-facie' because, as everyone knows, the
firsthand eye-witness account of a car accident, say, may be far less reliable than
the police report, written much later and compiled only from indirect evidence of
the event; and (to take another example) Goebbels's diary entries describing events
in Germany in 1939 may be less accurate than a later account compiled by a
historian who was not in Germany at the time. I'm grateful to Norman Kretzmann
for this point.

age will have to be mediated by historically oriented biblical scholarship which has the expertise in manuscripts and languages and in
the history of earlier cultures required to find and comprehend the
earliest sources.

There is one other thing to notice about Swinburne's account of
revelation, and that is the oddness of this deistic picture of revelation. When it comes to *secular* texts, Swinburne's picture of the
transmission of a message is understandable.[7] Take, for example,
Sophocles' *Oedipus Rex*. If we want access to Sophocles and his
ideas, it seems that we must proceed in just the way Swinburne
outlines, beginning with textual criticism and philology and ending
with an expert awareness of Greek history and cultural concerns. It
is crucial to be sensitive to the nuances of Greek terms, to grasp the
Greek notion of *hamartia*, or tragic error, to have an understanding
of the genre of Greek tragedy, and to be aware of common Greek
views on family, oracles, and gods. Without the expertise slowly
acquired by classical scholars since the end of the Middle Ages,
access to Sophocles' ideas will be unavailable to us. Furthermore, it

---

[7] Even for secular literary texts, there is considerable controversy over the
methods by which the text is to be interpreted, as recent developments in the field
of literary criticism make evident, and it is not clear whether the method Swinburne
advocates is the only or the primary method which should be employed in investigating even them. Furthermore, apart from recent developments in literary theory,
there are reasons for wondering whether Swinburne's approach is the right one, or
the only right one, where any text from another period is concerned. In an excellent
recent book, *Defenders of the Text: The Traditions of Scholarship in an Age of
Science 1450–1800* (Cambridge, Mass.: Harvard University Press, 1991), Anthony
Grafton details two stages in the recovery of ancient texts in the Renaissance. In the
first stage, philology and textual criticism were important, but the text resulting from
that scholarship was widely valued because it was thought to hold lessons for the
Renaissance society of the time; the text was consequently taken as an interlocutor
in the political or philosophical discussions of the Renaissance community. In the
second stage, scholars looked down on their predecessors, who seemed to them
historically naïve; these second-stage scholars added detailed historical enquiry to
philology and textual criticism to discover what an ancient text meant in its own
time, and they were reluctant to find in the ancient text any contribution to contemporary Renaissance discussions. Not surprisingly, it was in this stage of the recovery
of ancient texts that widespread interest in the texts began to die away, and that the
texts increasingly came to be the province of a small circle of scholars, who seemed
to others to have only antiquarian interests in the ancient texts. These two stages in
the Renaissance attitude towards texts have contemporary analogues: e.g., in current disagreements among philosophers as to the appropriate way in which to do the
history of philosophy. For the biblical texts, Swinburne's preferred methodology is a
second-stage approach; the methodology of some contemporary feminist or literary
biblical exegesis seems more like a first-stage approach. (I am grateful to Lynn Joy
for calling my attention to Grafton's book.)

is clear that Swinburne's approach is right for biblical texts if the purpose of the scholarship on the texts is only to learn more about those cultures and societies which gave birth to the traditions and documents on which biblical texts are based. So the programme of scholarship which Swinburne outlines and recommends is plausible as a means of studying texts from other times if what we want is information about those other times. What is notably odd is combining this conception of the right method for retrieving messages with the claim that the message is divinely revealed by God because the information in it is crucial for the salvation of all human beings, which is what God very much wants.

There is a certain oddness even in the deistic picture of creation. After all, master craftsmen tend to polish or adjust their creations as time goes by, without our thereby supposing that there was something deficient about their original productions. And even if we suppose that there is more power in producing a product which never needs any further attention, it is most perplexing to suppose that someone with the power and interest to produce persons would arrange for their production and then play no active role in the progress of their lives. Surely, the purpose in producing persons is undercut if the producer avoids active interaction with them. The deistic conception of *revelation* seems to me even odder. The basic explanation for God's making any revelation at all is that the information in the revelation is crucial for the salvation of human beings, which God desires, but that it would be at least very difficult for people to acquire this information if God did not reveal it. On the deistic conception of revelation, however, God reveals the crucial information in such a way that for virtually everybody the information is just as inaccessible as before, only now the difficulty is to gain access to the original revelation. Consequently, on the deistic conception of revelation, God's revealing information doesn't after all make that information readily available to ordinary people, and so the whole point of making a revelation in the first place seems defeated. In fact, one of the main changes effected by divine revelation, on this way of conceiving the process, is to introduce a new élite, the scholars whose expertise is needed to mediate access to God's revelation.

Until relatively recently, historically oriented biblical scholarship was largely a Protestant enterprise, and there is clearly something ironic in that fact. The movement which in its underdog era made biblical texts available to laymen in the vernacular as a revolutionary act and took as its anticlerical watchword 'the priesthood of all believers' insists now, in its establishment days, on the importance of reading the biblical texts in the original languages and requires the technical expertise of academics as intermediary between the unlearned and God's revelation. But the disconcerting sight of this Protestant about-face should not blind us to the real difficulties here. If there is something perplexing about unalloyed deistic conceptions of revelation, what alternatives are there? Even fundamentalist Protestants, whose conservative views of revelation have something in common with the early Montanist accounts, encourage their students to learn Greek and Hebrew in order to have better access to the original message, thereby showing that they share at least something of the deistic conception of revelation: a belief that the best access to the divine message requires reading it in the languages in which God originally conveyed it or caused it to be written down. And perhaps the whole notion of revelation compels this conception. If God has revealed truths at some point in history, then to have access to those truths, isn't it obvious that we need to retrieve the message as he put it into history? Swinburne's thesis, that the Church is the divinely appointed interpreter of Scripture, is an attempt to find some way around this view; but it seems to me not to sit well with the otherwise deistic cast of his understanding of revelation, and to have other problems as well. Certainly, in our own day it is not so easy to figure out what counts as the Church; and when it comes to the interpretation of Scripture, not even individual sects of Christianity speak with one voice.[8]

Historically oriented biblical scholarship seems to me right on this score, at any rate: knowledge of history is in general useful; and in this particular context, an interesting and useful alternative to the deistic conception of revelation can be found in the history of biblical scholarship itself. I want to look at the approach to biblical interpretation found in medieval philosophers and theologians as an alternative to the deistic conception prevalent in our time; in the interest of brevity, I will focus primarily on Aquinas and Augustine.

---

[8] I discuss these issues at more length in my review of Swinburne's book, in *The Philosophical Review*, Oct. 1994.

Aquinas's Approach to Biblical Interpretation

In his various treatments of prophecy and of grace, Aquinas discusses revelation at length, focusing on such issues as the method by which God communicates his message to the individuals who are the sources for, or the authors of, the written texts. These issues are not directly related to the point in question here, namely, the means by which other people retrieve the revealed message from the texts. To grasp Aquinas's thought on this point, it is more important, I think, to look at his biblical commentaries. First, however, it will be helpful to have some understanding of Aquinas's general account of the nature and purpose of revelation.

Aquinas holds the familiar view that revelation is necessary for salvation. Some of the truths revealed could not be found by human reason at all; but even for those truths which reason could attain, it was better that God reveal them. Otherwise, he says, these truths would be available only to a few people and after a long time, with a considerable admixture of error.[9] Unlike the deistic conception of revelation, which seems to hold that revelation is itself available only to a few people, after a long period of study (and, to judge from the lack of consensus in the field of biblical studies, even then with a considerable admixture of error), Aquinas's account of the purpose of revelation has an anti-élitist tone: the purpose of revelation is to make freely available to everyone those truths which otherwise would be inaccessible or which only specially trained intellectuals could attain by themselves.

Since salvation, which is the ultimate aim of revelation, is by faith, the primary purpose of revelation is to nourish faith.[10] Faith, in Aquinas's view, consists in a love of God's goodness and a hatred of our own sin.[11] A major part of the purpose of revelation, then, is to help us see and love God's goodness and to see and hate our own evil. One of the problems with human evil, however, is that it tends to reprogramme our consciences and cognitive faculties in such a

[9] St Thomas Aquinas, *Summa Theologiae* (hereafter *ST*), I, q. 1, a. 1: 'veritas de Deo, per rationem investigata, a paucis, et per longum tempus, et cum admixtione multorum errorum, homini proveniret.'

[10] *ST* I, q. 1, a. 2, sc, where he quotes Augustine to this effect with approval.

[11] I have discussed Aquinas's views on faith in my 'Faith and Goodness', in Scott MacDonald (ed.), *Being and Goodness* (Ithaca, NY: Cornell University Press, 1991), 179–201.

way that we find objectively evil things to be good, or at least acceptable.[12] But because salvation is salvation from sin, there is no salvation without at least as much turning away from sin as is involved in having faith—that is, in hating sin and longing for God's goodness—and both of these require a right recognition of what constitutes sin. Consequently, since sin corrupts moral judgement, our standards of good and evil need to be revised by something external to us. One important function of revelation is to serve as an external standard by which we can measure our judgement and correct for the distorting effects of the evil in us. Revelation constitutes a plumb-line that shows us where we need to tear down and rebuild our standards of good and evil.[13]

Aquinas's working principles with regard to the interpretation of Scripture are just what we might expect from a medieval thinker, but they involve an interesting caveat. Everything in the biblical texts is true, he says, and nothing is contrary to anything else. If it seems that there are contradictions in the biblical texts, there are two possibilities: either we don't understand the text, or our text is corrupt.[14] It is not surprising that with his view of the nature and purpose of the biblical texts Aquinas takes everything in Scripture to be true. On his view, revelation nourishes faith, and in order to do so, given his understanding of the nature of faith and the problem of human evil, revelation must constitute a measure by which we judge ourselves and our standards. If we suppose, however, that the biblical texts contain a mixture of truth and falsity, which it is up to us to separate, then we will have to use our own standards to

---

[12] See e.g. *Super ad Philippenses*, ch. 1, lectura 2, where Aquinas explains that false judgement follows from corrupt habits: 'Cuius ratio est, quia qui habet habitum, si rectus est habitus, sequitur inde rectum iudicium de his quae pertinent ad illum habitum; si vere corruptus, falsum.' I have discussed Aquinas's views on the relation of the intellect and the will in 'Intellect, Will, and the Principle of Alternate Possibilities', in Michael Beaty (ed.), *Christian Theism and the Problems of Philosophy* (Notre Dame, Ind.: University of Notre Dame Press, 1990), 254–85.

[13] Gregory the Great explicitly takes this approach also. At the start of book II of the *Moralia in Job*, he says: 'Holy Writ is set before the eyes of the mind like a kind of mirror, that we may see our inward face in it; for therein we learn the deformities, therein we learn the beauties that we possess; there we are made sensible what progress we are making, there too how far we are from proficiency' (Scriptura sacra mentis oculis quasi quoddam speculum opponitur, ut interna nostra facies in ipsa videatur. Ibi etenim foeda ibi pulchra nostra cognoscimus. Ibi sentimus quantum proficimus, ibi a provectu quam longe distamus) (CCSL 143 (Turnholt: Brepols, 1979), 59).

[14] *Super ad Titum*, ch. 3, lectura 2: 'si aliquid apparet contrarium, vel est, quia non intelligitur, vel quia corrupta sunt vitio scriptorum.'

judge the texts in order to determine which are true and which false. In that case, where our standards come into conflict with something in the texts, we won't struggle with the texts till our standards are revised and we have consequently changed in some way; rather, our standards are likely to lead us to reject passages in the texts as not true or authoritative. So Aquinas's views on the truth and consistency of the biblical texts are predictable. What is surprising is the caveat that our texts may be corrupt. If any given text may be corrupt, it seems that we have the very situation he wanted to avoid: we will have to use our own standards to separate the true texts from the corrupt ones. To understand why his caveat does not seem to him to undermine his position, there are two things that we need to see.

Aquinas and Corrupt Texts

The first thing to notice is that Aquinas is right to worry about the corruption of his texts. From our point of view, many of his texts appear corrupt; in his commentary on Job, for example, his text is often different from texts in common use today. Sometimes the differences are small, if significant, and may reflect translators' interpretations. For example, the RSV translation of Job 21: 30 includes the lines 'the wicked man is spared in the day of calamity, . . . he is rescued in the day of wrath'.[15] The text that Aquinas is commenting on has instead these lines: 'the wicked man is pre-served for the day of perdition . . . he is brought to the day of wrath.'[16] But sometimes the discrepancies are dramatic. Here is the RSV rendering of the lines about Leviathan in Job 41: 12–13: 'I will not keep silence concerning his limbs, or his mighty strength, or his goodly frame. Who can strip off his outer garment? Who can penetrate his double coat of mail?'[17] At this spot in the version of

---

[15] The Anchor Bible has: 'That the wicked is spared the day of disaster. They are delivered from the day of wrath?' The AV has fundamentally the same reading as Aquinas's text.

[16] *Expositio super Job*, ch. 21: 'in diem perditionis servatur malus . . . et ad diem furoris ducitur.'

[17] The AV has: 'I will not conceal his parts nor his power nor his comely proportion. Who can discover the face of his garment? or who can come to him with his double bridle?' The Douay Bible has: 'I will not spare him, nor his mighty words, and framed to make supplication. Who can discover the face of his garment? or who can go into the midst of his mouth?' (In the Douay the passage occurs at 41: 3–4,

the Vulgate that Aquinas is using,[18] the text has these lines: 'I will not spare him for strong words composed to placate. Who will reveal the face of his garment? Who will enter into the middle of his mouth?'[19] It is, of course, possible that both the RSV and the version of the Vulgate that Aquinas is using are based on the same Hebrew, which the translators are reading, or misreading, in different ways. But whether the fault lies in the Hebrew text being translated or in the translators' reading of the text, the upshot is the same. Either way, those whose access to revelation is (or was) mediated solely through the RSV or solely through the text used by Aquinas (or possibly both) have a corrupt version of the text. On the deistic conception of revelation, what we have to say is that if those passages are in some way a part of the divinely revealed message, then Aquinas or those dependent on the RSV (or both) have lost the message at those places.

It is worth pointing out here that we find an analogous situation in the New Testament with respect to the Old Testament. For example, Micah 5: 2 has 'But thou, Bethlehem Ephratah, though thou be little among the thousands of Judah'; whereas Matthew 2: 6, which is apparently citing Micah, says: 'And thou Bethlehem, in the land of Judah, art *not* least among the princes of Judah' (emphasis added)—apparently inserting a negative into the original text. Here the general point is preserved even if the texts are different, but this is not always the case. For example, Hebrews 11: 21 talks about the dying Jacob worshipping on the head of his staff, but Genesis 47: 31 says that he bowed in worship at the head of the bed.[20] And there are other well-known cases in which the New Testament is thought to include a corruption or misquotation of the

since the division into chapters is different at this point.) The Anchor Bible has: 'Did I not silence his boasting, By the powerful word Hayyin prepared? Who can penetrate his outer garment, Pierce his double mail?'

[18] For a discussion of the history of the Vulgate and the different versions of it available in Aquinas's period, see Raphael Loewe, 'The Medieval History of the Latin Vulgate', in G. W. H. Lampe (ed.), *The Cambridge History of the Bible*, ii (Cambridge: Cambridge University Press, 1969, repr. 1988), 80–154.

[19] *Expositio super Job*, ch. 41: 'non parcam ei verbis potentibus et ad deprecandum compositis . . . Quis revelabit faciem indumenti eius? Et in medium oris eius quis intrabit?'

[20] Here the Hebrew words for 'staff' and 'bed' have the same consonants but different vowel points; the Septuagint translators read the points as if the Hebrew word were 'staff'; the Masoretic text reads them as if the word were 'bed'. See Gleason L. Archer, *Encyclopedia of Bible Difficulties* (Grand Rapids, Mich.: Regency Reference Library, Zondervan Press, 1982), 421.

Old. Examples of this sort are often seen as an embarrassment for those Christians who take the biblical texts to be infallibly true.

The second, and more important, thing to notice is the way in which Aquinas handles texts he himself has some reason to suspect might be corrupt. In commenting on the passage in Hebrews which says that all things are open to God's sight, Aquinas is explaining why some things are not known to some cognizers. Sometimes, he says, a thing isn't known because it is hidden in something else; and in this way the things which are most hidden are those that lie concealed in the heart, because the heart is very deep and inscrutable.[21] He wants to support this claim about the nature of the heart with a biblical text, and in fact there is a passage about the heart in Jeremiah which is close to what he wants. It says: 'the heart of man is desperately wicked and inscrutable.'[22] 'However,' Aquinas says, 'the Septuagint translators render this passage, "the heart of man is *deep* and inscrutable".'[23] There is clearly an important difference between these two readings of the passage in Jeremiah, and any contemporary reader would naturally enough assume that only one of these readings could be right. But Aquinas makes no comment on the fact, worrisome to modern readers, that he has two versions of the same passage. On the contrary, he seems to accept *both* readings. Without calling into question the version which attributes wickedness to the heart, he goes on to support his interpretation with the Septuagint rendering of the passage in Jeremiah, apparently because it is the more helpful for understanding the passage in Hebrews that he is in the process of expounding.

It is not hard to find other cases in which Aquinas notes variant readings without any concern and certainly without any attempt to distinguish the genuine from the corrupt reading. For example, in commenting on one passage in Job, he has two readings for a single line, and he simply notes them both without comment: 'and he appends the cause: "for this is the joy of that way"—or "of that life"—that others sprout from the earth again.'[24] Here it seems

---

[21] *Super ad Hebraeos*, ch. 4, lectura 2: 'ex duobus autem contingit, quod aliquid non cognoscatur, scilicet aut quia est intra aliquod occultatum. Et sic maxime sunt occulta, quae latent in corde, quia ipsum est valde profundum et inscrutabile.'

[22] Ibid.: 'pravum est cor hominis et inscrutabilis.'

[23] Ibid.: 'secundum vero septuaginta interpretes habetur sic: profundum est cor hominis etc.'

[24] *Expositio super Job*, ch. 8: 'et causam subiungit dicens "haec est enim laetitia viae eius"—vel "vitae eius"—ut rursum deterra alii germinentur.'

apparent that the problem lies with a scribe, who has either added or omitted a 't' from the Latin word for 'way' (*via*) or 'life' (*vita*).[25] And in another place in the same commentary Aquinas notes two different readings for the same line: '[Elihu] adds: For you said "What is good (another text has 'what is right') does not please You".'[26] The variations between the texts in these cases is perhaps not large or significant. What is important and worth noticing is that Aquinas apparently has no interest in discerning which of the two disparate readings available to him is genuine; without comment or concern, he either cites both readings or simply picks one of the readings and makes it the basis for his subsequent interpretation.

A dramatic example of Aquinas's casual approach to variant readings occurs in his commentary on Titus. He is considering the line in Titus 2: 12 which contains an exhortation to repudiate 'impiety and worldly lusts', and he comments on the passage in this way.

> We should notice that [the Apostle] says 'impiety and worldly lusts' because all sins consist in one of two things. On the one hand, they may be directly against God, and then they are called sins of impiety. For, strictly speaking, piety is that whereby we cherish our parents and our country; but because God is our father most of all, piety pertains to the worship of God. In Job 28, where we have 'Behold, the fear of the Lord, this is wisdom', another text has 'Behold, piety, this is wisdom'. And therefore, sins against God are said to be instances of impiety.[27]

In this case, Aquinas is apparently accepting both variant readings as true and authoritative. However we understand the train of thought in his commentary here, it is clear that he wants to support his reading of the line in Titus with the alternate reading of the passage from Job. On the other hand, he undoubtedly does not mean thereby to reject the common reading which says that the fear of the Lord is wisdom; when he discusses wisdom in *ST*, he

[25] The RSV, the AV, the Douay, and the Anchor Bible have 'way' at this point.

[26] *Expositio super Job*, ch. 35: 'subdens: Dixisti enim "non tibi placet quod bonum est"—alia littera: "quod rectum est".'

[27] *Super ad Titum*, ch. 2, lectura 3: 'notandum est quod dicit impietatem et saecularia desideria, quia omnia peccata vel consistunt in his, quae sunt directe contra deum, quae dicuntur peccata impietatis. Pietas enim proprie est, secundum quam colimus parentes et patriam. Sed quia deus est principalis pater noster, ideo pertinet ad cultum dei pietas. Job 28: secundum aliam litteram, ubi nos habemus sic: ecce, timor domini ipsa est sapientia, habetur: ecce, pietas ipsa est sapientia. Et ideo peccata contra deum dicuntur esse impietates.'

cites the common reading with approval, and he analyses wisdom at least in part in terms of fear of God.[28]

In fact, in the discussion of wisdom in *ST*, he also cites the alternate reading in a way which makes explicit his simultaneous acceptance of both readings. The question is whether wisdom is a gift of the Holy Spirit distinct from other gifts. An objectioñ argues that it isn't and cites both readings of the line from Job. As part of his reply to this objection, Aquinas says: 'Piety manifests wisdom, and therefore it is said that piety is wisdom. So is fear, and for the same reason, because if a person fears and cherishes God, this shows that he has a right judgment about divine matters.'[29] In this case, too, Aquinas shows no interest in sorting out the genuine from the corrupt reading and is apparently content to accept *both* variant readings as true and authoritative.

Aquinas is hardly the only medieval who takes this approach to alternate readings. In commenting on Job 3: 11, Gregory the Great, for example, first gives the reading 'The tiger perishes for lack of prey', and explains the excellent lessons that the text teaches in this line, where Job is compared to a tiger. Then he points out that in a different version of the text the line reads 'The ant-lion perishes for want of prey'. According to Gregory, an ant-lion is an insect which preys on ants.[30] With no noticeable concern over the discrepancy between these two readings Gregory constructs a second, edifying interpretation of the same portion of the text, only this time the lesson is based on the text's comparing Job to the small, fragile ant-lion.[31]

A Dynamic Conception of Revelation

From the point of view of the deistic conception of revelation, this blithe unconcern over the genuine readings of biblical texts is

---

[28] *ST* II-II, q. 45, a. 1, ad 3.

[29] *ST* II-II, q. 45, a. 1, ad 3: 'pietas manifestat sapientiam. Et propter hoc dicitur quod pietas est sapientia. Et eadem ratione timor, per hoc enim ostenditur quod homo rectum habet iudicium de divinis, quod deum timet et colit.'

[30] In order to translate a peculiar Hebrew word, the Septuagint translators compounded Greek terms to produce *myrmekoleon*, 'ant-lion'. Today the term 'ant-lion' refers to any insect of the genus *Myrmeleon*, whose larvae prey on other insects, especially ants.

[31] Gregory the Great, *Moralia in Job*, book v, CLSL, 143, 245–6.

either lamentable or laughable. Only one of the variant readings, at
best, can constitute the text and be part of the original revelation,
and therefore access to divine revelation can come only through
that one reading. How do we account for the very different attitude
of Gregory and Aquinas?

It is helpful here to think again of the analogy between conceptions of revelation and theories of creation. On deistic theories of
creation, God acts once to create the world, and after that he lets
nature take its course. The medievals, on the other hand, favoured
more dynamic theories of creation. On medieval theories of
creation, God's activity is required constantly, at every instant of
time, to sustain and providentially order things in order to conserve
and promote the being of God's creatures. It seems to me that
Aquinas also assumes a dynamic, rather than a deistic, conception
of revelation. On Aquinas's view, the Holy Spirit works in the mind
and heart of every believer to guide, reform, and illuminate. We
can account for the great differences between his approach to
biblical interpretation and that of contemporary scholars by supposing that, on his view, help in getting access to the message of
revelation is included under the illumination of the Holy Spirit.
God puts his message into history in such a way that it serves
its function at that time. But then, rather than letting human
beings, with their unfortunate tendency to accidental or deliberate
distortion, bear the whole responsibility for transmitting the message to others, God also acts in making that message available to
people in different cultures and at subsequent times. Not only is
data input under divine guidance, on this view, but so is data
retrieval.[32]

Furthermore, on the view which seems to me to underlie the
practice of Aquinas's biblical commentaries, revelation is not a
single message. Because of human limitations in power and intel-

---

[32] A variation on this view seems to underlie the Old Testament itself. Michael
Fishbane has recently argued that scribes and exegetes working with the sources
underlying our version of the Hebrew Bible supposed their interpretations of the
text to be themselves inspired by God. They felt free to add interpolations to the
divinely revealed text or source bequeathed to them because they thought that their
reflections on the text were also divinely guided. See e.g. Michael Fishbane, *Biblical
Interpretation in Ancient Israel* (Oxford: Clarendon Press, 1985). This view is not
identical with Aquinas's, because as Fishbane explains it, the Hebrew exegetes felt
that their interpretations were on the same level as the texts they were exegeting. In
that case, we seem to have ongoing, divinely inspired data input, rather than divinely
guided data retrieval.

ligence, human communications are generally static and single-layered. No doubt Sophocles had a certain set of ideas to communicate in *Oedipus Rex*, and we can either get access to those particular ideas or else we fail to communicate with Sophocles. There is no reason, however, why a communication from a person of infinite power and intelligence couldn't be hydra-headed. On this dynamic conception of revelation, God in making his original revelation foresees (or even helps arrange) its coming to Aquinas in one form and to us in another and intends one layer of his message for Aquinas and a different layer of it for us. Even to a single individual, revelation need not take the form of a static message. On the dynamic conception of revelation, we can begin to understand the medieval willingness to embrace simultaneously two conflicting readings of the same text: the same God who allowed the text to flow into these disparate forms can provide (or has even intended) a good and useful layer of his message in each of the disparate readings. What looks like a pathetic indifference to accuracy from the point of view of the deistic conception of revelation seems, from the point of view of the dynamic conception of revelation, to be availing oneself of God's care and the riches of his revealed message.

The difference between the deistic and the dynamic conceptions of revelation can be seen most clearly, I think, by considering the conservative Christian claim that Scripture is the infallibly true revelation of God. On the deistic conception, if this claim should turn out to be true, it would be because in virtually miraculous ways God had provided for the error-free recording of his original message, the error-free scribal transmission of the original record, and the error-free communication of that scribally transmitted message to people in other periods of time. On the dynamic conception of revelation, this quasi-miraculous preservation of the original message is not necessary for the infallible truth of revelation. The claim that the biblical texts are infallible could be true just in virtue of the fact that the Holy Spirit makes available to individual believers some layer of God's infallibly true revelation, divinely intended for them, on the basis of the texts those believers have. On this view, the action of God's spirit in the hearts and minds of believing readers brings it about that what they can learn with their cognitive tools from the texts they have is true and constitutes a layer of revelation useful for them at that time.

The difference between the two conceptions of revelation also has implications for the history of biblical exegesis itself. When it comes to exegeting biblical texts, historically oriented biblical scholars have not had much interest in the history of biblical exegesis before the rise of their own discipline, and it is not hard to see why. On the deistic conception, there is little point in reading the biblical commentaries of exegetes such as Aquinas and Gregory who do not have access to critical editions and who lack understanding of the original languages. Their commentaries may be of antiquarian interest, but, given the deistic view of revelation, such medieval exegetes can provide very little help in understanding the biblical texts. On the dynamic conception of revelation, however, even Christian exegetes who employ allegorizing methods of interpretation on corrupt texts may have access to some significant aspect of the divine message. And so, on this view of revelation, one may profitably embrace a range of Christian exegesis, in somewhat the same spirit as Aquinas adopts different variants of the same biblical text, in the conviction that the different readings or interpretations make it possible for believing readers to find different layers of God's many-layered revelation.

Furthermore, on the dynamic conception of revelation, it makes no sense to hunt, as historically oriented biblical scholarship does, for the seams and joints of biblical texts in order to decompose them into their earlier and later parts. It isn't necessary to get back to the earliest sources in order to have access to God's revelation. Of course, if one does find the earliest sources and interpret the messages in them, one *will* have access to revelation—though only to one layer of it—but one can also have access to revelation in a fruitful form without that historical excavation. A similar point holds even for textual criticism and philology. On the deistic conception of revelation, we must read the message of revelation in the original languages as found in the best manuscripts available. But on the dynamic conception, the production of manuscripts and translations is also under the guidance of God, who means his message, or some layers of it, to be directly accessible also to the unscholarly. Augustine recognizes that the Septuagint differs widely in places from the Hebrew, whose authority he acknowledges. None the less, he says, 'in all the more learned churches it is now said that this translation was so inspired by the Holy Spirit that many men spoke as if with the mouth of one. . . . Therefore, even though something is found in Hebrew versions different from what they have set down, . . . it may be that the Holy Spirit judged that they should translate in a manner befitting the people whom they addressed.'[33]

Anaesthesia and Elephant Testicles

It is important to pause here to ward off one possible misconception concerning this view of revelation. It would be a mistake to suppose that on this view no interpretations are wrong; nothing in the dynamic conception of revelation entails that interpreters— even Christian interpreters—will always be *successful* in reading the text in such a way as to learn something good and true from it. This conception of revelation entails that interpretations don't *have to* go wrong because of deficiencies in the texts or their transmission; it doesn't follow that interpretations always have to be right and true to God's message. There are two sorts of ways in which interpretations can go wrong, even on this conception of revelation.

In the first place, as the proverb says, the Devil can quote Scripture for his own purposes; and it is abundantly clear that throughout the history of Christianity some Christians have produced devilish interpretations of biblical texts, citing them as warrant for malice and cruelty, torture and war, oppression and exploitation of the poor and helpless. To take just one example out of many that could be given, consider nineteenth-century objections to obstetric anaesthesia on the grounds of a particular construction of Genesis 3: 13–16. One nineteenth-century medical practitioner, opposed to the use of any anaesthesia during childbirth, warned that '*mothers* would consult their own happiness, to say nothing of health, by fulfilling the edict of bringing forth children "in sorrow"'.[34] What should be said about such cases?

---

[33] Augustine, *De doctrina christiana*, trans. D. W. Robertson, Jun., Library of Liberal Arts (New York: Bobbs-Merrill, 1958), 49; CCSL, 32 (Turnholt: Brepols, 1962), 47–8; 'qui iam per omnes peritiores ecclesias tanta praesentia sancti spiritus interpretati esse dicuntur ut os unum tot hominum fuerit. . . . Quamobrem etiamsi aliquid aliter in heraeis exemplaribus invenitur quam isti posuerunt . . . itaque fieri potest, ut sic illi interpretati sint, quemadmodum congruere gentibus ille . . . spiritus sanctus iudicavit.'

[34] See Martin S. Pernick, *A Calculus of Suffering* (New York: Columbia University Press, 1985), 50. Even if this interpretation is right about the text and its translation at this point, one might suppose that the very thought of the world into which one was bringing a helpless and vulnerable child would be enough to guarantee that any mother would bring forth her children in sorrow.

On the deistic conception of revelation, it is perfectly *possible* (whether ever actual or not) that immoral biblical interpretations, those warranting harmful or vicious actions, are not the fault of the interpreters but rather are the unfortunate result of problems with the texts themselves: editorial distortions, scribal errors, accidents of manuscript transmission, or bad translations, to say nothing of the problems resulting from readers' ignorance of the presuppositions of other cultures requisite for proper interpretation even of good translations of critical editions. On this way of understanding the nature of revelation, then, it is possible that even those who trusted in God and were obedient to what they took to be his revelation might find themselves, through no fault of their own, betrayed into actions which God himself would detest. On the dynamic concept of revelation, however, this possibility is ruled out, and the sort of excuse for evil made possible by the deistic conception is never available. Whatever the scholarly inadequacies of the text or the interpreter, the Holy Spirit makes *accessible* to the believing reader some message which is true and good.

But from the fact that a wholesome interpretation is made accessible, it doesn't follow that every believer will succeed in finding it. The medieval position here may be thought of as akin to certain medieval views of grace. From the fact that grace is available to all, it doesn't follow that all receive it. Just as the will and the intellect warped by sin may turn away from grace, so sin may block divine illumination for a reader of a biblical text and result in some reprehensible reading instead. When a reader draws a morally reprehensible interpretation from a text, on the dynamic conception of revelation the fault lies entirely with the reader, whose will and cognitive faculties are undermined by sin. Furthermore, in such a reader, faith is deficient, because even if he loves God's goodness (as faith requires), in virtue of his own sinfulness he has a wrong or perverted sense of what God's goodness consists of.[35]

---

[35] A good example of this sort of wrong exegesis can be found in some of the writings or sayings of Oliver Cromwell: e.g., Cromwell was convinced that Puritan England was the new Israel, and that therefore various Old Testament writings should be interpreted as referring to the Puritan army. Before the terrible Puritan massacres of the Irish, Cromwell told his men that they were 'Israelites about to extirpate the idolatrous inhabitants of Canaan' (see Antonia Fraser, *Cromwell. The Lord Protector* (New York: Donald I. Fine, Inc., 1973), 327). The consequences of this biblical interpretation on Cromwell's part are well known. In the slaughter at Drogheda, for instance, Cromwell ordered that no quarter should be given; and between 2,000 and 4,000 people died, including non-combatant Catholic religious,

In the second place, there are obviously interpretations which are just false, but not immoral as well. In so far as an interpreter arrives at such interpretations through some actions or dispositions for which blame is appropriate—stubborn disregard of evidence, proud unwillingness to change his mind, and so on—these cases may be assimilated to those involving sin. But there remain cases where the interpretation includes something false but not reprehensible and where no blame is to be imputed to the interpreter. So, for example, in interpreting Job 40: 10–19, which discusses behemoth (an animal Aquinas supposes to be an elephant), Aquinas has recourse to the best authority available to him on the biology of elephants—namely, Aristotle.[36] In weaving together the best scientific knowledge he can get with the best reading of the text he can produce, he interprets 40: 12 this way: it means that the tendons of elephant testicles are tangled. I have no knowledge of this subject, and, unlike Aquinas, I have no contemporary expert on the subject readily available to me. None the less, it seems to me entirely possible that Aquinas is wrong on the subject of the tendons of elephant testicles and therefore also wrong in his interpretation of this text. Suppose he is.[37] What account of such cases can be given by the dynamic conception of revelation?

On the dynamic conception of revelation, the point of revelation is the communication of a divine message necessary for the salvation and sanctification of human beings. On this view, God influences the access to his revelation in such a way that it is *possible* for readers to find interpretations which further the goal of salvation, even if they do not have the scholarly tools to get access to the original text or message. But the guarantee of access is for those parts of the message which are relevant to the purpose of revelation: sanctification and salvation. Nothing about this account entails that there also be guaranteed access to truths about the tendons of elephant testicles, for example, a subject that seems

women, and children. Cromwell's report to Parliament of this massacre summed it up in these words: 'I am persuaded that this is a righteous judgment of God upon these barbarous wretches' (reported in ibid. 338).

[36] It is noteworthy that Aquinas's procedure consists of reading a scientific authority in order to know how to interpret the biblical text, rather than interpreting the biblical text as a check on scientific authority.

[37] If he isn't wrong on the tendons of elephant testicles, then he is bound to be wrong somewhere in his long and rather bizarre explanation of the nature of elephant genitals and copulation practices.

irrelevant to sanctification and salvation. Where interpretations play a role in the process of salvation, the dynamic conception of revelation expects God to make accessible to readers interpretations which are good and true. Just because of the emphasis on this purpose of revelation, this conception of revelation provides no similar guarantees for those parts of interpretations which don't play such a role. So the goal of revelation is compatible with the existence of interpretations which are false but harmless, even in cases where it is not appropriate to blame the interpreter for the falsity of the interpretation.

Does this view, then, differ in any material way from that of Peter van Inwagen described earlier? I think it does. Van Inwagen supposes that since God had to tailor his original message to primitive people, the original divine message itself will be true only as regards those elements relevant to salvation. The difference between his view and the dynamic conception of revelation can be seen by considering what happens when some interpretation supposed to yield true information, such as Aquinas's interpretation involving the tendons of elephant testicles, is shown to contain falsehood instead.

On van Inwagen's view, we may simply have to recognize that the passage of the text on which that interpretation was based itself contains a part of the divine message which isn't true; even if the text accurately reflects the original divine message, the text itself is false. This view has the effect of, as it were, shrinking what counts as revelation: as scientific knowledge, for example, increases, more of the biblical texts will need to be rejected as false. On the other hand, on the dynamic conception of revelation, according to which revelation has many layers, there is no reason why God could not provide a message in such a way that it seemed true both to primitive people and to people in scientifically informed cultures, by making different layers of his message available to different groups at different times. On this view, when comparative anatomy shows that the tendons of elephant testicles are not tangled, what is to be rejected is not the text, but the interpretation which includes the wrong explanation of elephant testicles. Unlike the reader who holds van Inwagen's view, after his initial interpretation has been shown wrong (say, by comparative anatomy) a reader with the dynamic conception of revelation will continue to struggle with the text, looking for interpretations which are true and good.

Perhaps the most important practical difference between these two views is this: A reader coming to the biblical texts with van Inwagen's view must retain an attitude of suspicion towards the texts, which may contain a part of the original revelation which is false. A reader with the dynamic conception of revelation, on the other hand, trusts the texts to be true and good but is suspicious of himself as someone beset with ignorance and inclined to wrong judgement. If the medievals are right about the effect of moral evil on cognitive faculties, or if Aquinas and Gregory are right that one of the functions of the biblical text is to act as an external measure of human judgement, then the dynamic conception of revelation yields safer results.

Another Possible Misconception

Besides the philosophical misconception of the dynamic view of revelation just discussed, it is important also to ward off a historical misconception. It would be a misimpression to suppose that the medievals showed no concern whatsoever for the original message of revelation. They certainly did have such a concern. In 1236, for example, the Dominican Chapter General mandated that the Order's Bibles be standardized, to purge the corruptions which had crept into some versions of the Vulgate; and in 1256, when the earlier mandate had apparently remained unfulfilled, the Dominicans made another attempt at a standardization based on corrections made by Hugh of St Cher, prior of the Paris house.[38] Furthermore, the concerns of historical biblical scholarship, including its attendant emphasis on philology, were not unknown in the Middle Ages. Augustine in *De doctrina christiana* recommends that biblical exegetes acquire Greek and Hebrew, and some medievals did so. Robert Grosseteste, for example, learned Greek, studied the New Testament in Greek, and read Greek commentators. There were even some notable Hebrew scholars, particularly at the school of St Victor in Paris. And in 1311–12 the Church at the Council of Vienne decreed that chairs for the teaching of Greek, Hebrew, Aramaic, and Arabic should be established at Paris, Bologna, Salamanca, and Oxford.[39]

---

[38] Loewe, 'Medieval History of the Latin Vulgate', 146–9.
[39] See Beryl Smalley, 'The Bible in the Medieval Schools', in G. W. H. Lampe

Aquinas himself had a number of versions of the Vulgate available to him and used different ones as the occasion warranted. For example, in commenting on the Psalms he relied largely on the Gallican version of the Psalter, although elsewhere he also used the Roman Psalter.[40] Furthermore, perhaps more than most medieval biblical exegetes before him, Aquinas was concerned with the literal, rather than the allegorical, interpretation of biblical texts; and he showed some concern to understand the divine message in its original form. For example, in commenting on a passage in Hebrews Aquinas rejected an interpretation on the grounds that it isn't in accord with the 'intention of the Apostle'.[41] He even showed some concern with the historical setting of biblical texts; in one place in his commentary on the Gospel of John, for example, he explained a biblical passage by reference to what he took to have been a common theological position among ancient Jews.[42]

How are we to reconcile this evidence about the medieval attitude towards historically oriented biblical scholarship with the rest of what we have seen of the medieval approach to biblical exegesis?

The first thing to notice is that in spite of what this evidence might suggest, actual medieval interest in biblical history and biblical languages is slight. Augustine, for example, did not follow his own recommendation; he himself never acquired Hebrew and had only a small acquaintance with Greek. And, in general, Robert Grosseteste seems to have been something of an exception to the rule in his mastery of the original language of the New Testament. Furthermore, although there was a Jewish convert, John of Bristol, teaching Hebrew and Greek at Oxford in 1320–1, the injunction of the Council of Vienne to establish chairs in ancient languages remained something of a dead letter.[43] Aquinas was concerned to

(ed.), *The Cambridge History of the Bible*, ii (Cambridge: Cambridge University Press, 1969, repr. 1988), 197–220. Loewe, 'Medieval History', 152.

[40] James Weisheipl, *Friar Thomas d'Aquino. His Life, Thought, and Works*, 2nd edn. (Washington, DC: Catholic University of America Press, 1983), 369.

[41] *Super ad Hebraeos*, ch. 11, lectura 2: 'unde dicit et per illam defunctus adhuc loquitur, quia, ut dicit glossa, "post mortem adhuc commendatur fides eius, quia datur nobis materia loquendi de ipso, ut de fide eius, et patientia demus exempla ad exhortandum alios ad patientiam." Sed haec non est intentio apostoli, quia omnia, quae accepit hic sumit ex scripturis.'

[42] *Super Evangelium Johannis*, ch. 1, lectura 12; for a translation of this passage, see *Commentary on the Gospel of St John*, trans. James Weisheipl and Fabian Larcher (Albany, NY: Magi Books, 1980), 108.

[43] See Loewe, 'Medieval History'.

have good translations of Aristotle and made special efforts to gain access to Greek biblical commentators, but he did not show the same concern to make his way to the Greek of the New Testament. As for Hebrew, his knowledge of the nature of that language is so rudimentary as to be almost comic. In explaining why the same place is sometimes called 'Salem' in his biblical texts and sometimes 'Salim', he says: 'among the Jews a reader may use any vowel he chooses in the middle of his words; hence it made no difference to the Jews whether it was pronounced Salim or Salem.'[44] The historical concerns most often evinced by Aquinas are not directed towards the languages and cultures of the biblical texts but are focused instead, as we might expect on the dynamic conception of revelation, on acquainting himself with the efforts of earlier Christian commentators. He seems to have made little use of the *correctoria* of biblical texts available during his time. In his whole lengthy commentary on Job, he mentions alternate readings of the text only twice. On the other hand, Weisheipl, who has counted the citations in one of Aquinas's commentaries (on the Gospel of John), reports that he cites Augustine 373 times, John Chrysostom 217 times, and Origen 93 times.[45]

Augustine's attitude in *De doctrina christiana* is, I think, representative of the medieval approach to historically oriented biblical exegesis. After having explained for many pages what is necessary to find the intention of the human author of a biblical text—philology, history, and the rest—Augustine considers what happens if an exegete is not successful and does not manage to understand the biblical author's intention. In that case, he says, 'the Spirit of God, who worked through that author, undoubtedly foresaw that this meaning would occur to the reader or listener. Rather, he *provided* that it might occur to him' (emphasis added).[46] And in another place he says, 'Whoever finds a lesson there [in the biblical text] useful to the building of charity, even though he has not said what the author may be shown to have intended in that place, has not been deceived . . . [or] if he is deceived in an interpretation

---

[44] *Super Evangelium Johannis*, ch. 3, lectura 4; *Commentary*, tr. Weisheipl and Larcher, 208: 'apud iudaeos, lector pro voluntate uti potest vocalibus litteris in medio dictionum: unde, sive dicatur salim, sive salem, non refert apud iudaeos.' I have taken the translation from Weisheipl and Larcher.

[45] *Commentary*, tr. Weisheipl and Larcher, 12.

[46] *De doctrina christiana*, 102; CCSL, p. 100: 'dei spiritus, qui per eum haec operatus est, etiam ipsam occursuram lectori vel auditori sine dubitatione praevidit, immo ut occurreret, quia et ipsa est veritate subnixa, providit.'

which builds up charity, which is the end of the commandments, he is deceived in the same way as a man who leaves a road by mistake but passes through a field to the same place toward which the road itself leads'.[47]

Augustine's metaphor of a journey is helpful here, I think. The faithful traveller will recognize that he has a duty to do what he can to increase his chances of getting to his destination: he will consult maps, equip himself for the journey, and so on, as he is able. If he is able to take such prudent steps but doesn't, if in reliance on God's providence he simply sets out without any preparations whatsoever, or, worse, goes off in some direction he should or does know to be wrong, he is presumptuous, and the results of his expedition may be such as to teach him a better way of proceeding. On the other hand, if his ability to make the necessary preparations is limited and yet he must still make the journey, he may safely trust in God's care for him, even if like Paul he is assaulted, detained, or shipwrecked *en route*. Since divine activity is at work in the original input of revelation into history, the goal of an exegete includes gaining access also to that input; and he should take what steps he can to attain that goal. That is why Augustine recommends historical and philological study. On the other hand, since the message of revelation is many-layered and data retrieval is also under divine guidance, an exegete who misses the meaning of the original input may be taking a detour to the same goal. God will not only have foreseen but even have arranged affairs in such a way that it is *possible* for the exegete to have access to some layer of the divine message. In the case of the Septuagint, Augustine goes so far as to suppose that God prefers the Christians of that time to have the divine message derived from the translated text rather than the message in the original texts.

Given this sort of attitude, it is not surprising that in spite of his own recommendations, even Augustine apparently felt no urgency about acquiring scholarly tools for biblical exegesis or that interpreters such as Gregory and Aquinas felt free to accept simultaneously two or more conflicting readings of the same biblical

---

[47] Ibid. 30–1; CCSL, p. 29: 'Quisquis vero talem inde sententiam duxerit, ut huic aedificandae caritati sit utilis, nec tamen hoc dixerit, quod ille quem legit eo loco sensisse probabitur, non perniciose fallitur . . . si ea sententia fallitur, qua aedificet caritatem, quae finis praecepti est, ita fallitur, ac si quisquam errore deserens viam eo tamen per agrum pergat quo etiam via illa perducit.'

passage. On the dynamic conception of revelation, the divine message is accessible even without historically oriented scholarship; it is as available to the unlearned as to academic experts.

Augustine's Constraints and Requirements

At this point, any appeal which the dynamic conception of revelation may have by virtue of its anti-élitist approach to revelation may seem more than offset by the apparently alarming subjectivism of its approach. If revelation is many-layered and data retrieval is under divine guidance, then it seems as if any faithful interpretation based on any text, however corrupt, gives us equally good access to the divine message. Furthermore, it isn't clear any more why God should bother with a written revelation at all, since on the dynamic conception of revelation God provides different layers of the divine message for different individuals. Why shouldn't God omit public texts altogether and simply provide private revelations to each individual?

In one sense, Augustine accepts these implications of the dynamic conception of revelation. The common revelation in written texts is unnecessary for the holy, on his view. '[A] man supported by faith, hope, and charity, with an unshaken hold upon them, does not need the Scriptures . . . and many live by these three things in solitude without books. . . . in these persons . . . the saying is already exemplified, ". . . prophecies shall be made void, . . . tongues shall cease, . . . knowledge shall be destroyed". In them . . . such an erudition has been erected that, holding fast to that which is perfect, they do not seek that which is only partially so.'[48] On the other hand, for ordinary people, though God could make his message known through private revelation, the needs of human beings give him a reason not to do so. In private revelation there is a temptation to pride which is dangerous for ordinary people, and conversely, there is something humbling to pride about revelation which can be attained only by going through a common text. The

[48] Ibid. 32; CCSL, p. 31: 'Homo itaque fide et spe et caritate subnixus eaque inconcusse retinens non indiget scripturis. . . . Itaque multi per haec tria etiam in solitudine sine codicibus vivunt. Unde in illis arbitror iam impletum esse, quod dictum est: "*Sive prophetiae evacuabuntur, sive linguae cessabunt, sive scientia evacuabitur*" . . . tanta . . . in eis surrexit instructio, ut *perfectum* aliquid tenentes ea, quae sunt ex parte, non quaerant.'

communal nature of the texts of revelation also helps to draw people away from their focus on their own individual good and to remind them of the common good of all. In that way, the common, public means by which the divine message is transmitted helps to correct for corrupt human tendencies to prefer personal power and pleasure to greater goods.

What about the subjectivity of the medieval method for gaining access to this communal revelation?

The first thing to say about it, I think, is that it would be a great mistake to suppose there is any method whatsoever for dealing with texts which is not also highly prone to subjectivity. Certainly, historically oriented biblical studies thinks of itself as an objective—even a scientific—discipline, and nothing in its methodology for dealing with the texts obviously invites subjectivity. Anyone familiar with contemporary historical biblical scholarship, however, can testify to the enormous range of interpretations that the discipline has produced and the great variability of opinions within the field; there are often as many interpretations of a passage as there are scholars writing on it. Textual interpretations on any method, then, are unavoidably laced with subjectivity.

The second thing to say about this worry is that the medievals shared it and tried to provide some hedges against it. On the dynamic conception of revelation, the best access to the divine message in the texts is gained by an interpretation based on faith. It is, of course, not immediately clear what reading the text with faith amounts to; but in *De doctrina christiana*, Augustine lists a series of guide-lines for interpretation, which give some content to the notion of reading with faith and which help keep this method of interpretation from the worst perils of subjectivism. It is not possible in this short space to present and discuss all his guide-lines, but it will be useful to look at some of the most important ones.

To begin with, he assumes that all truth is God's truth and that faith and reason are therefore compatible. Consequently, he adopts the commonsensical requirement that the biblical texts must be intelligible; they must make sense. Human feet aren't sharp, though they can be swift; and so the reading of a passage which includes the claim that someone's feet are sharp to shed blood should be rejected in favour of the reading of that line which says that they are *swift* to shed blood.[49] Furthermore, for the same reason, Augustine

---

[49] Ibid. 45 CCSL, p. 44: 'Et ex ambiguo linguae praecedentis plerumque interpres fallitur, cui non bene nota sententia est, et eam significationem transfert, quae a

expects the biblical texts to be consistent with truths about the world, and he is quite capable of rejecting an interpretation on the grounds that it violates the best science of his day. Finally, because the biblical texts are common to all believers, interpretations should not contradict consensus among believers about religious doctrine. The more important the doctrine, the more weight should be given to the consensus, since it seems wrong to suppose that God would allow the great majority of believers to be altogether mistaken about important doctrines. So, for example, interpretations which deny some central attribute of God or salvific property of Christ which orthodox Christianity is committed to are for that reason to be ruled out.[50] For Christians of Augustine's time and later, then, Christian tradition forms a constraint on interpretation. These guide-lines can be summed up by saying that Augustine requires interpretations of biblical texts to be consistent with the rest of what we see—on the basis of reason or faith—to be the truth.

Because he thinks that faithful reading of the texts requires the assumption that the biblical texts are wholly true, Augustine also holds that an interpretation of a particular passage needs to be squared with all the rest of the biblical text. For Augustine, as for Aquinas, there is no inconsistency in revelation. This requirement doesn't provide much more than a general constraint on the philosophical and theological implications of interpretations, however, because of the way in which medieval exegetes find consistency in the texts. In this respect, medieval interpretation is just the mirror image of contemporary historically oriented biblical exegesis. Both the medieval and the contemporary approach to the texts consist in techniques for harmonizing apparent tensions in the texts, but the contemporary approach relies on division. At any point at which the contemporary approach detects a tension, it divides the text into at least two simpler, underlying sources, each tension-free. The medieval approach, on the other hand, relies on multiplication. Where biblical texts appear to assign different attributes to the same thing or event, the medieval interpreters assume that there were at least two such things or events with

sensu scriptoris penitus aliena est, sicut quidam codices habent: *Acuti pedes eorum ad effundendum sanguinem;* ὀξύς enim et acutum apud Graecos et velocem significat. Ille ergo vidit sententiam, qui transtulit: *Veloces pedes eorum ad effundendum sanguinem.*'

[50] Cf. ibid. 79; CCSL, p. 78.

somewhat different attributes. There must have been two places called 'Bethany', Aquinas says; that is why Matthew locates Bethany near Jerusalem but John has it on the far side of Jordan, a good way from Jerusalem.[51]

Augustine also has an overarching requirement which is just an explicit constraint on the theological and philosophical implications of any exegesis: if the point of revelation is to promote human salvation, then any faithful interpretation must also nurture love of God and goodness. 'Whoever . . . thinks that he understands the divine Scriptures or any part of them so that it does not build the double love of God and of our neighbour does not understand it at all,' Augustine says.[52] The same point serves him as a criterion for deciding on the appropriateness of allegorical interpretation: 'whatever appears in the divine Word that does not literally pertain to virtuous behaviour or to the truth of faith you must take to be figurative. Virtuous behaviour pertains to the love of God and of one's neighbour; the truth of faith pertains to a knowledge of God and of one's neighbour.[53] So, on Augustine's view, any interpretation which somehow hinders our love of God or our love of our neighbours is a mistaken one. This is a broad requirement on biblical interpretation, but it will rule out, for instance, any interpretation of a text which shows God cruel or unjust. According to Augustine, then, we should start by assuming not only that the biblical texts are true but also that they show us the goodness of God and encourage us to the love of other people. The difference here between Augustine and some contemporary Christian exegetes is that Augustine uses the requirement to rule out interpretations, whereas some contemporaries are inclined to use it to rule out texts. For example, one author in a recent book on revelation maintains that the Old Testament story in which God commands the killing of women and children is not part of revelation because it attributes a cruel and unjust action to

---

[51] *Super Evangelium Johannis; Commentary*, tr. Weisheipl and Larcher, 116–17: 'quod est duplex bethania: una quae est prope ierusalem . . . , alia trans iordanum, ubi erat ioannes baptizans.'

[52] *De doctrina christiana*, 30; CCSL, p. 29: 'Quisquis igitur scripturas divinas vel quamlibet earum partem intellexisse sibi videtur, ita ut eo intellectu non aedificet istam geminam caritatem dei et proximi, nondum intellexit.'

[53] Ibid. 88; CCSL, p. 86: 'quicquid in sermone divino neque ad morum honestatem neque ad fidei veritatem proprie referri potest, figuratum esse cognoscas. Morum honestas ad diligendum deum et proximum, fidei veritas ad cognoscendum deum et proximum pertinet.'

God.[54] On Augustine's requirement, the text is to be accepted as true and authoritative, but the interpretation whose implication is that God is cruel and unjust is ruled out as false or confused.

These and other requirements of Augustine's spell out the implications, as he sees them, of believing that the biblical texts constitute the revelation of an omniscient, omnipotent, perfectly good God who intends his revelation as an aid towards human salvation. Clearly, no method or set of rules can prevent considerable subjectivity in the interpretation of texts, but these requirements of Augustine's, which I think generally underlie the practice of medieval biblical exegesis, mitigate significantly the subjectivity of the dynamic conception of revelation.

A Remaining Difficulty

One serious difficulty remains, however, because on the dynamic conception it is hard to see how the biblical texts can serve the purpose which Aquinas (and other medievals) assign them. On Aquinas's view, revelation serves as a measure by which we assess and correct our view of ourselves and our standards of good and evil; it helps to correct for the warping effects of evil on judgement by showing us God's goodness and letting us revise our standards accordingly. The point of insisting that the texts contain only truths and no errors is in part to keep readers from using their standards to judge the text and to insist that the text serve as judge of its readers. But on the dynamic conception of revelation biblical interpretations can float free from the meaning of the text as intended by the original human author and yet still consist in access to revelation. It seems, then, that interpreters could simply read their own standards into the biblical text and use the dynamic conception of revelation to assure themselves that the resulting interpretations were what they were intended to glean from the texts. Augustine himself recognizes a problem very like this one.

---

[54] Stephen T. Davis, *The Debate about the Bible* (Philadelphia: Westminster Press, 1977), 96–7. Similarly, in a recent paper Philip Quinn argues that the story of Abraham and Isaac should not be accepted as a part of revelation, on the grounds that, according to the story, God puts Abraham into an insoluble moral dilemma, and such an action is incompatible with the goodness of God (Philip Quinn, 'Agamemnon and Abraham: The Tragic Dilemma of Kierkegaard's Knight of Faith', *Journal of Literature and Theology*, iv (1990), 181–93).

'[H]umanity', he says, 'is inclined to estimate sins . . . on the basis of their own customs, so that they consider a man to be culpable in accordance with the way men are reprimanded and condemned ordinarily in their own place and time. . . . [I]f Scripture commends something despised by the customs of the listeners, or condemns what those customs do not condemn, they take the Scriptural locution as figurative if they accept it as an authority [at all].'[55]

One way of handling cases in which a biblical text conflicts with a reader's moral standards, for both Augustine and Aquinas, is to abstain from judgement. A reader can decide that he does not understand the text and can consequently hold judgement in abeyance. But as a palliative for the problem that on the dynamic conception of revelation Christian readers will tend to produce interpretations which simply embody their own moral standards, Augustine also makes two recommendations.

Christian interpreters, he says, should approach with special diffidence any passage that appears to be in conflict with their own moral standards. In such cases readers should be wary of themselves and search particularly carefully for a literal interpretation of the text.[56] We must not contradict the text, he says, even when 'we feel as though we are wiser than it is and better able to give precepts. But we should rather think and believe that which is written to be better and more true than anything which we could think of by ourselves.'[57] The interpretation which stems from such a diffident struggling with the text must not overthrow a reader's standards of good and evil, as if God's standards were utterly alien from our own, but it might succeed in stretching or deepening the reader's standards. The resulting interpretation is still subject to Augustine's constraint that no biblical interpretation can deny the goodness of God or discourage love of neighbour, but it might refine a reader's views of the nature of divine goodness or human love.

---

[55] *De doctrina christiana*, 88; CCSL, pp. 86–7: 'Sed quoniam proclive est humanum genus non ex momentis ipsius libidinus, sed potius suae consuetudinis aestimare peccata, fit plerumque, ut quisque hominum ea tantum culpanda arbitretur, quae suae regionis et temporis homine vituperare atque damnare consuerunt . . . si quid scriptura vel praeceperit, quod abhorret a consuetudine audientium, vel quod non abhorret culpaverit, si animum eorum iam verbi vinxit auctoritas, figuratam lectionem putent.'

[56] Ibid. 87; CCSL, p. 86.

[57] Ibid. 38–9; CCSL, p. 37: 'nos melius sapere meliusque praecipere possimus, sed cogitare potius et credere id esse melius et verius, quod ibi scriptum est, etiam si lateat, quam id, quod nos per nos ipsos sapere possumus.'

In addition to this practical recommendation, Augustine addresses the problem of moral subjectivity in interpretation in a second, more comprehensive way. Before an exegete proceeds to interpret the biblical texts, Augustine says, he must exercise himself with fear of God, meekness and piety, knowledge of God's precepts, a hunger and thirst for righteousness, mercy, and moral purification. In other words, Augustine supposes that the danger of misconstruing revelation because of one's own moral evil is significant and that no formulaic constraint on interpretations is sufficient to remove it. That is why he supposes that the first business of exegetes, before any scholarly pursuits, must be moral training and moral growth.

Both these recommendations of Augustine's go some way towards alleviating the problem of the moral complacency of interpreters. But, given the main concern of this chapter, what is also worth noticing about this line of Augustine's is that it shows that Augustine does accept hierarchy with regard to the availability of revelation. Because, according to Augustine, the human tendency to moral evil is a hindrance in gaining access to revelation and because the best way around that hindrance is moral purification, those who have made more moral progress will have better or deeper access to revelation.[58] He is not claiming that only the morally good can interpret the texts appropriately, but he is suggesting that depth and excellence in interpretation are a function of moral progress. So the dynamic conception of revelation also recognizes some hierarchy when it comes to access to revelation, but the basis of the hierarchy is moral goodness.

Conclusion

A study of medieval philosophical biblical exegesis, then, is useful in the way all history of philosophy is useful: it shows us that our ordinary, unreflective way of approaching a concept or problem is not the only worthwhile way of doing so. In the dynamic concep-

[58] Perhaps it goes without saying that Augustine is committed to objective moral standards and that the moral progress at issue here is also an objective moral progress. Those who suppose that they are making moral progress but who in fact grow further away from the love of God's goodness and the love of their neighbours are simply mistaken in their view of themselves as making moral progress. I take those who supposed that they were making moral progress by burning witches or heretics as examples of such self-deceived people.

tion of revelation, study of medieval philosophers yields an interesting alternative to the deistic conception prevalent in our own day. Though the medieval approach recommends that those who have the ability and leisure to do so acquire the knowledge of history and languages needed for understanding the original message of revelation, it holds that these scholarly tools are not necessary for access to revelation. Revelation is a many-layered message, whose retrieval is under divine guidance as much as its original input was. Therefore, those saddled with corrupt texts or bereft of accurate translations, or those who are in general unlearned, may have equally good access to the divine message.

This approach has the worrisome feature of subjectivity; but some subjectivity is inevitable in the interpretation of texts, and the guide-lines for faithful reading which Augustine recommends provide a check on this tendency. The worst weakness of the medieval approach to revelation is apparent when we contrast it with the virtues of the historically oriented biblical studies current now. We have modern biblical studies to thank for the many useful scholarly tools which no reasonable person interested in biblical texts would part with, and that discipline has also given us insights into the culture and history of biblical peoples which Augustine himself would have valued. Although Augustine recommends scholarship on biblical texts, the dynamic conception of revelation provides no urgency for acquiring or producing that scholarship.

On the other hand, the deistic conception of revelation raises some of the same perplexities as the deistic theory of creation. The attributes and purposes attributed to the deity in the original divine act (of revelation or creation) are undermined or contradicted by the subsequent passivity ascribed to him on the deistic view. The dynamic conception thus seems to me a more consistent account of revelation. The most appealing element of the medieval approach is, in my view, its anti-élitism; what hierarchy it acknowledges is a hierarchy of saints, not of technical experts. Intellectual gifts fall within the realm of fortune, whereas moral goodness is rather more under our own control. It seems to me, therefore, more consistent with the divine attribute of justice, not to mention love, to suppose that God frames his hierarchies and distributes access to his revelation on the basis of moral goodness, over which we have some power, rather than on intellectual expertise, which stems in large part from the unmerited accidents of nature and nurture.

In whatever way we adjudicate the differences between these two conceptions of revelation, however, study of medieval philosophers is useful in helping us to reflect about the very notion of revelation. Both those who support and those who reject the idea that some truths are divinely revealed will argue their cases with more depth and sophistication if they are aware of the variety in the conceptions of the nature of revelation.[59]

[59] I am indebted to William Alston, Peter van Inwagen, and Alan Padgett for helpful questions and suggestions, and I am grateful to Norman Kretzmann for comments on earlier drafts.

PART III

Trinity and Incarnation

9

Not by Confusion of Substance, but by Unity of Person

PETER VAN INWAGEN

In an earlier essay, I showed how a part of the doctrine of the Trinity (that part that raises problems about counting, identity, and predication) could be given a statement in terms of 'relative identity'.[1] I did not contend that my statement of the doctrine was orthodox, although my tentative opinion, then and now, is that it is. I did not claim in any sense to have penetrated the mystery of the Trinity—to have proposed a non-mysterious formulation of the doctrine—but only to have formulated the doctrine in such a way that no contradiction could be formally derived from it. Here I propose to see whether the same methods can be applied to the mystery of the Incarnation: more exactly, to the doctrine of the hypostatic union of two natures—divine and human—in the person of Jesus Christ. I shall offer a formulation of a part of that doctrine in terms of relative identity. It is my hope that this formulation will be orthodox—that is, consistent with historical orthodoxy. I say 'part of' because I believe that there is no clearly demarcated set of propositions that can be called 'the doctrine of the Incarnation', or even 'the doctrine of the hypostatic union'. The 'part' of the doctrine that I shall be most concerned with is the part that raises grave metaphysical and logical problems: those propositions of

[1] Peter van Inwagen, 'And yet they are not Three Gods but One God', in Thomas V. Morris (ed.), *Philosophy and the Christian Faith* (Notre Dame, Ind.: University of Notre Dame Press, 1988), 241–78. Richard Swinburne's kind words about this paper—which approaches the philosophical problems raised by the doctrine of the Trinity in a way inconsistent with his own treatment of them—have encouraged me to contribute the present essay to this *Festschrift* dedicated to him. Swinburne's views on Trinitarian theology can be found in his essay 'Could there be more than one God?', *Faith and Philosophy*, v (1988), 225–41. The 'kind words' occur in n. 19, along with some words explaining why he prefers his own approach to mine. I will take this opportunity to say just a word (or twenty-one words) explaining why I prefer my approach to his: although I do not accuse him of tritheism, it seems to me that his Trinitarian theology is uncomfortably close to tritheism.

incarnational theology that appear to require violations of the principle of the transitivity of identity or of Leibniz's Law. (A violation of the former would be, a fortiori, a violation of the latter, since Leibniz's Law entails the transitivity of identity.) I shall not claim to have penetrated the mystery of the Incarnation, but at most to have shown that that doctrine can be stated without formal contradiction.

I

The present essay is best read as a sequel to 'And yet they are not Three Gods but One God'. But I shall do my best to make it self-contained. To this end, I present in this section a brief outline of the logic of relative identity ('RI-logic') that was developed in the earlier essay. For a fuller development of that logic, a discussion of the philosophical problems raised by the concept of relative identity, and a philosophical defence of the peculiar features of RI-logic, the reader will have to consult the earlier essay.[2]

Let us understand by 'quantifier logic' the logic of quantification developed as a system of natural deduction. The language of 'quantifier logic' will be understood to contain neither the identity sign nor any terms but variables (that is, it will contain neither names nor the description operator).

RI-logic is simply quantifier logic with its two-place predicate-letters partitioned into two classes, within one of which two special rules of inference apply. We indicate predicate-letters of the sort to which the two 'special' rules apply by underlining ('$\underline{F}$', '$\underline{G}$', ...). The two rules are:

Sym $\mathfrak{R}xy \vdash \mathfrak{R}yx$

Trans $\mathfrak{R}xy, \mathfrak{R}yz \vdash \mathfrak{R}xz$.

Here '$\mathfrak{R}$' represents any underlined predicate-letter.

The predicate-letters of RI-logic are intended to be replaceable only by ordinary-language predicates that satisfy the following restrictions: they do not contain denoting phrases, any ordinary-language equivalent of the identity sign, or, with one exception

---

[2] One very important question to which I can devote no space here is this: what, according to the philosophical defenders of RI-logic, is the status of the classical logic of absolute identity? This question is discussed at length in 'And yet they are not Three Gods but One God'.

that I shall mention in a moment, count-nouns. Underlined predicate-letters are to be replaceable only by 'relative-identity' predicates of ordinary language: phrases like 'is the same horse as' or 'is the same apple as', phrases of the form 'is the same N as', where 'N' represents the place of a count-noun. (This is the exception to the 'no count-noun' restriction. But we also allow one-place predicates of the form 'x is a(n) N', since these may be regarded as abbreviations for the corresponding phrases of the form 'x is the same N as x'.)

It will be noted that the inference rules of RI-logic do not include:

$$\vdash \mathfrak{R}xx.$$

If there were such a rule, then

$$\forall xx \text{ is the same horse as } x$$

would be an instance of a theorem. And an allowable reading of this sentence is 'Everything is a horse'. (In saying this, I assume that 'x is the same horse as y' is a relative-identity predicate of ordinary language, an appropriate substituend for '$\mathfrak{R}xy$'. I have said that a relative-identity predicate of ordinary language is a predicate of the form 'x is the same N as y', but this statement needs to be qualified. Identifying ordinary-language relative-identity predicates can be a tricky business in practice. 'Is the same colour as' functions as a relative-identity predicate in 'Magenta is the same colour as purplish-red' but not in 'Jane's skirt is the same colour as Alice's blouse'.[3])

If by Leibniz's Law, we understand the conditional

$$x = y \rightarrow (G \ldots x \ldots \leftrightarrow G \ldots y \ldots),$$

then it is obvious that the corresponding rule of inference is not a rule of RI-logic, owing to the fact that '=' does not belong to the vocabulary of RI-logic. A more substantive point is this: the rule

$$\mathfrak{R}xy \vdash (G \ldots x \ldots \leftrightarrow G \ldots y \ldots)$$

is not a rule of RI-logic. It was shown in the earlier paper that if this rule were added to the rules of RI-logic, then RI-logic would be without interest, being a mere notational variant of a fragment of

---

[3] Later, we shall have occasion to make use of the predicates 'x is the same breed as y' and 'x is the same price as y'. In the context in which we shall use them, these will not be functioning as relative-identity predicates, being equivalent to 'x is *of* the same breed as y' and 'x costs the same as y'. But it is not hard to imagine contexts in which they do function as relative-identity predicates: '*German shepherd* is the same breed as *Alsatian*', for example.

the classical logic of identity. (Roughly speaking, the addition of this rule would cause 'x is the same horse as y' to have the same logical properties as 'x is a horse and y is a horse and $x = y$'.)

Those who reason using RI-logic must regard any instance of the conditional that corresponds to this rule—for example,

> x is the same horse as $y \rightarrow (x$ is to the left of $z \leftrightarrow y$ is to the left of $z)$

—as a substantive metaphysical thesis, one whose truth the reasoner takes responsibility for. In this case, the RI-predicate '1 is the same horse as 2' is said to dominate the predicate '1 is to the left of 2'. Loosely speaking, if an RI-predicate dominates a predicate F, then it 'forces indiscernibility' with respect to F.[4] If an RI-predicate dominates all predicates, it is said to be 'dominant'. A statement made above may be rephrased using this term: if RI-logic is to be of any interest, then there must be some RI-predicate that is not dominant; or at least, there must be some RI-predicate that the user of RI-logic does not assume to be dominant.

The fact that the language of RI-logic contains no terms but variables constitutes a major stumbling-block for anyone who attempts to translate ordinary-language sentences into the language of RI-logic. But it should be clear that the language of RI-logic must have this feature. The language of RI-logic must not contain

---

[4] A small amount of technical apparatus is needed for an acceptable account of dominance. Remove the variables from an open sentence; replace them with boldface numerals, but use all of and only the first n numerals (use '1' or use '1' and '2' or use '1' '2'and '3' . . .). The result is a *predicate*. Thus, '1 is between 2 and 3' and '2 is between 1 and 1' are predicates. The former is a three-place (triadic) predicate, the latter a two-place (dyadic) predicate, owing to the fact that '3' is the highest numeral to appear in the former and '2' is the highest predicate to appear in the latter. The 'sites' in a predicate at which '1' appears are collectively called the predicate's first place, the sites at which '2' appears, its second place, and so on. An open sentence, which results from replacing the numerals in a predicate with variables, is called an 'instance' of that predicate, provided that a given numeral is always replaced with the same variable. Thus, 'y is between z and x' is an instance of the former predicate but not the latter; 'z is between x and x' and 'y is between y and y' are instances of both.

Strictly speaking, the truth of the formula in the text does not imply that '1 is the same horse as 2' dominates '1 is to the left of 2' *simpliciter*, but only that it dominates it with respect to its first place. If it is also true that

> x is the same horse as $y \rightarrow (z$ is to the left of $x \leftrightarrow z$ is to the left of $y)$,

then '1 is the same horse as 2' dominates '1 is to the left of 2' with respect to its second place as well. An RI-predicate dominates a predicate F (*simpliciter*) provided that it dominates F with respect to all its places.

singular terms. If *t* is a singular term that denotes both *x* and *y* then it follows that *x* is identical with *y*. The notion of a singular term is unintelligible without the notion of denotation (denoting things is what singular terms *do*—or at least, what they're supposed to do), and denotation is a many—one relation, and if *x* bears a many—one relation to *y* and to *z*, then *y* is identical with *z*. And, of course, this difficulty cannot be evaded by the ploy of eliminating singular terms by Russell's method, for that method essentially involves the use of the identity sign (which is no accident, given that denotation is a many—one relation). One can, however, employ relative-identity predicates to do more or less the work that Russell's method assigns to '='. One cannot translate 'Mr Ed told a lie' or 'The (unique) talking horse told a lie' into the language of RI-logic in a straightforward or unproblematic way. But one can say the following within the confines of the language of RI-logic:

$\exists x$ [*x* is a horse & *x* talks & $\forall y$ (*y* is a horse & *y* talks $\rightarrow$ *x* is the same horse as *y*) & *x* told a lie].

(The sentence '*x* is a horse' is short for '*x* is the same horse as *x*'.) Now this sentence comes to much the same thing as the sentence with which Russell's theory of descriptions replaces 'The talking horse told a lie' if 'is the same horse as' is dominant. And no doubt it is dominant. But perhaps not all RI-predicates are dominant.

II

The data of the doctrine of the Incarnation (other than the biblical data[5]) are, in my view, contained almost entirely in the following two statements. The first is from the *Quicunque Vult* and the

[5] The most important biblical data are, in my view, the opening passages of the Fourth Gospel, of the Letter to the Colossians, and of the Letter to the Hebrews. (Phil. 2: 5-11 has, I believe, less to tell us about the nature of the Incarnation than many have supposed.) The theologian, as I see matters, should regard the Bible as the physical scientist regards sense experience. Physical theories cannot be 'read off' sense experience, but they are in the last analysis responsible to sense experience, and must make sense of sense experience. Theological 'theories'—i.e., formulations of doctrine in abstract, theoretical terms, and even more abstract theoretical reflection on the allowable interpretations of doctrine and on the nature and methods of the interpretation of doctrine—cannot be 'read off' the words of Scripture, but they are in the last analysis responsible to the words of Scripture, and must make sense of the words of Scripture. Chesterton says somewhere that the New Testament is a riddle and the Church is the answer. I would say that the biblical passages cited

second from the Definition of Chalcedon. I know enough Latin to have satisfied myself that the language of the former is unproblematic, except in the matter of the meaning of individual theological terms. I therefore reproduce here the (reasonably accurate) translation of *The Book of Common Prayer*, which, better than anything else in English, captures the sensation of 'the great, roaring machine of Latin rhetoric' running at full throttle.

Furthermore, it is necessary to everlasting salvation that [one] also believe rightly the Incarnation of our Lord Jesus Christ. For the right Faith is, that we believe and confess, that our Lord Jesus Christ, the Son of God, is God and Man; God of the Substance of the Father, begotten before the worlds; and Man, of the substance of his Mother, born in the world; Perfect God and perfect Man, of a reasonable soul and human flesh subsisting; Equal to the Father, as touching his Godhead; and inferior to the Father, as touching his Manhood. Who although he be God and Man, Yet he is not two, but one Christ; One, not by conversion of the Godhead into flesh, but by taking of the Manhood into God; One altogether, not by confusion of Substance, but by unity of Person. For as the reasonable soul and flesh is one man, so God and Man is one Christ; Who suffered for our salvation . . .[6]

above are a riddle and that the Nicene Creed is the answer. (The Nicene Creed is in its turn a riddle, and the *Quicunque Vult* is the answer. The *Quicunque Vult*—largely a series of quotations from St Augustine—is a further riddle, to which the speculations of the medieval Trinitarian theologians are attempts at answers. Perhaps riddles come to an end only in the mind of God: there alone is Wittgenstein right: the *riddle* does not exist.)

[6] I do not believe that either the Apostles' Creed or the Nicene Creed adds anything of importance to what is contained in the *Quicunque Vult*. But the Nicene Creed (more properly, the Niceno-Constantinopolitan Creed) should perhaps be quoted, since, unlike the *QV*, it contains the famous word *homoousios*: 'And [I believe] in one Lord Jesus Christ, the only-begotten Son of God, begotten of the Father before all ages, God of God, light of light, true God of true God, begotten not made, through whom all things were made, *consubstantial with* the Father. Who, for us human beings and for our salvation, came down from heaven, and was incarnate by the Holy Spirit of the Virgin Mary, and was made man: crucified also for us under Pontius Pilate, he suffered and was buried: and on the third day he rose again in accordance with the Scriptures and ascended into heaven, sits on the right hand of the Father, and will come again with glory to judge the living and the dead; whose kingdom shall be without end.' This section of the Nicene Creed is a slightly expanded version of the section of the Creed actually issued by the Council of Nicaea. The earlier Creed, unlike the later one, contained a gloss on the phrase '*homoousios* with the Father': *ek tes ousias tou Patros*, which would seem to be the source—perhaps some scholar will correct me on this point—of the phrase '*ex substantia Patris*' ('of the Substance of the Father' in the Prayer Book translation) in the *QV*.

But the meaning of the Greek of the Definition is a more delicate matter, and since I know almost no Greek, I use a more scholarly translation:

> In agreement, therefore, with the holy fathers, we all unanimously teach that we should confess that our Lord Jesus Christ is one and the same Son, the same perfect in Godhead and the same perfect in manhood, truly God and truly man, the same of a rational soul and body, consubstantial with the Father in Godhead, and the same consubstantial with us in manhood, like us in all things except sin; begotten from the Father before the ages as regards his Godhead, and in the last days, the same, because of us and because of our salvation begotten from the Virgin Mary, the *Theotokos* [God-bearer], as regards his manhood; one and the same Christ, Son, Lord, only-begotten, made known in two natures without confusion, without change, without division, without separation, the difference of the natures being by no means removed because of the union, but the property of each nature being preserved and coalescing in one *prosopon* [person] and one *hypostasis* [subsistence], not parted or divided into two *prosopa*, but one and the same Son, only-begotten, divine Word, the Lord Jesus Christ, as the prophets of old and Jesus Christ himself have taught us about him and the creed of our fathers has handed down.[7]

Our job is to attempt to show how to translate the central statements of the theology of the Incarnation into the language of relative identity, and to show that the whole set of these statements is free from logical contradiction—at least in the sense that no contradiction can be derived from them by the rules of RI-logic. We adopt the following criterion of adequacy: the translations (and the whole set of their logical consequences) must be in accord with the biblical and creedal data. (And what is the criterion of *that*? Who is to say whether our translations are true to the letter and the spirit of the Bible and the Creeds? We must leave that a subjective matter. Those who are interested in such things must judge for themselves. Obviously we are not going to convince everyone. There are certainly plenty of theologians who think that the Creeds themselves are inconsistent with the biblical data; these people will therefore say a priori that we have set ourselves an impossible task: our translations will, of necessity, be untrue to the Bible or untrue to the Creeds—or, of course, untrue to both.)

---

[7] Trans. in J. N. D. Kelly, *Early Christian Doctrines*, 2nd edn. (London: A. and C. Black, 1960), pp. 339 ff. I have added the words in square brackets; Kelly's translation has only the transliterated Greek words. The word *prosopon*, incidentally, like the Latin *persona*, originally meant 'mask' or 'face'.

In 'And yet they are not Three Gods but One God', I made use of the following primitive vocabulary:

x is the same being (substance, *ousia*) as y,
x is the same person as y,
x is divine,
x begets y,
x proceeds from y through z.

(We also introduce by definition the predicates 'x is a being' and 'x is a person': something is a 'being' if it is the same being as something, and similarly for 'person'.) The first two of these predicates are relative-identity predicates, and the rest are ordinary predicates. The fourth and fifth express the relations that individuate the Persons of the Trinity. The idea of 'individuating the Persons' by means of these relations is roughly this: the Father is the unique Person who begets; the Son is the unique Person who is begotten; and the Holy Spirit is the unique Person who proceeds. Thus, for example, the sentence 'The Father made us' is translated into this vocabulary as:

Something begets (that is, begets something), and anything that begets is the same person as it, and it made us.

The sentence 'All things were made through the Son' is translated into this vocabulary as

Something is begotten (that is, is such that something begets it), and anything that is begotten is the same person as it, and all things were made through it.

The sentence 'The Holy Spirit is the Lord, and giver of life' is translated as:

Something proceeds (that is, proceeds from something through something), and anything that proceeds is the same person as it, and it is the Lord, and giver of life.

I will use the fourth and fifth predicates without any regard for how they might be explained.[8]

---

[8] If I *were* to attempt some sort of explanation of them, it would be along the following lines: 'x begets y' would be understood as meaning something like 'x is divine, and does not receive its divinity from another; and x imparts divinity to y'; 'x proceeds from y through z' would be understood as meaning something like 'y is divine, and does not receive its divinity from another; and y imparts divinity to z, and z imparts divinity to x'.

In sentences containing 'God', 'God' is understood as 'the unique divine being'. Thus we translate 'God made the heavens and the earth' as

Something is divine, and anything that is divine is the same being as it, and it made the heavens and the earth.

I will make only one other comment about any of these predicates. In my view, 'person' in the predicate 'is the same person as' means just what it means in ordinary speech. (But a little caution is needed here. One ordinary meaning of 'person' is, apparently, 'human being'. I have often talked at cross-purposes with philosophy students who have been puzzled by my speaking of intelligent non-human extra-terrestrials as 'persons'. C. S. Lewis somewhere records the statement of an uneducated man who said that he did not believe in a 'personal devil'; it transpired that he meant only that he regarded the devil as a spiritual being, and not as the horned and tailed biped of popular iconography. Let us say that if we are using 'person' in such a way that the devil and Wells's Martians are 'persons', then we are using the word in its 'inclusive' sense. My thesis is that 'person' in the Creeds ought to be understood as meaning no less and no more than it does in everyday speech, provided that we understand the everyday word in its inclusive sense.) This position of mine has met with the following criticism: '[Van Inwagen's] doctrinal formulations seem almost naïve: while he has heard that 'person' in Trinitarian theology does not mean what it means in everyday English (as indeed it does not), he is content to brush this aside with a remarkably ahistorical quotation from Geach.'[9] I will leave it to Geach to defend himself against the charge of having written something remarkably ahistorical, if that charge in fact means anything and is not simply a hostile noise. As to what I have been charged with—'seeming near doctrinal naïveté', we might call it—my first reaction to reading these words was to wonder what their author would come up with if he were asked to give an account of what 'person' does mean in everyday English. One is not in a position to write words like those quoted above unless one can give some sort of account of what 'person' means in everyday English. And this point applies to everyone, no

---

[9] James Wm. McClendon, Jr, review of *Philosophy and the Christian Faith*, ed. Thomas V. Morris, *Faith and Philosophy*, ix (1992), 109–16. The quoted passage occurs on p. 113.

matter how learned he or she may be about the history of the doctrinal employment of terms like 'hypostasis' and 'prosopon'. (The following objection to what I have just said misses the point: 'Since I am a native speaker of English, I have a perfect understanding of the ordinary sense of "person".' This objection misses the point because one can have all sorts of false *beliefs* about the meanings of words one understands perfectly: witness the famous case of 'by accident' and 'by mistake'.)

The doctrinal meaning of 'person' can be specified 'functionally' as follows: persons are what there are three of in the Trinity.[10] The ordinary sense of 'person' is best explained by means of pronouns. Persons are those things to which personal pronouns are applicable: a person can use the word 'I' and be addressed as 'thou' (we can address a skylark or an urn or a flower or a city or an abstraction like learning or fame as 'thou'—'Thou still unravished bride of quietness'—but this is the rule-proving exception, for we call it 'personification'). A person, if he is male or female, or if we are willing to regard him as male or female for certain purposes, is called 'he' or 'she', as opposed to 'it'.[11] (Many languages, of course, do not face the unfortunate gender difficulty raised by third-person singular pronouns in English.) And it is not only personal pronouns and the closely related possessive and reflexive pronouns that mark a distinction between persons and non-persons. Consider the indefinite pronoun 'one', which is used in generalizations applying only to persons. Consider the contrasting pairs, 'which' ('that')/ 'who', 'something'/'someone', and 'everything'/'everyone'. We could easily introduce a count-noun 'someone' by means of the

---

[10] Or, to employ a syntactical device that is used with great subtlety and flexibility by 6-year-olds, persons are what the Father, the Son, and the Holy Spirit are three ones of.

[11] I say 'as opposed to' and not 'and not'. The pronoun 'it' can be used in generalizations that are supposed to include persons but which apply to other things as well. We may say of Alice that whenever she admires something, she wants to write a poem about it. This implies that if Alice admires Jack, then she wants to write a poem about him. Exercise for the reader: connect this observation with the use of 'it' in the renderings in the text of 'The Father made us' and 'All things were made through the Son' and 'The Holy Spirit is the Lord, and giver of life' and 'God created the heavens and the earth'.

Ordinary usage is very complicated in the matter of 'he' and 'she'. We use these pronouns when we talk about our pets, and we may use them when talking about very primitive animals in contexts in which their sexes are particularly relevant. But note that we can say, 'It's hurt' or 'Don't go near it' when speaking of a dog of unknown sex; we cannot use these words of a human being of unknown sex.

definition 'x is a someone' $=_{df}$ 'x is someone'. And this count-noun, I maintain, would mean exactly what the count-noun 'person' (understood in its 'inclusive' sense) means, for there is a person—'a someone'—having the feature F if and only if someone has the feature F. (If the devil tempted Sally, then someone tempted Sally. If a Martian can prove Goldbach's Conjecture, then someone can prove Goldbach's Conjecture.) It is evident that the Persons of the Trinity *are* in this sense 'persons', *are* 'someones': if the Father loves us, then someone loves us, and if the Son was incarnate by the Holy Ghost of the Virgin Mary, then someone was incarnate by the Holy Ghost of the Virgin Mary. But this does not prove that 'person' in Trinitarian theology means 'person' in the ordinary (inclusive) sense. After all, all three Persons are *invisibilia*, but this does not entail that 'person' in Trinitarian theology means *invisibile*. The real question is whether 'persons' in the ordinary sense are 'what there are three of' in the Trinity.

In order to investigate this question from the perspective provided by an appeal to relative identity, we must remind ourselves that in our relative-identity language, count-nouns appear only in relative-identity predicates. (We should also remind ourselves that, from a relative-identity perspective, there is no such thing as absolute counting, a fact that has the consequence that, from a relative-identity perspective, the phrase 'what there are three of' has to be approached very carefully.) What we need to do is to explain what the relative-identity predicate 'x is the same person as y' means, using the pronominal resources of ordinary English. (A solution to this problem that exploited the pronominal resources of Latin or Greek would differ only in irrelevant detail.) The clearest, most idiomatic pronominal phrase of English that can be used to express propositions concerning the identities of persons is, to my mind, the negative phrase 'someone else'. Accordingly, I offer the definition:

> x is the same person as y $=_{df}$ x is someone and y is someone but not someone else.

(Another possibility would be, ' ... but not someone other than x'.) Having this predicate at our disposal, we are able to count by persons—by 'someones'. To say, for example, that exactly two persons sinned in Eden is to say:

> Someone x sinned in Eden, and someone y sinned in Eden, and y was someone other than x, and anyone who sinned in

Eden was either not someone other than *x* or not someone other than *y*.

And is it not true that when we count Persons of the Trinity we are counting 'someones'? The Father is someone. The Son is also someone. And, surely, he, the Son, is someone *else*? If he were not someone else, could he not say truly, using the *personal* pronoun 'I', 'I am the Father'? In general, if someone can say truly, 'I am F', then anyone who is *not someone else* can say truly 'I am F'. And if there is one undeniable datum in Trinitarian theology it is this: the Son (though he can say 'I and the Father are one') cannot say 'I am the Father'. And, of course, the Father cannot say 'I am the Spirit', nor the Spirit, 'I am the Son'. Each of the Father, the Son, and the Spirit is 'Thou', not 'I', to the other two. That is to say, each of the Father, the Son, and the Spirit bears the following relation to the other two: *being someone else*. (And it is in fact this very relation that we are counting by when we use the phrase 'the other two'.)

I do not wish to maintain that a technical term of Trinitarian theology like 'hypostasis' is an exact equivalent of 'person' (understood in its inclusive sense). 'Hypostasis', as it is used by many theological writers, no doubt carries a lot of metaphysical baggage that is not carried by the ordinary 'person'. And it may well be that many other writers use it as simply a convenient general term to cover the Father, the Son, and the Spirit, and do not trouble themselves too much about its content. What I do maintain is that any theologian of whatever period who says, for example, that the Father and the Son are distinct hypostases says something that entails that the Father and the Son are distinct persons (in the ordinary, inclusive sense), or is at any rate consistent with their being distinct persons in that sense, or is simply heretical. (As to the second possibility: it *may* be that the theologian is simply using 'hypostasis' as a place-holder, its use sanctified by tradition, with very little content, no more than this: (a) by definition, the Father, the Son, and the Spirit are 'distinct hypostases'; (b) whatever its meaning, 'distinct hypostases' does not entail 'not consubstantial'.) And here is a pair of far more important theses: any theological treatise on the Trinity whose propositions do not entail that the Persons are three distinct persons in the ordinary sense is gravely incomplete; any treatise whose propositions entail that they are *not* three distinct persons is simply heretical. And I am willing to argue

that anyone who denies these two theses is philosophically confused, probably about the everyday meaning of the word 'person'.
I suspect that anyone who denies these two theses thinks that
'person' in ordinary English means something more or other than
it does.[12] (Of course, my being willing to argue for this implies a
willingness to listen to arguments for the conclusion that I ought to
change my mind.)

[12] Theologians do not seem to me to speak with one voice on these matters. Here
are two quotations. The first is from Van A. Harvey's *A Handbook of Theological
Terms* (New York: Macmillan, 1964), 246: 'It is important to note that no important
Christian theologian has argued that there are three self-conscious beings in the
godhead. On the contrary, Augustine's favorite analogy for the triune God was one
self-consciousness with its three distinctions of intellect, will, and the bond between
them' (article 'Trinity'). The second from Edmund Hill's *The Mystery of the Trinity*
(London: Geoffrey Chapman, 1985), pp. 101 ff.

'Now in God [according to Thomas] what are distinctly subsistent are the mutually opposed and corresponding relationships. So the words "person" and "hypostasis" can properly be used in talking of God to refer to these relationships, even
though in themselves they do not signify any kind of relationship. Thomas adds that
since "person" means that which is most perfect in the whole of nature, namely what
subsists in rational (or intelligent) nature, it is particularly apt for use in talking
about God. . . . But Aquinas adds a most important proviso. . . . "But the word
cannot be used in the same way of God as of creatures, but in a superlative way. . . ."
What this superlative . . . way actually means is that . . . to call the Father, the Son,
and the Holy Spirit three persons [adds] nothing to what we already know from
calling them the Father, the Son, and the Holy Spirit, apart from being our way of
saying that they are really distinct from each other. . . And this is really the point
that Augustine is making when he concludes that these words are no more than just
labels . . . so that we might just as well, in answer to the question "Three what?",
reply "Three Xs", or, more elegantly, "Three someones".'

I take the second quotation more or less to support my position, with the following important qualification: Hill seems not to be aware that, or, to choose my words
more judiciously, does not accept my thesis that, the meaning of the ordinary word
'person' is just 'a someone'. My difference with Thomas, as Hill represents him,
would be just this: I think that the word 'person' *can* be predicated univocally of
God and creatures. (Note that the 'superlative sense' point would apply if we spoke
of God without using Trinitarian language at all; if Thomas is right, then when, say,
Alvin Plantinga defines atheism as the thesis that there is no such person as God, the
word 'person' in this thesis cannot have the same sense as the sense it has in the
thesis that there was no such person as King Arthur—or in the thesis that there is no
such person as Satan. This I would deny, for reasons having nothing to do with
Trinitarian theology.)

As to the first quotation, I probably do subscribe to various theses that, in the
view of its author, no important Christian theologian has held. It is true that I would
deny that there are three self-conscious beings in the Godhead, since I would deny
that there are three beings of any description in the Godhead. But I would say that
the Father is self-conscious (he knows of himself that he is the Father, and that
would seem to be sufficient for self-consciousness) and that the Son is self-conscious,
and the Son is not the Father but rather someone else. And I *think* that Harvey
would deny that any important Christian theologian has held this. Whether or not

In the earlier paper, I translated a fair number of sentences in traditional Trinitarian language into a language whose entire vocabulary comprises sentential connectives, brackets, variables, the quantifiers, and the above five predicates. I contended that these sentences (together with their logical consequences) included all the Trinitarian sentences that implied any seeming contradictions relating to counting, identity, or predication. And I showed that this set of sentences is formally consistent; I showed this by finding a model on which all these sentences are true. One striking consequence of this result, the single consequence that I find the most interesting, is this: the translations of the following three sentences make up a formally consistent set:

The Father is the same person as God.[13]
God is the same person as the Son.
The Father is not the same person as the Son.

And this result holds despite the fact that the transitivity of personal identity (if that is the abstract substantive that corresponds to 'is the same person as') is an immediate consequence of the rule Trans.

III

I now turn to the theology of the Incarnation. Our first problem is the problem of how to use the sparse referential capacities of our language (supplemented by whatever ordinary predicates may be useful) to refer to particular human beings. How, for example,

---

he is right about this, the appeal to Augustine's psychological analogy is not to the point. The relations between intellect and will pertain, in Augustine's analogy, to the nature of the relations in which (as which?) the Father and the Son subsist. The Father and the Son are, for Augustine, *subsistent* relationships, and the mutual relations of intellect and will in human beings, by which we can reach a dim analogical understanding of them, are *not* subsistent relationships. Because the latter are not subsistent, any question about their consciousness makes no more sense than a question about the consciousness of a number or a quality. If there could be subsistent relationships, however, there would be no logical or metaphysical barrier to their being self-conscious. In my view, what Augustine says about the three subsistent relationships in the Godhead commits him to the thesis that each of them is a someone.

[13] That is: for some x and for some y, x begets, and anything that begets is the same person as x, and y is divine, and anything that is divine is the same being as y, and x is the same person as y.

restricted as we are, shall we talk about Abraham Lincoln? The question is in a way ill-formed, for, if we are really restricted to our 'referentially sparse' language, we cannot ask it. But we can observe that there are various sets of ordinary predicates (like 'ended slavery' and 'saved the union' and 'once practised law') such that, or so we believe, there is one and only one human being who satisfies all of them. Let 'L' be the conjunction of the members of some suitably comprehensive one among these sets. (Perhaps 'L' is the predicate that, according to the description theory of names, expresses the meaning of 'Abraham Lincoln' in the usage of some reasonably knowledgeable person—if there is such a predicate.) If we take 'being' in the phrase 'human being' seriously, it would seem plausible that a sentence of the form 'Lincoln is F' would best be represented in our referentially sparse language by the corresponding sentence of the form

$$\exists x \, (Lx \, \& \, \forall y \, (Ly \rightarrow \underline{B}xy) \, \& \, x \text{ is F}).$$

(In this formula, $\underline{B}$ abbreviates 'is the same being as'.) Now it is no doubt true that all of us would accept the thesis that if x and y are human beings, then, x and y are the same being if and only if x and y are the same person. Accordingly, we would accept a sentence of the above form if and only if we were willing to accept the corresponding sentence of the form

$$\exists x \, (Lx \, \& \, \forall y \, (Ly \rightarrow \underline{P}xy) \, \& \, x \text{ is F}).$$

(In this sentence, of course, $\underline{P}$ abbreviates 'is the same person as'.) And we should no doubt therefore regard the sentence of the second form as an equally good representation of the corresponding sentence of the form 'Lincoln is F'. It is, however, sentences of the first form that I shall be primarily interested in. The reason for this will soon transpire if it is not already evident.

In order to represent the propositions of Incarnational theology using the apparatus of relative identity, we require only two predicates (both of them ordinary) in addition to the five that figured in our representation of the propositions of Trinitarian theology. The first is 'J', which we shall use for a predicate that stands to the historical figure Jesus of Nazareth as 'L' stands to the historical figure Abraham Lincoln. (The exact list of predicates of which 'J' is a conjunction is of no great interest—but the list is restricted to predicates that neither imply divinity nor involve any of the concepts of incarnational theology. The list might include 'was born of a virgin', 'was crucified', and 'was raised from the dead'. But it may not include 'is God', 'is the Son of God', or 'is possessed of a human nature that enters into a hypostatic union with the Godhead'. I leave the question of the list of predicates that define 'J' unresolved, because the facts of Jesus' biography are controversial, and because even a controversial list would be very long. I assume, however, that everyone who believes that there was a historical Jesus at all will be able to devise a list of predicates that he believes applies to Jesus and to no other historical figure.) Having introduced J, we allow it immediately to disappear into an abbreviation:

$$Jx =_{df} Jx \ \& \ \forall y \ (Jy \rightarrow \underline{B}xy).$$

'Jx' may be read 'x is Jesus (of Nazareth)'. Any sentence of ordinary English of the form 'Jesus is F' may be represented in our vocabulary as the corresponding sentence of the form '$\exists x \ (Jx \ \& \ x \text{ is } F)$'.

The only other predicate that we shall need to add to our list of predicates is 'is human'; we shall abbreviate 'x is human' as 'Mx'. We abbreviate 'x is divine' as 'Dx'. And (as in the earlier paper) we introduce the abbreviations (read, respectively, 'is God', 'is the Father', 'is the Son', and 'is the Holy Spirit'):

$$Gx =_{df} Dx \ \& \ \forall y \ (Dy \rightarrow \underline{B}xy),$$

$$Fx =_{df} x \text{ begets} \ \& \ \forall y \ (y \text{ begets} \rightarrow \underline{P}xy),$$

$$Sx =_{df} x \text{ is begotten} \ \& \ \forall y \ (y \text{ is begotten} \rightarrow \underline{P}xy),$$

$$Hx =_{df} x \text{ proceeds} \ \& \ \forall y \ (y \text{ proceeds} \rightarrow \underline{P}xy).$$

The earlier paper listed a set of theological assertions and 'conceptual truths' that were held to comprise that part of Trinitarian theology that concerns counting, identity, and predication. The theological assertions were the formal equivalents of 'There is exactly one God' and 'There are exactly three divine Persons'. The 'conceptual truths' included some more or less trivial assertions ('Anything that is divine is both a being and a person'; 'All persons are beings') and some more substantive ones. The latter comprehend the assertion that sameness of being dominates divinity (formally: $\underline{B}xy \rightarrow . Dx \leftrightarrow Dy$) and various assertions whose collective import is that the relations of begetting and procession hold only among divinities, that these relations uniquely specify the three divine Persons, and that nothing besides the three divine Persons enters into these relations. We must now expand this set of statements. We begin with four conceptual truths (the numbers are continuations of the numbering in the earlier paper).[14]

$$CT13 \ Mx \rightarrow \neg Dx,$$

$$CT14 \ Jx \rightarrow Mx,$$

$$CT15 \ Mx \rightarrow \cdot Px \ \& \ Bx,$$

$$CT16 \ \underline{B}xy \rightarrow \cdot Mx \leftrightarrow My.$$

Thus, humanity is like divinity in that it entails both personhood and being and in that it is dominated by 'ontic identity' or sameness of being. In the earlier essay, I explicitly and pointedly refrained from assuming that personal identity dominated divinity. I now explicitly and pointedly refrain from making the corresponding assumption as regards personal identity and humanity. In the earlier essay, I explicitly and pointedly refrained from assuming that ontic identity dominated personal identity. I now explicitly and pointedly refrain from assuming that personal identity dominates ontic identity.

We require two theological assertions. The first is (as I shall call it) the Dogma of the Incarnation:

$$\exists x \ \exists y \ (Sx \ \& \ Jy \ \& \ \underline{P}xy).[15]$$

That is to say, God the Son and Jesus of Nazareth are one and the same person. And this in the ordinary sense of the words 'same person': the Son is someone and Jesus is someone, but not someone else; the Son can say 'I am Jesus whom thou persecutest', and Jesus can say 'I am (*ego eimi*) God the Son'. (Perhaps, as many have contended, Jesus did not, during his earthly ministry, possess the concept that theologians were later to express by the words 'God the Son'; if not, I expect he does now.) More exactly, these two sentences are ambiguous. The word 'am' that occurs in each *could* be taken to express an ontic identity between the human being

---

[14] No doubt there are other conceptual truths involving the concepts that are represented formally in our language. One candidate for such a truth would be a proposition that has already been mentioned: that sameness of person and sameness of being coincide on human beings. For all we can show, therefore, it may turn out that even though (as we shall see) the truths of Incarnational theology, as they are specified here, are formally consistent, there are plausible candidates for conceptual truths that, if added to our set of truths, would yield a formal inconsistency. But the same might be said of any formal system that is intended to capture the relations that hold among the members of some set of concepts.

[15] In unabbreviated form: $\exists x \ \exists y \ [\exists z \ z$ begets $x \cdot \& \ \forall y \ (\exists z \ z$ begets $y \cdot \rightarrow \underline{P}xy) \ \& \ Jy \ \& \ \forall x \ (Jx \rightarrow \underline{B}xy) \ \& \ \underline{P}xy].$

from whose lips the word issues and God the Son; if it is taken in that sense, then what is expressed by the two sentences does not follow from the Dogma of the Incarnation (and is, of course, heretical). But if the copula expresses personal identity (much the more natural interpretation, to my mind, owing to the fact that its subject is a personal pronoun), then what is expressed by these sentences— leaving aside the part about persecution—does follow from the Dogma of the Incarnation.

The second theological assertion that we shall require is the thesis that no more than one divine Person is incarnate:

$$\text{D}x \ \& \ \text{D}y \ \& \ \exists z \ (\text{M}z \ \& \ \underline{\text{P}}xz) \ \& \ \exists z \ (\text{M}z \ \& \ \underline{\text{P}}yz) \cdot \rightarrow \underline{\text{P}}xy.$$

We shall now consider a fairly comprehensive set of English sentences that pertain to the theology of the Incarnation, sentences that can plausibly be said to be parts of or logical consequences of the doctrine of the Incarnation. We shall show how to translate these sentences into our formal vocabulary; we shall then show that they are formal consequences of our conceptual truths and our two theological assertions (taken together with the conceptual truths and the theological assertions that were endorsed in 'And yet they are not Three Gods but One God'), and that no contradiction is a formal consequence of this set of sentences.

The most difficult problems of translation arise in connection with sentences containing the name 'Jesus Christ'. Let us begin by considering sentences that do not involve this name. I follow each sentence with a proposed translation.

—God was incarnate in Jesus of Nazareth[16]

$$\exists x \ \exists y \ (\text{G}x \ \& \ \text{J}y \ \& \ \underline{\text{P}}xy).$$

Or, in unabbreviated form:

$$\exists x \ \exists y \ (\text{D}x \ \& \ \forall y \ (\text{D}y \rightarrow \underline{\text{B}}xy) \ \& \ \text{J}y \ \& \ \forall z \ (\text{J}z \rightarrow \underline{\text{B}}yz) \ \& \ \underline{\text{P}}xy).$$

—God the Son was incarnate in Jesus of Nazareth

$$\exists x \ \exists y \ (\text{S}x \ \& \ \text{J}y \ \& \ \underline{\text{P}}xy).$$

Or, in (almost) unabbreviated form:

$$\exists x \ \exists y \ (x \text{ is begotten} \ \& \ \forall y \ (y \text{ is begotten} \rightarrow \underline{\text{P}}xy) \\ \& \ \text{J}y \ \& \ \forall z \ (\text{J}z \rightarrow \underline{\text{B}}yz) \ \& \ \underline{\text{P}}xy).$$

(From now on, I will given only the abbreviated forms of sentences.) The next sentence,

---

[16] Our formal apparatus does not extend to the representation of tenses.

—God the Father is not incarnate

is ambiguous. It could be read either as a predication of 'is not incarnate' of God the Father, or as a denial of the thesis that God the Father is incarnate: as

$$\exists x \ (Fx \ \& \ \neg \ \exists y \ (My \ \& \ \underline{P}xy))$$

or as

$$\neg \ \exists x \ (Fx \ \& \ \exists y \ (My \ \& \ \underline{P}xy)).$$

Some sentences containing the word 'God' are ambiguous in ways that have led to theological controversy. I given two examples. First,

—God died on the Cross.

This might be represented in either of the following ways:

$$\exists x \ (Gx \ \& \ x \ \text{died on the Cross});$$

$$\exists x \ \exists y \ (Gx \ \& \ y \ \text{died on the Cross} \ \& \ \underline{P}xy).$$

The second of these sentences follows from the sentences we have endorsed (given that Jesus of Nazareth died on the Cross) and, I believe, represents something like the position that those who have looked favourably on language like 'God died on the Cross' were defending. The first does not follow from the sentences we have endorsed. In fact, its denial follows, given the additional premiss that anything that dies on a cross is a human being. I would suppose that it represents something like the position that those who opposed language like 'God died on the Cross' were trying to guard against. ('God the Son died on the Cross' can be seen to be ambiguous in almost the same way. But all reasonable representations of the sentences 'God the Father died on the Cross' and 'The Holy Spirit died on the Cross' in our formal language can easily be seen to be 'false'.[17])

Our second example of an ambiguous sentence is

—Mary was the God-bearer (*Theotokos*).

Let us invent a predicate 'Vx' that stands to Mary as '$Lx \ \& \ \forall y \ (Ly \rightarrow \underline{B}xy)$' stands to Lincoln and 'Jx' stands to Jesus. And let us suppose that 'x bears y', whatever precisely it may mean, is satisfied by a pair of objects only if the first is biologically female and the

---

[17] I will call sentences that follow from the sentences we have endorsed 'true' (in scare-quotes) and sentences whose denial follows from the sentences we have endorsed 'false' (in scare-quotes).

second is a living organism (for dualists: has a body that is a living organism) that develops from a gamete supplied by the first. Our sentence may be represented in either of the two following ways:

$$\exists x \, \exists y \, (Vx \,\&\, Gy \,\&\, x \text{ bore } y)$$

$$\exists x \, \exists y \, (Vx \,\&\, Gy \,\&\, \exists z \, (x \text{ bore } z \,\&\, \underline{P}zy)).$$

Remarks similar to the above remarks about the two representations of 'God died on the Cross' apply to these two sentences.

Let us now turn to sentences containing the name 'Jesus Christ'. How are we to understand this name? Logic and etymology would suggest that 'Jesus Christ' means 'Jesus the Messiah'. If that were so, we should represent sentences of the form 'Jesus Christ is F' in our formal language by the corresponding sentences of the form '$\exists x \, (Jx \,\&\, x \text{ is F} \,\&\, x \text{ is the Messiah})$'. But in theology, as in all other areas of human discourse, established usage laughs at logic and etymology. It may well be that there is no one meaning that covers all theologically legitimate uses of 'Jesus Christ', but it seems to me that the term has a 'central' meaning in Christian theology, and that whatever else may be true of this central meaning, it somehow involves the idea of the Incarnation, the union of the divine and human natures in a single Person. (I take it that this is not part of the meaning of 'Messiah': if it had pleased God so to arrange matters, the Messiah might be, or might have been, a human being in whom he was not incarnate.) It would seem that 'Jesus Christ' does not mean the same as either 'God the Son' or 'Jesus of Nazareth' but something more like 'the Person who is both God the Son and Jesus of Nazareth'. I would suggest that we represent sentences of the form 'Jesus Christ is F' by the corresponding sentences of the form

$$\exists x \, (\exists y \, (Sy \,\&\, \underline{P}xy) \,\&\, \exists y \, (Jy \,\&\, \underline{P}xy) \,\&\, x \text{ is F}).$$

If this is what we mean by 'Jesus Christ', then the formal representation of the sentence

—Jesus Christ is God and man

is 'true'. Or, at any rate, it is true if we regard it as the conjunction of the two sentences 'Jesus Christ is God' and 'Jesus Christ is man', and not as predicating of Jesus Christ the impossible property *being-both-God-and-man* (that is, the property expressed by the open sentence 'x is God and x is man'). In other words, we must distinguish between

$$\exists x \ (\exists y \ (Sy \ \& \ \underline{P}xy) \ \& \ \exists y \ (Jy \ \& \ \underline{P}xy) \ \& \ Dx) \ \&$$
$$\exists x \ (\exists y \ (Sy \ \& \ \underline{P}xy) \ \& \ \exists y \ (Jy \ \& \ \underline{P}xy) \ \& \ Mx)$$

and

$$\exists x \ (\exists y \ (Sy \ \& \ \underline{P}xy) \ \& \ \exists y \ (Jy \ \& \ \underline{P}xy) \ \& \ Dx \ \& \ Mx).$$

The former sentence follows from the endorsed sentences, and is, I believe, orthodox. The second does not follow from the endorsed sentences; in fact, its denial follows.

One traditional device that is used in discussions of the truth-values of sentences of the form 'Jesus Christ is F' is a threefold distinction marked by the use of sentences of the following forms:

Jesus Christ is *simpliciter* F (is F without qualification).

Jesus Christ is *secundum divinitatem* F (is F 'as touching his divinity').

Jesus Christ is *secundum humanitatem* F (is F 'as touching his humanity').

I shall adopt this distinction. What I have so far discussed is the representation of *simpliciter* sentences. The other two types of sentences are represented as follows:

$$\exists x \ (\exists y \ (Sy \ \& \ \underline{P}xy) \ \& \ \exists y \ (Jy \ \& \ \underline{P}xy) \ \& \ Dx \ \& \ x \text{ is F})$$
$$\exists x \ (\exists y \ (Sy \ \& \ \underline{P}xy) \ \& \ \exists y \ (Jy \ \& \ \underline{P}xy) \ \& \ Mx \ \& \ x \text{ is F}).$$

On this reading, the following theses are true:

Jesus Christ is *simpliciter* human.

Jesus Christ is *simpliciter* non-human.

Jesus Christ is *simpliciter* divine.

Jesus Christ is *simpliciter* non-divine.

Jesus Christ is *simpliciter* such that there never was a time when he was not.

Jesus Christ is *simpliciter* such that in 10 BC he did not yet exist.

It is important to realize that there is neither contradiction nor (in my view) unorthodoxy in these theses. Consider, for example, 'Jesus Christ is *simpliciter* non-human'. This thesis is not equivalent to (nor does it entail) the thesis

It is not the case that Jesus Christ is *simpliciter* human.

If this equivalence did hold, then some theses in the above list (the second if no other) would be unorthodox, and the whole list would be self-contradictory. But the formal representation of 'Jesus Christ is *simpliciter* non-human' is:

$$\exists x\ (\exists y\ (Sy\ \&\ \underline{P}xy)\ \&\ \exists y\ (Jy\ \&\ \underline{P}xy)\ \&\ Mx),$$

while the formal representation of 'It is not the case that Jesus Christ is *simpliciter* human' is:

$$\neg\ \exists x\ (\exists y\ (Sy\ \&\ \underline{P}xy)\ \&\ \exists y\ (Jy\ \&\ \underline{P}xy)\ \&\ Mx).$$

And these two sentences are not equivalent. The first follows from the set of sentences we have endorsed. The second does not follow from those sentences. Is there anything unorthodox about the sentence 'Jesus Christ is *simpliciter* non-human'? I should say that there was not. The sentence—or what is meant by it on my reading of it—does not deny the full humanity of Jesus Christ, for it is consistent with 'Jesus Christ is *simpliciter* human'. The truth of what is expressed by 'Jesus Christ is *simpliciter* non-human' is simply a consequence of the fact that God the Son, Begotten Divinity, although he is the same person as a certain member of our species, is not (being, as he is, eternal, omnipresent, and so on) 'in the strict and philosophical sense' a member of our species. The truth of what is expressed by 'Jesus Christ is *simpliciter* human' is simply a consequence of the fact that Jesus of Nazareth, not begotten of the Father but rather conceived by the Holy Ghost, although he is the same person as a certain Person of the Trinity, is not (being, as he is, temporal, locally present, and so on) 'in the strict and philosophical sense' a Person of the Trinity. In the words of the *Quicunque Vult*, Jesus Christ is 'One altogether; not by confusion of Substance, but by unity of Person' (*unus omnino non confusione substantiae, sed unitate personae*). As there are in the Holy Trinity three distinct persons who are one by unity of being, so there are in Jesus Christ two distinct beings who are one by unity of person.

It is often confusing to predicate properties of Jesus Christ in the 'ontologically promiscuous' manner provided by the form of words 'Jesus Christ is *simpliciter* F'. It is often a more perspicuous procedure to employ an idiom that segregates the properties of Jesus Christ according as they belong to him in virtue of his divine or his human natures. This is, of course, the function of the other two idioms of predication, predication *secundum divinitatem* and predication *secundum humanitatem*. We may thus say that Jesus Christ is begotten of the Father before all worlds *secundum divinitatem*, but is not begotten of the Father before all worlds *secundum humanitatem*, and that Jesus Christ was conceived by the Holy Ghost and born of the Virgin Mary *secundum humanitatem*, but was not conceived by the Holy Ghost and born of the Virgin Mary *secundum divinitatem*, and that Jesus Christ is equal to the Father as touching his Godhead and inferior to the Father as touching his manhood. (And so on; there would seem to be no particular difficulty in deciding whether a property that belongs to Jesus Christ according to one or the other nature belongs to him *secundum divinitatem* or *secundum humanitatem*. There are, of course, many properties that he possesses both *secundum divinitatem* and *secundum humanitatem*: consciousness, free will, and moral perfection, for example. Or, at least, this is true if these terms can be predicated of God and humanity in the same sense.)

It would seem that a sentence of the form 'I am F' spoken by Jesus of Nazareth should express a truth just in the case that the corresponding sentence of the form 'Jesus Christ is *simpliciter* F' is true. Thus, Jesus could say truly both 'I am meek and lowly of heart' (presumably, being meek and lowly of heart belongs to Jesus Christ *secundum humanitatem* and not *secundum divinitatem*) and 'Before Abraham was, I am'. This is because 'I' is a personal pronoun and 'attaches semantically' to all the properties of the *person* who utters it; more exactly, if it is uttered by one of two beings who are the same person, that utterance comprehends the properties of both of those beings.[18]

It is time now to show that the whole set of sentences we have endorsed is consistent—that no contradiction can be deduced from its members by RI-logic. It will not be surprising if this is so, for the deductive resources of RI-logic are rather weak, owing to the fact that the inference rules of RI-logic do not include anything corre-

---

[18] There may have been some attempt, either by Jesus or by the Evangelists, to divide his self-ascriptions into those true of him *simpliciter*, those true of him *secundum divinitatem*, and those true of him *secundum humanitatem*. I have in mind his (or their) use of, respectively, the first-person-singular pronoun, 'the Son', and 'the Son of Man'. I do not mean to suggest by this speculation that anyone in the first century was in possession of a fifth-century Christology. I mean, rather that his, or their, use of these terms may have been a response to the same divine/human reality that was later conceptualized in developed Christologies. (It should not be necessary to make this disclaimer, but one is liable to be accused of just such an anachronism if one says anything that implies that a developed Christology can be of some use in understanding the Gospels.) This speculation faces severe textual difficulties (consider, e.g., Mark 13: 32 = Matt. 24: 36), but I nevertheless think that it is worthy of careful consideration.

sponding to Leibniz's Law (and owing to the further fact that we have not assumed that identity of person dominates either humanity or divinity or identity of being). Our method is simple. We shall tell a story, a story that is obviously internally consistent, and we shall give each of our formal predicates an interpretation in that story—being careful to interpret both our RI predicates as expressing symmetrical and transitive relations. We shall see that all our endorsed sentences are true on this interpretation. It will follow, by a well-known property of quantifier logic, that if a contradiction follows from the endorsed sentences by quantifier logic, then our story is internally inconsistent—which it is obviously not. Since, moreover, our two RI predicates are interpreted as expressing symmetrical and transitive relations, our story will be internally inconsistent if a contradiction can be deduced from the endorsed sentences by the rules of quantifier logic plus Sym and Trans. It follows that no contradiction can be deduced from the endorsed sentences by RI-logic.

The story is an elaboration of the story used for the same purpose in the earlier paper:

Our universe of discourse comprises four animals. There are three dogs of the same breed, A, B, and C, and one cat, a jet-black Manx. None of the dogs is jet-black. Each of the dogs is for sale at a different price, and the cat is for sale at the same price as dog B. A barks at B and at nothing else, and nothing else barks. C prances from A to B and does no other prancing, and nothing else prances.

Here are our interpretations:

$\underline{B}xy$	: x is the same breed as y.
$\underline{P}xy$	: x is the same price as y.
Dx	: x is a dog.
Mx	: x is a Manx.
Jx	: x is jet-black.
x begets y	: x barks at y.

x proceeds from y through z: x prances from y to z.

These interpretations of our undefined predicates settle the interpretation of our defined predicates:

Bx : x is of some breed.

Px : x is for sale at some price.

Gx: x is a dog of the only breed.

Fx : x barks, and anything that barks is the same price as x.

Sx : x is barked at, and anything that is barked at is the same price as x.

Hx: x prances from something to something, and anything that prances is the same price as x.

Jx : x is jet-black, and anything that is jet-black is the same breed as x.

It is an easy, if somewhat tedious, exercise to verify that all our endorsed sentences are true in the story of the four animals, provided that the predicates they contain are interpreted according to this schema.[19] It follows from this fact and from the fact that 'is the same breed as' and 'is the same price as' are symmetrical and transitive, that the story of the four animals is internally inconsistent if a contradiction can be derived from the endorsed sentences in RI-logic. But that story is obviously internally consistent. Therefore, no contradiction can be derived from the endorsed sentences in RI-logic.

As I said I should at the beginning of this chapter, I have shown how a part of the doctrine of the Incarnation (or of the Hypostatic Union) can be represented in a way that is free from formal contradiction. But, as I said, I have done nothing to make the mystery of the Incarnation any less a mystery. Just as 'And yet they are not Three Gods but One God' left the mystery of the Trinity untouched, so the present chapter leaves the mystery of the Incarnation untouched. Indeed, I have done little more than provide a vocabulary in which the mysterious aspect of the doctrine can be stated precisely. But perhaps this vocabulary has the advantage of suggesting a precise description of the relationship between the mystery of the Incarnation and the mystery of the Trinity. The mystery of the Trinity is this: how can it be that ontic identity (which dominates humanity and divinity) fails to dominate personal identity? The mystery of the Incarnation is this: how can it be that personal identity fails to dominate ontic identity—and humanity and divinity as well? These questions raise more general and abstract questions that are no less mysterious: how can *any*

[19] As one would expect, the four dominance assumptions that we have 'explicitly and pointedly' refrained from making—Pxy → · Dx ↔ Dy, Pxy → · Mx ↔ My, Bxy → · Pxz ↔ Pyz, and Pxy → · Bxz ↔ Byz—are false on this interpretation.

relative-identity predicate fail to dominate *all* predicates? (That is to say, how can the whole topic of relative identity be of any interest, for relative identity is interesting only if some relative-identity predicate is not dominant?) And given that ontic identity and personal identity fail to dominate certain predicates, what is the reason for the fact that they interact differently with humanity and divinity? To none of these questions have I an answer.[20]

[20] My thinking about the questions addressed in this chapter has been stimulated by correspondence with Timothy Bartel.

10

Neither Confounding the Persons nor Dividing the Substance

C. J. F. WILLIAMS

Richard Swinburne is the only colleague I have had, in thirty-one years of teaching philosophy in British universities, who has shared my belief in God. There was an occasion when our familiarity with atheistic milieux was thought enough to make us experts on the 'phenomenon of non-belief', and we were summoned to a meeting in Manchester organized on behalf of a Vatican body rejoicing (perhaps it still rejoices) in the name *Il Segretario per i Non-Credenti*. And we are indeed fellow Christians. That in itself gives him a special place in my affections. As young men we were members of a small but rapidly growing philosophy department in the University of Hull. We later collaborated in running the journal *Analysis*, and we have often discussed each other's work. I think that Richard's paper on the Trinity was what chiefly prompted me to put into words the thoughts I have been having for some time on the same subject. I offer them here in the hope that they may do him honour, and in the confident expectation that they will in due course receive the benefit of his judicious criticism.

If my memory can be trusted, I remember singing the words that form my title, coming as they do from the so-called Athanasian Creed, as part of the service of Morning Prayer at the simple parish church that my family used to attend in my Anglican childhood. I suspect that you need to be old enough to have pre-war memories to be able to say that. Like much else that is in the *Book of Common Prayer*, this practice had fallen into desuetude long before that book was replaced by the *Alternative Services Book*; and that, as far as I can see, does not contain the Athanasian Creed. But it is not only Anglicans whose liturgical devotion no longer finds expression in the *Quicunque Vult*. In my twenties, as a member of the novitiate at Downside Abbey, I recited it again at the monastic office of Prime on Trinity Sunday. There is no Prime now at Downside, and I wonder whether there is any Catholic church where the Athanasian Creed is still recited as an act of worship. Ironically, the Orthodox, who adopted the Creed for liturgical use only in modern times and do not regard it as a standard of faith, may be the only Christians who retain it as a liturgical formula.

But let us get down to business.

'Firmly I believe and truly God is three and God is one.' Should this be sung with defiance, with a proud consciousness of having contradicted oneself? Do we say, with Tertullian, '*Credibile est, quia ineptum est . . . certum est, quia impossibile*'. ('It is believable, because it is absurd, certain because impossible'?[1]) Or should one ask Gerontius to be a little more precise: three what and one what? Frege's *Foundations of Arithmetic* was published in 1884, and Newman did not die until 1890; but it is doubtful whether Newman took advantage of this fact to improve his understanding of statements of number.

Theologians were in fact quite capable of talking sensibly about number centuries before Frege had produced an adequate theory of the meaning of number statements. From the Council of Nicaea onwards it was standard practice to connect threeness with *Person* and oneness with *God*. 'Firmly I believe and truly there are three Persons in the Godhead and there is one God' may not fit the tune, but it is much more accurate as a statement of the Catholic Faith— which, unless a man keep pure and undefiled, without doubt he shall perish everlastingly (women may give a sigh of relief at this point)—and it is less likely to give scandal to the tender consciences of logicians. Counting divine Persons is a different matter from counting Gods.

Put like that, however, the difficulty seems to recur. What is a God if not a divine Person? Richard Swinburne, for one, has in recent years defined 'God' as 'a spirit, that is, a non-embodied person who is omnipresent'[2]—that is, as 'a divine person'. Accordingly, he has been less troubled than traditional theologians about

---

[1] Tertullian, *De carne Christi*, V, quoted by Bernard Williams in 'Tertullian's Paradox' in Antony Flew and Alastair MacIntyre (eds.), *New Essays in Philosophical Theology* (London: SCM Press, 1955), 187–211.

[2] Richard Swinburne, *The Existence of God* (Oxford: Clarendon Press, 1979), 90. Cf. also Swinburne's *The Coherence of Theism* (Oxford: Clarendon Press, 1977), 99: 'That God is a person, yet one without a body, seems one of the most elementary claims of theism.'

speaking of there being three Gods.[3] Brian Davies, who has more scruples in this matter, has suggested that Aquinas himself might have been willing to dispense with the word 'person' as the appropriate way of expressing what there are three of in the Blessed Trinity.[4]

In my view we do better to begin, not by consulting our intuitions about the meaning of the word 'person', but by looking at the reasons we have for affirming oneness and threeness, respectively, and then seeing where these reasons lead us. I believe that the reasons we have for insisting on the unity of the Godhead do not militate in the least against our recognizing three divine Persons. Indeed, the relationships whose revelation demands this recognition of Trinity themselves provide an understanding of what it is for God to be one. It is not, as seemed likely, a case of antinomy. An antinomy is a pair of arguments one of which seems to constitute a proof of a proposition, the thesis, and the other to constitute an equally cogent proof of its contradictory, the antithesis. We should note, however, that in metaphysical contexts the arguments for a conclusion are often the best guide for showing us what that conclusion really means. And in this case, the arguments for the unity of God make it clear that their conclusion in no way contradicts the doctrine to which we are led by the reasons we have for affirming the Trinity of divine Persons. Unity and Trinity are not related as thesis and antithesis: no antinomy here.

What are our reasons for affirming that there is a God at all? Following St Thomas, I would say that we affirm the existence of God because we need an explanation of certain facts about the world, the fact of its changeableness, the fact of its contingency, the fact of its limited perfection, the fact of its order. The first of the five ways starts from the premiss that what is in process of change must be caused to change by something else. Where we are prompted to look for explanations, it is not too difficult to know where to begin; but it is not so easy to know where to stop. Every atheistic philosopher who puts pen to paper (or switches on his word processor) recycles the Schopenhauer canard that those who use the principle of causality to prove the existence of God are like people who hire

[3] Cf. Richard Swinburne, 'Could there be more than One God?', *Faith and Philosophy*, v (1988), 225–41.

[4] Brian Davies, OP, *The Thought of Thomas Aquinas* (Oxford: Clarendon Press, 1992), 202.

a cab and dismiss it when they have reached their destination. I start with the present state of the world, and trace that back and back through a vast number of previous states until I reach, perhaps, a big bang. What, I ask, produced the big bang? The only explanation is that the big bang was made by God. Ah, says Schopenhauer, but who made God? As though a philosopher as considerable as St Thomas would have left himself open to the charge that he had used the premiss 'Everything has a cause' to obtain the conclusion 'There is an uncaused cause'.

But of course he did *not* use the premiss 'Everything has a cause'. He used the qualified premiss 'Everything that is in process of change has a cause', or 'Everything that has a beginning of existence has a cause'. It is only something which is in process of change or which began to exist which calls for an explanation in this way. If we reach a cause which is not itself in process of change, which had no beginning of existence, and whose existence is necessary, the pressure to take the series of *explanantia* further and further back comes to an end. The same principle applies where an explanation is sought for something having a 'perfection' to a limited degree: why just so much and no more? But possession of unlimited perfection does not cry out for explanation. How could there be an *explanation* of someone's possessing all knowledge? One could hardly say 'How did you come to know *all that*?'

The same issue arises when a plurality of causes combine to produce some phenomenon. David Hume, discussing the so-called Argument from Design, suggested that we might just as well look to a designing committee as to a single designer for our explanation of the order in the universe. It might indeed provide us simultaneously with an explanation of the disorder which is so conspicuously mixed in with that order, giving rise to the problem of evil. Committees are notorious for producing botched work. The difficulty with a committee as an explanation of order is that, even if the decisions of the individual members of the committee are not regarded as needing explanation, we need to know why the fact that they do agree, or that a majority of them agree, should itself explain anything. Even a unanimous decision needs some machinery to make it effective. Committees can bring things about only when there is some institution which gives them this power. That there is such an institution is a fact, if indeed it is a fact, which calls for an explanation.

Might there not be the same difficulty about tracing the order back to the activity of a single mind? Is there not such a thing as a divided mind, a will opposed to itself? Hume again objected to the suggestion that we could find in the ideas of the mind of a designer the explanation of the order observed in the supposed artefact. The blueprint of the building, even if it exists only in the mind of the architect, is a blueprint only to the extent that it exhibits the same pattern, the same organization, as the building that is being produced. But here again, Hume claimed, the phenomenon of order calls out for explanation. A design for a building, existing in someone's mind, is a collection of ideas; and Hume thought that the organization of these ideas in such a way as to constitute them a plan for a building was an instance of exactly the same sort of order as the existence of the building in which the architect's vision results.

Here, I believe, Hume is mistaken. The inventor of the internal combustion engine had a thought. I am not the person to spell out with any degree of accuracy what that thought was; but let us suppose that it was something like this: 'There could be a machine which would use liquid fuel to move pistons in cylinders by making small explosions, and the movement of the pistons could be transferred to that of a turning wheel.' This is no doubt highly simplified, but even so, it involves considerable complexity. Without such complexity it would not be *that* thought. And without some complexity it would not be a thought at all. Hume's idea of an idea is more than usually confused at this point. He thought that ideas were mental pictures which, like playing cards, might or might not be arranged in a regular pattern. There is the idea of *machine* and the idea of *fuel* and the idea of *using x to y*, and so forth, and they need to be arranged just as carefully as the sparking plugs and the pistons and the cylinders if we are to have even the idea of the internal combustion engine.

The supposed idea of *using x to y* ought to give us pause. The concept of something being a means to something else is not a picture which can sit around all on its own like the King of Spades, waiting to be put into some arrangement. To use terminology helpfully provided by Gilbert Ryle, the words 'in order to' can be *extracted* from the sentence 'Fuel ignites in order to produce explosions', but the concept expressed by those words can only be *abstracted* from the thought expressed by the sentence. The concepts, the ideas, that compose a thought exist only potentially until they are actualized by the occurrence of some thought to which they contribute. Ideas do not occur side by side like playing cards laid out for a game of patience. Nor do they occur serially like notes in a tune. The concept of *using x to y* is a capacity possessed by someone for making judgements of a certain sort, judgements about ends and means. Unless they take their place in a judgement, they do not exist. They do not lie about waiting for someone to order them in a certain way, like cards that have been well shuffled. They exist only as part of an organization.

So it is idle to ask for an explanation of the order exhibited by a given thought. Without order there is no thought. The order that exists between the elements of a thought is necessary, not contingent. It needs explanation only to the extent that the occurrence of the thought itself needs explanation.

A thought may occur as what is affirmed, 'It is the case that so and so', or as what is decreed, 'Let it be the case that so and so'. In the first case, '*Est*', we have description: in the second, '*Fiat*', we have prescription.[5] Where a thought occurs as a *Fiat*, it is an act of will. Such is the act of creation.

It is an infirmity of the human mind which sees creation as a series of acts of will spread out over seven days of creation or millions of years. What God creates has a history; one event takes place after another; the dinosaurs give place to the mammals. But God is not literally working his purposes out as age succeeds to age. God's purpose is all one, a single act of will that this possible world should be enacted, this history unfold. What is willed takes aeons to develop, but the will that this should happen is eternally complete; it exists *tota simul*. And this single perfect act of will is not the sort of thing for which an explanation can be demanded. It is the only thing for which an explanation cannot be demanded. The buck of explanation stops here.

There can, therefore, be only one God, the God whose will is the creative act before which our 'Why' questions subside. Nothing but unity could have this finality. A plurality of Gods could not be the creator, and it is only as Creator that we have reason to affirm God at all. Apart from unity God has no *raison d'être*—although after all I have been saying it is infelicitous to talk of a *raison d'être*. One

---

[5] Cf. Anthony Kenny, 'Practical Reasoning', *Analysis*, xxvi (1965–6).

should speak here not of a *ratio essendi*, a reason for his existing, but of a *ratio credendi*, a reason for our believing in him.

Things that occupy space are identified, picked out, by their relationships with other things or places. From where I am now, in Blackfriars, Oxford, St John's is across the road. Beyond that is Balliol, followed by the College of the Holy and Undivided Trinity, and so on past Blackwell's to the New Bodleian. Objects in the physical world are identified by me by the spatial relations in which they stand to other objects and, ultimately, to where I am now. Natural numbers are identified in terms of their relationships to their predecessors: thirty-three is the successor of thirty-two. It makes no sense to suppose that any other number, or that several numbers, might have succeeded thirty-two in the way that thirty-three does. We do not have to choose between candidates for this position. It is the same with God. We cannot say that Jehovah just happens to be God, that in other possible worlds Baal got the job. All possible worlds lead to, and stem from, the one God, just as all lines of longitude in the Northern Hemisphere converge on the North Pole. In God's case, as in the others, the identification proceeds via a certain relationship or set of relationships.

But God lived here on earth some 2,000 years ago. He was born and grew up and worked and taught and died and was raised from the dead in the place that we now call Israel. And he talked all the time of his Father, whom he told us too to call Father, and who was most certainly God. Father and Son were clearly distinct persons. The Father proclaims that the Son is his beloved. The Son reiterates that he has come to do the will of his Father. Love and obedience—these are ways in which *persons* relate to each other. The Father communicates knowledge to the Son; he reveals things to him; he tells him things. And this is one of the principal ways in which persons are related to persons—they tell each other things. We have here another set of relationships, which again provide the foundation for identification. The Father is identified as such, and as he who has sent the Son into the world. The Son is identified as such, and as he in whom the Father is well pleased. And a third person is identified: another, the Paraclete, who is also sent by God the Father, and, as we in the West say, by God the Son too. Traditional theology speaks of these relationships as constituted by 'processions', and speaks of those who proceed and those from whom they proceed as 'subsistent relations'.

When I first met this phrase 'subsistent relation' I thought it was utter nonsense. *Being underneath* is a relation. How could something like *being underneath* be subsistent? Surely a relation was a way in which *things*—subsistent entities—were related, the last sort of entity that could be supposed to exist in its own right—to subsist. Then I read Aristotle's *Categories*. That made me realize that when Aquinas speaks of a relation, he means something like *being the teacher of Plato* or *being underneath the carpet*—what we should call a relational property. Now *being the teacher of Plato* is something that can be said of Socrates, but it is not what Socrates *is*. Socrates might have existed, even if Plato had died in infancy and had never been taught by anyone. But if there were someone whose whole identity consisted in being related to someone in a certain way, we might express this fact by speaking of this being as a 'subsistent relation'. What it is to be the Second Person of the Trinity just is to be begotten of the Father. What it is to be the First Person just is to be he of whom the Son is begotten. If the analogy may be forgiven, what it is to be thirty-three just is to be the successor of thirty-two.

Now we have come close to the formulation that seems hardest to accept as consistent. For we have spoken of Christ as God the Son, and we have spoken of the one who is his Father as God. If the Church speaks of the Holy Spirit also as God, the logical strain is no greater than it already is. In the words of the Athanasian Creed: The Father is God, the Son is God, and the Holy Ghost is God; yet they are not three Gods but one God. So the Son and the Holy Ghost are not different Gods. Should we say, therefore, that the Son is the same God as the Father? St Thomas asks the question 'is the Son different from the Father', where 'different' represents the Latin masculine form *alius*.[6] His answer is 'Yes', but he hastens to add that the answer would have been 'No' if the questioner had used the neuter form *aliud*. In English we might represent the distinction by saying that the Son is *what* the Father is, but not *who* the Father is. This is the distinction between specific and numerical identity: the Son is specifically, but not numerically, the same as the Father.

If, however, we take the Athanasian formula to mean that the Father is the same as God, the Son is the same as God, and the

---

[6] *Summa Theologiae*, Ia, q. 31, a. 2.

Holy Ghost is the same as God, it seems to follow that they are numerically the same God—that is to say, for example, that the Son is in the numerical sense the same God as the Holy Ghost. But perhaps what is wrong with the words 'The Son and the Holy Ghost are different Gods' is not that they say something false, and that we must therefore assert what appears to be the contradictory, but that both they and their apparent contradictory alike fail to be truly intelligible.

Can we assume without question that when we say 'The Father is God' we mean just what would be meant by saying 'The Father is the same as God'? St John's Gospel begins: 'In the beginning was the Word, and the Word was with God, and the Word was God.' I think we tend to read the last clause here as though it had the same sense as 'The Word was the same as God'. 'God' feels to us like a proper name. But the Greek makes a difference: literally it says, 'In beginning was the Word, and the Word was with *the* God, and God was the Word.'[7] Not only is there a definite article before the first occurrence of the word for God—θεός—which is omitted before the second occurrence of that word, but the word 'God' comes first in the last clause. Word order in Greek at this point indicates if anything the opposite of what is indicated by the English word order. In English the word that comes first in the sentence is naturally taken to be the subject. In Greek it is often an indication of its being the predicate. It is certainly so here, as the omission of the definite article makes clear. 'God' is being predicated of the Word. St John is telling us that the Word was divine. *Deus*, says St Thomas, is a *nomen naturae*. When we say 'The Father is God' we are saying *what* the Father is, not *who* he is. What the Father is, is the same as what the Son is and the same as what the Holy Ghost is: each is God. Each is ὁμοούσιος, 'of one substance' with each of the others. Just so, Peter is what Paul is, a man.

But wait. Are we then to say that the Son is what the Father is, a God? Should we translate St John's Greek, 'Θεὸς ἦν ὁ λόγος' as 'The Word was a God'? Greek and Latin give us no help here, because neither has an indefinite article.[8] Greek-speakers and

<hr />

[7] Cf. Karl Rahner, 'Theos in the New Testament', in *Theological Investigations*, 2nd edn. (London: Darton, Longman and Todd, 1965), 136 n. 1.

[8] Peter Geach pointed out to me years ago that there was something strange about the relation between the authorized Latin and English translations of the clause in the Nicene Creed recording the Incarnation. The English, 'was made man', which is one of the few clauses of the Creed where we still use the translation made

Latin-speakers did not have to pronounce on the appropriateness
or inappropriateness of anything analogous to the English sentence, 'The Word was a God' or 'The Son is what the Father is, a
God'. But that does not mean that we English-speakers do not have
to make up our minds about these matters.[9] The indefinite article is
appropriate where the plural is appropriate. To say 'The Son is
what the Father is, and what the Holy Ghost is, a God' is to suggest
precisely what the Creed denies: 'They are not three Gods, but one
God.' But this remark, surely, is what Wittgenstein would call a
grammatical observation. It is not like saying 'I haven't got three
cars, but just one car'. It is more like saying 'There aren't three
North Poles. There couldn't be more than one.' Unity is part of the
raison d'être of deity, as I was maintaining earlier. 'God' is not a
count-noun like 'man' or 'car' or 'symphony'; nor is it a mass-noun
like 'water' or 'cheese' or 'misery': you can't speak of a parcel of
God as you can of a parcel of water, or of a lump of God as you can
of a lump of cheese, or of a great deal of God as you can of a great
deal of misery. And since it is neither a count-noun nor a mass-
noun, it cannot be substituted for 'A' in the phrases 'is the same A
as' or 'is a different A from': this can be the same car as the one I
came in last year; this can be different water from the water I
washed in yesterday; but we cannot say that the Father is the same
God as, or a different God from, the Son.

  'God' is, for all that, a name, a *nomen naturae*. But names of
this sort, like 'frog' and 'oak' and 'silver', seem to be either count-
nouns or mass-nouns. What is 'God' the name of, a sort of stuff or
a kind of thing? The answer is that we don't rightly know, although
neither of these alternatives looks promising. We don't know, because 'God', in Aristotelian terms, signifies God's essence, 'what it
is to be God', or 'what it is for God to be'. St Thomas, following

---

in the sixteenth century, was obviously taken from the Latin, '*homo factus est*'—the
Greek original uses the single word '*ἐνανθρωπήσαντα*'. But there is nothing in '*homo
factus est*' to justify the omission of the indefinite article in English: no reason not to
say 'he was made a man', or more correctly still 'he became a man'.

  [9] Greek-speakers may not have had an indefinite article, but they had plural
forms of nouns. These forms were available, as in English, only for what are now
called 'count-nouns'. And the speaker of Homeric Greek would have seen no
difficulty in *counting* gods and using plural forms like '*τρεῖς θεοί*'. The interesting
question is whether the Hebrew concept of *God* was such that it would have been
appropriate for their word for it to function as a count-noun. The form of the word,
haelohim, is plural with the definite article. How would St John have written '*θεὸς ἦν
ὁ λόγος*', in Hebrew or Aramaic?

Aristotle, says that what it is for living things to be is to live. God is a living God, so God's essence, what it is for God to *be*, is his life. But we do not know what God's life is like. St Thomas tells us that no one this side of death knows what the divine essence is. And if what it is to be God is something that we cannot fully grasp, what it is for there to be one God must also be hidden. Unity follows essence.

How then do we know what we mean by 'God', what our nominal definition is of the world 'God'? We know this, in St Thomas's view, in terms of the way the world is related to God. God is that to which the world is related as its Creator. More precisely, God is that whose act of will, eternally willing by a single, complete, perfect act, brings it about that our universe comes into existence, if so it does, and continues to exist. All the attributes which natural reason ascribes to God are derived from this primary reason that we have for saying that there is a God at all. And that goes for unity, in so far as it can be called an 'attribute'.

God is known to us in terms of a relation. But what God is, is not a relation. God is that, whose essence we do not know, to which we are related as creatures. 'Holy Ghost' is the name of a subsistent relation (meaning, as we have seen, in this context, relational property): 'God' is the name of a substance. However, we lack a *real* definition of 'God', and in default of this the *nominal* definition, which is the best we can come up with, has to treat 'God' as the name of a relational property, the relational property of being creator to each and every creature. It is part of our understanding of the relation involved here that its divine term is the same for every possible creature, just as the North Pole is the point on which all lines of longitude in the Northern Hemisphere converge. So there is no more sense in talk about Gods or 'the same God' than in talk about North Poles or 'the same North Pole'.

But do we have to say that we know nothing of the life of God? Is not St John telling us about this when he says in his first Epistle, 'God is love'?

How does St John know that this is what God is? His reply is given in the opening words of that Epistle: 'That which was from the beginning, which we have heard, which we have seen with our eyes, which we have looked upon, and our hands have handled, of the Word of life; (For the life was manifested, and we have seen it, and bear witness, and shew unto you that eternal life, which was

with the Father, and was manifested unto us;) That which we have
seen and heard declare we unto you.'

Aquinas thought, however, that 'God is love' was knowable by
the light of reason, that it was part of that knowledge of God which
could be obtained by philosophical proof reflecting on the world in
which we live.[10] If he is right, it looks as though reason, not revelation, is the source of our awareness of a plurality of Persons in the
heart of the Godhead. If love is God's nature, his love must have an
object other than his creation, or any part of it: to believe otherwise
would be to make God dependent for his innermost activity on
something that is not himself. But love is relational, and the relation in question is irreflexive: that is to say, it makes no sense to
talk of a person loving herself.

Eyebrows may be raised at this. Do we not talk constantly of self-
love? Are we not enjoined to love our neighbour as ourselves? This
is in fact how St Thomas deals with the consequence of supposing
that natural theology can prove that God is love. The love that
philosophical proof can establish as being identical with God is, in
Aquinas's view, the love that God has of himself. In my view this
will not do. I believe that talk of self-love is analogical, if not
metaphorical. When we are told to love our neighbour as ourselves,
the point is that we are to look after the interests of our neighbour
as we look after our own, and looking after someone's interests is a
typical manifestation of love for her. Again it is said that someone
who is unable to love herself is unable to love anyone else. But lack
of self-love is here, surely, a way of talking about a failure to value
oneself properly. It is the same as self-disgust, self-depreciation,
self-neglect—a syndrome that is more hinted at than adequately
described by the phrase 'failure to love oneself'. But real love, love
in the literal sense, requires more than one person.

So if God is love, that love must involve the love of one person
by another. And if creatures cannot be the only ones who are the
objects of God's love, there must be a plurality of Persons in the
Godhead.[11] If God is love, there must be distinction of Persons in

---

[10] *Summa Theologiae*, Ia, q. 20, a. 1. Strictly speaking, the article proves only that
love is in God; but since Aquinas also believes himself to have proved that each of
the divine attributes is identical with God himself, he may be said to have claimed
to possess a proof of the proposition that God is love.

[11] This conclusion is drawn by P. T. Geach, *The Virtues* (Cambridge: Cambridge
University Press, 1977), 75 ff. This view is compatible with St Thomas's insistence
that the doctrine of the Trinity, the doctrine that there are just three Persons in the

the unity of the divine nature. And just as the unity is complete, so the distinction is absolute. There is no I–thou relation if the I might any moment split into a they or merge with thou to become an it. The one I love is utterly distinct from me. Only so is there any power in the drama of love. But in desire the lover is totally one with the beloved.

I wish at this point to call to your attention the problem of other minds. I can never have your experiences. If I know that you have them, this can only be because you tell me of them or because I see your reaction to your surroundings and the way you behave. But are these sources of information good enough to provide me with knowledge? Should I not need for this an awareness of your thoughts and feelings as direct as that which you have yourself?

This is not just a dry conundrum to keep philosophers happy. It can be an agony felt by human beings who are in love, an expression of longing for the overcoming of separation. Nothing will serve except a free entrance into the heart and mind of the beloved. The distance between the self and the other is felt as a barrier which in some way must be broken down. Browning's poem 'Two in the Campagna' is well known, but perhaps it is worth quoting nevertheless.

> How say you? Let us, O my dove,
>   Let us be unashamed of soul,
> As earth lies bare to heaven above!
>   How is it under our control
> To love or not to love.
>
> I would that you were all to me,
>   You that are just so much, no more.
> Nor yours nor mine, nor slave nor free!
>   Where does the fault lie? What the core
> O' the wound, since wound must be?
>
> I would I could adopt your will,
>   See with your eyes, and set my heart
> Beating by yours, and drink my fill
>   At your soul's springs,—your part my part
> In life, for good and ill.
>
> No. I yearn upward, touch you close,
>   Then stand away. I kiss your cheek,

Godhead, is accessible only by revelation. Plurality of Persons must be distinguished from trinity of Persons.

Catch your soul's warmth—I pluck the rose
  And love it more than tongue can speak—
Then the good minute goes.

Already how am I so far
  Out of that minute? Must I go
Still like the thistle-ball, no bar,
  Onward, whenever light winds blow
Fixed by no friendly star?

Just when I seemed about to learn?
  Where is the thread now? Off again?
The old trick? Only I discern—
  Infinite passion, and the pain
Of finite hearts that yearn.[12]

'The good minute' is, perhaps, the brief period when consummation seems to be achieved. For that short space the two wills are one, the lover sees with the eyes of the beloved. It passes, and the finite hearts are left with the yearning of infinite passion.

The life of God is for all eternity, I suggest, what Browning's lover achieved only for a minute. Each of the Persons of the Trinity has knowledge and will of his own, but is entirely open to those of the other, so that each adopts those of the other, sees with his eyes, as it were. The barriers that keep us from knowing each other's hearts, save fleetingly, in 'the good minute', are there down eternally.

There is, in any case, an 'other minds' problem for those who ascribe to God complete knowledge of the human soul, amongst them the Psalmist. God alone, he tells us, *scrutat renes et corda*, 'searches the heart and reins'. (Ps. 7: 10). We can hardly suppose that this scrutiny begins and ends with our behaviour. God's knowledge of the conscious life of his creatures must already be supposed to overcome the difficulties that trouble the 'other minds' sceptic. Still less can there be fences to prevent any Person of the Trinity from penetrating into the inner life of another. And yet the love of the Father is distinct from the love of the Son, and both from that of the Holy Ghost. If there were no distinction, the joy of sharing would be absent. Where there is no *meum* and *tuum*, there is no giving. We must not admit any confusion of the divine Persons.

---

[12] Francis Palgrave (ed.), *The Golden Treasury* (London: Macmillan, 1943), no. ccclxxviii.

And we, who are promised a share in the divine life, shall we in this way obtain release from the pain of hearts that yearn with infinite passion? Is the bliss of heaven chiefly this: that the impossibility of entering into the mind of another, of welcoming another into my own mind, is overcome without the minds themselves being merged? Is it the breaking down of the barrier between what is self and what is not?

Eastern religions, to the small extent that I know anything about them, seem to speak in ways that resemble these. In Hinduism the great enlightenment is the realization that Atman (self) is the very same as Brahman (deity). In Buddhism enlightenment consists in getting rid of the illusion of self, in accepting Anatta, the no-self doctrine. But neither Hinduism nor Buddhism seems to me to preserve the diversity in unity that makes the consummation of love, either in the inner life of God or in the bliss of heaven, answer to the longing at which Browning hints. The Hindu speaks not of a loving union, but of an identification of Atman with Brahman. And the Buddhist dispenses with the self altogether. In recent years Derek Parfit and his friends have not hesitated to claim agreement between their own 'low' doctrine of the self and the Buddhist Anatta. Philosophers and Buddhologists differ on the question of how far this analogy may be pressed. But Buddhists and Parfittians seem to agree at least in this: they are trying to get rid of me. And this matters. Not because I cling to my own identity, my uniqueness, my separateness. Quite the contrary. It is because I want to give full access to my heart—which seems the most natural word for it—to the God who loves me and to those with whom, by participation in the divine life, that love can be extended. To give and to receive. To know and to be known. To be an I confronting a thou, though not merely confronting, but totally open, all barriers down. And if they get rid of me before my desire is fulfilled, I am deprived of 'the one thing necessary'. Where love is concerned, whether human or divine, to confound the persons is to destroy its very essence.

The unity which Browning sensed in the fleeting moment is, as he saw, a unity not only of knowledge but of will. In love my will is identified with yours. I not only want what you want, but I want it with your wanting. The satisfaction of your desire is always the satisfaction I desire, and it is *qua* the satisfaction of your desire that I desire it, though not only *qua* the satisfaction of your desire. (We do not just conveniently both happen to like the same film.) In

God, to will is to act. So just as the divine Persons in their mutual love will the same thing with the same will, so they act in one and the same act. This is why, in the classical terminology, all the *operationes ad extra* are acts of the Godhead and acts of each of the divine Persons. It is in fact inaccurate to speak here of *acts* in the plural, of *operationes*. The act of creation is one act, a single decree which says '*Fiat*' to the entire history of the universe. And the voice which utters that '*Fiat*' is at once the voice of the Father and the voice of the Son and the voice of the Holy Ghost. Each speaks with the voice of the others which have become his own voice. For the voice of God is an inner voice, the very thought of the divine Mind. To us God says, 'My ways are not your ways, neither are my thoughts your thoughts.' But to the other Persons of the Holy Trinity each Person says, 'My thoughts, like my ways, just *are* your thoughts, my will your will, my act your act.'

Since love is the essence of God, what it is for God to be, it is no accident that the wills of the divine Persons are united. Their unanimity is not a passing phase but eternally present, not contingent but necessary, and therefore not something which needs to be explained. It is a unanimity which is actually a unity: there is no possibility of disunity between the acts of will of the divine Persons in their *operationes ad extra*. Indeed, unanimity is too weak an expression to describe what is meant. The will of the lover and the beloved coincide so completely that there is a single act of willing. 'Let us make man in our own image' is not the record of a decision arrived at after long hours of negotiation, like the decisions of the European Community. 'I would I could adopt your will,' says Browning. But the Father, the Son, and the Holy Ghost have each other's will, not by adoption, but by nature.

And this unity, which is the consequence of the fact that love is the very life of God, corresponds to the unity, which, as we saw, is a necessary attribute of deity, because only when it reaches unity— and a necessary unity at that—can the pressure to take explanation further be relieved. We must affirm that God is one, not because there was a clear winner in the competition for the post, not because this was an office that was not put into commission, but because plurality can never be the resting-place where the quest to explain the universe can come to an end. The reasons that we have for affirming the existence of a God at all are reasons for affirming that there cannot be many Gods. What we know of the life of God through revelation confirms this: God is the love of three Persons for each other. It is no use objecting that the unity which consists in the love of the three Persons is not enough to constitute that oneness of substance, of οὐσία, to which the definitions of the Councils commit us. We do not know by reason in this life what this οὐσία, what it is for God to be, or to be one, is. We cannot, on the basis of knowledge of this οὐσία, say that the unitedness of love is inadequate to constitute what it is for God to be one. And what other reason could we have for rejecting it? This, then, is the substance, the οὐσία, which must not be divided. It is precisely as Creator, as the source of all contingent being, that God must be one. How could this unity be more gloriously manifested than in the love of the utterly distinct and unconfounded Persons who together constitute the Holy and undivided Trinity?

PART IV

Atonement

II

Is the Doctrine of the Atonement a Mistake?

JOHN HICK

One can wish to honour a thinker because one agrees with his work or because one disagrees with it but nevertheless sees it as important and therefore as needing to be discussed. My own motivation in contributing to the present volume in honour of Richard Swinburne is the latter. He is a major figure in the philosophy of religion today, exercising his powerfully logical mind with immense energy, and is now producing in a series of volumes what will amount to a new *summa* of Christian dogma. My own view is that this new *summa*, produced at the end of the twentieth century, is a vast anachronism, representing the thought-forms out of which Christianity is developing rather than the kind of new thinking that is needed as we approach the twenty-first century. But Swinburne's growing *summa* is nevertheless a very considerable intellectual achievement, and those who see this as misapplied should present reasons for so thinking. The present chapter attempts to do this on one particular topic.

The term 'atonement' is so deeply embedded in Christian discourse that every systematic theologian feels obliged to have a doctrine under this heading. And yet the word is so variously used that some of these doctrines have little in common except the name. In its broad, etymological meaning, at-one-ment signifies becoming one with God—not ontologically but in the sense of entering into a right relationship with our creator, this being the process or state of salvation. But in its narrower sense, atonement refers to a specific method of receiving salvation, one presupposing that the barrier to this is guilt. It is in this context that we find the ideas of penalty, sacrifice, oblation, propitiation, expiation, satisfaction, substitu-

This chapter is adapted, with permission, from John Hick, *The Metaphar of God Incarnate* (London: SCM Press, 1993; Louisville: Westminster John Knox, 1994).

tion, forgiveness, acquittal, ransom, justification, redemption, and remission of sins, forming a complex of ideas which has long been central to the Western or Latin development of Christianity.

In this narrower sense, Jesus's crucifixion was an act of atoning, or making up for, human sin. On the other hand, in the broader sense in which atonement simply means salvation, or entering into a right relationship with God, Jesus's death may or may not be separated from his self-giving life as a whole, as having a special significance on its own. As a rough approximation we can say that the broader sense has been more at home in the Eastern or Greek development of Christianity, the narrower sense in its Western or Latin development.

In my view it would be best, in the interests of clarity, to restrict the term 'atonement' to its narrower, more specific meaning. The basic notion is then that salvation requires God's forgiveness, and that this in turn requires an adequate atonement to satisfy the divine righteousness and/or justice. This atoning act is a transaction, analogous to making a payment to cancel a debt or to remit an impending punishment. In the background is the idea of the moral order of the universe which requires that sin, as a disruption of that order, be balanced or cancelled either by just punishment of the offender or a substitute, or by some adequate satisfaction in lieu of punishment.

I am going to argue that in this narrower sense the idea of atonement has played itself out; although of course the broader sense, in which atonement simply means salvation, is alive and indeed vitally important. In so arguing I am, I think, reflecting a widespread contemporary perception. Indeed, were it not for its recent revival by some Christian philosophers who, unlike most contemporary theologians, see Church doctrine as a set of immutable truths, one could easily think that the notion of atonement, in its narrower sense, had died out among thoughtful Christians. For modern treatments of salvation seldom centre upon Anselm's doctrine of a satisfaction to cancel the insult to God's majesty caused by creaturely disobedience or the penal-substitutionary idea of an imputed justification won by Christ's having taken upon himself the punishment due for human sin.

However, as with other traditional doctrines, it is important to try to go back in historical imagination to the original experience out of which it grew. It is evident that the profound and all-absorbing experience of the early post-Easter Christian community was of a living spirit, which they identified as the spirit of the risen Jesus, welling up within them, individually and corporately, and drawing them into a new, joyous and exhilarating stream of life, full of positive meaning and free from the besetting fears of the ancient world—of demons, of fate, of sin, and of death. This new, liberated life, brimming with meaning and hope, was the religious reality that was to be expressed, first in what seem to us today a cluster of bizarre images, and later, within medieval Latin Christianity, in various sophisticated theories of a transactional atonement. However, we in the Western Churches today, both Catholic and Reformed, may well feel that none of these inherited theories retains any real plausibility, and that we should look again at the alternative development within Eastern Christianity of the idea of a gradual transformation of the human by the divine Spirit, called by Orthodox theologians 'deification' (*theosis*).

These two conceptions do not of course entirely exclude each other. Latin theology has also held that the justification won by Jesus's death leads to sanctification, which is the gradual transformation of the sinner into a saint. And Orthodox theology also holds that Jesus's death was somehow crucial in bringing about our deification. And since both traditions use the same stock of biblical images, one can find much the same language somewhere within each. But nevertheless, their basic tendencies move in markedly different directions, one guided by a transactional atonement understanding, the other by a transformation understanding of salvation.

We shall come back later to the Eastern tradition and its transformational conception, but in the meantime let us look more closely at the transactional model. Richard Swinburne has recently made an impressive attempt, in his *Responsibility and Atonement*,[1] to retrieve a transactional conception. His understanding of salvation can be summarized as follows:

1. Guilt in relation to God is the great barrier to salvation: that is, to receiving God's gift of eternal life. (This is assumed throughout Swinburne's discussion.)

---

[1] Richard Swinburne, *Responsibility and Atonement* (Oxford: Clarendon Press, 1989). References to this book are included in the text. Another such attempt is that of Eleonore Stump, in 'Atonement According to Aquinas', in Thomas Morris (ed.), *Philosophy and the Christian Faith* (Notre Dame, Ind.: University of Notre Dame Press, 1988), and 'Atonement and Justification', in Ronald Feenstra and Cornelius Plantinga (eds.), *Trinity, Incarnation, and Atonement* (Notre Dame, Ind.: University of Notre Dame Press, 1989).

2. In the case of wrong done by one human being to another, reconciliation requires four things: repentance, apology, whatever reparation (that is, undoing of the harm done) is possible, and penance—that is, some additional act, such as the giving of a costly gift, which is not part of the reparation but is an expression of the reality of one's regret and sorrow at having done the wrong (chapter 5).

3. God is a personal being—though absolutely unique in nature—with whom we exist in the same kind of moral relationship as to our fellow human beings, and the same general conditions for reconciliation apply. (This is assumed throughout part II, though not explicitly stated.)

4. All wrongdoing to fellow humans is also wrongdoing to God. For 'Man's dependence on God is so total that he owes it to him to live a good life. Hence when a man fails in any objective or subjective duty of his fellows, he also fails in his duty towards God, his creator' (p. 124).

5. We can repent and apologize to God for our sins, but we cannot on our own offer adequate atonement—that is, reparation and penance. For, 'Since what needs atonement to God is human sin, men living second-rate lives when they have been given such great opportunities by their creator, appropriate reparation and penance would be made by a perfect human life' (p. 157).

6. That 'perfect human life' is provided by Christ, who lived without sin and voluntarily endured a death which he openly intended as a sacrifice that we, accepting it from him, can offer to God as atonement for our sins, both individual and corporate. Christ's death is thus 'an offering made available to us men to offer as our reparation and penance'. 'There is no need', Swinburne adds, 'to suppose that life and death [of Christ's] to be the equivalent of what men owe to God (or that plus appropriate penance), however that could be measured. It is simply a costly penance and reparation sufficient for a merciful God to let men off the rest' (p. 154).

7. To be sanctified, and thus saved ultimately, is possible only to those who (as well as repenting and apologizing) participate in the Christian worship of God and plead the atoning death of Christ, thereby throwing off their guilt. To be saved, we must thus be joined—either in this life or hereafter—to the Christian Church, which is the Body of Christ (p. 173).

I think it must be granted that all this is possible; and indeed, those of us who were once fundamentalist Christians, 'washed in the blood of the Lamb', are likely to feel a certain emotional tug towards this set of ideas. The question is not, however, whether such a schema is logically possible, but whether it is religiously plausible; and to many of us today it is likely to seem highly implausible, even though also to have elements of truth within it. I shall comment from this point of view on the seven points listed above.

1. That the idea of salvation revolved around the issues of guilt and atonement is a central theme of the Latin theological tradition, launched above all by St Augustine. By contrast, the Greek tradition, stemming from the early Hellenistic Fathers of the Church and preserved within Eastern Orthodoxy, thinks of salvation as deification or (more precisely) spiritual transformation. Forgiveness is of course an element in this, but it does not have the central place that the Latin tradition, followed by Swinburne at this point, gives to it. Swinburne prefers the Greek to the Latin development on a number of issues; but he does not seem to have considered the radical alternative which the Eastern theological projectory offers. If one sees salvation as the transformation of human existence from self-centredness to a new orientation centred in the ultimate divine Reality, then transaction theories of salvation appear as answers to a mistaken question.

2. Swinburne's analysis of guilt and reconciliation between human beings is excellent; this is one of the 'elements of truth', as it will seem to less conservative Christians, within his total theory.

3. Clearly, for Christianity, God is personal. But that God is another person who is subject to the same moral requirements as ourselves and thus with obligations and duties and possibilities of supererogatory deeds, that God's probable procedures can be predicted by means of a human analogy, and that the proper human analogy leads to the belief that God's saving work is confined in its fullness to the Christian strand of history—strikes me as anthropomorphic, parochial, and unimaginative to a degree that renders it massively implausible. But I shall say more under point number 5 about Swinburne's transfer of the conditions for reconciliation with a fellow human being to reconciliation with God.

4. That our relationship to fellow human beings involves our relationship to God, so that in all that we do we are also ultimately

having to do with God, is from a less conservative point of view another 'element of truth' in Swinburne's theory.

5. When we do wrong, the kind of reparation required is that we do what we can to nullify or reverse the consequences of our action. Thus, when we contribute—as we do almost all the time—to the common evils of the world, we can do something to counter this by contributing to the common good of the world. When we wrong an individual, we can usually do something to recompense the person wronged. And, as Swinburne points out, in such a case it is also appropriate to do something extra, which he calls penance, by offering some additional service or gift to express the reality of our regret and sorrow at having wronged the other person. But the question that has to be asked is whether this fourfold schema—repentance, apology, reparation, and penance—can be carried over unchanged into our relationship with God. Swinburne's fundamental error, in my view, is in assuming that it can. Repentance, confession, and apology as an expression of repentance still apply; the sinner should truly and deeply repent and ask God's forgiveness. But is there also scope, specifically in relation to God, for reparation and the extra that Swinburne calls 'penance'? I suggest that when we have offered reparation plus penance to the human beings whom we have injured, there is no further reparation plus penance to be made solely for God's benefit. In doing all we can to repair matters with our wronged neighbour, we are doing what genuine repentance requires. For God cannot be benefited, and thus recompensed and atoned to, by any human acts in addition to those that benefit God's creation. In relation to God, the truly penitent person, genuinely resolving to do better in the future, can only accept forgiveness as a free gift of grace, undeserved and unearned. It may well be Jesus's life and teaching that prompt someone to do this. But it is not, in my view, appropriate to express that fact by depicting his death as an atoning sacrifice that benefits God and so enables God to forgive humanity.

In this connection Swinburne emphasizes that 'One man can help another to make the necessary atonement—can persuade him to repent, help him to formulate the words of apology, and give him the means by which to make reparation and penance' (p. 149). True; and the divine Spirit may prompt us to a true repentance which wants to make reparation to the human individual or community that we have wronged and to offer some additional service or gift that may be appropriate. But what the Spirit will thus prompt us to do is some act in relation to those human neighbours. It is this that satisfies the principle, which Swinburne rightly stresses, that to take a wrongdoer and his or her wrongdoing seriously entails the need for whatever restitution and whatever additional gift or service is appropriate. But the idea that something further, corresponding to this reparation plus penance towards our human neighbour, is required by God for God's self seems to me groundless. It rests upon a category mistake by which God is treated as another individual within the same moral community as ourselves. For a moral relationship with another person presupposes the possibility of actions that can benefit or injure that other person; but we cannot benefit or injure our creator over and above our actions in benefiting and injuring our fellow creatures.

Further, even if, despite this, a benefit solely to God were possible and required, Swinburne's unargued assumption that a perfect human life would constitute it is, surely, illogical. A perfect life, fulfilling every 'objective and subjective duty', is already, according to Swinburne, owed by all of us to God, and therefore could not constitute a reparation plus penance for not having lived such a life in the past. And yet again, even if *per impossible* it could, how would one single perfect human life—namely, that of Jesus—count as all human beings having led perfect lives? Swinburne's answer at this point is that God was free to accept whatever God wished as an atonement for human sin. 'God could', he says, 'have chosen to accept one supererogatory act of an ordinary man as adequate for the sins of the world. Or he could have chosen to accept some angel's act for this purpose' (p. 160). This is a deeply damaging admission, rendering it truly extraordinary that God should require the agonizing death of his Son. For on Swinburne's view there was no necessity for the Cross, such as was provided in their own way by the satisfaction and penal substitution theories. Swinburne is abandoning the idea of a moral law that could only be satisfied by Jesus's death. For it was, according to him, entirely within God's free choice to establish the conditions for human salvation. But in that case God's insistence on the blood, sweat, pain, and anguish involved in the crucifixion of his innocent Son now seems to cast doubt—to say the least—on the moral character of the Deity.

6. Swinburne says several times that Jesus openly intended his death as 'an offering to God to make expiation in some way for the

sins of men' (p. 122). There is, in fact, no consensus among New Testament scholars as to how Jesus understood his own death. To what extent did he think of it as having religious significance? There is a range of possibilities. A (theologically) minimalist view is expressed by E. P. Sanders.[2] He lists it as 'conceivable' (p. 326) or even 'possible' (p. 332) (in distinction from 'probable', 'highly probable', or 'virtually certain'), that Jesus 'may have given his own death a martyrological significance' (p. 326). Acknowledging—indeed, emphasizing—the historical uncertainties, he notes that 'the idea that a martyr's death is beneficial for others and that his cause will be vindicated is attested in Judaism. . . . It is not necessary to assume that Jesus indicated to his followers that they should think in this way. Once he died, it probably seemed entirely natural to attribute benefit to his death and look for vindication' (pp. 324–5).

At the other end of the scale is the older view of Joachim Jeremias, developed in his influential treatment of the Last Supper.[3] He recalls that a lamb was killed at the original Passover, and its blood smeared, at Yahweh's command, on the Israelites' doors:

As a reward for the Israelites' obedience to the commandment to spread blood on their doors, God manifested himself and spared them, 'passing over' their houses. For the sake of the passover blood God revoked the death sentence against Israel; he said: 'I will see the blood of the passover and make atonement for you'. In the same way the people of God of the End time will be redeemed by the merits of the passover blood. Jesus describes his death as this eschatological passover sacrifice: his vicarious death brings into operation the final deliverance, the new covenant of God. (p. 226)

And Jeremias concludes: 'This is therefore what Jesus said at the Last Supper about the meaning of his death: his death is the vicarious death of the suffering servant, which atones for the sins of the "many", the peoples of the world, which ushers in the beginning of the final salvation and which effects the new covenant with God' (p. 231).

On Jeremias's interpretation we have to suppose that Jesus, in E. P. Sanders's words, 'conceived in advance the doctrine of atonement' (p. 332), a supposition which Sanders regards as highly im-

---

[2] E. P. Sanders, *Jesus and Judaism* (London: SCM Press, 1985). References to this book are included in the text.
[3] Joachim Jeremias, *The Eucharistic Words of Jesus* (1965), trans. Norman Perrin (London: SCM Press, 1966). References to this book are included in the text.

probable. 'Aspects of Jeremias' view, for example that Jesus identified himself with the Suffering Servant of Isaiah, have', he says,
'been disproved, but there are general objections to the whole line
of thought that has Jesus intending to die for others, rather than
just accepting his death and trusting that God would redeem the
situation and vindicate him' (p. 332). However, let us nevertheless,
for the sake of argument, suppose that Jesus did understand his
coming death as a sacrifice to God, analogous to the original
Passover blood-shedding, and that he thought of this as required to
inaugurate God's coming kingdom. Such a self-understanding
could only occur within the context of Jesus's apocalyptic expectation, which was itself a variant of contemporary Jewish restoration
eschatology. But Jesus's expectation, confidently taken up by the
early Church, was not fulfilled, and had faded from Christian consciousness before the end of the first century. The identification of
Jesus as the eschatological prophet inaugurating God's kingdom
went with it, being progressively superseded by his exaltation to a
divine status. This in turn made possible the various atonement
theories which presuppose his divinity, eventually seeing the Cross
as (in the words of the Anglican liturgy) 'a full, perfect, and sufficient sacrifice, oblation, and satisfaction, for the sins of the whole
world'. However, even conservative New Testament scholarship
today does not suggest that Jesus thought of himself as God, or
God the Son, Second Person of a divine Trinity, incarnate; and so
we cannot reasonably suppose that he thought of his death in any
way that presupposes that. It is therefore much more believable, as
a maximal possibility, that Jesus saw himself as the final prophet
precipitating the coming of God's rule on earth than that he saw it
in anything like the terms later developed by the Church's atonement theories.

It is, incidentally, noteworthy that Swinburne departs from the
traditional view that the value of Jesus's death was equal to, or
exceeded, the evil of human sin, so as to be able to balance it.
Swinburne says: 'It is simply a costly penance and reparation sufficient for a merciful God to let men off the rest' (p. 154). But if a
merciful God can properly 'let men off the rest' without a full
punishment having been inflicted or a full satisfaction exacted, why
may not God freely forgive sinners who come in genuine penitence
with a radically changed mind? Traditional atonement theories
explained *why* God could not freely forgive penitent sinners. But

what was intelligible—whether or not acceptable—on those theories becomes unintelligible, and doubly morally questionable, on Swinburne's view.

7. Swinburne also modifies the traditional exclusivist doctrine that salvation is confined to Christians (*extra ecclesiam nulla salus*) by adding that non-Christians may have an opportunity to be converted beyond this life. This epicycle of theory, although departing from established teaching about the finality of death, is the natural next step for one who does not wish to have to defend a manifestly morally repugnant position. It is a form of the Christian 'inclusivism' that I have criticized elsewhere,[4] and I shall not pursue it further here.

The basic fault, as I see it, of the traditional understandings of salvation within the Western development of Christianity is that they have no room for divine forgiveness! For a forgiveness that has to be bought by the bearing of a just punishment or the giving of an adequate satisfaction or the offering of a sufficient sacrifice or reparation is not forgiveness at all, but merely an acknowledgement that the debt has been paid. But in the recorded teaching of Jesus there is, in contrast, genuine divine forgiveness for those who are truly penitent and deeply aware of their own utter unworthiness. In the Lord's Prayer we address God directly as our heavenly Father, and ask for forgiveness for our sins, expecting to receive this—the only condition being that we in turn forgive one another. There is no suggestion of the need for a mediator through whom to approach God or of an atoning death to enable God to forgive. Again, in the Lukan parable of the prodigal son, the father, when he sees his penitent son returning home, does not say, 'Because I am a just as well as a loving father, I cannot forgive him until someone has made adequate atonement for his sins', but rather he 'had compassion, and ran, and fell on his neck, and kissed him. And the son said unto to him, Father, I have sinned against heaven, and in thy sight, and am no more worthy to be called thy son. But the father said to his servants, Bring forth the best robe, and put in on him and put a ring on his hand, and shoes on his feet: and bring hither the fatted calf, and kill it; and let us eat and be merry: For this my son was dead and is alive again; he was lost, and is found' (Luke 15: 20–4). And again, in the Lukan parable of the Pharisee

---

[4] John Hick, *Problems of Religious Pluralism* (London: Macmillan, 1985), ch. 3.

and the publican, the latter 'standing afar off, would not lift up so much as his eyes unto heaven, but smote upon his breast, saying, God be merciful to me a sinner. I tell you, this man went down to his house justified' (Luke 18: 13–14). And yet again, there is the insistence that Jesus came to bring sinners to a penitent acceptance of God's mercy: 'go ye and learn what that meaneth, I will have mercy, and not sacrifice: for I am not come to call the righteous, but sinners to repentance' (Matt. 9: 13).

This was fully in accord with contemporary Judaic understanding. E. P. Sanders, in his authoritative work on Jesus's Jewish background, says: 'The forgiveness of repentant sinners is a major motif in virtually all the Jewish material which is still available from the period' (p. 18). And it continues today in this prayer from the service on the Day of Atonement:

O do thou, in thy abounding compassion, have mercy upon us, for thou delightest not in the destruction of the world . . . And it is said, Let the wicked forsake his ways, and the man of iniquity his thoughts; and let him return unto the Lord, and he will have mercy upon him; and to our God for he will abundantly pardon. But thou art a God ready to forgive, gracious and merciful, slow to anger, plenteous in loving kindness, and abounding in goodness; thou delightest in the repentance of the wicked and hast no pleasure in their death . . . turn ye, turn ye from your evil ways; for why will ye die, O house of Israel? And it is said, Have I at all any pleasure in the death of the wicked, saith the Lord God, and not rather that he should return from his way, and live?'

For Judaism sees human nature as basically good, yet also with an evil inclination that has continually to be resisted. However, God is aware of our finitude and weakness, and is always ready to forgive the truly penitent. In Islam there is an essentially similar view. God is always spoken of in the Qur' an as *Allah rahman rahim*, God the gracious and merciful. God knows our weakness, and forgives those who, in the self-surrender of faith, bow before the compassionate Lord of the universe. Again, in the most widely influential of the Hindu scriptures, the *Bhagavad Gita*, we read,

Please, God, be patient with me.
As a father with his son, a friend with his friend,
A lover with his beloved.[5]

⁵ *The Bhagavad Gītā*, trans. Kees Bolle (Berkeley: University of California Press, 1979), p. 141 (ch. XI, V, 44).

This sense of divine mercy is found throughout the world's monotheistic faiths, with the Latin Christian belief in the need for an atoning death standing out as exceptional. Indeed, within modern Protestant thought, outside the continuing fundamentalist stream, there is now a general acceptance of the idea of a free divine forgiveness for those who truly repent. In an attempt to reconcile this with the traditional language about Jesus's death as the instrument of our salvation, various 'moral influence' theories have been proposed in the modern period. Their essence is admirably expressed in the old preacher's story about the tribal chief who urges his people to abandon cannibalism. When his urgings are ineffective, he tells them that if they must kill someone, they should go to a certain clearing the next day at dawn and kill the man they find there wrapped in a red blanket. They do so, and on opening the blanket find that they have killed their own beloved chieftain; and they are so struck with remorse that they are at last motivated to give up their cannibalism. Likewise, it is suggested, remorse at having crucified the Son of God can lead to repentance and hence God's forgiveness. Thus Auguste Sabatier wrote that Jesus's Passion and death 'was the most powerful call to repentance that humanity has ever heard, and also the most operative and fruitful in marvellous results. The cross is the expiation of sins only because it is the cause of the repentance to which remission is promised.'[6]

This is no longer a transactional conception of atonement, and indeed is no longer a conception of atonement, in the sense of expiation, at all. It is rather a suggestion about how Jesus's death may have helped to make salvation possible. The limitation of this suggestion is that remorse at having (collectively) killed God the Son can be felt only by that minority of human beings who believe that Jesus of Nazareth was indeed the Second Person of a divine Trinity. The notion, which the older satisfaction and penal substitution theories made possible, of an atonement offered on behalf of all humanity, is here lost. The moral influence conception of atonement is in fact one of those theological epicycles whereby it is sought to abandon an untenable traditional idea—in this case the transactional conception of salvation—while at the same time retaining the traditional language.

---

[6] Auguste Sabatier, *The Doctrine of the Atonement* (1901), trans. Victor Leuliette (London: Williams and Norgate; New York: G. P. Putnam's Sons, 1904), 127.

We can now move from a critique of the Western/Latin understanding of salvation as hinging upon sin and guilt and as requiring the atoning sacrifice of Christ, to build upon the work of the Hellenistic Fathers, treating this, however, not as a fully developed theological option but as a movement of thought which can be continued today.

For Christianity is richer and more varied than most Christians, immersed within their own particular strand of it, have commonly been aware. Thus, those of us formed by Western Christianity or its missionary extensions are often ignorant of the rather different Eastern development of Christian thought. The Orthodox Churches themselves, which are guardians of this tradition, have remained more or less moribund, both theologically and ecclesiastically, for many centuries; and I am not advocating acceptance of their whole theological package. But buried in their history is the groundwork of a profound and attractive alternative to the medieval theology of the Roman Church as well as that of the sixteenth-century Reformers and their successors. The difference is between salvation as hinging upon an atoning transaction that enables God to forgive and to accept the fallen human race, and salvation as the gradual transformation of human beings, who are already in the 'image' of God, into what the Hellenistic Fathers, on the basis of Genesis 1: 26, called the 'likeness' of God. Thus the eighth-century John of Damascus wrote: 'The expression "according to the image" indicates rationality and freedom, whilst the expression "according to the likeness" indicates assimilation to God through virtue.'[7] This 'assimilation to God' was also frequently called *theosis* (deification). In the words of the seventh-century Byzantine theologian Maximus the Confessor, 'A man who becomes obedient to God in all things hears God saying "I said: you are gods" (John 10: 34); he then is God and is called "God" not by nature or by relation but by [divine] decree and grace.'[8] Accordingly, to quote a contemporary Orthodox writer, 'The Christian faith . . . is understood to lead to the transfiguration and "deification" of the entire man; and . . . this "deification" is indeed accessible, as a living experience, even now, and not merely in a future kingdom.'[9] It is this actual human

---

[7] John of Damascus, *On the Orthodox Faith*, II. 12.
[8] Maximus the Confessor, *Ambigua*, cited by John Meyendorff, *Byzantine Theology* (New York: Fordham University Press, 1987), 164.
[9] Meyendorff, *Byzantine Theology*, 125.

transformation, or 'deification', that constitutes salvation. Thus, while on the Latin view, to be saved is to be justified—that is, relieved of guilt—by Christ's sacrificial death; on the Orthodox view, to be in process of salvation is to be responding to the presence of the divine Spirit, and thus undergoing a gradual transformation from natural self-centredness to a radically new centring within the divine life. It should be noted that this Eastern understanding largely coincides with the modern 'liberal' Western approach initiated in the nineteenth century by Friedrich Schleiermacher, who viewed the saving influence of Christ in the context of God's total creative work, so that Christ's 'every activity may be regarded as a continuation of that person-forming divine influence upon human nature'.[10]

In Orthodox thought the deification theme is embedded in a comprehensive theology in which the ideas of Incarnation and Trinity are central elements and in which the resurrected Christ plays a vital role in the process of transformation. That role was described only in broad metaphorical terms, however. Thus Athanasius said that humans 'could not become sons, being by nature creatures, otherwise than by receiving the Spirit of the natural and true Son. Wherefore, that this might be, "The Word became flesh" that He might make man capable of Godhead';[11] and again, 'He was made man that we might be made God.'[12] But the way in which God becoming human enables humans to become divine was not spelled out. Indeed, perhaps it cannot be intelligibly spelled out other than in terms of the experience, known within all religious traditions, of being influenced and changed by the life and words of a great exemplar. There is a continuity here with what Adolf Deissmann called St Paul's 'mysticism',[13] which involves humans undergoing a transformation (*metamorphosis*) in Christ; for we 'are being changed into [Christ's] likeness from one degree of glory to another' (2 Cor. 3: 18). We are to be transformed from the state of slavery into the state of sonship (Romans 8: 15–17); or again, conformed (*symmorphosis*) to the image of Christ (8: 29).

---

[10] Friedrich Schleiermacher, *The Christian Faith*, trans. H. R. Mackintosh and J. S. Stewart (Edinburgh: T and T Clark, 1956), para. 100, p. 427.

[11] Athanasius, *Discourses Against the Arians*, II. 21. 59, trans. in *The Nicene and Post-Nicene Fathers*, iv. 380.

[12] Athanasius, *On the Incarnation of the Word of God*, para. 54, trans. in ibid. 65.

[13] Adolf Deissmann, *The Religion of Jesus and the Faith of Paul*, trans. William E. Wilson, 2nd edn. (London: Hodder and Stoughton, 1926), 193 ff.

'Do not be conformed to the world', Paul urges the Christians in Rome, 'but be transformed by the renewal of your mind' (2: 12). And indeed, we may say that to be a Christian is to be one in whose life Christ is the major, the largest single, influence (often among a variety of influences) for salvific transformation.

Jesus's death has indeed played no small part in this transforming influence. Although the meaning of that death was pictured during most of the first Christian millennium in the early ransom imagery, and during most of the second millennium in terms of the morally questionable satisfaction and penal substitution theories, the Cross has continued throughout as the central Christian symbol because it stirs deeper, more complex emotions than are captured by any of these official doctrines. It is for many people a self-evident intuition that an authentic religious leader is willing to be martyred, if necessary, by those who fail to recognize or accept the challenging truths which he or she embodies. It is indeed because true prophets and gurus embody, or live out, or incarnate, their teaching that to reject the message is to reject the messenger; and the most emphatic form of rejection is by inflicting death.

To illustrate this from recent history, in the moral and political conflicts of India and the United States in the twentieth century there was a certain tragic appropriateness in the fact that both Gandhi and Martin Luther King, teaching the universal requirements of love and justice, were assassinated by fanatics motivated by religious and racial prejudice. Likewise, there was a tragic appropriateness to the death of Jesus. He taught the way of life of God's kingdom and the imminent coming of that kingdom on earth. This was to the ruling Roman power a potential incitement to rise up against it in the name of God, as was to happen in 66–70 and again in 135 CE. He also prophesied the destruction of the Jerusalem temple, thus deeply antagonizing its priestly guardians, who collaborated in his arrest and trial.

But these historical factors were soon submerged in the Christian consciousness by a religious understanding of the Crucifixion. Jesus's acceptance of his death as having some positive meaning inevitably evoked, in the thought-world of his time, the universal language of sacrifice. In the Judaism of Jesus's period, a sacrifice made as a sin offering to God involved the shedding of blood as a giving of the life essence. However, as a cumulative result of the teaching of Jesus, as well as of Hosea and Amos before him and many others after him, can we not now see that the sacrifice of animal or human blood pointed, in a crude and inadequate way, to the much deeper sacrifice of the ego point of view in becoming a channel of divine grace on earth? The real meaning of Jesus's death was not that his blood was shed—indeed, crucifixion did not involve much bloodshed—but that he gave himself utterly to God in faith and trust. His Cross was thus a powerful manifestation and continuing symbol of the divine kingdom in this present world, as a way of life in which one turns the other cheek, forgives one's enemies 'unto seventy times seven', trusts God even in the darkness of pain, horror, and tragedy, and is continually raised again to the new life of faith.

And yet even this does not exhaust the felt impact of Jesus's death. For the voluntary death of a holy person has a moral power that reverberates beyond any words that we can frame to express it. Even on a lower level, when someone knowingly gives his or her life for the sake of another—say, in a rescue from fire or avalanche or bomb or an oncoming train or car or in some other way— something has happened that is awe-inspiring and, in an indefinable way, enriching and enhancing to the human community. And so it was, in a much greater way, with the death of Jesus. This is no doubt why the mythological pictures of a ransom paid to the Devil or of a sacrifice to appease the divine honour or justice—or indeed any idea of an atoning sacrifice being required to gain God's forgiveness—have been able to last so long; for, since we cannot fully articulate the impression made upon us by the crucifixion of one who was so close to God, no ecclesiastical language about it has been ruled out as too strange or too extravagant.

Nevertheless, we have to insist that these ecclesiastical theories are all misleading. It is misleading to think that there is a Devil with legitimate rights over against God. It is misleading to think of the heavenly Father on the model of a feudal lord or a stern cosmic moralist. And it is misleading to see acceptance of the Christian mythology of the Cross as the only way to salvation for all human beings. Let the voluntary sacrifice of a holy life continue to challenge and inspire us in a way that transcends words. But let us not reduce its meaning to any culture-bound theological theory.

To summarize and conclude: Jesus's death was of a piece with his life, expressing a total integrity in his self-giving to God; and his cross continues to inspire and challenge us on a level which in no way depends upon atonement theories developed by the Church. Those theories have no doubt helped people in the past to rationalize the immense impact upon them of the cross of Christ, and they did so in ways that cohered with the plausibility structures of their time. But our own intellectual world is so different, both within the Church and without, that traditional atonement theories, including their contemporary variations, no longer perform any useful function.

12

Reflections on the Atonement

J. R. LUCAS

The cross claims to speak to everyone, but different people have different needs, and therefore different ideas of salvation, and hence different understandings of what Jesus' death signifies. As they try to explain what happened at Calvary they naturally make sense of it in accordance with their own needs and own idea of what was effected for them by Jesus' coming down for us and our salvation and dying a criminal's death. The Doctrine of the Atonement is therefore articulated in many various ways, which to some Christians seem profoundly true, but often are reckoned deeply unsatisfactory by others, also moved by the cross, but to whom it speaks in some very different way, answering to different needs, and offering a different sort of salvation.

Different accounts of the Atonement should be assessed stereoscopically. They are not necessarily rivals, and may sometimes be seen as different metaphors, each bringing out some facet of the truth. But they are not all equally valid either; some involve presuppositions, or carry implications, which on a fuller view of Christianity must be rejected. What may be suitably sung at Eastertide may be dangerously misleading if taught as literal truth in catechism. A philosopher's account, while recognizing the meaningfulness of the metaphors, should itself eschew poetry and aim to express the truth, so far as possible, in pedestrian prose.

For many modern Christians the great day of the year is not Good Friday but Easter Sunday. If Jesus really rose from the dead, then the materialist view of the universe is falsified by the facts, and Christian theism vindicated. God proves His existence by this one, fundamental and indisputable, miracle. Other miracles might have done—the stilling of the winds and waves, the raising of Lazarus, the taking up of Elijah into heaven—but this one is more appropriate. Jesus was done to death in the messy happenstance of Jewish history, but God showed that the last word is with Him. On the strength of the resurrection we know that God reigns and the teaching of Jesus is true, and that we can lead our lives accordingly, trusting in the power of God and the love shown in the life and teaching of Jesus Christ.

The resurrection also speaks to many in a more personal and interested way. It shows that death is not the end we all naturally fear that it is. Christ triumphed over death. It is not fully clear what that triumph will mean in their own future lives, but at least they can live as men not without hope. They are freed from the fear of death. The fundamental message of Christianity for them is not the cross but the empty tomb, and, as in the case of those whose chief fear is the fear that atheism might be true, the importance of Good Friday lies not in itself but in its preparing the scene for the victory of Easter Day.

But although Easter is the great festival of the Church, it does not attract as much attention as Christmas among modern people at large, or as much devotion among the religiously minded as Good Friday and Holy Week generally. The symbol of Christianity has always been the cross, and it was Christ crucified that was preached by St Paul. Yet to many it remains obscure what the attraction of the cross is.

For some Christians the salvation secured by the cross is liberation. They know themselves to be in bondage to sin, and find freedom in the cross: derelicts saved from drink by the Salvation Army are in such case now, and throughout its history Christianity has shown remarkable power to speak to, and save, those who have ended up at the bottom of the pile as a result of their own addictions and fecklessness. If I am freed from slavery, it is natural to think of myself as ransomed, or redeemed (literally 'bought back'). A ransom theory then makes sense. I was in thrall to sin, and if I am freed by Jesus' death on the cross, it was the price he paid for my release. 'There was no other good enough to pay the price of sin.' Jesus paid a terrible price, and I am in consequence liberated from my previous state. These two facts the ransom theory expresses powerfully. But it has other implications that are not easy to accept. To whom was the price paid? Why did it have to be paid? Why could not God just liberate me by *force majeure*?

Answers are available, but themselves raise further awkward questions. The price was paid to the Devil, because he had, by reason of human sin, become legitimate owner of sinners' souls.

God would have being acting immorally if He had just snitched what was properly the property of the Devil. A moral God must respect the rights of everyone, even of the Devil himself. But the hypothesis of a personal Devil with rights sits uneasily with the sovereignty of God. Jesus Himself talks of Satan, but only in a metaphorical way. The metaphor of the sinner being enslaved, and hence, presumably, enslaved to someone, is more telling, but it is much more a matter of fact than of right, and the rights of the Evil One seem perilously close to a contradiction in terms. Moreover, in many versions, most accessibly in the story of Aslan and the White Witch in C. S. Lewis's *The Lion, the Witch and the Wardrobe*, there is an element of deceit in God's tricking the Devil into accepting the offer of Jesus' life in exchange for that of the sinner, a trickiness which sits ill with our faith in God the non-deceiver.[1] The ransom theory expresses the great cost of the Crucifixion and the great benefit obtained for us, but fails to give an adequate account of how the two are connected.

If we adopt a hardline retributivist theory of punishment, we can say why a price has to be paid: it is not a payment to the Devil which will induce him to loosen his grip on me, but a punishment for the wrongdoing I have done, and undergone by Jesus instead of me. Such an account makes sense to those overwhelmed by a sense of guilt. Their prime need is not liberation but forgiveness. In order to be forgiven they need to do penance: but no penance they could do by themselves could possibly make up for the enormity of their wrongdoing. Only a divine death could make up for what they take themselves to have done.

But the penal theory of the Atonement again raises awkward questions. Who is satisfied by Christ's self-offering on the cross? God the Father? That all too easily portrays God the Father as a wrathful power demanding the death of Jesus because other people deserve punishment. If the Prodigal Son could be forgiven, why not other sons too? Retributivists tell us that it is part of the fabric of the universe that debts incurred by wrongdoing must be paid, and if that were so, we could just see why the Father could not simply let us off the hook; but hard-line retributivism is itself implausible, even though espoused by great philosophers. Although we can see how it is that the penal theory speaks to those overwhelmed by a

---

[1] For a sympathetic exposition, see Charles Taliaferro, 'A Narnian Theory of the Atonement', *Scottish Journal of Theology*, xli (1988), 75–92.

sense of their own misdeeds, it comes unstuck as we examine it further.

Actually, the sins of those who claim to be sinners are mostly not very original, and even rather dull. By any ordinary reckoning, most of those who seek forgiveness live moderately good lives. They have a strong sense of worthlessness, but this is because they crave for more than mere right-doing. Some seek inspiration, and in Jesus' self-sacrificing example find it. Other historical figures—Socrates, St Francis—have also had High Inspirational Value, but it is not implausibly partisan to claim supreme influentiality for Jesus and His self-sacrifice on the cross. Its power to draw men, as Jesus had Himself predicted (John 12: 32), has proved enormous. Whatever account we give of the cross, its influence as an example cannot be denied, and the exemplar theory that Abelard put forward contains an important truth.

The exemplar, or moral influence, theory has been widely accepted in this century. Hastings Rashdall was a strong advocate, and certainly it has the two powerful commendations of evidently expressing at least part of the truth and of not carrying with it the awkward implications of the ransom or penal theory. Nevertheless, it has been reckoned unsatisfactory by many contemporary Christians. It is held to be too subjective, and not to register the objective difference that the crucifixion effected. Moreover, if the only reason for the crucifixion was to set us an example, it seems rather phoney. If I do something for real, it may indeed be a good example to others, but if I do it only to set an example, I am just play-acting, and it would not be right to let oneself actually be killed in a play just for the benefit of the spectators. We can certainly allow that the cross has had a great influence, and that the example Jesus set has continued to lead men away from sin and into the paths of righteousness and peace: but Jesus did not die in order to set an example, and the importance of what He did then is not constituted by what we have done since.

Richard Swinburne espouses a sacrifice doctrine of the Atonement. He makes trenchant criticisms of the ransom and penal theories, and reckons that the moral influence theory fails to register the objectivity of what happened once and for all time on Calvary. Moreover, the understanding of Jesus's death as a sacrifice goes back to New Testament times. The Epistle to the Hebrews makes explicit use of it, and much of the imagery of the Apocalypse is in terms of the lamb that was slain for us. Sacrifice was still a living part of Jewish religion, and even in our attenuated modern usage, it makes perfect sense to say that Jesus sacrificed His life, and if in consequence we are now at one with God, we can put the result together with the deed, and say that Jesus sacrificed His life *for us*. But though we believe it was for us He hung and suffered there, the language of sacrifice only describes, and does not explain, Jesus' dying on the Cross. The same questions obtrude as with the ransom and penal theories. To whom was the sacrifice made? Why should the death of Jesus make up for alleged wrongdoing on our part? What real difference does it make to the situation of Plato, who lived a long time before, or us, who live a long time after? Once again, attempts to give answers to these questions lead us into further difficulties. Nor is it just that we are failing to appreciate the thought-forms of New Testament times: although sacrifice was still part of Jewish religious practice in New Testament times, it had long been known that God was not to be appeased by sacrifices, and that we should not presume to offer the fruit of the body for the sin of the soul. Like the ransom and penal theories, the sacrifice theory expresses the great cost of the crucifixion, and identifies a cause, in our sin, and a consequence, in the sin's being remitted, but again describes rather than explains the real connection between them.

A better account of the significance of the cross is available in terms of *identification*. Much of Christian theology is concerned with identification. It is implicit in the etymology of the word 'at-one-ment', and is invoked to answer the question raised by the Incarnation: why did God become man? The very word 'Adam' has a suggestion of our all being caught up in a common human predicament, and our Christian destiny is expressed in the same terms: 'For as in Adam all die, even so in Christ shall all be made alive' (1 Cor. 15: 22). Only if we can be identified with humanity generally, can we plausibly be held to have committed great wrongs. And if Jesus could reconcile us with God, then that identification would, for many people, amount to salvation.

What sort of salvation is it rational to want? There are many different answers, depending on where people are and what they have got. Each of those good things sought by people thus far described, though good, is not always completely adequate. To know that God exists, that death is not the end, to be free from the slavery to sin, to have the example of someone like St Francis before one's eyes and enabled to lead the moral life, are all good. But the devils believe and tremble, and everlasting life has seemed to some to be unending tedium; a lot of people manage to lead a moral life, but do not seem to enjoy it much, even when told about other people much more moral than they can ever hope to be. Although the moral law is important, it lacks the personal touch—it does not say it with flowers. We need to be responsible, but yearn to go beyond responsibility and operate in a world of personal relations in which we are not merely well thought of for our reliable performance of duties, but actually liked.

If once we allow that we want to be loved, then it is natural for us to want to be loved by God, and to construe this as the greatest good there could be. But even if God does love us, it is difficult to believe that He does. We are told in the Old Testament, 'Like as a father pitieth his own children, even so is the Lord merciful unto them that fear him' (Ps. 103: 13); but it is easy for God to tell us, indeed easy for God to love us from afar, so long as it does not really cost Him all that much. The Old Testament is full of words, but words are always likely to fall on deaf ears, because it is always easy to say them, and often difficult to mean them. 'He would say that, wouldn't he?' is an ever-available *riposte*.

By the time of Jesus the Old Covenant was wearing rather thin: although most Jews were remarkably scrupulous in their observance of the Law, it was becoming more and more an external observance of an externally formulated code, undertaken for prudential or other unauthentic reasons, and they were often showing the effects of *mauvaise foi*, being whited sepulchres without, but full of corruption within (Matt. 23: 27). It was a bargain rather than a means of identifying oneself with God, and the best efforts of the Old Adam were directed to seeing how much one could get away with, while not actually breaking the terms of the contract.

In the incarnation God started a new dispensation, in which He did not just tell us, but threw His lot in with us. If it worked, we should be whole-heartedly sharing in God's purposes for us, not just toeing the line in order to keep on the right side of Him. In the later formulation of the Fathers, God became man, in order that man might become God.[2]

---

[2] Athanasius, *De Incarnatione*, ed. F. L. Cross (London, SPCK, 1939), ch. 54.

But it did not work, and perhaps could not have worked. The gospels tell of growing conflict with the established authorities. It is possible even to sympathize with them in their efforts to keep things on an even keel, and avoid trouble, either with the Romans or with the populace. They were not outstandingly wicked, but were acting in the way men naturally act when they have got a stake in the established order and feel that it is threatened.

Jesus confronted the authorities, and foresaw the outcome; yet He resolutely set His face to go to Jerusalem. He could have done otherwise. He could have kept out of harm's way, confining His mission to country areas out of the reach of the Jerusalem hierarchy. Elijah had bided his time: why not Jesus? It is difficult to say. He was not courting death. He prayed that the cup might pass from Him. But He felt impelled to go on to Jerusalem. In modern parlance we might say that it was a matter of integrity for Him. He could not back down without unsaying all that He had been preaching and teaching about the Kingdom. The Scribes and Pharisees had taken issue with Him, and He had to have it out with them. Confrontation was inevitable, if the truth was to be maintained. Granted the tenor of Christ's teaching and the nature of the powers-that-were, there had to be a show-down, and in any show-down, Jesus would be worsted. It is part of the way of the world when uncomfortable truth comes up against entrenched interests.

Jesus' death was part of His life, and in so far as we use the language of sacrifice to describe His death, we need to make it clear that it was His whole life that He dedicated to the Father.[3] Living that life, it was humanly inevitable that He should die that sort of death. It was a human inevitability, not a necessitarian one. Judas could have not betrayed His Lord; the Sanhedrin could have heeded the advice of Gamaliel, not Caiaphas; Pilate could have remembered Roman canons of justice, or at least taken notice of his wife's warning. But although then Jesus would not have died on Calvary, He would still have died: some leading Jews might have bound themselves by a great oath, that they would neither eat nor drink until they had killed Jesus, and carried out their plan while He was daily teaching in the Temple. Or if the Chief Priests had recognized that the word of the Lord was with Jesus, the Zealots would have got Him for failing to lead a crusade against

[3] I owe this point to Professor Swinburne, in the course of a discussion of an earlier version of this chapter at Leeds on 5 Aug. 1992.

the Romans. It was not foreordained that Jesus should die exactly when and how He actually did, but, men being what they were, a life like His was bound in first-century Palestine to end in a bloody death.

But still, we protest, it might have been different. Jesus might have been born in Athens, where new truths were always welcome, or in Victorian Britain, dividing His time between the ancient and the new universities, sure of obtaining a respectful hearing somewhere or other, and certainly safe from arrest and execution. But would we have believed Him then? There is a market for high-sounding idealism, and those who cater for it manage fairly well, thank you. My bread is buttered on the side of benevolence, and I can hope to make a reasonable living out of being nice. If God had been incarnate as an acquaintance of Xenophon, a rival to Epicurus, or a Fellow of Bracton College, Edgestow, we again could doubt His sincerity in taking His place among us: He had taken a fairly cushy pad. But if one were to lay down his life for his friends, we could be sure that His love was great. If the purpose of the Incarnation was to be achieved, God must become man not in the best circumstances human society could afford, but in some situation sufficiently typical for all to relate to.

Different explanations of the crucifixion become available, answering different questions at different levels. There is a historical account, of worldly powers getting rid of a dissident. There is a personal account, from Jesus' point of view, showing how, although not courting death, He was the sort of person who had it coming to Him, and had no alternative but to go to Jerusalem and accept His fate. There is a God's-eye account, of God needing to identify Himself with the human condition, and undergo the worst that could befall Him. Each account explains why Jesus was done to death, but in a different way, picking on a different cause, and eliciting a different response. Jesus died because men put Him to death. Jesus died because He was a man, and all men die. Jesus died, voluntarily but unwillingly, because His mission required it. Jesus died because only so could God's love towards man be made known in such a way that it would be believed. And if we press further and seek to explain the last explanation, we see that it was because of the hardness of our hearts that Jesus had to die: we had been told, but would not listen, and needed to be shown in the one incontrovertible way how much God cared for mankind.

We have different agents, different explanations, different purposes. We therefore also have different identifications, and different understandings. Most naturally we identify with Jesus. We feel for Him, and in feeling for Him are strengthened in our own miseries. Even in death, even in the dark night of the soul, we have an assurance that He, too, has been there before us, and that we are not alone in what we undergo. And suffering shared is suffering less insupportable. In a sense, then, Jesus dies for us—we are the beneficiaries of His death, though it was not for that end He died. Rather, He died as a consequence of sharing our lot, and exposing Himself to the ills of the human condition.

No sense of Jesus' having died for our *sins* arises from this identification. But we can also identify with those who put Jesus to death, the ecclesiastics, the local government officials, the Occupying Power. The British have much to answer for. We washed our hands of Poland at Yalta; we sent innumerable East Europeans to their deaths by repatriating them in 1945. We still repatriate Vietnamese boat people; we are about to consign the inhabitants of Hong Kong to the murderous mercies of those who organized the massacre of Tiananmen Square. Of course, there are excuses. We could not do much about the Poles. We had to try and trust the Russians. We had to consider consequences. All true, all partly exculpatory. But the good things of our civilization have been secured at great cost to others, and we enjoy them at their expense. Although individually I may have kept my hands clean, corporately we have touched pitch and are defiled.

Of course, also, it remains true that I myself did none of these things: most of them happened long before I was born. But if I insist on this, and disclaim all responsibility for the world I have inherited and whose benefits I enjoy, and shrink from shouldering the burdens and want only to make the most of what I have got, I opt out from all corporate identity and thereby diminish myself. So we are faced with a dilemma: either I disclaim corporate responsibility, and say, truthfully, that it all happened *ohne mich*; and then I am separating myself from the rest of humanity, and am becoming a self-isolated unlovable soul: or I come out of my shell, begin to expand my identity, and pick up the tabs for my fellows. It was because of the former possibility that Jesus had to die to prove His sincerity, since I was so tough-minded that only a death would get through to me, and in that sense it was because of my individual sin that Jesus died. In so far as I accept the latter identification, I accept responsibility for our corporate sins which led, among other things, to Jesus being executed. So either way, Jesus died on my account. And He died to the end that I, along with all other human beings, might be reconciled to God, realizing that God's will for us was not just the edict of a distant potentate but was the working-out of a love for us which was lived in our world under our conditions, even the condition of mortality.

Although I can see how, either way, Jesus died on my account, the accounts are very different. In the one case, I am retrospectively taking responsibility for what Pilate and the Chief Priests did, recognizing that in doing as they did, they did the sort of thing I might well have done had I been there, and acted in a typically human way, a way I am implicated in by the way I have joined in, and have benefited from, human society. I am saying that Jesus died because *we* killed him, extending my first-personal responsibility back to cover the events of AD 29. In the other case I am interpreting the whole Incarnation as a plan of God's to reconcile the whole of humanity; and since human selfishness, exemplified in my own selfishness, is the great barrier to our being at one with God, that plan needed God to undergo the worst fate that can happen to man, both to demonstrate His sincerity and to be someone we can identify with, however bad our own lot is.

If I identify with Jesus, I can be at one with God, and live a new life in Christ. But also, if I identify with Jesus, I shall begin to feel for Him and with Him in His suffering. I shall, though only to a small extent, enter into His Passion. The more I identify, the more I shall suffer. St Francis felt His sufferings so keenly that they actually imprinted their stigmata on his flesh. Such suffering is inevitable: it is the price of love. The more we make ourselves vulnerable by love, the more we expose ourselves to feeling wounded by all the things that go wrong for the beloved. But it is easy also to construe it in terms of punishment or penance. I am unsaying the values of the old man, now recognized by the new man to be worthless, but I need to express the disavowal in the values of the old man. I am able to do this, by identifying with Christ, and in so doing, make manifest my repudiation of the worldly values that led to His crucifixion, and the human self-centredness that left God no other way to get through to us than living among us, and suffering the worst that can befall a man. My vicariously joining in Christ's suffering is my penance for my sin; in which case, once again, it is easy to say that His actual suffering was a punishment for my sin.

Many different explanations of the crucifixion can be given, answering different questions, and articulating different understandings of its deepest significance. According to the identification theory the crucifixion should be seen not as a separate event but in the context of the birth, life, and teaching of Jesus and His subsequent resurrection and ascension; and the reason for the incarnation and all that followed was that man should be able to be at one with God, not merely, as under the old dispensation, through trying hard to conform his outward actions so as to walk in the way of the Lord, but by sharing fully in His purposes, and being able to accept the fact that he is accepted by God. This was the Good News. But, though gladly received by some, it was not acceptable to all, and perhaps could not be, in view of what human nature is like, and the way society is organized. Confrontation led to Jesus' arrest, trial, condemnation, execution, resurrection, and founding of the Church. If we ask within the whole complex pattern why Jesus died, we can explain it in terms of the ecclesiastical and Roman authorities, and identify with them. If we ask why Jesus did not avoid confrontation, we can explain that too, but need—in contrast with the moral influence theory—to distinguish final from consecutive clauses, and make it clear that although Jesus' death on the cross had, as a result, an influence on mankind, it was not in order to have that influence that He died. He died because He could no other, consistent with His mission. We can identify with that too, and see in His integrity a proof of His sincerity and absolute commitment. We can be sure that it was not mere play-acting, and that God really means what He says, and in spite of all our doubts and cynical suspicions, accept after all the fact that we are accepted.

There are many different identifications involved. Often we identify with different people in the course of the same explanation. The concept of identification is itself sometimes unclear and often fuzzy-edged. But it is a concept we use none the less, and it can give us a way of expressing different explanations of the crucifixion at different levels, in a way which reveals the force of traditional theories and metaphors without committing ourselves to their unfortunate, and often unchristian, implications.

13

Swinburne on Guilt, Atonement, and Christian Redemption

PHILIP L. QUINN

Richard Swinburne's work in philosophy of religion has already made important contributions to natural theology. His earlier trio of volumes, consisting of *The Coherence of Theism*, *The Existence of God*, and *Faith and Reason*, is concerned mainly with issues common to the theistic religions. In these books Swinburne defends the coherence of theism, argues that theism is more probable than not, and makes a case for the rationality of living by theistic belief. He is currently engaged in elaborating a specifically Christian philosophical theology. His recent books, *Responsibility and Atonement* and *Revelation*, are the first two of a planned quartet of volumes about distinctively Christian doctrines. Other volumes in the quartet will deal with the doctrines of the Trinity and the Incarnation and with providence and the problem of evil. *Responsibility and Atonement* is devoted to the topic of moral relations between God and human creatures. Among the theological issues it addresses are sin and original sin, redemption, sanctification and corruption, and heaven and hell. Swinburne's large project invites comparison with the great medieval *Summa*s, particularly Thomas Aquinas's *Summa Theologiae*; it is systematic philosophical theology on a grand scale. I know of no other project in contemporary analytic philosophy of religion with such lofty ambitions. When it has been completed, this will be an impressive constructive achievement that will deserve evaluation as a systematic whole. In the interim, critical discussion must focus on the parts of the edifice as they are added to the construction in successive volumes.

My modest aim in this chapter is to set forth an interim evaluation of the account of the Christian doctrine of the Atonement that Swinburne proposes in *Responsibility and Atonement*. The chapter is divided into four parts. In the first I describe the methodology which Swinburne employs in the book, and raise some questions about it. In the second I give an exposition of the moral theory he advances in part I, paying particular attention to the connections among guilt, atonement, and forgiveness that hold according to this theory, and to the theological consequences for Christ's atonement he derives in part II. The third section is devoted to criticism of Swinburne's theology of the Atonement. I argue that his account of this doctrine leaves unanswered questions to which a more complete account would respond. And in the fourth and final section I sketch an account I believe to be better than Swinburne's because it leaves unanswered fewer of these questions.

An Archimedean Methodology

One of the things that is most striking about the architecture of *Responsibility and Atonement* is the way in which it is neatly divided into two parts, the first of which has a kind of methodological privilege relative to the second. In part I Swinburne sets forth a moral theory that is meant to be evidentially independent of any theological assumptions. Thus he does not appeal to the existence of God or to any distinctively Christian doctrine in order to justify any component of the theory; nor do the scriptures or the traditions of particular religious communities or denominations play any role in justifying the theory. As the footnotes indicate, Swinburne's chief conversation partners at this stage of the game are secular moral philosophers, from whom he selectively appropriates theoretical ideas and distinctions and with whom he sometimes sharply disagrees. Moral intuitions or widely shared moral opinions provide the bulk of the evidence on which the theory rests. Indeed, Swinburne's appeal to intuition is quite explicit when he remarks that 'a satisfactory theory of ethics should try to take on board, albeit in a modified form, as many human intuitions about moral matters as it can'.[1] Modifications will be necessary, of course, if intuitions conflict; or they may be required to achieve coherence with a theory that seems likely to be correct on independent grounds. Since the intuitions to which Swinburne appeals are

[1] Richard Swinburne, *Responsibility and Atonement* (Oxford: Clarendon Press, 1989), 20. Hereafter page references to this book will be made parenthetically in the body of the text.

shared in our culture by non-religious and religious moral enquirers, it is not surprising that the moral theory he works out to take
them on board is not a distinctively Christian—or even a specifically religious—ethics.

Swinburne describes the enterprise of part II of the book as
drawing consequences from the results of part I. His own account
of his procedure goes as follows:

> I introduce a theological assumption that there is a God with certain
> characteristics who became incarnate as Jesus Christ and did certain
> things, including allowing himself to be crucified by men. I then examine
> what follows when all this is added to the results of part I, for the tra-
> ditional Christian doctrines concerned with the moral relations between
> man and God; concerned, that is, with sin and original sin, with our
> redemption by Christ and our sanctification through the means of grace
> provided in the Church, with Hell as an eternal punishment for the wicked,
> and Heaven as an eternal reward for the good. (p. 2)

One noteworthy feature of this procedure is that the results of part
I are not up for reconsideration or revision in the light of the
theological assumption, the traditional Christian doctrines under
consideration, or the scriptural and traditional sources from
which these doctrines derive. Instead, these results function
as Archimedean fixed points throughout the remainder of the discussion, in consequence of a methodological decision. It is this
feature of Swinburne's treatment I mean to highlight by referring
to a methodological privilege. I want to question the legitimacy
of this privilege.

But before doing so, I need to make two points in the interests of
fairness to Swinburne. The first is that the evidential independence
of his moral theory from theological assumptions does not imply
that it is causally independent of religious influences. The theory is
supported by widely shared moral intuitions. But our moral
intuitions are shaped by our culture, and our culture in turn has
been shaped by historical factors that include, prominently, theism
in general and Christianity and Judaism in particular. Hence it is
only to be expected that theism has influenced the moral intuitions
widely approved in our culture, and so it should come as no surprise that a moral theory committed to taking on board as many of
these intuitions as it can turns out to agree with explicitly theological moralities at many points. However, the culture of modernity
has also been influenced by many non-religious factors. So we

should also expect there to be some conflict between a moral theory that is sensitive to the full range of intuitions widely shared in the culture of modernity and an ethics with a narrower religious or theological basis. An important methodological question is this: how are religious moral enquirers to resolve such conflicts when they arise?

The second point I want to make is that Swinburne himself is well aware that introducing his theological assumption makes a moral difference. Though he rejects the radical theological voluntarism of Occam and even the more moderate voluntarism proposed by Scotus, he affirms that the existence of God 'shifts the boundaries between the obligatory and the supererogatory good, and the good, the indifferent, and the bad' (pp. 125–6). Thus, for example, worship is a duty of gratitude if God exists and is our creator, but it is a pointless activity and so not even good if God does not exist. And just as human parents may command their children to do what they ought to do anyway, so also God as our creator may command us to do what we ought to do anyway; in both cases the act thus commanded becomes doubly a duty, and failure to perform it doubly wrong. But there are limits to how far even God can shift these boundaries, and they are the results of independent moral constraints. So, for instance, even God cannot make it morally permissible to torture or to deceive another for no good purpose. And the existence of God does not collapse the distinction between the obligatory and the supererogatory, although it does, by increasing the number of our obligations, narrow the scope for works of supererogation. More generally, 'our theological assumption can only refine and deepen our views about what is obligatory and what is good, it cannot lead to their total replacement' (p. 128). We are not forced to choose, however, between total replacement and mere refinement of our moral views when they are brought into contact with theological claims. If adjustment is necessary in order to achieve coherence between religious beliefs and independent moral beliefs, it would seem that revision of the moral beliefs is another alternative.

The coherence method prescribed for ethics by John Rawls and Norman Daniels provides a model of how such revision of moral beliefs might proceed.[2] The goal of the first stage of the procedure

---

[2] See John Rawls, *A Theory of Justice* (Cambridge, Mass.: Harvard University Press, 1971), 19–21, 48–51, and Norman Daniels, 'Wide Reflective Equilibrium and Theory Acceptance in Ethics', *Journal of Philosophy*, lxxvi (1979), 256–82.

is narrow reflective equilibrium within ethics between considered moral judgements and the principles of a moral theory. Coherence is to be achieved by resolving conflicts on a case by case basis; the moral enquirer is to retain the belief that, on reflection, seems more likely to be true and revise the belief that seems less likely to be true. Neither considered judgements nor theoretical principles are immune from revision, and neither sort of belief is systematically privileged by the method. The coherent system of moral beliefs arrived at in narrow reflective equilibrium is apt to include both moral intuitions modified in the light of theory and theoretical principles modified in the light of intuition.

The goal of the second stage is to be reached by reiterating the procedure in order to achieve wide reflective equilibrium between moral beliefs and background theories of other kinds: for example, scientific accounts of human psychology or metaphysical theories of the nature of the moral agent. As in the first stage, there is no systematic methodological privilege; moral beliefs are not to be regarded as fixed points. Conflict resolution proceeds in terms of revising the belief that seems less likely to be true, and moral beliefs will not necessarily always win out over beliefs of other sorts in cases of conflict. Distinctively religious beliefs feed into the process at this stage of the quest for global coherence, and moral beliefs are to be revised if they seem to the reflective enquirer less likely to be true than religious beliefs with which they conflict.

There is an interesting contrast to be drawn between the way this method recommends that we proceed from narrow to wide reflective equilibrium and the way Swinburne argues from the moral theory of part I of his book to the theological conclusions about sin and redemption, sanctification and eternal reward, in part II. If one is a thoroughgoing coherentist in method, one must remain open to revising one's moral beliefs if there is conflict when they make contact with one's religious beliefs and it seems on reflection that one's religious beliefs are more likely than one's moral beliefs to be true. Moral beliefs do not become immune from revision at the point of narrow reflective equilibrium, and so do not thereafter serve as fixed points in the course of progress toward wide reflective equilibrium. According to Swinburne, by contrast, once one has the non-theological moral results of part I in hand, all that remains to be done is to add a theological assumption and then examine the consequences that follow for various traditional

Christian doctrines. There seems to be no room in this view for even the possibility that traditional Christian doctrines should rationally dictate reconsideration and, in certain circumstances, revision of antecedently and independently acquired moral results.

The question I want to raise is whether it is legitimate to preclude this possibility on methodological grounds. Consider an example. I share with Swinburne the view that we do not inherit guilt for the sins of others. This view conflicts with the Augustinian account of original sin, according to which all of Adam's descendants, except Christ, are guilty for Adam's original sin. When I consider how to resolve this conflict, it seems to me more likely that my moral intuition about the non-transference of guilt by inheritance is on target than that Augustine's account of original sin is true. So in this particular case I concur with Swinburne in rejecting what he calls 'the doctrine of original guilt' (p. 144). But I would regard it as only rational for someone whose estimate of the relative likelihoods in the case was the reverse of mine to revise the moral intuition in question in order to make an exception to the general rule that moral guilt is not inherited. Moreover, I do not want to generalize from cases of this sort to the conclusion that similar conflicts should always be resolved in favour of moral beliefs based on non-religious grounds. As I shall argue later on when I criticize Swinburne's account of the Atonement, there is a traditional account of that doctrine which conflicts with normal intuitions widely shared in our culture, though not in the culture in which the account originated, but which is attractive enough in theological terms to make reconsideration—and perhaps even revision—of moral views prevalent in our culture a prospect worth taking seriously.

But before I can begin to criticize Swinburne's account, I must first explain a bit about his views concerning how we humans atone to one another for moral offences and the bearing of these views on his conception of Christ's atoning work. I now turn to this task.

Moral and Theological Atonements

Swinburne's moral theory is Kantian in its general contours, although it does not coincide with Kant's actual views on all points of detail. Thus, for example, he explicitly dissents from Kant's 'stern view that there are no supererogatorily good acts' (p. 19). Nevertheless, as Swinburne acknowledges repeatedly in both his text and his footnotes, he agrees with Kant about many things. For instance, he considers libertarian freedom to be a necessary condition of moral responsibility, and so his moral theory, like Kant's, is metaphysically grounded in a commitment to this kind of human free will. Like Kant, Swinburne stresses the importance of good intentions—that is, 'the goodness of doing or trying to do what the agent believes to be good, which exists despite any error in the agent's factual beliefs or moral principles' (p. 27). The deontological concept of obligation or duty plays a key role in his moral theory. And Swinburne even endorses the idea of there being a special moral value in struggle against contrary inclinations that provoked the so-called sour duty objection to Kant. As he puts the point, 'it is good that an agent do the objectively morally good action for the reason that it is morally good; and indeed we value such pursuit of the morally good the more if it is done despite contrary desire' (p. 24).

For present purposes the most significant part of Swinburne's moral theory consists of its account of guilt, atonement, and forgiveness. An agent acquires objective guilt in virtue of objective wrongdoing, either failing to do what it is obligatory to do or doing what it is obligatory not to do. One acquires subjective guilt in virtue of doing what one thinks is wrong, either failing to do what one believes it is obligatory to do or doing what one believes it is obligatory not to do. When one knowingly fails with respect to one's obligations, the two kinds of guilt are both present, but each can be present in the absence of the other. To be guilty is, in a sense, to be unclean. According to Swinburne, 'both subjective and objective guilt are stains on a soul requiring expunging; but subjective guilt is embedded in the soul while objective guilt lies on the surface' (p. 75). Moreover, when one's wrongdoing involves wronging someone, one puts oneself in a situation resembling the legal situation of a debtor who owes money. The wrong needs to be righted just as the debt needs to be repaid. The wrongdoer thus acquires an obligation to atone whose fulfilment is a necessary condition of the removal of the stain of guilt from the soul. In addition to atonement on the part of the wrongdoer, forgiveness on the part of the victim is required for the perfect removal of guilt.

According to Swinburne, atonement normally involves four components: repentance, apology, reparation, and penance. Not all of them have to be present in every case. Repentance and apology distance the wrongdoer from a past wrong act. They involve the wrongdoer's acknowledgement of having done the act and of its wrongness, as well as a resolution of future amendment. The sincere expression of these things to oneself is repentance; their sincere, public expression to the victim is apology. If subjective guilt is present, the wrongdoer must repudiate past bad intentions; whereas the wrongdoer's apology should stress the continuity of past and present benevolent purposes if the guilt is purely objective. The wrongdoer makes reparation by compensating the victim for the harm done if possible. Penance consists of a costly gift to the victim above and beyond what is owed by way of reparation. The giving of such a gift is a performative act whereby the wrongdoer disowns the wrong act in a way that is not achieved by mere words of apology; by doing something costly to disown the wrong act, the wrongdoer makes the act of penance a serious act. Reparation and penance are not always required. Insults do not demand reparation, and small wrongs do not call for penance. But sincere apology is always needed.

Swinburne regards the victim's acceptance of the wrongdoer's atonement as forgiveness. If the wrongdoer makes the atonement appropriate in the circumstances and is forgiven by the victim, the wrongdoer's guilt is eliminated, and the stain associated with it is removed from the soul. So atonement and forgiveness are jointly sufficient for the removal of guilt. However, forgiveness is not in all circumstances necessary for the elimination of guilt. If the wrongdoer makes the appropriate atonement but the victim fails to forgive, the guilt remains for a while. But, according to Swinburne, 'if the apology is pressed, the penance increased, and still the victim refuses to forgive, the guilt disappears' (p. 87). By contrast, some sort of atonement is a necessary condition of the removal of guilt. To be sure, the victim can decide to disregard the wrongdoer's act, to treat it as if it had never happened, even in the absence of any atonement. But Swinburne holds that such a decision 'will not then suffice to remove guilt, for the wrongdoer has not distanced himself from that act' (p. 85). In the interest of regimenting ordinary language, which is not clear on this point, Swinburne suggests that we say that 'a victim's disowning of a hurtful act is only to be called forgiveness when it is in response to at least some minimal attempt at atonement such as an apology' (p. 87). Such a minimal attempt at atonement is therefore always necessary, and in some cases sufficient, for the elimination of guilt.

Within limits, it is within the victim's power to determine how much atonement is required before the forgiveness that removes guilt is granted. The wrongdoer has to do something to set the wrong act at a distance—for example, repent and apologize. But the victim may choose to let the wrongdoer off from doing more, and forgiveness granted in such conditions would be efficacious in eliminating the wrongdoer's guilt. Swinburne insists that the victim is not obliged to exercise this kind of leniency. As he sees it, 'the victim can insist on substantial reparation, and sometimes it is good that he should do so, that he should insist on the victim [*sic*: the wrongdoer, I presume] for his sake making a serious atonement; for that allows him to take seriously the harm that has been done' (p. 86). It may thus be good that the victim exercises this discretionary power on the side of leniency in some circumstances and on the side of greater severity in others. Forgiving the serious penitent and thereby contributing to the removal of guilt is a good thing for the victim to do. Though forgiveness is a work of supererogation for some people, Christians have an obligation to forgive all those who sincerely seek their forgiveness. This is because Christianity teaches that God's forgiveness can be had only by those prepared to forgive others. Hence Christians who accept God's forgiveness thereby undertake the obligation to forgive others.

Atonement is radically individual: one person cannot atone for another. According to Swinburne, 'I can help my friend to make atonement by encouraging him to repent and apologize, and providing the means for him to make reparation and penance if he does not have them himself' (p. 91). But it is the friend who must repent and apologize; it is the friend who must make use of the means of repentance and penance I have provided. Otherwise the atonement would not be the friend's. I cannot do more than help, and, in particular, I cannot replace or substitute for my friend in atoning for wrongdoing.

When Swinburne's theological assumption is added to this account of the morality of atonement, wrongdoing becomes doubly a fault because it is also a failure to do one's duty to God. When humans fail in their objective or subjective duties to one another, they also fail in their duty to their creator, to whom they owe it to lead good lives. Failure in a duty to God is sin, and all mere humans are sinners. Human sinners owe atonement to God for their sins. God could, of course, forgive human sins in return for repentance and apology without demanding reparation or penance, and God would not have done wrong if he had chosen to do so. But, according to Swinburne, 'it is good that if we do wrong, *we* should take *proper* steps to cancel our actions, to pay out [*sic*] debts, as far as logically can be done' (p. 149). Moreover, 'if we are in no position to make proper atonement for what we have done, it is good that someone else (even the victim) put us in that position and thereby allow us to make proper atonement' (p. 149). Repentance and apology for their sins are within the power of humans, but humans require help with reparation and penance. God provides the reparation and penance whereby humans may properly atone to God for their sins in the form of the life and death of Christ, especially in the suffering which Christ endured in his Passion and Crucifixion.

But how exactly does the life and death of Christ furnish us with reparation and penance for our sins? As Swinburne explicitly notes, Christian theology has never had a 'formal definition of what was effected on the Cross with the kind of stamp of orthodoxy upon it possessed by the Chalcedonian definition of the Incarnation' (p. 150). Instead, it has made use of a variety of models, each of which is rooted in scriptural language, to illuminate the mystery of Christ's Atonement. With one exception, according to Swinburne, each of these models taken by itself, seriously and literally, fails as an explanation of how the death of Christ on the Cross helped to deal with the problem of removing human guilt for sin. Two of them can be seen to have a point, however, if they are reinterpreted metaphorically in the light of the exceptional model, which is Swinburne's primary device for making sense of the doctrine of the Atonement.

Swinburne criticizes four theories of the Atonement that are rivals of the account he favours. According to the first, Christ's Atonement is a victory in battle over cosmic evil, either in the form of impersonal forces or in the form of personal demons. Swinburne raises two difficulties for this theory: first, it offers no explanation of how such a victory could remove the guilt of sin from the human soul; second, it furnishes no explanation of why such a victory needed to be so costly in terms of Christ's suffering unto death. After all, it would seem that God, being the omnipotent creator of

evil beings or forces, could have effortlessly annihilated them
simply by ceasing to exert divine conserving power. The second
theory Swinburne objects to supposes that God has promised Satan
dominion over human sinners and thereby granted him rights over
them. Though God could, of course, liberate human sinners from
bondage to Satan by force, it is inconsistent with divine justice to
break a promise or violate anyone's rights, and so God is constrained to proceed in some other way. On one variant of this
theory, Christ's suffering and death are a price paid to Satan in
order to ransom human sinners from bondage. On another variant,
Satan went beyond what was his by right in attempting to assume
dominion over Christ, who was no sinner, and thereby forfeited his
rights over other humans. Swinburne's main objection to accounts
of this sort takes the form of a rhetorical question: why should God
have made so foolish a promise? According to exemplarism, which
is a theory that some historians attribute to Abelard, Christ's life
and death are efficacious solely in virtue of inspiring us to penitence and good acts.[3] Swinburne is at pains to insist that the life and
death of Christ are inspiring examples; he asserts that the supreme
example which Christianity 'presents for imitation is the example
of Jesus Christ sacrificing himself to atone for human sins' (p. 171).
But he regards exemplarism as less than the whole truth of the
matter, because it contains no objective transaction, no act performed by Christ that 'makes an objective contribution to removing our guilt which we ourselves were in no position to make'
(p. 162).

The theory of penal substitution, according to which Christ, who
is innocent, pays a penalty owed by human sinners by undergoing
the punishment they should have undergone, is the fourth account
which Swinburne criticizes. On one version of this theory, Christ
somehow assumes the guilt of human sinners, which is then removed from him after he has paid the debt of punishment for it by
his Passion and Crucifixion. On another version, which does not
involve transfer of guilt, God insists that the full penalty be paid,
but not that those who owe it pay it, and so the stain of guilt is
removed from sinners who repent and apologize once Christ has

---

[3] I argue that this attribution is unfair to Abelard in Philip L. Quinn, 'Abelard on
Atonement: "Nothing Unintelligible, Arbitrary, Illogical, or Immoral about It"', in
Eleonore Stump (ed.), *Reasoned Faith* (Ithaca, NY: Cornell University Press, 1993),
281–300.

paid the debt of punishment they owe by his suffering and death. Swinburne has two objections to theories of this type: first, since the only role sinners have to play in this process is to repent and apologize, it would seem better that God should simply remit the debt of punishment and let us off without anyone suffering punishment than that God should arrange for the debt to be paid by the suffering and death of Christ; second, the theory's 'talk of law courts and punishment makes the whole process too "mechanical" for a means of reconciliation which ought to be intimate and personal' (p. 152).

The biblical model which Swinburne develops in his own account of Christ's Atonement centres on the motif of sacrifice. The idea of sacrifice in the Hebrew Bible is, roughly, that worshippers offer God something valuable as a gift of reconciliation whose benefits God may then share with them. If Christ were completely distinct from God, we could think of Christ's sacrifice as a gift to God of both a life lived in obedience to God and a life voluntarily laid down on the Cross, a present whose benefits will eventually flow to others. According to Swinburne, however, in so far as Christ is God, he cannot offer a sacrifice to himself, and so the model needs a bit of revision. On the revised model, 'God makes available the sacrifice (of himself), but it is we who have to offer it'; hence, 'Christ's death has no efficacy until men choose to plead it in atonement for their sins' (p. 153). It is therefore God's way of providing sinners with the means to make reparation and penance. But there is no need to suppose that Christ's life and death are equivalent to what human sinners owe God by way of reparation plus something extra by way of penance. They are 'simply a costly penance and reparation sufficient for a merciful God to let men off the rest' (p. 154). Of course, once a sinner has sincerely repented and made an apology, it is within limits up to God to choose how much reparation and penance to require before granting forgiveness. So, as Swinburne explicitly acknowledges, 'God could have chosen to accept one supererogatory act of an ordinary man as adequate for the sins of the world'; alternatively, 'he could have chosen to accept some angel's act for this purpose' (p. 160). Indeed, since on Swinburne's account of the morality of atonement, reparation and penance are not always necessary for atonement to be successful in rendering the response of forgiveness appropriate, it would seem to be possible for a merciful God to forgive sins in the absence of any reparation or penance without doing wrong. What is it, then, that makes the life and death of Christ a fitting sacrifice to offer in atonement for human sin? Two observations made by Swinburne appear to be responsive to this question. First, he remarks that 'if it is good that there be reparation and penance, it is good that these be substantial; that the atoning sacrifice be not a trivial one' (pp. 160–1). Second, he immediately goes on to say that 'it is good too that our creator should share our lot, and of his generosity make available to us his sacrificial life' (p. 161).

In the light of this positive account of Christ's Atonement, Swinburne is able to make some sense of the scriptural motifs of victory and ransom. Christ's life and death are a victory over evil because, as a result, sinners are not fated to remain guilty in the eyes of God for ever. Having repented and apologized, we have only to plead Christ's Atonement in order to be rid of such guilt. And, speaking metaphorically, Christ's life and death ransom us from evil because we have only to offer them in atonement in order to be freed from its prison. But, Swinburne cautions us, Christ's Passion and Crucifixion are only a 'punishment' in the remote sense that this part of his earthly existence 'replaces the punishment which we would otherwise have deserved (though not one which God would necessarily have inflicted)' (p. 162).

This completes my exposition of Swinburne's account of the morality of atonement and its application to the Christian doctrine of the Atonement. The next item on my agenda is a critical discussion of his treatment of that theological doctrine.

The Parity of Sacrifice and Substitution

There are moral intuitions that count against the idea that the suffering and death of Christ constitute part of a fitting sacrifice to offer in atonement for human sin. Abelard points at them by posing two powerful rhetorical questions:

So what compulsion, or reason, or need was there—seeing that by its very appearing alone the divine pity could deliver man from Satan—what need was there, I say, that the Son of God, for our redemption, should take upon him our flesh and endure such numerous fastings, insults, scourgings, and spittings, and finally that most bitter and disgraceful death upon the cross, enduring even the cross of punishment with the wicked? In what way does the apostle declare that we are justified or reconciled to God through the death of his Son, when God ought to have been the more angered against man, inasmuch as men acted more criminally by crucifying his Son than they ever did by transgressing his first command in paradise through the tasting of a single apple?[4]

Those scourgings and spittings, that bitter and disgraceful death, to which Abelard's words compel us to give due weight, are surely very bad things, especially horrible if Christ is indeed God incarnate. It certainly seems possible that God should become incarnate without having to endure them; it appears to be possible that Christ should live a life devoted to doing extraordinary works of supererogation and then die without suffering more than an ordinary portion of the ills to which human flesh is subject. Assuming that these things are possible, if God could have chosen to accept a single supererogatory act of an ordinary human or an angel as adequate reparation and penance for the sins of the world, such a life replete with supererogatory goodness could have served the purpose too. As Swinburne has reminded us, God need not act in accord with the principle of equivalent compensation in determining how much reparation is required before divine forgiveness is granted.

I agree with Swinburne's suggestion that it is often good that reparation and penance be substantial rather than trivial. But even if the life of Christ had not ended with the evils of the Passion and the Crucifixion, the immense supererogatory goodness contained in it would have added up to a substantial reparation and penance if it were then made available to us to plead in atonement for our sins. And I agree that it is good that our creator should share our lot and generously make available to us a sacrifice to offer in atonement for sin. But that good, too, could have been achieved if the life of God incarnate had not ended with those scourgings and spittings and in that bitter and disgraceful death but none the less had contained the supererogatory goodness to make up such a sacrifice. So it seems that the particular goods to which Swinburne refers could have been attained without the evils of the Passion and the Crucifixion. If they could, it would clearly be better that these

---

[4] Peter Abelard, *Commentary on the Epistle of Paul to the Romans*. I quote from the translation of selections from this work in *A Scholastic Miscellany: Anselm to Ockham*, Library of Christian Classics, 10, ed. and trans. Eugene R. Fairweather (Philadelphia: Westminster Press, 1956), 282.

goods should exist without those evils than that both exist. Hence
there remains something morally counter-intuitive in the view that
the suffering and death of Christ comprise part of a fitting sacrifice
for us to offer in atonement for our sins.

It is of course possible that the evils of the Passion and the
Crucifixion serve other divine purposes that could not be achieved,
even by an omnipotent God, in the absence of evils at least as bad,
if not worse, than they are. And if there are such divine purposes,
there is no special reason to think that we humans would be able to
figure them out or even understand them if they were revealed to
us. So when I make the point that Swinburne's account of the
Atonement is morally counter-intuitive in some respects, I am
under no illusion that I have refuted or discredited it. At this stage
of the argument I only want to make the point that Swinburne's
account, like the rivals to it which he rejects, leaves questions
unanswered and mysteries unsolved. Perhaps this is bound to be a
feature of any account of the Atonement that we humans are
capable of framing, because it is, after all, often said to be a mystery
of faith. If so, alternatives to Swinburne's account should not be
dismissed from consideration merely because they possess this
feature.

I want next to argue that one version of the theory of penal
substitution is neither better nor worse than his theory of sacrifice
when judged in terms of counter-intuitive features or unanswered
questions. My conclusion will be that there is parity between these
two theories with respect to their coherence with moral intuitions
that are immune from revision.

In a way, such parity, if it exists, should come as no surprise to
those sympathetic to Swinburne's general moral outlook. On his
view, Christ's Atonement provides us with a means we can use to
make a reparation with penance for our sins. Morally speaking,
when we do not voluntarily make appropriate reparation for
wrongdoing, others may take the reparation from us by force, along
with compensation for the costs of extracting the reparation and for
the obdurate attitude manifested by the failure to repent and
apologize. Swinburne proposes that 'compensation beyond the
reparation owed by one who makes voluntary atonement we may
call the penalty; and the exacting of reparation, including the penalty, we may call the exacting of retribution' (p. 93). He defines
punishment as any infliction of harm, whether by the victim or by

an authority such as the State, as retribution for wrongdoing. Hence, punishment in Swinburne's sense will 'include exacting the reparation which would be owed by one who made voluntary atonement but will go beyond it' (p. 94). And since, on this view, punishment is defined in terms of reparation, we can make use of the idea of owing reparation to help us make sense of the notion of owing a debt of punishment. If one who is obliged to make reparation fails to do so voluntarily, then others are morally permitted to extract from the wrongdoer the amount of the reparation owed plus the appropriate penalty. To summarize matters in a simple formula, the debt of punishment owed equals the amount of the reparation owed plus the appropriate penalty.

When these ideas are extended to the theological realm and incorporated into a theory of penal substitution, some complications arise. I have no intention of defending the variant of that theory according to which Christ assumes the guilt of all the world and it is removed from him after he has paid the debt of punishment for it. Comparing the moral intuition that guilt cannot be transferred from the wrongdoer to an innocent party with the claim that Christ somehow acquired the guilt of the sins of other humans, I find myself judging that the former proposition is much more likely to be true than the latter. So, in accord with the coherence methods outlined above, I stick with the former and reject the latter. But I do think that there is a case to be made for the variant of the theory according to which, though guilt for the sins of others is not transferred to Christ, it is removed from those among them who repent and apologize for their sins once Christ has paid the debt of punishment they owe, if they acknowledge Christ's action on their behalf.

To the extent that we think of serious sins as analogous to crimes and respect the practices embodied in our own system of criminal law, we are bound to find even this version of penal substitution counter-intuitive. Though a parent can pay her child's pecuniary debts, a murderer's mother cannot pay his debt of punishment by serving his prison term. If he does not serve the term, but his mother, out of love for him, voluntarily remains in prison for a period at least as long as his term, she does not succeed in paying his debt of punishment even if he repents and apologizes for the murder and tries to authorize her to act on his behalf. The debt of punishment remains unpaid as long as he does not pay it. So it seems that debts of punishment, like guilt, are not transferable even to those who would willingly pay them. But I do not think that these considerations are decisive. We know of or can imagine other legal arrangements that would evoke intuitions which point in the opposite direction. Imagine, for example, a legal system in which the punishment for murder is not a term in prison but a term as an indentured servant of the victim's family or clan. Ignoring the ways in which such arrangements might be abused by the victim's relatives, it is at least arguable that such a system would serve justice by compensating the victim's household for the loss of a productive member, and hence making some reparation for the harm done by the murder. Within a system with this sort of rationale for punishment, it is important that debts of punishment be paid; however, it is not essential that those who owe them pay them. If a murderer does not serve his term as an indentured servant, but his mother, out of love for him and with his consent, voluntarily serves as a substitute for him, she does, I think, succeed in paying his debt of punishment. And if, in addition, he repents and apologizes for the murder, I am inclined to say that the burden of guilt is lifted from him. Because contrasting legal analogies can be used to mobilize conflicting moral intuitions about punishment, it is not clear to me that coherence methods of the sort I have described will yield widespread agreement on the conclusion that the penal substitution theory presently under discussion is to be rejected. When I compare the moral intuition that debts of punishment can never be transferred from the wrongdoer to an innocent party with the theological claim that Christ's life and death were sufficient to pay the debt of punishment for all human sin, I do not find myself stuck with the conclusion that the moral intuition is more likely to be true than the theological claim. So I, at least, am willing to reconsider the moral intuition and perhaps to revise or even to abandon it in the light of the theological claim.

There are some interesting parallels between this penal substitution theory and Swinburne's sacrifice theory. Just as, on Swinburne's account, there is no need to suppose that Christ's life and death are equivalent to what human sinners owe God by way of reparation plus penance, so also, on this view, there is no need to suppose that they are equivalent to the reparation plus penalty which together add up to the full debt of punishment for human sins. And just as it would seem to be possible for a merciful God to forgive sins in the absence of any reparation or penance without doing wrong, so also it would seem to be possible for a merciful God to forgive sins, and do no wrong thereby, without any part of the debt of punishment, either reparation or penalty, having been paid. As Swinburne notes, it is often, morally speaking, 'objectively meritorious if I do not exact retribution from an enemy who has hurt me—any retribution at all, that is, even within the suggested permissible limits' (p. 99).[5] It thus appears to be morally permissible, at the very least, for God to forgive sins without further ado, once the sinner has repented and apologized, and simply to remit the whole debt of punishment.

Swinburne's first objection to penal substitution theories builds on this point. It would, he thinks, seem better that God should simply remit the debt of punishment than that God should arrange for it to be paid by the suffering and death of Christ. Or, to put the point in a slightly different form, it would seem better that God should collect at most that part of the debt which would be covered by the supererogatory goodness in Christ's life minus the Passion and Crucifixion than that God should collect the larger part, if not the whole, which would be covered by that supererogatory goodness plus the Passion and Crucifixion. When the objection is put in this form, it becomes clear that it is essentially the same as the objection I directed against Swinburne's own sacrifice theory earlier. In both cases, the problem is understanding why it would be good for God to receive, or what reason God has for wanting to receive, reparation and penance or penalty that includes the spittings and scourgings, the bitter and disgraceful death, in light of the fact that God could mercifully and without injustice forgive sins which had been repented of and apologized for without receiving any reparation and penance or penalty. I find the objection equally forceful in both cases, but decisive in neither. At any rate, since I have already conceded that it is not decisive against Swinburne's sacrifice theory, I can insist without being unfair that it is not decisive against the penal substitution theory under consideration. All it shows in either case is that the theory in question leaves questions unanswered.

---

[5] Swinburne suggests that the limits alluded to are defined by the following principle of moral prohibition: 'it is wrong to cause anyone a harm which serves no good purpose, and it is wrong to cause anyone a great harm unless it serves a very good purpose' (p. 98).

Because there is no definition of the doctrine of the Atonement with the stamp of orthodoxy on it, the history of theological reflection on this topic is richly pluralistic in character. Numerous scriptural motifs and theological elaborations upon them appear in a bewildering variety of permutations and combinations. It is useful to impose some taxonomic order on this variety of accounts of the Atonement by thinking of them as falling at various places along a spectrum. At one end of this spectrum would be monistic accounts that emphasize one motif to the exclusion of all others. Swinburne's account falls fairly close to this end of the spectrum because of its emphasis on the motif of sacrifice. Other motifs such as victory over evil or ransom from evil are subordinated to the sacrifice motif; they enter into Swinburne's account only under metaphoric reinterpretation. As one proceeds along the spectrum, the accounts one encounters grow increasingly pluralistic. Thus, for example, though Aquinas thinks that the principal function of Christ's Atonement is to satisfy for human sin by paying a debt of punishment that human sinners cannot pay, he also holds that Christ's Passion and Crucifixion have several other functions. In particular, the Passion contributes to the salvation of sinners by meriting grace for them on account of its voluntary character, by redeeming them from bondage to Satan by means of a ransom paid to God, and by reconciling them to God because it is an acceptable sacrifice.[6] If the argument of this section of the chapter is on target, there is no conclusive reason for rejecting a certain version of the penal substitution theory. If this is right, it seems natural to ask next whether the ideas of sacrifice and penal substitution can be combined to yield an account that is richer and more pluralistic than Swinburne's.

I think they can. Suppose Christ's Atonement provides whatever reparation is needed to supplement our own efforts to atone to God for sin. If we repent, apologize, and properly acknowledge Christ's Atonement, then God will forgive our sins. As Swinburne says, proper acknowledgement involves offering the gift of reparation that God has made available to us. Hence Christ's Atonement

---

[6] I develop this interpretation of Aquinas in Philip L. Quinn, 'Aquinas on Atonement', in Ronald J. Feenstra and Cornelius Plantinga, jun. (eds.), *Trinity, Incarnation, and Atonement* (Notre Dame, Ind.: University of Notre Dame Press, 1989), 153–77. Further support for it is contained in Romanus Cesario, *Christian Satisfaction in Aquinas* (Washington, DC: University Press of America, 1982).

does function as a sacrifice offered to God when we plead it. But it also has at least one other function. We must recognize that it is we who owe God reparation for our sins. This is a debt of punishment we owe God, because there would be nothing unjust in God extracting payment from us by force and thereby retributively punishing us. Hence Christ's Atonement also functions to pay that debt, provided we repent and apologize. The proviso is important. If Christ's Atonement served to pay the debt for sinners who do not repent or apologize, then God would unjustly collect payment of the debt twice, so to speak, if God were to punish unrepentant and unapologetic sinners. Since we have assurances that God means to punish such sinners, we must assume that doing so is not unjust. Hence we must conclude that Christ's Atonement does not serve to pay the debt for sinners who fail to repent and apologize. It should also be noted that no penalty is involved in paying the debt in this fashion, because no penalty would be appropriate. Since the sinner has repented and apologized, compensation for the obduracy manifested by failure to repent and apologize is not needed. And because what serves to make reparation is voluntarily offered by Christ rather than extracted by God using force, there is no question of compensation for the costs of exacting the reparation.

An advantage of thinking about the reparation provided by Christ's Atonement in terms of both sacrifice and substitution is that it allows us to respond to Swinburne's second objection to penal substitution theories. Considered in isolation, the idea of penal substitution suggests a legalistic process that might terminate with the sinner unreconciled to God. But if we go on to say that the sinner's atonement includes repentance, apology, and offering a sacrificial gift, we can dispel the impression that the sinner need not take steps to seek God's forgiveness. Using the ideas of substitution and sacrifice in combination also allows us to answer an objection that could be lodged against Swinburne's theory. It might be taken to portray God as resembling a judge who plays favourites by relaxing just demands for reparation in cases in which guilty sinners give the judge a particular costly gift but not in other cases. To construe the theory this way would, of course, be to misunderstand Swinburne's intentions; he certainly does not mean to suggest that God resembles a judge who is open to being bribed. And we can guard against this misunderstanding by going on to say that this particular gift, because it functions to make reparation for sin, pays the debt of punishment sinners owe, to the extent that it is fitting that it should be paid, so that divine forgiveness of those who offer it does not represent unjust partiality.

My critical appraisal has not uncovered any insurmountable difficulties for the account of Christ's Atonement that Swinburne bases on the scriptural motif of sacrifice. I have merely argued that Swinburne dismisses the idea of penal substitution too quickly, and thereby overlooks material in the theological tradition that could be used to round out and strengthen that account. But even if one grants that both sacrifice and substitution are themes that have something to contribute to our imperfect grasp of the mystery of the Atonement, one is left with the problem of understanding why it is good that God receive by way of reparation for human sin a sacrifice and payment that includes the horrible suffering and death of Christ. I conclude by trying to solve that problem.

Counterfactual Reparation

Up to this point in the discussion, I have followed Swinburne in assuming that Christ's life and death in some fashion count as the reparation, including penance or penalty if they are needed, owed to God for human sin. My disagreement with him has so far been narrowly focused on the question of the propriety of conceiving of this reparation as payment, at least in part, of a debt of punishment that sinners owe to God while also functioning as a sacrifice available for them to offer to God. But now I propose to challenge that assumption.

Suppose that God, for reasons beyond our ken, would have insisted on reparation being made for sin, though he could forgive sin without such reparation, if Christ had not lived, suffered, and died in the manner he did. My suggestion is that we treat this subjunctive supposition as a counterfactual. We may then go on to assume that Christ's life and death persuade God to be lenient rather than severe in his treatment of human sinners. Just because the supererogatory goodness in Christ's life and his voluntary submission to suffering and death are a sacrifice that is enormously pleasing to God, their effect is to forestall the severe but just demand for reparation and not to make the reparation that would be demanded in their absence. They function not to remove a debt of punishment that human sinners owe by paying it, but to persuade God to remit or cancel the debt. On this view, those spittings and scourgings, that bitter and disgraceful death, are not part of a reparation that satisfies a just divine demand. So we are relieved of the burden of wondering how it could be good for God to receive such terrible things by way of reparation for human sin or why God might want to or even insist on receiving them as a reparation before considering it fitting to forgive human sinners. We need only think that God discerns such great value in the life and death of Christ that they serve to persuade God to forgo receiving a reparation for sin that God is entitled to demand. And it certainly seems good that God should be thus persuaded.

I find the picture of personal relations reflected in this way of thinking about the Atonement morally attractive quite apart from its theological application. Perhaps I can best mobilize the moral intuitions that support this picture by telling a revised and expanded version of a story I have used elsewhere for a similar purpose.[7] Imagine that a great magnate makes his two sons stewards of the two finest farms on his estate. The elder son irresponsibly neglects and thus ruins his farm, while the younger son conscientiously makes his farm flourish. As a result of his negligence, the elder son owes it to his father to make reparation by restoring his farm to its former prosperity. It would be severe but just for the father to punish him by disinheriting him if he does not repair the ruined farm. Unfortunately, the elder son is not a good enough farmer to be able to accomplish this task, though he is good enough that he could have prevented the ruin of the farm had he but tried to do so. Acknowledging his responsibility and guilt, the elder son repents of his negligence, and sincerely apologizes to his father. But as the father contemplates the now desolate fields of the ruined farm, he cannot help thinking that repentance and apology are not enough. He is poised to exercise his right to disinherit his guilty elder son.

Then the younger son intervenes. Moved by love for his brother as well as by devotion to their father and the welfare of his estate, the younger son undertakes to restore the farm that his brother has ruined to its former prosperity. This new endeavour requires tremendous sacrifices from him; he must now maintain his own

---

[7] Quinn, 'Aquinas on Atonement', 174–6.

farm while trying to rehabilitate another. His guilty elder brother joins with him in this undertaking, but his feeble efforts contribute almost nothing. And then a senseless tragedy occurs. At harvest time the younger son has to work late into the evening to finish mowing the hay in his brother's fields. Just as he is completing this chore, marauding outlaws catch him in the open, slay him, and set the hay ablaze. His heroic attempt to restore the ruined farm ends in failure. But his sacrifices so work upon the grieving father's heart that he is persuaded to be merciful, rather than severe, toward his surviving elder son. He forgives his elder son for the damage he has done to the estate, even though that damage has not been repaired, and he mercifully refrains from exercising his right to disinherit his erring elder son.

By design, this small fable contains echoes of scriptural parables. If it serves to make its intended point, it will make it intuitively plausible to readers that the father in the tale acts with supererogatory goodness in responding to the life and tragic death of his younger son by forgiving his repentant and apologetic elder son, despite the fact that neither son has actually made the reparation which the father's rights would allow him to insist on before extending forgiveness. I therefore propose that this story provides the basis for a model of the morality of a particular sort of atonement that shows promise of both cohering with widely shared moral intuitions and helping us deepen our understanding and appreciation of the mystery of Christ's Atonement. My claim is that this way of thinking about the doctrine of the Atonement constitutes an advance over Swinburne's rather monistic sacrifice theoretic account, though I hasten to add that it is influenced by, deeply indebted to, and deliberately incorporates elements of that account.

Indeed, it might be thought that the account of Christ's Atonement that I have sketched reduces to Swinburne's account. But as I see it, they differ in two important ways. First, on Swinburne's account, Christ's life and death function to make reparation for human sin to the extent that God requires it; whereas, on mine, they serve to persuade God not to require it of repentant and apologetic sinners. Second, my account does not claim, as Swinburne's does, that Christ's death has no efficacy until sinners choose to plead it in atonement for their sins. I grant, of course, that Christ's death is efficacious if sinners choose to plead it; but I allow that Christ's death may also be efficacious for at least some repentant and apologetic sinners who do not choose to plead it. Thus my account permits the efficacy of Christ's Atonement in persuading God to forgive sins to extend to repentant and apologetic sinners who do not plead it because, through no fault of their own, they are not Christians.

However, I do not claim that my model furnishes us with anything like a full account of the Atonement, or even that it penetrates as far into the mystery as we humans are capable of going. After all, it helps us to understand only one of the effects of Christ's Atonement: the contribution it makes to securing divine forgiveness and thus to removing guilt for past human sin. It is therefore wholly retrospective in orientation. I think a full account of the doctrine of the Atonement would also have a prospective dimension. It would stress the idea that divine love, made manifest throughout the life of Christ but especially in his suffering and dying, has the power to transform human sinners, with their cooperation, in ways that fit them for everlasting life in intimate union with God. As Swinburne puts the point, 'Christ's atoning death must be the supreme means of human sanctification' (p. 171). About this, he and I are in complete agreement.[8]

[8] I am grateful to William Hasker and Richard Swinburne for helpful comments on an earlier version of this chapter that was presented at an Author Meets Critics session of the 1992 American Philosophical Association Central Division meeting.

PART V

Theological Anthropology

14

Body And Soul: Physical Properties and Cartesian Mind

ROM HARRÉ

Introduction

It is a special pleasure to contribute to a volume honouring the work of Richard Swinburne. As our most recent joint venture, we gave a university class in which we explored a wide variety of very fundamental concepts, fundamental to any physical theory. These included the concepts involved in space, time, causality, thinghood, and property. Though we are poles apart over the question of the viability of the notion of the Cartesian mind (soul), we are generally of similar opinions about many of the concepts involved in the physical sciences, in particular about the necessity to treat the physical properties of material things and substances as grounded dispositions, and thus as powers and liabilities. This idea has been around since the time of Aristotle. It was the dominant doctrine during the seventeenth and eighteenth centuries. Revived by a number of authors, including Madden and myself in 1977, it has since been taken up by both Shoemaker and Cartwright.[1] Heisenberg and Popper have used something akin to a causal powers notion to explicate their interpretations of quantum mechanics.[2] In this chapter I want to situate the discussion in a sequence of proposals, beginning with that of Locke, for treating physical properties as powers. This sequence ends, I believe, with what I shall call the 'quasi-realism' of a Kantian-style interpretation

---

[1] R. Harré and E. H. Madden, *Causal Powers* (Oxford: Blackwell, 1977); S. Shoemaker, 'Properties, Causation and Projectibility', in L. J. Cohen and M. B. Hesse (eds.), *Applications of Inductive Logic* (Oxford: Clarendon Press, 1980), 291–312; N. Cartwright, *Nature's Capacities and their Measurement* (Oxford: Clarendon Press, 1989).

[2] W. Heisenberg, *Physics and Philosophy* (New York: Harper, 1958); K. R. Popper, *Quantum Theory and the Schism in Physics* (Totowa, NJ: Rowan and Littlefield, 1982).

which is foreshadowed in Bohr's philosophy of physics. More controversially, I shall try to show that the generalization of this treatment of properties to the metaphysics of human personhood is fatal to Swinburne's Cartesian enterprise.[3] The long history of the interplay between philosophy of physics and philosophy of theology must culminate, in my view, in no less than a return to something like the Socinianism of Joseph Priestley.

Traditionally the metaphysics of nature has been based on the notion of substances and their properties. This reflects and is reflected by a traditional analysis of descriptive discourse into propositions of subject/predicate form. Subject expressions denote substances, both individual (things) and mass (stuffs). Predicate terms are used to ascribe properties to those substances. Two broad classes of properties have been recognized by philosophers in our discourses about nature, both scientific and lay: occurrent properties which an entity displays to an observer at the moment of observation, and dispositional properties the possible (or future) display of which is conditional on the obtaining of certain material or physical conditions. This distinction is reflected in the logical forms of the respective types of proposition with which each kind of property is ascribed to a subject. Occurrent properties are ascribed in indicative propositions of the form 'A is (was, will be) F', and dispositional properties in propositions of the form 'If C then A will (would) be F'.

The distinctions invoked in the last paragraph, that between substance and property (subject and predicate) and that between occurrent and dispositional properties have both been subject to 'imperialistic' reduction. According to both Mach and Russell, there is nothing to a substance but its properties.[4] In the end the subject expression reduces to an indication of spatio-temporal location as we transfer properties from the substance to that which is ascribed to it. Thus the apple which was said to be ripe is replaced by a mere location at which the properties that distinguish apples are all collocated. There is a certain subset of those properties which must be found there without which the collocated totality would not properly be called 'an apple'. I propose to follow this line

---

[3] R. Swinburne, *The Evolution of the Soul* (Oxford: Clarendon Press, 1986), ch. 5.
[4] E. Mach, *The Analysis of Sensations* (New York: Dover, 1959); B. Russell, *Our Knowledge of the External World as a Field for Scientific Method* (Chicago: Open Court, 1914).

of analysis, and shall take it for granted that to refer to sodium or Mars is to refer to a set of properties which, for convenience of exposition, are assimilated to a substance. Entities and stuffs appear in the ontology of physics as a discursive expedient only. Properties, too, have been subjected to an imperialistic reduction. It has been claimed that, for the physical world as it can be described by human beings, all properties which can be ascribed to the entities and stuffs of that world are dispositional. Occurrent properties occur only in human consciousness. This is not to say that the entities and stuffs of the world as it is conceived in the physical sciences are devoid of occurrent properties. This would be absurd, since that physical world certainly exists now. The dispositionalist reduction proposed by Greene, Kant, Faraday, Popper, and Shoemaker must be taken as a doctrine about the limits of human knowledge.[5] All a human being can know about the real nature of the entities and stuffs that we encounter in our explorations of the world are their dispositions to affect us or our instruments in certain ways. It is these effects which are occurrent, and which we naïvely ascribe to the entities and stuffs which are their source. If we now bring together the two reductionist 'tendencies', we arrive at the position I wish to argue for in this chapter: namely, that the only possible ontology for the science of physics, as it could be practised by any sentient being, recognizes only spatio-temporal distributions of a certain class of dispositions—namely, causal powers and liabilities.

What Conditions must a Property Satisfy to be Counted as 'Real'?

For science, a real property must have the following characteristics:

(1) It must exist independently of human sensibility.
(2) It must be knowable by human beings, in some way, directly or indirectly.

This seemingly innocent pair of desiderata are full of thorny puzzles and difficulties. With respect to the first requirement, the

---

[5] R. Greene, *The Principles of the Philosophy of the Expansive and Attractive Forces* (Cambridge: Cambridge University Press, 1727); I. Kant, *Metaphysical Foundations of Natural Science*, trans. J. Ellington (Indianapolis: Bobbs–Merrill, 1970 [1786]); M. Faraday, *A Course of Six Lectures on the Various Forces of Matter* (London: Harper, 1860); Popper, *Quantum Theory*; Shoemaker, 'Properties'.

most obvious problem concerns the way in which a vocabulary for describing and referring to such properties could be created. If all our meaningful descriptions must somehow be rooted in experience, how could a vocabulary, the point of which is to describe something which exists independently of human experience, be constructed? A preliminary answer might be that the fulfilment of desideratum 2 ensures that there are conditions under which a situation exists in which meaning could be created. But what of those properties of which we have only indirect knowledge, those that figure in our instructions for indirect manipulation of unobservable entities and processes? I shall return to this problem when a more developed account of the logical form of property ascriptions has been set out.

The second requirement will need considerable elaboration to take account of the qualification that some of the most important properties that we need for the physical sciences can be known only indirectly. This desideratum is, moreover, compatible with the idea that there could be all sorts of properties that could never become part of the knowledge field of the physical sciences, because they could be known to human beings neither directly nor indirectly, neither by ostensive definition nor by metaphor. No vocabulary for ascribing them could be created. In this discussion we need not trouble to consider this possibility, since it is to the problem of the nature of the properties that can figure in the physical sciences, as developed by human beings, that the argument is addressed.

The defence of scientific realism, in the broad sense, must surely include a defence of the claim that there are real properties. But it seems at first sight that there is a tension between the two desiderata that I have sketched above. How could something that is capable of existing independently of human sensibility be knowable by human beings?

Since the time of Galileo's discussion of the nature of physical properties in *Il Saggiatore*[6] there has been one account that has been sustained and refined and has persisted: namely, that the way to achieve the fusion of these two apparently profoundly incompatible desiderata is by use of the idea of a dispositional property. This idea has taken various forms, and has been expressed in a variety of concepts. For instance, the concept of a dispositional property has

---

[6] G. Galileo, *Il Saggiatore* (Milan: Feltrinelli, 1965).

taken the form of a 'causal power', a 'tendency', a 'capacity', a 'propensity', and so on. I shall proceed to develop the notion of a dispositional property by working through some of the main historical moments in which the notion has been proposed. I shall look critically at some of its major forms, in particular the versions proposed by Locke and by Kant. From these I shall jump to more recent proposals, particularly those of Polanyi and Niels Bohr.

Dispositional Concepts in the Seventeenth and Eighteenth Centuries

Locke's philosophy of science was proclaimed by its author as a kind of philosophical foundation to the physics of Newton.[7] Locke distinguished sharply between knowledge proper and mere conjecture, nescience. We could never know the real essences that constituted the true reality or natures of the types of material things we come across or of the stuffs of which they are made. Only the nominal essences of things can be known. The nominal essence of gold, for instance, is that set of observable properties which are the prescribed requirements for a metal to be called 'gold'. Yet the physical sciences do pretend to offer explanations of the appearances of things in terms of their unobservable corpuscular constitutions, their ultimate physical properties. However, the relation between the properties of bodies supposed by physicists—that is, the bulk, figure, texture, and motion of the said corpuscular constituents, which were their real properties—and their appearances needed a subtle explication.

Locke saw clearly that there could be no explanation in the physical sciences as to why a certain texture of surface looked a certain hue to a human being. One could know only that it looked that way and draw on corpuscularian theory to give an account of causes of the experience in terms of the physical properties of the surface. But what was one to say of the proposal about the real property that produced the hue? How was the fact that a surface did look just that way to a human being to play any essential part in physics?

[7] J. Locke, *An Essay Concerning Human Understanding*, ed. J. Yolton (London: Dent, 1964 [1690]).

The solution to the problem was to introduce dispositional properties, in the form of causal powers, as the real properties of bodies responsible for certain of their appearances to a human being. The property that a surface had by virtue of which it looked, say, yellow to a human being was a power to produce just that sensation in an observer. This was the real property. But surely this sort of dispositional concept is empty of useful empirical content? What is gained by this shift? The answer is that this ascription is not just the assertion of the existence of a simple disposition, a kind of physical *virtus dormitiva*. These dispositions are powers—that is, causally active states of material bodies. It is these states that serve to ground the dispositions of material things to look this hue or that in the properties of the surfaces in question. These properties are occurrent. But where do our ideas of them come from? To answer this question, Locke took over the popular theory of primary and secondary qualities. He drew his repertoire of primary qualities from Boyle's corpuscular theory of nature (rather than from Galileo's version of the theory[8]). Our ideas of the real properties of material things came from our sensory experience of some of the qualities of things as we perceived them. These were the ideas of the primary qualities. Unlike our ideas of secondary qualities, like hue and taste, the material causes of which had to be treated dispositionally, the properties in things which produced the experiences or ideas of primary qualities resembled those ideas. They could be treated non-dispositionally.

It was evident to some, at least, of Locke's contemporaries that this account of properties had two fatal flaws. The trouble lay in the use of primary qualities as the alleged groundings for the necessary causal powers. In Locke's terminology, a property as it was experienced by a human being, as some attribute of an observed thing, for instance, was an idea of a quality. Corresponding to it, in the thing itself, was a quality. Ideas of secondary qualities, like hues, did not resemble the secondary qualities of coloured things, the qualities that produced the ideas. All that could be ascribed to the thing itself was a power to produce the idea. However, a thing had a power only by virtue of its physical nature. According to the philosophy of science that Locke inherited from Boyle, that nature must be specified in terms of the mechanical properties of an array

---

[8] Galileo, *Il Saggiatore*.

of corpuscles, the elementary constituents of everything to which the power had been ascribed. It was essential for Locke's theory that the unobserved primary qualities of things could be known. But that would require a one-to-one relation between ideas and primary qualities and the qualities 'themselves'. Locke boldly claimed that this relation was resemblance. Since human beings are confined to their sensory experiences for their knowledge of the world, and this Locke himself acknowledges in his doctrine of nescience, one can never know whether the hypothesis that ideas of primary qualities resemble the qualities themselves is true. At best, this is a bold conjecture.

To the second flaw we cannot be so charitable. It was realized first by Greene in 1727 that if the resemblance doctrine has to be dropped as untenable at worst, reckless at best, then all the perceived properties of things must be secondary in Locke's sense; that is, for example, both perceived colour and perceived shape are the effects of causal powers.[9] So when a human being is aware of some of the properties of a material thing, that person can ascribe to the thing itself—that is, as it exists independently of human sensibility—only the appropriate power. Reality, then, for Greene and many who have come after him, is material, but it is characterized by powers, dispositions, tendencies, and so on, not by occurrent properties. At least, this is as far as one may go as a scientific investigator of nature whose bent is realist. Notice that Berkeley, though he started from a denial of the distinction between the ideas of primary and secondary qualities, reached a quite different terminus in the denial of matter of any kind.

The Causal Structure of Dispositions as Powers

A statement of the form 'If p then q', read causally, is usually taken to mean that what p describes or refers to is the cause of that which q describes or refers to. So we frequently adopt the conditional form for expressing causal hypotheses, particularly when the causes and effects we have in mind are events, including the comings to be of permanent states. However, when the conditional appears in the spelled-out form of a description of a grounded disposition, that is, in the form

---

[9] Greene, *Principles.*

If C, then M by virtue of N

the conditional part of the statement does not express the causal element. The point of a causal power attribution to some particular A is that it is the state N, an occurrent property of A, that is causally efficacious in the production or generation of M. The conditions, C, though necessary for the state N to work, are merely enabling or background. It is not the coming to be of C that causes M. Rather, the statement above expresses the fact that only when C obtains can N act causally. So another way of laying out a description of a causal power would be as follows:

N will cause M only if C obtains.

By shifting the mood of the verbs in this statement-form, various levels of possibility can be expressed. Thus

N would cause M were C to obtain

suggests that the obtaining of C is less likely than in the case described in the indicative.

It is this feature of the logical form of causal power attribution that lends the concept of a causal power a special aptness for describing such physical entities as fields or the charges from which they emanate. The very notion of a 'potential' is of a power that would or will be exercised; that is, will or would cause something to happen if the appropriate circumstances obtain. In removing the support from a heavy body in a gravitational field, we bring it about that the body falls. But it is the gravitational potential that causes the downwards acceleration, not the removal of the support. This alone would be enough to make the Humean regularity account of causality inapt for physics.[10] It would require us to call the relation between the removal of the support and the falling of the heavy body causal. This would seriously distort the physics of fields and the phenomena that they can bring about. As Gower has argued, the insistence that there must be a metaphysics of active powers 'behind' appearances was one of the moving forces not only in the developing physics of fields but also in the origins of the Hegelian tradition in the general dialectics of nature.[11]

---

[10] D. Hume, *A Treatise of Human Nature* (Oxford: Clarendon Press, 1978 [1789]), I. 3. 14.
[11] B. Gower, 'Gravity, Polarity and the Dialectic Method' (forthcoming).

Ending the Regress: How to Interpret 'Bare' Dispositions

In applying the concept of a grounded disposition to the analysis of physical properties in a real case—say the behaviour of metals as described in solid state physics—we find that the physical sciences display a hierarchical structure. The natures of the things and substances that are causally efficacious in the circumstances which define this or that causal power or liability are themselves to be analysed in terms of clusters or structures of powerful particulars, the description of the properties of which follows the same form. At any time the physical sciences rest on a common ontology defined by the choice of certain classes of beings as the ultimate or atomistic individuals of the world. So far, this choice of a stopping-point to physical analysis has proved only temporary. However, suppose that at some moment in the history of the physical sciences the quest, from a human point of view, were felt to be ended. How would the deepest level of beings be described? We should certainly wish to ascribe causal powers to them. But the argument so far has been to show the need to treat power ascriptions as complex casual hypotheses in which the grounding state of the disposition was causally efficacious. But, by hypothesis, the ultimate entities are without structure. There will be no further concepts to ascribe properties to them other than those which appear in the bare disposition 'If such and such conditions obtain, beings of type N will produce effects of type M'. But the only characteristic left by which beings of type N can be identified is that they have this causal power—that is, produce this type of effect. Here we run into Armstrong's objection to ontologies in which the basic particulars are bare dispositions: namely, that the world cannot be made of possibilities. This objection can be met if we keep in mind the logical structure of the causal interpretation of dispositional statements. The modality of possibility does not qualify the causal power, but only the conditions under which it is manifested. Thus, even at 'ground level', so to say, the power attribution can be expressed as follows:

A, the powerful particular, will bring about B, if such and such conditions obtain.

And that is its nature. This is an occurrent property. The only conditional thing about the ascription is to do with when and under what circumstances it will manifest that property. To think that the property is a cluster of possibilities is to miss the point of ascription of a causal power and to misplace the point at which causal efficacy is ascribed. Dan Robinson has pointed out to me that Thomas Reid remarked that a scientific law does not reveal the cause of an event, but only the 'rule' whereby the cause operates. This is certainly compatible with—indeed, best interpreted in terms of—a causal powers ontology.

An Alternative Reading of Locke's Philosophy of Science

Taking Locke as an epistemologist, the combination of the doctrine of real and nominal essences with the theory of primary and secondary qualities and their relations to ideas seems to be seriously flawed. How could one possibly know that the primary qualities resembled our ideas of them? We seem to be required to believe that when taking account of our ideas of primary qualities, we are in touch with reality via the resemblance relation, and yet we are also required to accept that real essences, clusters of primary qualities, are, in general, unknown. Sometimes Locke writes as if this is just a contingency, a failure consequent on the weakness of our sensory systems. However, there is another philosophical context within which Locke's various principles and doctrines can be set in which they make perfect sense. This is the theory of models. Suppose that the resemblance thesis, which seems so hopeless when set in the context of a theory of knowledge, were to be interpreted as the thesis that, in theorizing, physicists conceive a model of the unknown real essences that are needed to ground causal powers of material things. Boyle's bulk, figure, texture, and motion are the concepts needed to construct a model of the world, which, if the real world resembled it, would account for the phenomena we do observe, clusters of Lockian 'ideas'. According to Way, the most powerful way of expressing the relation between a model and its source is to take them to be subtypes at the same level in a type-hierarchy.[12] So the physicist's 'corpuscles' are a subtype of the supertype 'material thing', the defining qualities of which are bulk, figure, texture, and motion. As a subtype of this supertype, material

[12] E. C. Way, *Knowledge Representation and Metaphor* (Dordrecht: Kluwer, 1991).

corpuscles 'inherit' all the properties of the supertype, so they too are characterized as having bulk, figure, texture, and motion. The resemblance doctrine is a trivial consequence of the fact that all material things, observable and unobservable, are subtypes of the same supertype. This, in updated form, is the main point of the recent proposal that Locke's *Essay* could be—and indeed should be—read, as a sketch of a general conceptual system, formulated a priori but not in complete independence of how the world appears to human perception. I called this system a 'quasi-definition', finding its origins in the metaphysics of Galileo's *Il Saggiatore*. With the type-hierarchy account of the semantics of models available now, this proposal seems an even more attractive way of reading Locke as a philosopher of physics.

A World of Powers: The Kantian Metaphysics of Nature

In his *Metaphysical Foundations of Natural Science* Kant offers a thoroughgoing dispositionalist account of the world to be investigated by the methods of physics.[13] There are two fundamental 'forces' or tendencies, and the net effect of the joint actions of these forces is what we take to be a world of solid, impenetrable material things. Where the tendency to attract and the tendency to repel are equal, a human being will experience a surface as of a solid. For instance, at that point a test object will encounter a net force of repulsion, experienced as a resistance to further 'penetration' of whatever solid it seems to be approaching. Effectively this ontology deletes human sensibility from the story of the physical world, which could be told wholly in terms of systems of opposing tendencies or 'forces', in Kant's slightly misleading terminology. In ascribing a property to the physical world on the basis of our sensory experiences, we humans need not suppose that the state of the world producing our experiences resembles those experiences in any way at all. All we need to do is to ascribe a tendency or power to the world to produce that state of sensibility (or experienced quality) in us. The distinction between primary and secondary qualities vanishes from the metaphysics and epistemology of the physical sciences. Neither reading of Locke is required to create a metaphysical foundation for the natural sciences.

[13] Kant, *Metaphysical Foundations*.

The attempt to build a world out of dispositions alone seems to suffer from a fatal flaw too. But it is not the flaw that David Armstrong thought he saw in dispositionalism, the 'dynamicist' view of the world. Armstrong thought that dispositions needed grounding in permanent material conditions, since one could not make a world out of possibilities.[14] But the flaw goes much deeper. In Locke's dispositionalist philosophy of physics there are refinements which must now be acknowledged. He realized that there are some dispositions which are active, for which I will reserve the term 'power', and some which are passive, a readiness to be acted upon, for which I shall reserve the term 'liability'. So far, the account seems to be compatible with a world of powers and liabilities, be they properties of some ubiquitous stuff or taken entitatively, as in the manner of Greene,[15] or by Berkeley in invoking 'spirits.' The second matter of importance concerns the problem of the existence of powers and liabilities when they are not being exercised. We would like to be able to say that the acid has the power to etch a copper plate while it is still in the bottle, and that the copper plate has the liability to be corroded by that acid, even when it is not in contact with it. We would like to be able to say that a surface of beaten gold, at this moment unilluminated or unobserved or both, would look yellow under the appropriate conditions.

What is wrong with an ontology of bare dispositions? In any ontology we need to give an account of the criteria of individuation, identity, and continuity of the beings in question. The bare disposition is described in a simple conditional statement: that if such and such conditions occur, then such and such a phenomenon will be perceived or detected. There is nothing in this formulation which could answer the question of whether it is numerically the same or a different disposition which is activated on another occasion. Nor is there anything in the formulation that would enable one to claim that the disposition existed all along even when not activated. However, when grounded in some permanent state of the powerful particular which has the property ascribed in the dispositional statement, both questions are easily answered. A disposition is numerically the same not only if it has qualitatively the same manifestation in similar circumstances, but also if it is grounded in numerically the same state of the particular in ques-

---

[14] D. M. Armstrong, *A Materialist Theory of the Mind* (London: Routledge and Kegan Paul, 1968).
[15] Greene, *Principles*.

tion—say, the arrangement of the parts in its surface as the grounding of its tendency to resist sliding motion. A similar answer can be given to the question of how the disposition exists in the intervals between its manifestation. It exists in the stable grounding property of the particular in question.

But dispositions are also distinguished by whether they are active (properties of agents) or passive (properties of patients). There is nothing in the bare disposition which can answer the question of whether a disposition expressed in the bare 'If . . . then . . .' formulation is active or passive—that is, whether the particular in question is an agent or a patient. This question is not answered by adverting to the grounding state of the particular. In fact, I do not believe that it can be answered except by reference to the details of the physical theory applicable in any particular case. I do not see how there could be any general criterion for whether a disposition is to be taken as active power or passive liability, and for the being of which it is a property of an agent or of a patient.

To these and other requirements for a physics of dispositions, Locke offered the doctrine of real essences.[16] If we knew the material constitution of substances, we would know why they had the powers and liabilities that they displayed when activated. But that doctrine, as we have seen, is capable of more than one interpretation. In the standard, or 'epistemological', interpretation it seems fatally flawed, since, to give it content, Locke had recourse to his unsatisfactory notion of primary qualities. However, the Lockian idea can be both strengthened and weakened to become somewhat more convincing. It can be strengthened by dropping the notion of primary qualities as the way of giving content to the real essences of material substances. Instead, we say that a substance has this or that power by virtue of its nature, whatever that should prove to be. It may be, as I have suggested in my 'ontological' interpretation of Locke's philosophy of science, that physicists can make use of the mechanical properties of observed bodies as a model for their unobserved properties, in part. But more exotic properties may also be needed, and in the end may displace the mechanical properties altogether. A history of the physics of the eighteenth and nineteenth centuries could be focused on the way that the mechanical model for the real natures of things hung on. The generic notion that has developed in physics for the grounding of disposi-

---

[16] Locke, *Essay.*

tions in the natures of things is 'charge'. A charge, in its most general reading, is that property of a material thing that grounds its electrical, mechanical, and other dispositions. Locke's notion can also be weakened, by dropping the requirement that the grounding be made specific by reference to the qualities of the world as we observe it. Again, the notion of 'charge' fulfils this desideratum.

We have thus withdrawn from the somewhat extremist position that Greene and Kant arrived at. The world is not a world constituted by some set of dispositions or ungrounded powers and liabilities. It is not a world wholly of possibilities. Powers and liabilities are grounded in the natures of material beings, though the property we ascribe to them may be schematic—in particular, the important schematic property of charge. By making a strategic withdrawal from a pure dynamicist metaphysics upon which to base the concepts of physical science, we achieve another advantage. The final problem for the Kantian position is that of providing convincing criteria for the identity and individuation of powers and liabilities. When and how can we say that the same power is being exercised or that the powers of a thing have changed? To answer this question, we need to invoke the whole panoply of clauses implicit in the full-blown powers concept. The dispositional part would be written as a conditional:

> If certain conditions are fulfilled a certain phenomenon will be manifested,

to be followed by a grounding clause;

> By virtue of the nature of the substances involved, whatever that turns out to be,

A manifestation of a power is display of the same power if and only if

> (i) there is a display of the same phenomenon (*ceteris paribus*)
> (ii) the grounding state of the powerful particular is preserved.

The *ceteris paribus* qualification to the first desideratum is needed because there may be different ways in which a power is displayed, depending on the circumambient conditions. Gravitational potential may be displayed either in accelerated motion or in downward pressure on a support.

However, it is still not clear that the Armstrong objection has been fully met. It might seem as if the introduction of the explicit grounding condition dealt with the problem of the seeming impossibility of finding anything existent in a world of possibilities. But in reflecting on the grounding states of powerful particulars, one seems driven to reintroduce another set of dispositions. If the chemical properties of a substance are grounded in its atomic constitution, is this not because the atoms are possessed of certain powers and liabilities, grounded in their natures, whatever those might be? And so on. How could such a regress be ended?

At this point we have two pathways ahead. If the question of ending the regress is posed as an ontological problem, it seems that the only solution is to assert that there must exist a class of ultimate beings, powerful particulars whose nature is identical with their powers. Or, to put this requirement another way, there must be a class or classes of beings whose defining properties are their natures—that is, whose real essences are identical with their nominal essences. Again, via the dispositionalist analysis of the claims to the existence of observed properties, we again reach the point of asserting that the only properties they have are dispositional. This terminus seems to be just the very proposal that we have tried to escape. However, there is another pathway. It might be that the problem of the termination of the regress could be resolved by seeing the citation of the progressive structure of powers and natures as a discursive device rather than as an ontological hypothesis. It represents our ways of expressing our beliefs about the powerful particulars with which we are dealing. Our beliefs about the ultimate entities proposed by the physical sciences are beliefs about what these entities can do in this or that circumstance. To say that their natures are their powers is to say something no more baffling than to say that, so far as we can know them, our knowledge is only of what they can do, within the limits of the conditions which we can impose upon them. There may be many other things that they can do, but we shall never know them. These are the ultimate entities for human beings, and perhaps for God.

The Relativity of Dispositions to their Modes of Manifestation

The rough formula 'If C (conditions) then M (manifestation) by virtue of N (nature)' expressing some aspects of the content of a dispositional attribution has already led us to ponder the consequences of the way in which the natures of things need to be treated. There are equally important observations to be made about the M, or manifestation, term. Consider an electrically charged particle. By virtue of that charge it has a tendency to move towards a particle of opposite charge, but it also has a tendency to move at right angles to a magnetic field. With the same nature a thing has more than one disposition, and that disposition depends on the conditions in which the powers of a thing are to be displayed. There are also cases in which we would say that the very same disposition is manifested in different ways in different circumstances: for instance, the acidity of vinegar can be displayed in the corrosion of copper or in the taste of vinaigrette. In both cases the disposition is grounded in the powers of the H^+ ions of the acid in solution.

These examples illustrate a general difficulty with dispositional treatments of properties: namely, the relativity of a disposition to the manner of its manifestation in human sensibility or to the choice of apparatus in the reactions of which this or that disposition is made manifest. I shall examine two attempts to develop a theory of properties which manages to deal both with the problems sketched in the last section and with the problem raised in this. Both Polanyi and Bohr proposed accounts of properties that are dispositionalist and are sensitive to the relativity of dispositions to their modes of manifestation, be it in apparatus or in human perceptual systems.

Tacit Knowing: Polanyi and the 'Probe Ploy'

Polanyi was among the first to insist on the 'active shaping of experience performed in the pursuit of knowledge'.[17] Polanyi's main technique in philosophy was to take some feature or aspect of the psychology of perception, in his case the Gestaltist version, and generalize it to all forms of knowing. According to Polanyi, all forms of knowing have a common structure, the structure of 'tacit knowing', exemplified in the phenomenon of the use of a probe to examine the shape of a surface.

Tacit knowledge has two terms:

[17] M. Polanyi, *Personal Knowledge* (Chiacgo: University of Chicago Press, 1958), 6.

(1) The first or proximal term is known by our awareness of it, though in knowing we do not attend to it. We are aware of the pressures on our fingers and wrist when we are feeling something with the tip of Descartes's walking-stick. But we do not attend to them.

(2) The second or distal term is what we attend to via our awareness of the proximal term. In the case of the Cartesian walking-stick it is the shape of the hole in the ground which we are using the stick to probe. What is revealed about the world by the use of a probe is not felt in the palm of the hand or the joints of the fingers.

In this scheme the first term is tacit, the second explicit.[18] The first term is known only through its meaning—that is, through the second term. Finally Polanyi introduced the human observer explicitly in the thesis that the human body (and of course experimental apparatus in interaction with the physical world) becomes that from which we attend to the states and conditions of the material world.

It should be clear from this sketch that Polanyian 'tacit knowing' is a realist theory of perception. Sense-data are necessary for knowing the world, but are means and not ends, tacit (proximal) not explicit (distal). What we experience are things and their properties and relations, not bodily sensations. Generalized to the epistemology of natural science, it becomes a realist theory of scientific knowledge. We know the world (distal) via the behaviour of instruments (proximal), through which we attend to physical reality. The final step in Polanyi's account of experience comes directly from Gestalt psychology. It is the thesis of structural isomorphism between the 'structure of comprehension' and the 'structure of that which is comprehended'.

There are several points of interest about this account. The structural isomorphism principle seems to me to be none other than Locke's notorious resemblance doctrine of primary qualities and their corresponding ideas in Gestalt dress. If we delete that from Polanyi's analysis, we get a dispositionalist account directly. The variety of modes of manifestation of a disposition is taken care of by the thesis of tacit knowing. That from which we attend can be as various as the sensory modalities or the kinds of relevant experi-

---

[18] M. Polanyi, *The Tacit Dimension* (New York: Doubleday, 1986), 11–13.

mental apparatus. It drops out of the features of the world as experienced, since it is that through which we attend to what is distal—namely, that state of things that brought it about that we had the proximal (tacit) bodily states, experienced as sensations (or generalizing this, as reactions or readings of instruments).

There are some serious objections to this attractive theory of knowledge. The state explicitly known should figure as the ground of a disposition to elicit or produce the proximal or tacit effects in an observer or apparatus. But to say this is to go beyond the psychology of perception. This is indeed Polanyi's move. I think it is not too much of a distortion to give Polanyi's theory of scientific knowledge a dispositionalist twist. If we do so, it will read something like the following: Knowing the dispositions of things via the phenomena they cause us to experience is not a matter of perception but of discursive knowledge. I know that a surface has a disposition to look red because I know that it looks red. What I do not experience are the grounding conditions in the molecular structures of the surface that would complete the content of the disposition as a causal power. It seems as if the analogy with the Gestalt theory of perception is too fragile to bridge the gap from perceptual knowing to discursive knowledge.

Bohr and Physical Affordances

At first glance Bohr's philosophy of science seems to owe little to the psychology of perception. He takes it for granted that a human observer can look at or otherwise attend to the state of an apparatus and know what it is, and then record that knowledge discursively. The leading idea in Bohr's philosophy of physics is that of the 'phenomenon'. From this idea all else, including his well-known Principles of Complementarity and Correspondence follow. A Bohrian phenomenon is an observable state of the world brought into being in the interaction between apparatus and world. The topic of the science of physics is phenomena. Apparatus is not transparent. There is no way of eliminating it from physics, no way of reading back from phenomena to some *Ur*-state of the world which in a one-to-one way determinately produces that which we observe. Bohr begins, then, with a (tacit) rejection of Locke's doctrine of primary qualities and their alleged relation to a corresponding set of ideas, though he does not put the matter like that. I believe it is an essential part of Bohr's philosophy of science that we should regard the world as indeterminate with respect to any and all of our possible descriptive categories until it interacts with an apparatus. An apparatus is itself determinate only in so far as its states can be observed and thereby become capable of being described in the terms of classical physics, the most refined vocabulary for describing phenomena, that is, that which can be perceived by a human being.

I believe that Bohr's philosophy of science can be made much clearer by taking a leaf out of Polanyi's book and incorporating into it one of the leading concepts of the contemporary psychology of perception—namely, Gibson's notion of an affordance.[19] Affordances are a class of dispositions, the main feature of which is their incorporation of some human relevance in their content. For example, a cup has, amongst many other dispositions, the ability to hold a quantity of liquid for easy transport to the mouth. This disposition is relevant to, and indeed a necessary condition for, the role of the cup in drinking. We could say that because of its physical characteristics and the way it is regarded by people, a cup affords drinking. Floors afford walking, and scissors afford cutting. However, an affordance is not an inference from the physical characteristics of the cup and the task that some people have in mind. It is how the cup strikes someone, as an object which has a definite part to play in our ways of life. An affordance is a perceptual category, not a theoretical concept.

Let us now extend the notion of affordance to the context of Bohrian phenomena and their genesis in indissoluble apparatus–world complexes. We link the phenomenon and the apparatus–world complex by this notion. We can say that this apparatus–world complex affords electron phenomena (tracks of a certain sort) in these conditions, while this apparatus–world complex in these conditions affords X-ray phenomena, or this one in these conditions W particles, and so on. The world is indeterminate relative to our conceptual system, limited as it must be to the human affordances of our apparatus and more primitively to our perceptual systems. The relativity of dispositions to the mode of their manifestation is now neatly incorporated in a quasi-realist theory of science. Each

[19] J. J. Gibson, *The Ecological Approach to Visual Perception* (Boston: Houghton Mifflin, 1970).

affordance is defined in such a way that tacitly or explicitly the apparatus in which the relevant phenomena are made manifest is included in that definition. But it is a quasi-realist theory since, although the world plays an ineliminable role in the genesis of the phenomenon, its current state is indeterminate for us. It is not apparatus that affords electron phenomena, but apparatus–world complexes.

A generic principle of complementarity follows directly. There will be as many affordances described in physics as there are kinds of apparatus. In some cases conjunctions of kinds of apparatus will be compatible, and in others not. It is the latter case that crops up in subatomic physics and is expressed in the rules of combination of observables that are characteristic of quantum mechanics. A generic principle of correspondence also follows directly. If apparatus is ineliminably involved in the definition of affordances, then the descriptive concepts appropriate to apparatus will also be ineliminable from physics. Since these are necessarily classical concepts, the building blocks of the physics of the world of observable material interactions, then every physical theory must be expressible in classical concepts, though, from the Principle of Complementarity, it follows that the rules for their joint use may be more restrictive than the laws of classical physics.

This theory of physics is a quasi-realism. A certain apparatus–world complex affords particulate electron phenomena. Another apparatus–world complex affords wave-like phenomena. 'Is the world particle-like or wave-like?' This is the wrong question. The world is neither. Affordances are simple or bare dispositions of apparatus–world complexes. There is no room, in physics, for the question of the grounding of whatever are the ultimate affordances in any state of the world alone. Some state of the world is implicated, but it is indeterminate until made determinate in the relevant apparatus–world complex. Can it be made more determinate in thought? All attempts to do so have failed.

Kinds of Dispositions

From this survey of the development of the use of dispositional concepts in the philosophy of physics, a taxonomy of alternative interpretations can be extracted.

1. Dispositional concepts might be appearing in physics as a way of describing otherwise indescribable features of the natural world. This interpretation was the backbone of the treatment of those dispositional properties that have found their way into physics since the seventeenth century. However, I have come to think that the way in which dispositional concepts have displaced occurrent property concepts should be seen as having a deeper significance. They may be appearing so ubiquitously because they are the appropriate concepts for a more fundamental kind of physical state, property, or entity than the occurrent properties revealed or displayed in human experience.

2. If we follow the second proposal in (1) there are again two main ways of interpreting dispositional concepts. They might be used for a certain class of properties—for instance, all those properties which are other than those that have their being in human sensibility, such as the attributes of the powerful particulars that bring about changes in the world. Or they might refer to powers as entities—for instance, as the basic beings from which the world is constructed. I believe that we can find examples of both interpretations in contemporary physics.

In commenting on these distinctions, there is one important matter to be borne in mind: namely, that dispositions are what lie dormant until activated by something, perhaps the human being *qua* scientist, or for that matter *qua* cook. They satisfy the double desiderata with which this discussion began; that is, if there are real properties, they must be knowable by human beings and yet must exist independently of human sensibility. Dispositions, as properties, fulfil this double requirement perfectly. We come to know them by activating them. They exist, whether we activate them or not.

The Kantianism of Bohr's Point of View

It is well known that there is a natural-seeming parallel between Bohr's general philosophy of science and the structure of cognition that one finds in Kant's *Critique of Pure Reason* and in his *Metaphysical Foundations of Natural Science*.[20] It is worth briefly spell-

[20] I. Kant, *Critique of Pure Reason*, trans. N. K. Smith (London: Macmillan, 1929 [1781]); idem, *Metaphysical Foundations*.

ing this out. By doing so, I will be able to home in more closely on the structure of Bohr's position. Phenomena, for both Kant and Bohr, are the constituents of the world as we experience it. They are not constituents of the world as it is in itself—that is, how it would be independent of human sensibility or the probing reactions of humanly constructed instruments. Kantian phenomena come into being through the schematization of the flux of sensation by the application of the concepts, which are themselves fixed a priori by the possible forms of judgement. Bohrian phenomena come into being through the interaction of apparatus and world. Apparatus is a realization of certain principles, concepts, and laws which are themselves fixed a priori by the possible applications of classical physics, the only acceptable science of the material world as human beings experience it.

Apparatus makes determinate some state of the world that is indeterminate with respect to the only array of empirical concepts we can have. Thus, as we have seen, the world must be described in terms of the affordances of apparatus–world complexes, in which the first member of the pair is determinate and the second indeterminate. Looked at from this Kantian slant, two features of importance in Bohrian philosophy of physics can be seen.

1. In the sentential structure of dispositional attributions there must be a reference to the apparatus (or for that matter to the human perceptual or motor system) in all three clauses. Thus, in

If C then M by virtue of N,

the conditions for the display of M include the presence and the running of the apparatus; the manifestation of the affordance is to be observed in the state of the apparatus; and the grounding of this affordance is in some partly indeterminate state of the apparatus plus world. It follows that what we can know about the world is relative to the apparatus we have available to explore it. And since the concepts by which we are limited in our powers of describing the affordances of the world are also relativized to the very same apparatus, this account of physics yields the thesis of the 'theory-ladenness of observation' very directly.

2. So far I have analysed only those properties which, as physicists, we would wish to ascribe to the world, but find ourselves, *faut de mieux*, ascribing to apparatus–world complexes with which we explore the world. But what of the determinate states of the apparatus which are afforded by these complexes? Ought they not too to

receive exactly the same treatment? A certain state of the apparatus in question affords a certain perceptual experience to a human observer, as it might be of a pointer coinciding with a certain graduation on a scale. This is indeed so. The consequence is that just as in Polanyi's account of science a certain theory of perception, the Gestaltist, appears and reappears both in the general epistemology and in the account of how a human observer knows anything about what is going on in the world, so it is in this version of Bohr's philosophy of science. The Gibsonian psychology of perception must now be invoked to deal with the 'interface' between the human observer and some determinate state of the apparatus–world complex. However, it ought to be clear that this interface is not part of the subject-matter of physics. Physics is about Bohrian phenomena, not about the perceptual uptake of the human perceptual system. To assume that it is would be to confuse Kantian phenomena with Bohrian phenomena.

How Relativist is Quasi-Realism?

We must all acknowledge that however sophisticated and historically and pragmatically validated our methods of enquiry might be, each can reveal only a limited aspect of that which exists independently of human powers and interests. The generalization of this insight yields 'relativism'. To adjudicate between various answers that might be given to the question that forms the title of this section, it will be necessary to delve a little more deeply into the possible forms that the relativist insight can take.

There is what I shall call a 'benign relativism', which can be expressed in the following four principles:

1. Different aspects of a person-independent world are revealed by the use of different kinds of instruments and to different kinds of perceptual systems. One kind of instrument in manifesting tracks reveals particle-like affordances, while another in manifesting spatially distributed interference patterns reveals that there are wave-like affordances. (One quantum number phenomenon is afforded by the spectrometer, while another is afforded by the Stern–Gerlach apparatus. Both, as affordances, are aspects of atomic reality.) Human beings see a garden with both red and blue flowers. Bees probably see only shades of blue and ultraviolet.

2. We continually strive for an ideal empirical result in which a robust and determinate empirical grounding permits the deletion of the term expressing human sensibility or the choice of a specific apparatus from the expression of the ascribed dispositional property.

3. We now have good reason to believe that no one instrument/ conceptual system could give a complete account of the grounding of what can be afforded by some natural entity.

4. We also have reason to believe that no set of instrument/ conceptual systems could be proved to give an exhaustive account of the grounding of all possible affordances to people and to their apparatus.

This benign relativism is quite compatible with such realist ideas as the progress of science. If does not serve to justify the kind of anti-foundationalism preached by such as Rorty.[21]

But there is a malign relativism. Starting from the same observations about the ways in which knowledge is garnered, the malign relativist arrives at a seemingly startling conclusion: Different instrument/conceptual systems bring different aspects of nature into existence. In this observation the term 'nature' can be deleted without loss of content. It plays no role.

The obvious objection to this move is to point out that it ignores the necessity of grounding dispositions in some state or other of the world independently of human sensibility. Without this grounding condition we have no criteria for the identity, individuation, or continuity of dispositional properties, without which even the dedicated relativist has no world at all. It also treats affordances as if they were simple dispositions of the apparatus. The Bohrian affordances with which I have constructed a quasi-realism allow us to accept the limitations on our scientific hubris that are expressed in the four principles of benign relativism, without falling into the follies of the anti-realism of malign relativism.

Could the Mind be a Cluster of Dispositions?

I dare say that Cartesians and dispositionalists agree that much of the psychology of human beings is best expressed in terms of the

---

[21] R. Rorty, *Philosophy and the Mirror of Nature* (Princeton, NJ: Princeton University Press, 1979).

manifestation of dispositions and the intentional use of skills. Locke was not the first to ask whether it was incoherent to suppose that a material entity could possess cognitive skills and moral dispositions.[22] Like Socinus before him, he thought that there was no contradiction in the supposition but that as a matter of fact it was not true. This was in sharp contrast to the line of Descartes himself: namely, that the properties of cognition were such that the substance in which they inhered could not be extended and material.

At this point in the argument one must identify some principle of rational thought that would be compelling enough to enable me to impose the pattern I have identified in the metaphysics of nature on ways of thinking about the mind. In this context, the outlines of which have been set by Swinburne's own line of argument, imposing this metaphysics on the mind is also imposing it on the soul. The principle of rationality that one might at first sight advert to would be analogy. The argument would be played out in terms of the relative weights of the similarities and differences that would be revealed by considering the dispositions of the Bohrian apparatus–world complexes and the dispositions of human beings. Lately this mode of analysis has been refined by the introduction of a general way of expressing the structure of both analogical reasoning and the use of metaphor as a discursive device. This is the technique of representation in a type-hierarchy.[23]

Can we construct a supertype of which Bohrian complexes and human beings are subtypes? This will be a generic entity characterized by the fact that its dispositions are simple or bare, that they are not grounded in structures of constituent beings characterized by further dispositions. It is easy to see that Bohrian complexes satisfy this requirement, as I have tried to show above, and so are subtypes of the generic supertype. But what are human beings with respect to their characteristic cognitive and moral dispositions? This question takes us to the heart of the main current controversy in cognitive science. Cognitive activity results in the creation of discourses of various kinds, jointly constructed by the members of the local community. The ability to take a proper part in discursive interaction (often a conversation) is a skill or cluster of interrelated skills. The justification for putting the category 'human being' in a

---

[22] J. W. Yolton, *Thinking Matter: Materialism in Eighteenth-Century Britain* (Minneapolis: University of Minnesota Press, 1983).
[23] Way, *Knowledge Representation*.

subtype slot in the same type-hierarchy as Bohrian apparatus–world complex will require an argument to the effect that human skills are not grounded in anything that is itself cognitive. For the Socinian (and in some important respects Gassendi was also a Socinian in his psychological theory) these skills are grounded in the structure of the material nervous system. Acquiring a cognitive skill involves reshaping the neural structures of that system, just like the reshaping that we know occurs when we learn a motor skill. The subjective use of symbolic systems for reasoning, deciding, imagining, and so forth is just a privatized version of the public use of these skills in conversation and other discursive interactions. This is no mental mechanism behind the use of cognitive sills. We must not mistake a private use of our skills for a mental process that lies behind their public use. To make a cast-iron case for this view, it would be necessary to follow the lead of Wittgenstein and undertake a case by case study to show that in every realm of thought there were basic skills and dispositions resting on no more fundamental skills. And that is the project of discursive psychology. In the ultimate fate of that programme lies the means for finally deciding between Socinians and Cartesians.

15

The Problem of Evil: A Deontological Perspective

DAVID McNAUGHTON

I

How is it that an omnipotent, omniscient, and wholly good God has created a world in which there is anything bad or evil? In particular, what could justify his allowing his creatures to suffer? For it seems that a morally good being would eliminate evil as far as he could, and an omnipotent being could eliminate all evil. Faced with this difficulty, theists have produced a number of responses. Varied though they may be in content, they nearly all share a common argumentative structure. While agreeing that God would eliminate all pointless or unnecessary evils, they claim that the evils in this world are neither pointless nor unnecessary—these evils are the price we pay for the existence of certain goods whose value is at least sufficient to outweigh the evils needed to produce them.

The two most common arguments of this kind are the higher-order goods defence and the freewill defence. The first argues that suffering is a necessary condition for the existence of some very good things, especially for the existence of many valuable human traits, such as compassion, courage, loyalty, and so on. The second claims that much suffering is the consequence of human sin. In creating beings with genuine (incompatibilist) free will, God ran the risk that they would sin; this is a risk which could only have been avoided by not granting them free will. In each case, the argument continues, the good in question is arguably sufficient to outweigh the evil needed to produce it.

To put the matter a little more formally, many theists claim that, in order for God to have had good reason to permit the evils that exist in his creation, the following claims (or something very like them) must be true:

(1) There are evils which it is not logically possible for God to eliminate without thereby eliminating a good.

(2) All the evils in this world are of this kind.

(3) The attendant goods which those evils bring outweigh those evils.

(4) An agent would be morally justified in not eliminating an evil if he could not eliminate it without thereby eliminating a good greater than the evil he would thereby prevent.[1]

If (1)–(4) are true, then there are no evils in this world which God has good reason to eliminate.

The two defences I mentioned exhibit this structure, although, as I have already suggested, they differ in the way in which the goods and evils involved are related to each other and also in their explanation of the fact that God could not have eliminated the good without eliminating the evil. In the higher-order goods defence the actual existence of suffering in various forms is a logically necessary condition for the exercise of virtues such as compassion, fortitude, and self-sacrifice. The existence of the evils is not, of course, sufficient to elicit these virtues; the presence of evil merely makes room for the display of such qualities. This structural feature raises a question as to just what good it is whose presence is supposed to outweigh the attendant evils: is it the actual display of these virtues which is the good in question, or, as Swinburne suggests, is the opportunity to display such virtues, whether or not it is seized, itself a good of the right kind?[2] The advantage of the second answer is that the opportunity for the exercise of virtue is a good whose presence is guaranteed by the occurrence of evil in a world containing beings like us. The disadvantage is that the mere opportunity might be thought a good insufficient to outweigh the evils necessary for such an opportunity to exist.

In the freewill defence, by contrast, the actual good of free will makes possible, in our kind of world, the existence of sin and wrongdoing, with their harmful consequences; but the actual existence of sin and wrongdoing is not a logically necessary condition of free will. This raises a difficulty for the proposed justification: if it is

---

[1] The fourth claim is close to a formulation in R. Swinburne, 'Knowledge from Experience and the Problem of Evil', in W. J. Abraham and S. Holtzer (eds.), *The Rationality of Religious Belief* (Oxford: Clarendon Press, 1987), 142. For a similar formulation see K. Yandell, *Basic Issues in Philosophy of Religion* (Boston: Allyn and Bacon, 1971), 47. I am not here distinguishing, as I later do, between eliminating a greater good or bringing about a greater evil.

[2] Swinburne, 'Knowledge from Experience', 148.

only the *possibility* of evil which is a necessary consequence of the good of free will, then how does the defence justify the actual existence of evil? Surely God could have created a world like ours in which there were free beings who never sinned, so that the possibility of evil was not actualized. There are two well-known strategies in response to this obvious objection. One claims that it may be that God could not create creatures who would not sin, perhaps because, as Plantinga suggests, all creaturely essences suffer from trans-world depravity.[3] The other, favoured by Swinburne, claims that, in creating any world containing free beings, God could not eliminate the risk of wrongdoing, since it is not logically possible for anyone, even God, to foresee with certainty what free beings will do.[4]

Claim (I) is largely accepted;[5] it is the second and, to a lesser extent, the third claims which have provoked the most controversy, and much ingenuity has been exercised in their defence. Defenders tend to adopt one of two main strategies. The minimalists, of whom Plantinga is a leading example,[6] offer an account of God's purposes which attempts to show merely that it is conceivable that the second and third claims are true. If this is the case, then the theist can at least be cleared of the charge of inconsistency. The theodicists, of whom Swinburne is a leading example, go further, and offer a detailed account of God's providential plan which aims to show that we have good reason to believe that the second and third claims are true.[7]

The fourth claim, by contrast, has received comparatively little attention.[8] Here I will try to remedy this omission. What I

---

[3] A. Plantinga, *God, Freedom and Evil* (London: George, Allen and Unwin, 1975), 48 ff.

[4] R. Swinburne, *The Coherence of Theism* (Oxford: Clarendon Press, 1977), 167–78.

[5] Although M. M. Adams denies that God is only justified in permitting an evil to exist if its existence is a logically necessary condition of the good, on the grounds that one good, the beatific vision, is incommensurate with earthly suffering, so that no one who received such a benefit could have any claim against God's justice. See her 'Redemptive Suffering: A Christian Solution to the Problem of Evil', in R. Audi and W. Wainwright (eds.), *Rationality, Religious Belief, and Moral Commitment* (Ithaca, NY: Cornell University Press, 1986), 263.

[6] See e.g. Plantinga, *God, Freedom and Evil.*

[7] See R. Swinburne, *The Existence of God* (Oxford: Clarendon Press, 1979), 180–224, and *idem*, 'Knowledge from Experience'.

[8] Which is not to say that it has been neglected. Apart from the authors mentioned in the text, the worries I have about (4) have been raised by D. Z. Phillips, *The Concept of Prayer* (London: Routledge and Kegan Paul, 1965), esp. 93.

shall seek to show is that (4) as it stands, while acceptable to consequentialists, is not acceptable to any mainstream version of deontology. This poses a difficulty for many theists since, as Robert Adams has pointed out,[9] Christians (and others) have usually employed a deontological ethical framework when thinking not only about their own actions but also about God's. Both Richard Swinburne and Robert Adams have offered important and substantial theodicies which try to meet these deontological worries. While both are open to objection, I shall argue that Adams's view is defensible if suitably amended. I shall then tentatively canvass a third option, which I derive from the work of Marilyn Adams, which, though capable of standing on its own, can also be seen as supplementing Robert Adams's view.

II

Consequentialists are in the business of trading off evils against goods. Claim 4 is a specific version of a principle which would find its place in any act-consequentialist theory.[10]

> P In a choice between two courses of action, an agent is *permitted* to choose the one which will produce the most good.

Indeed, the most common form of the theory, optimizing act-consequentialism, commits us to something stronger than this: it tells us that, of all the actions open to him, the agent is *required* to do the one which produces the greatest balance of good over evil. Other, weaker versions, such as satisficing consequentialism, which only requires us to produce a satisfactory balance of good over evil, still entail the permissive version of the principle.

Consequentialism has often been criticized for taking insufficient account of the claims of individuals. A defence of theism which appeals to (4), or some principle akin to it, is open to similar complaints, for it appears to take insufficient account of the suffering of the individual victims of a policy which is designed to make the world a better place overall. Would not a just and loving God be

---

[9] R. M. Adams, 'Must God Create the Best?', *Philosophical Review*, lxxxi (1972), 318.

[10] I shall ignore indirect consequentialism here. In any case, none of the reasons standardly given for being an indirect consequentialist could apply to God.

concerned not only about the good of his creation as a whole, but also about the good of each individual in it? This objection may take one of two forms. The first is the concern that some people suffer such horrific evils that their lives are not worth living. To this objection, the Christian has an obvious response. We must not restrict our view to the present world, but must take into account the world to come. It may be that God offers to all, including, of course, those who have suffered dreadfully in this life, the prospect of a post-mortem life of communion with him so fulfilling that the good of it will, at the very least, outweigh any harm, however great, that the person may have suffered in his earthly life. Overall, the life of each person (or, at least, each person who accepts God) may thus turn out to be both deeply meaningful and supremely worth living.

This response, however, does not, on its own, meet the second kind of objection, which poses more difficulty for the theist. In essence, it is the objection that the policy wrongs innocent people by making them suffer horrendous evils for some purpose other than their own good. It seems that their suffering is being used as a means to an overall good end. The suffering may be necessary to make the world a better place, but the suffering of the individual is not a necessary condition of his own life going better. To the contrary, his life goes worse because of the suffering. While it may be justified to do extremely painful or unpleasant things to someone for their own good—to save them, say, from even worse suffering— many, including many Christians, think it wrong for any agent to inflict such suffering in order that the world may be a better place. It is this objection, which lies at the root of many people's worries about the problem of evil, which I wish to explore. The problem is a difficult one, which perplexes believer and unbeliever alike. I cannot do more here than explore certain avenues to see if any look promising.

The problem is particularly poignant in the case of children, a point which is brought out in Ivan's famous and arresting protest in *The Brothers Karamazov.*

But there are the children, and what am I to do about them? That's a question I can't answer. For the hundredth time I repeat, there are numbers of questions, but I've only taken the children, because in their case what I mean is so unanswerably clear. Listen! If all must suffer to pay for the eternal harmony, what have children to do with it, tell me, please? . . . Why should they too furnish material to enrich the soil for the harmony of the future? . . .

Imagine that you are creating a fabric of human destiny with the object of making men happy in the end, giving them peace and rest at last, but that it was essential and inevitable to torture to death only one tiny creature . . . and to found that edifice on its unavenged tears, would you consent to be the architect on those conditions?[11]

So understood, Ivan's objection is, I believe, essentially deontological in character. Deontologists deny even the weaker, permissive version of P, and thus deny (4). They characteristically hold that there are constraints on action which limit what we may do even in the pursuit of the good, so that the condition in (4), though it may be necessary for an act to be morally justified, is not sufficient. There are many kinds of action which we ought not to perform. For example, each of us ought not to lie, cheat, break promises, torture, murder, and so on. Some deontologists hold that (at least some) constraints are absolute; others maintain that all constraints are threshold constraints.[12]

As I have already suggested, most deontological systems contain a number of constraints, and there are variations between them both as to what kinds of constraint are to be included and as to the precise form that any particular constraint is to take. It seems to me, however, that Ivan's protest can be formulated in terms of a constraint some version of which is likely to be included in any plausible deontological system: the constraint against (seriously) harming an individual by causing him considerable or severe pain or disability.[13] Much would need to be said in qualification to make this claim plausible. There are, for example, various circumstances in which it might be held that we would not be wrong to harm

---

[11] F. Dostoevsky, *The Brothers Karamazov*, trans. C. Garnett, book 5, ch. 4; repr. in N. Pike (ed.), *God and Evil* (Englewood Cliffs, NJ: Prentice-Hall, 1965), 15–16. An almost equally poignant plea is found in a letter of St Augustine's quoted in C. Kirwan, *Augustine* (London: Routledge and Kegan Paul, 1989), 68–9. This was, of course, before he formulated his notorious claim that infants are not innocent and so their suffering, however great, is not unjust.

[12] A threshold constraint has a 'cut-off point' beyond which, if the circumstances are sufficiently pressing, it may be 'relaxed'. See S. Kagan, *The Limits of Morality* (New York: Oxford University Press, 1989), 5.

[13] Here I shall not look at other constraints which deontologists hold should govern our conduct, most notably the constraint against killing the innocent. I think that there may be reasons for thinking that this constraint does not apply to God in the way in which it applies to us.

others, so that the constraint might need amendment. Among these circumstances are the following: that the suffering is inflicted to save the person from worse suffering; that the sufferer is a willing, autonomous, and fully informed volunteer, seeking to achieve a considerable good; that the person who is to be made to suffer represents a genuine but innocent threat to others; that the person who is to be made to suffer has been found guilty of a serious crime and deserves punishment. I excuse myself from the difficult task of refining the constraint against harm, because these special circumstances do not appear to apply in the kind of case which concerns us here.

Deontologists, unlike many but not all consequentialists, hold that the way in which harms, or other bad consequences, are brought about by our actions is morally significant. A distinction is often drawn between harms we (intentionally) inflict and harms we merely fail to prevent or eliminate. A constraint against harm would typically forbid agents to inflict various kinds of harm on others. Although an agent may be justified in not eliminating an evil if to do so would eliminate a greater good, he ought not to inflict such an evil, even if that prevents him from bringing about a greater good. This distinction, between the harms we inflict and the ones we merely fail to prevent or eliminate, though intuitively appealing, is notoriously difficult to draw, and I shall not attempt to make it precise here. The distinction gets its grip, in the case of finite beings, because there are many events that are brought about not by my agency but by natural causes or the choices of others, over which I may have little or no control. Since God is the creator and sustainer of the universe, and nothing happens except through his will, it might at first appear that any harms in his creation are ones which God inflicts on us, in apparent breach of the constraint, not merely ones which he fails to eliminate or prevent.[14] To anticipate the conclusions of the next section, I think that this is true of natural evils but not of evils brought about by the human abuse of free will.

An absolute constraint is one that must not be breached. To be in breach of a threshold constraint, however, is not necessarily to have

---

[14] Formulating (4) in terms of eliminating evils, as Swinburne does, may be misleading, since it directs our attention away from the thought that God inflicts evil. Swinburne himself, however, is not misled. The relevant section in *The Existence of God* is entitled 'God's Right to Inflict Harm'.

acted wrongly; for to say that it has a threshold is to allow that there are circumstances in which it is right to act against it. This might appear to offer a loophole to the deontological theistic defender who does not believe that the constraint against harm is absolute. But two points need to be noted. First, the more horrific the suffering, the more weighty the countervailing considerations must be in order to justify its infliction. It seems doubtful that the kind of good secured by God's policy would justify the breach of the constraint to the extent of the imposition of horrendous suffering.[15] Second, and most important, I do not think that promoting a great good and averting a great harm can be treated on a par, as (4) implies. Most deontologists think that the constraint against harm may be breached to avert a catastrophe. It is quite another thing to say that it would be acceptable to impose horrendous suffering in order to bring about a great good. A world without free will and higher-order goods need contain no great evils; it is merely a world which lacks many good things found in ours. It is not at all clear that it would ever be right to inflict horrendous suffering on anyone simply to make the world a better place. If I am right, this makes the deontological worry much stronger.

I conclude that the theistic defender must deny one of three things. He must either deny that there is a constraint against causing harm, or admit that there is such a constraint but deny that it applies to God, or else deny that God is in breach of it. Since, in this chapter, I am putting as forcefully as I can a deontological worry about solutions to the problem of evil, I am taking the existence of the constraint as given. Hence, in the remainder of the chapter I shall explore the second and third responses.

III

I begin with a partial defence of the third kind. Theodicies standardly distinguish between moral and natural evils. The former are evils brought about by the free choices of created beings. The defence I shall consider in this section aims to show that, in allowing the existence of moral evils, God is not breaching the constraint against inflicting harm.

---

[15] Indeed, the more horrendous the suffering, the more tempting it is to say that there is an absolute constraint against inflicting suffering of that kind.

Humans frequently act in ways that bring about, or contribute to bringing about, harm to others. Deontologists traditionally distinguish between ways of bringing about harm which are licit and not in breach of the constraint against harm, and ways that are forbidden by the constraint. To my mind, a plausible, as well as possibly the most historically influential, way of drawing the distinction is to be found in the principle of double effect. This principle, as is well known, distinguishes between those effects of one's action the bringing about of which can be seen as part of one's plan and those effects which are foreseen but form no part of the plan. The former consist of any effects at which I aim as my goal and any effects which I aim at as a means to achieving that goal. The doctrine states that there are some effects, such as serious harm to the innocent, which must not figure in my plan, but which it may be permissible to bring about where they are merely foreseen side-effects. An additional constraint on my action is that the good to be achieved (or the harm averted) by my action must be suitably proportionate to the harm caused. I shall not defend this doctrine here, but will show how an appeal to it can be used to argue that God is not in breach of the constraint against harm in allowing moral evil.[16]

It is no part of God's plan, so the defence runs, that humans should sin. If Adam and Eve and their descendants had remained morally pure, God's purposes would not have been frustrated. Indeed, God commands humans to act rightly. God permits sin because it is part of his plan that there should be free creatures who can choose either to live rightly or to do wrong. In sinning, humans cause great harm to others which could have been avoided. The harm that comes from sin is foreseen by God (at least as a real possibility), but its occurrence is no part of his plan.[17] The good to be achieved, the existence of creatures who freely choose the right, is a good that is arguably sufficient to be suitably proportionate to the foreseen but unintended harm. So, in allowing harm brought about by sin, God is not, according to the doctrine of double effect, in breach of the constraint against harm.

---

[16] It was M. M. Adams, in 'Horrendous Evils and the Existence of God', in *idem* and R. M. Adams, *The Problem of Evil* (Oxford: Oxford University Press, 1990), 213 n. 11, who drew my attention to the fact that St Augustine uses the doctrine for just this purpose.

[17] This position is defensible if we assume, as freewill defenders do, an incompatibilist account of free will.

I said that this defence is partial, in that it covers only moral evils. It would, of course, be a complete defence if all evils turn out to be moral evils, and there is an extension of the freewill defence, suggested by Plantinga, which claims just that.[18] On this account, evil in the world not caused by us is caused by very powerful sinful creatures, such as fallen angels. The very same defence may then be mounted to show that God is in breach of no constraint by allowing the effects of that sin.

Swinburne rejects Plantinga's solution, since he regards the inclusion of fallen angels in the theistic hypothesis as an *ad hoc* addition which offends against Occam's razor.[19] He thinks the theist best advised to admit the existence of natural evil, which he defines so that it includes not only suffering not caused by humans but suffering unwittingly and non-culpably caused by human action. He then ties the solution to the problem of natural evil to the freewill defence in an ingenious way, by claiming that the existence of natural evil is a necessary condition of humans having significant free choice; that is, of humans being in a position to make informed and responsible choices about matters that deeply affect the welfare of themselves and others. They can do this only if, first, there are serious harms which people can suffer and if, second, they can learn from experience how harms are brought about and how they can be prevented. In turn, they can do this only if there is suffering not brought about by human wrongdoing. Only if there are accidental poisonings can there be deliberate poisonings. Someone cannot be culpably negligent, careless, or reckless unless she could have known the consequences of her actions, and she could only have known these if there had been previous similar actions or happenings which brought about similar harmful consequences unforeseeably. The obvious response to this line of defence is to suggest that God could have imparted this knowledge in some other way. Swinburne argues with considerable force that he could not have done this without revealing his presence in a way so obvious as to deprive humans of the epistemic room to freely accept or reject him.

The freewill defence argues that free will is a great good, and that that fact justifies God in creating free beings, despite the miseries they can bring. Since the presence of natural evil is, on Swinburne's

---

[18] Plantinga, *God, Freedom and Evil*, 58 ff.
[19] Swinburne, 'Knowledge from Experience', 148–9.

account, a necessary condition of genuine free choice, then God, so the argument runs, would be justified in creating a world with natural evil in it if this were the only way he could bring about this great good. This defence runs foul, however, of the principle of double effect. In using that doctrine to defend God against the charge of having breached the constraint against harm, it was claimed that it was no part of God's plan in giving us free will that people should actually sin and thus cause suffering. But if Swinburne's argument is correct, then it is part of God's plan that people and animals should suffer all kinds of natural evil; for if they did not, then people would not be able to have the great good of morally significant choice. The infliction of suffering, not just the presence of hazards, is a means to the goal of giving us all genuine free will; the plan would not work if, despite the existence of poisons, viruses, and volcanoes, no one was ever poisoned, infected, or incinerated. But the infliction of suffering as a means to the achievement of a good is ruled out by the principle of double effect.

Is there any way in which the natural evils necessary for us to have the knowledge which enables us to exercise morally significant free will might enter into God's creation without his being in breach of the constraint against harm? Here we might return to the suggestion about fallen angels; for God might avoid moral censure if these harms were brought about through the free choice of another. It would not help if God were to have it as part of his plan that some other powerful being, such as Satan, were to inflict those evils, for it does not affect the wrongness of my act, on the principle of double effect, if the execution of my plan depends on the will of another. The person who actually inflicts the harm shares the blame, but I am not exonerated. It is legitimate, however, for an agent to respond to someone's wrongdoing, without either condoning it or conniving at it, by using it to bring about a good end, even an end which might not otherwise have been possible. So the plan would be legitimate if it were no part of God's original purpose that Satan rebel and bring suffering to the world. The following possibility is thus left to the theistic defender. God created powerful angels who have significant free will. He also created humans who had free will but who did not yet have the knowledge needed to make significant choices, because no serious evils existed in their world. That they had some freedom was good, but not as good as their having morally significant free choice. Some of the angels acted contrary to God's will and rebelled; their rebellion took the form of introducing evils into God's good creation. While it was not God's intention that this should happen, he had devised things so that good would come out of evil. For the introduction of natural evil now gave humans scope for significant moral choices.

This account of God's plan, it seems to me, exonerates him, given the principle of double effect, from the charge of having breached the constraint against harm. But it does so only by making Swinburne's defence of the existence of natural evil redundant. For, on this account, what we think of as natural evils are seen to be really moral evils, and so are already explained by the freewill defence.[20] We would merely have used Swinburne's epistemic argument to show the way in which God could bring a further good out of Satan's evil choices.

This still leaves the extended freewill defence intact. It is, however, open to severe, though not fatal, criticism. First, as Swinburne claims, it is, as a piece of natural theology, *ad hoc*. Second, it needs considerable work before it can be turned into a satisfying theodicy, because there are so many unanswered questions. Why did God choose to create and sustain in existence an enormously powerful being who is, apparently, irredeemably evil? How could Satan rebel when he must have been able to see the consequences of his folly very clearly? I share Swinburne's view that this line of thought is unattractive, so I will explore other possible defences.

IV

In the last section I offered a partial defence, in terms of double effect, against the charge that God breaches the constraint against harm, and then showed that Swinburne's solution to the problem of natural evil cannot avail itself of it. This is not, however, the defence which Swinburne espouses. He offers a version of the second line of defence which I sketched out at the end of section II.[21] His defence is that the difference between our position and God's means that God does not have the same duties and is not subject to the same constraints as we are. He puts the

[20] As Swinburne points out in 'Knowledge from Experience', 148.
[21] Swinburne, *Existence of God*, 216–18.

deontological objection with characteristic force. 'Surely no one has the right to inflict harm on an agent for his greater good, let alone for the greater good of another, without the agent's consent.'[22]

His reply is threefold. First, it matters whether the agent who inflicts the suffering could in fact gain the sufferer's consent. Where consent cannot be obtained, we may be justified in imposing the suffering to obtain the good. When God decided to create a world in which people were to have morally significant choices and were to be responsible for each other's welfare, he could not, of course, consult us. This remark, though true, fails to address the point. It is sometimes in order, as we have seen, to inflict suffering on someone without his consent, for his own future good, in a case where he is unable to consent. In particular, we may do so to prevent an even worse harm befalling him. What is at issue here is whether it is justified to inflict suffering on someone without his consent for someone else's future good. This is precisely the kind of action which the constraint against harm rules out.

Second, Swinburne argues, we are often unsure of how much someone will suffer and what its effects on him will be. This makes us rightly cautious. But God is not ignorant of these matters, and so is not subject to such inhibitions. This reply is relevant to cases where we would not take a risk of inflicting severe suffering because of our ignorance, but where God is in a better position to judge. But this reply is utterly beside the point when we are considering the infliction of horrendous evils. Here our conviction that it would be wrong to act in this way is not based on any worries we might have about our ignorance of the extent of the suffering involved.

Third, Swinburne suggests that 'God as the author of our being would have rights over us which we do not have over our fellow men'.[23] These are essentially parental rights, stemming from one's being the begetter or creator of a child. While I have no general right to let someone suffer for the sake of the good of his soul or the soul of another, parents do have *some* right to let one of their children suffer for the good of his soul or for the good of his sibling's soul.[24] God, who as our creator is more than a

---

[22] Ibid. 216.   [23] Ibid. 217.

[24] Swinburne's use of the word 'let' here is revealing. For what is at stake, as he admits in the title of the section, is whether God has the right to inflict pain.

parent, has such rights to a greater degree, and he has them over all people.

This suggestion has merit, but I do not think that it will deal with the vexed problem of natural evil. As before, we must distinguish between a child suffering for the good of his own soul and suffering for the good of another's. We certainly think the former is legitimate in a limited fashion; we allow a child to suffer a little in order to teach him to be more careful in future. We even impose punishments in order to improve a child's moral character. If these sufferings or punishments serve as an object-lesson to others, well and good, but that is not their primary purpose. Making a child suffer for the good of his sibling's soul alone, however, seems more problematic. I think there are cases where a parent may risk harm to the child in order to develop the moral character of a sibling. Here are a couple of cases. First, a parent might encourage an older child to take his younger sibling out for a walk, to develop the older child's sense of responsibility. Here the parent foresees that the risk of the younger child's getting hurt is slightly greater than it would be if there were an adult present, but judges the risk worth taking, in part because of the moral effect on the older child. Second, a parent might refrain from offering a child needed help so that a sibling could be given the chance to take responsibility for supplying the help. Young Ivan is having problems with his homework; the parent may know how to help but, wishing to encourage the child's older sister to take more responsibility for Ivan, lets her help him, even though she may not do as good a job as the parent would have done.

Now these, and cases like them, seem to me to be examples where, to draw on the discussion in the last section, harm to the child is no part of the parent's plan. The parent is prepared to risk harm or risk the fact that no one will help, but the success of the plan does not depend on the child being harmed. By contrast, the infliction of undeserved suffering on a child as a means to bettering the soul of another is surely wrong. One would not make a normally contented child miserable so that a sibling could learn the importance of comforting him.[25] It seems to me that parents have no right to inflict suffering on some of their children as part of a

---

[25] Nor do I think that our reluctance to do such things is merely because there is a lot of misery around already for us to practise our virtue on, without our creating any more.

plan to improve the moral character of other of their children.[26] And if they don't have that right *qua* parents, then God does not, as creator, have that right either.[27] Yet Swinburne's justification of the presence of natural evil requires that God's plan will be a success only if some people suffer, and suffer horribly. It is that fact which justifies the complaint that, on his account, God is in breach of the constraint against harming.

V

So far, we have been assuming that, in creating a world with many natural evils, God has harmed or injured us in ways that require justification, because they seem to be in breach of the constraint against harm. Robert Adams, in an impressive and important paper, denies this claim.[28] As an avowed non-consequentialist, he seeks to show that God has not injured, but has rather benefited us by bringing us into existence in this world, with all its attendant evils. In addition, he argues that God is neither unjust nor unkind in his allocation of burdens and benefits. An important part of his argument rests on a highly plausible claim about personal identity: that had my parents not met and had sexual relations, I would never have existed. Indeed, given the biological facts, it seems plausible that I would not have existed had not the particular sperm and egg from which I derive met and fused. I agree with Adams that an even stronger, but more controversial, metaphysical claim is probably true: namely, that 'no-one who was not produced from the same individual egg and sperm cells as I was *could* have been me', but his main argument does not depend on that strong claim.[29]

---

[26] Apart from the fact that this would be a very strange form of moral education—to show by our example that it was alright to inflict suffering on one person for another's good.

[27] I think it mistaken to hold, as Swinburne does, that one has the limited right I am prepared to concede simply in virtue of being a biological parent. As a parent one has a duty to look after one's children; the proper exercise of that duty gives one the right to let the child suffer for its own and others' good. If one hands over the duty to a foster or adoptive parent, one hands over the right. And if one does not fulfil one's duty as a parent in other ways, one does not retain the right in question.

[28] R. M. Adams, 'Existence, Self-Interest and the Problem of Evil', in his *The Virtue of Faith* (Oxford: Oxford University Press, 1987), 65–76.

[29] Ibid. 67, my emphasis. If his argument does need the stronger claim, then it would rest on a metaphysical premiss which many Christians, including Swinburne,

He offers three main arguments, of which only two are germane here.[30] The first is that we cannot have been injured by most of the evils which, though they may affect our lives now, came into being before we were conceived. For, were there no famine, disease, earthquakes, or wars, the history of the world would have been entirely different, in which case the patterns of procreation in the past would have been different, and, plausibly, none of the people alive now would ever have been born; instead, some completely different set of individuals would have existed. Subject to the important proviso that each person has a life that is, on balance, worth living, this argument shows that none of us have been injured by these pre-existing evils.[31] For, if they had not existed, we would not have been born. Even if they have brought sorrow or suffering into our lives, we have not been injured by them, for to injure us, such evils would have had to make our lives worse than they would otherwise have been. So 'we cannot have been wronged by the creation of a natural and historical order that has these features; for we could not have existed without them'. At this point in the argument, however, it is still open to us to 'ask why God does not intervene in the natural and historical process in our lifetime to protect us from the consequences of those facts'.[32]

Adams's second claim is that each person now alive has benefited from the policy of permitting evil that God has followed so far. Each of us has benefited, even if we have not all benefited equally, by having a life worth living, a life we would not otherwise have had.[33] This thought provides a way of dealing with the question left open after the first argument. There is no reason to think that we are going to suffer from these evils more than have our ancestors who lived under the same policy. It does not, therefore, seem to be 'a demand of fairness that God should end the policy that has benefited us'[34] and give up the worthwhile goals that he is pursuing,

do not accept. See R. Swinburne, *The Evolution of the Soul* (Oxford: Clarendon Press, 1986).

[30] The third is a defence of the claim that God has been good to us.

[31] That proviso may not be met in this life, but it will be met if we add the bliss of a life to come, from which no one will be excluded except, perhaps, through their own fault.

[32] R. M. Adams, 'Problem of Evil', 67.

[33] We may be doubtful about this claim, for the sorts of reasons given by Derek Parfit in *Reasons and Persons* (Oxford: Clarendon Press, 1984), 487–90. I am, however, persuaded by Parfit's arguments that these reasons are not conclusive.

[34] R. M. Adams, 'Problem of Evil', 71.

in order to spare us the unpleasant consequences of the continued implementation of the policy.

To take Adams's second argument first. He admits that unfairness is not the only charge which might be made against God's justice. My objection is not that God has been unfair in distributing burdens inequitably, but that he has wronged individuals in breaching the constraint against harm. What Adams has shown is that each individual is a net beneficiary of that policy, since without it he or she would not have had a life worth living. This may mitigate the complaint, but does not, I think, eliminate it. This is a claim I shall try to make good in my discussion of his first argument, to which I now turn.

The claim that, if my life is worth living, I could not be wronged by a decision, action, or policy which was a necessary condition of my coming to exist has been contested.[35] Woodward argues, rightly in my view, that

people have relatively specific interests (e.g. in having promises kept, in avoiding bodily injury, in getting their fair share) that are not simply reducible to some general interest in maintaining a high overall level of well-being and . . . many moral requirements function so as to protect against violations of such specific interests. That an action will cause an increase in someone's overall level of well-being is not always an adequate response to the claim that such a specific interest has been violated.[36]

He argues the point forcibly with respect to several of the examples discussed by Derek Parfit in part IV of *Reasons and Persons*, but one of his own will serve to illustrate the point. Acme Chemical Corporation discovers that, in order to continue operating profitably, it must adopt a policy of dispersing pollutants which it foresees will kill or injure many people over the years. A couple who work for the plant meet and have a child. If the plant had not existed, they would never have met. As a result of exposure to the pollutants, the child develops cancer. The parents claim that the company has wronged their child, and they are surely right in this. The company cannot reasonably defend itself by saying that, but

[35] What I say on this difficult topic is too brief. Much discussion has been generated by Parfit's discussion of population policy and resource allocation in part IV of *Reasons and Persons*. I am grateful to Professor Adams for drawing my attention to two important papers which bear on these issues: J. Woodward, 'The Non-Identity Problem', *Ethics*, xcvi (1986), 804–31; M. Hanser, 'Harming Future People', *Philosophy and Public Affairs*, xix (1990), 47–70.
[36] Woodward, 'Non-Identity Problem', 809.

for their factory continuing to operate, the child would never have existed, and that, since he has had a worthwhile life on balance, no harm or wrong has been done to him, because he is no worse off than he would have been if the company had ceased production and he had never existed. Woodward is surely right to claim that a wrong has been done to the child; his right not to have his health injured has been violated. The claim that the company's policy leaves him no worse off than he would have been under alternative policies is simply irrelevant.[37]

There is, however, a significant difference between this example and the case of God's policy to his creatures. For, as Woodward points out, although the Acme Corporation Board's policy may be a necessary condition for the existence of the child, the worthwhile character of that child's life is not achieved or created by the Board's policy but by the many actions and choices of his parents, teachers, and others. Thus, he says, we cannot appeal to the worthwhile character of that life as somehow cancelling the wrongfulness of the planners' choice, for the connection between the policy and the benefit is purely accidental. But the worthwhileness of our lives is mainly, if not wholly, attributable to God, who ensures that our lives will be worth living (except, perhaps, through our own fault). So, even if it is conceded that we *can* be wronged by a policy which was a necessary condition of our coming into existence, it may still be the case that God has not in fact wronged us when he lays burdens upon us, since the worthwhile character of our lives is a part of his plan.

I have already agreed that an act of harming which would otherwise be wrong may be justifiable if, as well as being necessary to achieve a good end, it was also intended to benefit the person harmed. Thus it may be permissible to operate on a young child without anaesthetic if this is the only way to save her life. What is at issue is whether the non-accidental connection between the horrendous evil someone suffers and the benefits she receives are of the right kind to exonerate God from the charge of wrongdoing in creating a world with disease, earthquakes, and so on. I wish to argue that the fact that it is part of God's plan that we lead worthwhile lives is not, on its own, sufficient to exonerate him. I shall try to illustrate this contention by a further example.

---

[37] See ibid. 813–14.

Suppose there is a virulent childhood disease which causes great pain, severe physical handicap, and an agonizing early death for a significant proportion of the population. Its effects are so bad that we reasonably believe that, in their earthly life, the children who suffer from this disease do not have a life worth living. We have on hand a research programme which, we can reasonably hope, will lead to the eradication of the disease in a number of generations, say ten, so that no child need ever again suffer in this way. Unfortunately, the research will have to be carried out on children who do not have the disease; it is very painful, and it will lead to their being handicapped in some fairly serious way, though they will be less severely handicapped than those who contract the disease. This research programme will lead, for familiar reasons, to predictable changes in who is conceived. We fear that the children on whom the research is carried out may not have lives worth living unless we intervene to assist them, so we decide to compensate those children by giving them resources to cope with their handicap and plenty of love and affection. It is thus part of our policy to give all children, including those in the programme and those whose disease will later be cured when our research is complete, a life worth living.

After the policy has been in place for several generations, someone questions its moral legitimacy.[38] It seems reasonable to suppose that, had the policy not been pursued, none of the children now alive would have been born. All have lives worth living, and so all have benefited from the policy. What is more, this is not accidental; that they should have lives worth living is a central aim of the policy. Is there no reason to doubt the morality of the policy? It seems to me that such a policy would do the children on whom the experiments are performed a great wrong in inflicting suffering on them, admittedly in order to achieve a good end, the eradication of disease, but not in order to achieve a good for them. It seems, then, that the fact that it is an aim of the policy to produce lives worth

---

[38] Adams's defence would not be available when the policy started, because the first generation of children have not benefited from the policy. If there was a first generation of humans, then Adams's theodicy cannot justify God's allowing evil to happen to them; in which case, God's policy of introducing evil into the world could never get started. This point might be met, however, if we suppose that humans evolved from other animals and that the world always contained suffering, for then the first humanoid creatures would not have existed without the existence of the policy.

living is not sufficient to justify it if it involves the infliction of severe harms.

Note that, as I have already suggested, the policy would be morally acceptable if the research we were undertaking on the children were therapeutic. Suppose that the only method of treatment currently available saved the child from worse suffering and death at the expense of pain and handicap, and that each child who was saved had a life worth living. While treating each child, we also conduct research to develop ways of improving the treatment. Here the benefit to each child is a direct result of the painful and harmful treatment; if he is not treated, then things will be worse for him. Therapeutic research is justified because the specific harm that the patient undergoes is a necessary means to a specific benefit within her life. It is true that the children who are handicapped as a result of the original non-therapeutic research programme also receive a benefit after their ordeal. But here their suffering is not the causally necessary condition of their receiving that benefit; they receive the benefit as compensation for the injury we inflicted on them. Similarly, although those who suffer horrendous evils in this life are benefited by a blessed post-mortem existence, their suffering is not, on Adams's picture, a necessary condition of their receiving that benefit.

We might, on reflecting on the contrast between therapeutic and non-therapeutic research, be tempted to the more general conclusion that any policy which involves the inflicting of serious harm can only be justified if the harm each individual receives is necessary for that individual to receive a proportionately greater benefit within her life. And that would seem to rule out Adams's theodicy, in which each of us is merely an intended net beneficiary of the policy. But that dismissal of Adams's position would, I think, be too swift.

Adams, in his discussion of whether God is fair in the allocation of burdens under his policy, holds that it is crucial that there be a non-accidental connection of an appropriate kind between the burden and the benefit. His rather brief characterization suggests a closer connection than the one I have just rejected as inadequate.

It is also important to the argument that the evils be necessary for an end that is good and of which the benefits already received by those who suffer the evils are in some way instances. If the end were not good, or if the benefits already received were accidental consequences or mere means in relation to it, the argument would lose much or all of its force. . . . But the creation of persons such as we are is presumably among the ends for whose sake God lets evils happen.[39]

What I take him to be suggesting here is this. The evils in the world may be necessary in order that lives of a certain kind can exist—the lives of persons in which there can be, for example, the goods of significant choice, of virtue, and, most important, of communion with God. Without the evils, there could, perhaps, be less valuable lives, but not lives which have this kind of value. Each person benefits from the policy, not simply by having a life worth living, but by living a particular kind of valuable life which would otherwise not be available. The good end of the policy is the creation of personal life, and each of our lives is an instance of it. The connection between the evil and the benefit here seems sufficiently close to justify the policy. For the good which my life embodies is a specific kind of good which the policy alone makes possible. Some, but not all, have to pay a high price for that specific benefit, but none has to pay so high a price that her life is not worth living.

The difference between this policy and the one of carrying out non-therapeutic research is that the latter policy, though it sought to ensure that everyone had a life worth living, did not have as its aim the creation of a different and more valuable kind of life. That kind of life was available before the policy was in place. The policy sought merely to extend it to all. The lives of the children who suffered under the research programme were not instances of a kind of life which could not otherwise be realized.

I conclude that Adams's theodicy, suitably amended, is defensible, even though the horrendous evils which a particular individual may suffer are not a necessary condition of the particular benefits which that individual receives within her life. But we might hope to do more. We might hope to show that the suffering of each person who experienced horrendous evil in her earthly life was also the necessary condition for some great and specific benefit within her life which she could not otherwise receive. I want finally, therefore, to sketch very briefly a theodicy which, though it can stand independently of the one we have just been examining, can also be seen as a supplement to it.

[39] R. M. Adams, 'Problem of Evil', 71.

VI

This theodicy incorporates a direct connection, of the kind we found in the case of therapeutic research, between the suffering of the individual and his eventual benefit.[40] It draws its inspiration from Marilyn Adams's paper 'Horrendous Evils and the Goodness of God'.[41] Her concern is to deal with the objection that a loving God would not, even in pursuit of a good goal, allow people to live lives rendered meaningless by suffering; but her point can easily be adapted to meet the deontological worry. Following Chisholm,[42] she distinguishes between a case where a good balances or outweighs an evil and one where it defeats it. In the former, there is simply as much or more good than bad in a situation; the value of the whole is just the sum of the values of the two contributing parts taken separately. In the latter, there is an organic unity between the parts, such that the presence of the bad part is necessary to the goodness of the whole of which it is a part; the whole is the better for the bad part. She suggests that God would wish, in the post-mortem existence of someone who had suffered a horrendous evil, not merely to give her a good which would outweigh her earlier suffering, but to defeat that suffering by making it possible for it to be seen as contributing to the good of her whole life. She suggests that this could be done only by 'integrating participation in horrendous evils into a person's relationship with God'.[43] Thus, for example, it may be that God suffers, and that only those who have suffered horrendously will be able to enter deeply into that aspect of the divine life. The sufferer will then see her suffering not as something she would prefer not to have experienced, but as a necessary part of what makes her life particularly good. Another suggestion, particularly relevant to our concerns, might be that the sufferer sees the goodness of God's plans and retrospectively identifies with them, glad that she has been able, though unknowingly at

---

[40] Not of exactly the same kind, for, although the suffering of some great evil may be a necessary condition (for beings such as us) of entering fully into the divine nature, the suffering of the particular evil(s) which that person suffered do not seem to be such a necessary condition. (The necessity in question here must be logical, and not merely causal, for the reasons given in section I.)

[41] See n. 16.

[42] R. M. Chisholm, 'The Defeat of Good and Evil', *Proceedings of the American Philosophical Association*, xlii (1968–9), 21–38.

[43] M. Adams, 'Horrendous Evils', 218.

the time, to participate in the plan—an act of retrospective self-sacrifice.

Two aspects of horrendous suffering particularly concerned the deontologist. First, the suffering was imposed to make the world a better place, and not for the specific benefit of the victim. Second, the victim was in no position to consent to or, in the case of very small children, even to understand the suffering. Both worries are, perhaps, met in this theodicy. First, the sufferer is offered a great benefit which can be attained only by someone who has suffered as she has suffered. So it turns out that the suffering was, and was intended to be, a necessary condition of her attaining a great blessing. Second, though there was not, and could not be, consent at the time, there is at least retrospective consent.[44] Undeserved suffering, which would constitute a very great wrong if it were inflicted on someone against their will, can be a very great good if undergone as a voluntary self-sacrifice.[45]

---

[44] Woodward raises many difficulties for this kind of use of retrospective consent which I cannot begin to tackle here; see his 'Non-Identity Problem', 822–5.

[45] I am grateful to members of the Keele Philosophy Department and to the editor, Alan Padgett, for helpful comments on an earlier version of this chapter. I have benefited greatly from discussions with Eve Garrard, who has offered encouragement and argument in equal measure.

A Select Bibliography of the Works of Richard Swinburne

Since we fully expect more publications from the pen of Professor Swinburne, a comprehensive bibliography would be premature. Included here are all books (but not translations) and articles (but not reprints, anthologies, or book reviews) up to 1993. A.G.P.

BOOKS

1968   *Space and Time.* London: Macmillan. 2nd edn., 1981.
1971   *The Concept of Miracle.* New Studies in the Philosophy of Religion. London: Macmillan.
1973   *An Introduction to Confirmation Theory.* London: Methuen.
1974   *The Justification of Induction* (contributing editor). Oxford Readings in Philosophy. London: Oxford University Press.
1977   *The Coherence of Theism.* Clarendon Library of Logic and Philosophy. Oxford: Clarendon Press. Rev. edn., 1993.
1979   *The Existence of God.* Oxford: Clarendon Press. Rev. edn., 1991.
1981   *Faith and Reason.* Oxford: Clarendon Press.
1983   *Space, Time and Causality* (contributing editor). Synthese Library vol. 157, Royal Institute of Philosophy conference vol. Dordrecht: D. Reidel.
1984   *Personal Identity* (with Sydney Shoemaker). Oxford: Blackwell.
1986   *The Evolution of the Soul.* Oxford: Clarendon Press.
1989   *Responsibility and Atonement.* Oxford: Clarendon Press.
1989   *Miracles* (contributing editor). Philosophical Topics. New York: Macmillan.
1992   *Revelation: From Metaphor to Analogy.* Oxford: Clarendon Press.
forthcoming   *The Christian God.* Oxford: Clarendon Press.

PAMPHLETS

1973   *Sense and Nonsense in Physics and Theology.* Inaugural Lecture, University of Keele.
1984   *Evidence for God.* Oxford: Mowbray, for the Christian Evidence Society.
1987   *A Selective Bibliography of the Philosophy of Mind.* Oxford: Subfaculty of Philosophy.

ARTICLES

1961 'Three Types of Thesis about Fact and Value', *Philosophical Quarterly*, 11, 301–7.

1962 'The Presence-and-Absence Theory', *Annals of Science*, 18, 131–45.

1963–4 'Privacy', *Analysis* (supplement no. 2) 24, 127–36.

1964 'Falsifiability of Scientific Theories', *Mind*, 73, 434–6.

1964–5 'Times', *Analysis*, 25, 185–91.

1965 'Galton's Law—Formulation and Development', *Annals of Science*, 21, 15–31.

1965 'The Timelessness of God', *Church Quarterly Review*, 116, 323–37, 472–86.

1965–6 'Conditions of Bitemporality', *Analysis*, 26, 47–50.

1965–6 'Knowledge of Past and Future', *Analysis*, 26, 166–72.

1966 'Affecting the Past', *Philosophical Quarterly*, 16, 341–7.

1966 'The Beginning of the Universe', *Proceedings of the Aristotelian Society*, supplementary vol. 40, 125–38.

1966 'Horizons', *Philosophy of Science*, 33, 210–14.

1967–8 'Grue', *Analysis*, 28, 123–8.

1968 'The Argument from Design', *Philosophy*, 43, 199–212.

1968 'Miracles', *Philosophical Quarterly*, 18, 320–8.

1968–9 'Primary and Secondary Tenses', *Analysis* 29, 203–5.

1969 'The Christian Wager', *Religious Studies*, 4, 217–28.

1969 'Projectible Predicates', *Analysis*, 30, 1–11.

1969 'Vagueness, Inexactness, and Imprecision', *British Journal for the Philosophy of Science*, 19, 281–99.

1969 'Whole and Part in Cosmological Arguments', *Philosophy*, 44, 339–40.

1970 'Choosing between Confirmation Theories', *Philosophy of Science*, 37, 602–13.

1970 'Physical Determinism', in G. N. A. Vesey (ed.), *Knowledge and Necessity*, London: Macmillan, 155–68.

1971 'The Paradoxes of Confirmation—A Survey', *American Philosophical Quarterly*, 8, 318–30.

1971 'Popper's Account of Acceptability', *Australasian Journal of Philosophy*, 49, 327–43.

1971 'Probability, Credibility, and Acceptability', *American Philosophical Quarterly*, 8, 275–83.

1971 'The Probability of Particular Events', *Philosophy of Science*, 38, 327–43.

1972 'The Argument for Design—A Defence', *Religious Studies*, 8, 193–205.

1972 'Cohen on Evidential Support', *Mind*, 81, 244–8.

1972–3 'Confirmability and Factual Meaningfulness', *Analysis*, 33, 71–6.

1973 'Omnipotence', *American Philosophical Quarterly*, 10, 231–7.

1973–4 'Personal Identity', *Proceedings of the Aristotelian Society*, 74, 231–47.

1974 'Duty and the Will of God', *Canadian Journal of Philosophy*, 4, 213–27.

1974–5 'Meaningfulness without Confirmability—A Reply', *Analysis*, 35, 22–7.

1975 'Analyticity, Necessity and Apriority', *Mind*, 84, 225–43.

1976 'The Objectivity of Morality', *Philosophy*, 51, 5–20.

1976 'Persons and Personal Identity', in H. D. Lewis (ed.), *Contemporary British Philosophy* (Fourth Series), London: Allen and Unwin, 221–38.

1976 'Reply to Wallace's "On Making Actings Morally Wrong"', *Canadian Journal of Philosophy*, 6, 551–2.

1977 'The Problem of Evil', in S. C. Brown (ed.), *Reason and Religion*, Ithaca, NY: Cornell University Press, 81–102.

1978 'Natural Evil', *American Philosophical Quarterly*, 15, 295–301.

1979 'God's Action in the World', *Epworth Review*, 6, 89–100.

1979 'Der kosmologische Beweis', in N. Hoerster (ed.), *Glaube und Vernunft*, Munich: Deutscher Taschenbuch Verlag, 37–44.

1980 'Conventionalism about Space and Time', *British Journal for the Philosophy of Science*, 31, 255–72.

1980 'Properties, Causation and Projectibility', in L. J. Cohen and M. Hesse (eds.), *Applications of Inductive Logic*, Oxford: Clarendon Press, 313–20.

1981 'The Evidential Value of Religious Experience', in A. R. Peacocke (ed.), *The Sciences and Theology in the Twentieth Century*, Notre Dame, Ind.: University of Notre Dame Press, 169–82.

1982 'Are Mental Events Identical with Brain Events?', *American Philosophical Quarterly*, 19, 173–81.

1982 'Science is both Inductive and Realist', in D. R. Gregory (ed.), *The Questions Behind the Answers*, Washington, DC: University Press of America, 105–12.

1983 'A Theodicy of Heaven and Hell', in A. J. Freddoso (ed.), *The Existence and Nature of God*, Notre Dame, Ind.: University of Notre Dame Press, 37–54.

1983 'Causality', and 'Theism', in John Bowden (ed.), *Dictionary of Christian Theology*, London: SCM.

1983 'Mackie, Induction, and God', *Religious Studies*, 19, 385–91.

1984 'Analytic/Synthetic', *American Philosophical Quarterly*, 21, 31–42.

1985 'Desire', *Philosophy*, 60, 429–45.

1985 'Original Sinfulness', *Neue Zeitschrift für systematische Theologie und Religionsphilosophie*, 27, 235–50.

356   *Select Bibliography*

1985   'Thought', *Philosophical Studies*, 48, 153–71.

1986   'Indeterminism of Human Action', *Midwest Studies in Philosophy*, 10, 431–49.

1987   'Analogy and Metaphor', in G. J. Hughes (ed.), *The Philosophical Assessment of Theology*, Tunbridge Wells, Kent: Search Press, 65–84.

1987   'Knowledge from Experience and the Problem of Evil', in W. J. Abraham and S. Holtzer (eds.), *The Rationality of Religious Belief*, Oxford: Clarendon Press, 141–67.

1987   'The Origin of Consciousness', in J. M. Robson (ed.), *The Origin and Evolution of the Universe*, Montreal: McGill–Queens University Press, 211–26.

1987   'The Structure of the Soul', in A. R. Peacocke and G. Gillett (eds.), *Persons and Personality*, Oxford: Blackwell, 33–55.

1988   'The Christian Scheme of Salvation', in T. V. Morris (ed.), *Philosophy and the Christian Faith*, Notre Dame, Ind.: University of Notre Dame Press, 15–30.

1988   'Could there be more than One God?', *Faith and Philosophy*, 5, 225–41.

1988   'Does Theism Need a Theodicy?', *Canadian Journal of Philosophy*, 18, 287–312.

1988   'The Free Will Defense', *Archivo di Filosofia*, 56, 585–96.

1989   'Meaning in the Bible', in S. R. Sutherland and T. A. Roberts (eds.), *Religion, Reason and the Self*, Cardiff: University of Wales Press, 1–33.

1990   'The Argument from the Fine Tuning of the Universe', in J. Leslie (ed.), *Physical Cosmology and Philosophy*. New York: Macmillan, 154–73.

1990   'Could God Become Man?', in G. N. A. Vesey (ed.), *The Philosophy in Christianity*, Cambridge: Cambridge University Press, 53–70.

1990   'Faith and the Existence of God', in A. P. Griffiths (ed.), *Key Themes in Philosophy*, Cambridge: Cambridge University Press, 121–33.

1990   'God's Necessary Being', *Archivo di Filosofia*, 58, 533–42.

1990   'The Limits of Explanation', in D. Knowles (ed.), *Explanation and its Limits*, Cambridge: Cambridge University Press, 177–94.

1990   'Tensed Facts', *American Philosophical Quarterly*, 27, 117–30.

1991   'Necessary A Posteriori Truth', *American Philosophical Quarterly*, 28, 113–23.

1992   'Revelation', in K. J. Clark (ed.), *Our Knowledge of God*, Dordrecht: Reidel, 115–29.

1993   'God and Time', in E. Stump (ed.), *Reasoned Faith*. Ithaca, NY: Cornell University Press, 204–22.

1993 'Interpreting the New Testament—Comments on the Paper of Attridge', in T. P. Flint and E. Stump (eds.), *Hermes and Athena*, Notre Dame, Ind.: University of Notre Dame Press, 225–34.

1993 'The Vocation of the Natural Theologian', in K. J. Clark (ed.), *Philosophers Who Believe*, Downers Grove, Ill.: InterVarsity Press, 179–202.

Index of Names and Scripture

N.B.: Biblical titles are set in italics, and listed in alphabetical (not canonical) order.

Printed in the United Kingdom
by Lightning Source UK Ltd.
132605UK00005B/9/A